T   H   E

Word For Windows™ 2.0

PRINT AND PRESENTATION KIT

How to Create

Brochures, Ads, Flyers,

Newsletters,

Reports, and Slides

Christine Solomon

Addison Wesley Publishing Company

Reading, Massachusetts • Menlo Park, California • New York

Don Mills, Ontario • Wokingham, England

Amsterdam • Bonn • Sydney • Singapore

Tokyo • Madrid • San Juan • Paris

Seoul • Milan • Mexico City • Taipei

For
FJW, PH, and JR.
Thanks, folks.

Library of Congress Cataloging-in-Publication Data
Solomon, Christine, 1962–
        The Word for Windows 2.0 print and presentation kit : how to
    create brochures, ads, flyers, newsletters, reports, and slides /
    Christine Solomon.
            p.   cm.
        Includes index.
        ISBN 0-201-58108-6 : $26.95
        1. Desktop publishing--Computer programs. 2. Microsoft Word for
    Windows (Computer program)   I. Title.
    Z286.D47S64   1992
    686.2'2544536--dc20   91-38193
                                                                  CIP

Permission was granted to the author by the following companies for use of their material(s):

The Graduate School of Political Management
Essential Information
RJE Consulting
Micro Modeling Associates, Inc.

Sponsoring Editor: Julie Stillman
Project Editor: Elizabeth Rogalin
Cover design: Skolos/Wedell, Inc.
Text design: David F. Kelley
Set in 11 point Times by Carol Woolverton and CIP

1 2 3 4 5 6 7 8 9 -MW- 9594939291
First printing, December 1991

Table of Contents

Acknowledgments   vi

Introduction   vii

Part 1   **Making Everything You Do Look Like a Designer Did It**   1

Chapter **1**   **Rules of Thumb**   3
The dos and don'ts of great-looking documents, explained in common-sense terms.

Chapter **2**   **Desktop Designs**   15
A collection of designs that just about anybody can do with Word for Windows, including layouts for brochures, newsletters, reports, catalogs, and much more.

Chapter **3**   **Typography Versus Typing**   67
How to turn type into graphics, and how to get those graphics into your documents without hiring—or being—an artist.

Chapter **4**   **From Start to Print Shop**   91
Explains the process of planning a publication and getting it ready for the print shop.

Part 2   **Looking Great with Word for Windows**   109

Chapter **5**   **Tools of the Trade**   111
How to use Word for Windows' basic typographic and desktop publishing tools—the Ribbon, the Ruler, the Toolbar, the Character and Paragraph dialog boxes—as well as the capabilities of those tools, including fonts, type styles, and line spacing.

Chapter 6   **Those Special Typesetting Characters**   153
Getting the most out of the special characters, dingbats, and symbols that give your work a professionally-typeset flair.

Chapter 7   **Looking Stylish**   183
How to use styles to format your document as you type it.

Chapter 8   **Designing with Tables**   227
How to use tables to create great-looking designs, from ads to informational presentations.

Chapter 9   **Let Those Presses Roll!**   249
Pointers on printing so that your publications turn out just the way you planned.

Chapter 10   **Graphs and Graphic Touches**   259
How to use Microsoft Draw and Microsoft Graph to add real graphic appeal without a lot of hassles or expense.

Chapter 11   **Graphically Speaking**   287
How to use graphs and artwork created in other programs—such as Microsoft Excel, Lotus 1-2-3, and CorelDraw!—in your Word for Windows documents and publications.

Chapter 12   **Good Design is in the Details**   299
How to use headers and footers, margins, page numbers, facing pages, and other "details" to create the professional look you want.

Chapter 13   **Designing a Page**   325
How to use Word for Windows' most sophisticated page layout features—frames and newspaper-style columns—and how to create drop and stick-up caps.

Chapter 14   **Templates Save Time**   349
How to create and revise templates to make complex designs come out perfectly.

Chapter 15   **Tips for Handling Long Documents**   357
Tricks for working with longer publications, including creating a table of contents and index.

Part **3**	**Do It Yourself**	367

Chapter 16 Create Your Own Form   369
How to create a computerized expense report.

Chapter 17 Create Your Own Marketing Materials   377
How to create two classic marketing pieces—a letter-fold brochure and a flip sheet.

Chapter 18 Create Your Own Reports   387
How to create two practically-perfect report layouts—one in portrait and one in landscape orientation.

Chapter 19 Create Your Own Newsletter   395
How to create a professional-looking newsletter. Only you will ever know it was done in a word processing program.

Chapter 20 Create Your Own Slide Show   403
How to create great-looking presentation materials, including tips for creating slides, handouts, and other visuals.

Chapter 21 P.S. PostScript   415
How to edit a PostScript file to create high-quality special effects such as outlining and screening text.

Visual Glossary   427

References   435

Index   436

Acknowledgments

I have often read the long lists of acknowledgments that clog the opening pages of many books with a feeling that the author was going overboard. Now that I've written a book, I understand how many people's efforts went into it. In the course of getting the words, graphics, and disk between these two covers, many people got to work early, stayed late, and took piles of pages home on the weekend.

This book series got its start when Claudette Moore agreed to be my agent. And then Julie Stillman at Addison-Wesley actually liked the idea, for which I will always be grateful.

Since then, Elizabeth Rogalin has read, edited, and re-edited every page I've written. For several weeks she carted the raw manuscript (which was not a pretty sight, by the way) between the office and her home. Somehow she managed to piece together paragraphs sent separately by fax, Fed Ex, and answering machine, and turn them into chapters. She was still making needed corrections to the manuscript right up to the end, when I couldn't bear to look at it.

Vicki Hochstedler produced this book. Unless you know what it takes to turn an edited manuscript into something people are able to read, you might pass this by without further thought. Let me just say, then, that this is a big deal, especially when the book in question is authored by someone who thinks she knows a lot about production.

I also want to thank:

- Pat Wheeler and Jeff Shlager at Tiger Information Systems for the opportunity to write a training manual on Word for Windows, and for turning me on to Windows in the first place;

- Janet King at Mary O'Brien Kukovich & Associates and RJE Consulting, who somehow found time to do a technical edit for the first part of this book;

- Paul Hoffman who managed to do the technical edit for the second and third parts of this book in between writing his own;

- Megan Moyer and Mark Walls at Autographix, who didn't have any trouble imagining that it's possible to create good-looking slides with a word processing program;

- Kevin, Mike, and Steve at MicroPage—the best service bureau I know; and

- Andy Mehring and Roy Wetterstrom at Micro Modeling Associates, who gave me a lot of reasons to push Word's desktop publishing capability to its limit.

Introduction

I am not a designer. Sometimes I think that, because I *didn't* go to a graphics arts school, I got to learn design the best way—by doing it. I had a computer and a job where I was responsible for producing a fair number of quality documents and publications. So I started to pay attention to how others did similar publications. I picked out the ideas I liked, mixed them together, figured out what I could actually do on the computer, and then added my own touches. The results weren't that bad.

Over the years, I've done a great deal of work on heavy-duty desktop publishing programs like PageMaker and QuarkXpress. But recently, a number of clients have started desktop publishing with powerful word processors, such as Word for Windows. And now I keep getting questions about translating Word's power into the professional-looking work they want to turn out: "How do I make my documents look better?" To help my clients get started, I developed a large collection of designs that just about anybody can do with Word for Windows.

The first part of this book draws from that collection. *Making Everything You Do Look Like a Designer Did It* explains the different elements and techniques that make up each design so that you'll be able to adapt them easily to the things you do yourself. It also gives some rules of thumb to make it simpler to create your own reports, brochures, fancy forms—whatever—from scratch. The first part of the book also explains some of the basics of planning a document or publication, and preparing it for printing—whether it's the printer sitting on your desk; the copy shop down the street; or even a full-service, commercial printer.

The second part of the book, *Looking Great with Word for Windows*, teaches you, step-by-step, how to use Word to produce great-looking stuff. At some point, you'll probably want to use clip art, graphs from Lotus 1-2-3 or Microsoft Excel, scanned images, and the like; this section gives clear examples of how to do all these things. There's also a chapter on how to use Microsoft Draw and Microsoft Graph (two programs that come with Word for Windows), so that you can add some nice graphic touches without a lot of hassles or expense.

The last part, *Do It Yourself*, walks you through creating your own report, form, brochure, newsletter, and even a slide show. Each project is developed so that you can work on it whenever you have time. If you happen to be on deadline, however, you can use the instructions to produce the report or brochure you're actually trying to get out the door.

This book is written for beginners. However, it does assume you know a *few* things about Word for Windows—for instance, how to highlight (or select) text; how to select commands from menus; how to open, close, and save files; how to print. If you can do that much, don't worry—you'll be able to create great-looking publications in no time.

Like so many other computer books, this one was written using a beta (or test) version of the software. Practically speaking, this means that there may be a few differences between the version I was working with and the one you have now. In addition, there are no doubt instances where I could have explained things better. In a classroom, students can stop me right away when such foul-ups occur. While you can't do that, you can drop me a note at P.O. Box 1343, Old Chelsea Station, New York, NY 10011. If you send a stamped, self-addressed envelope, I'll send a corrected explanation. If you have any comments, suggestions, or publications you created using Word, send them along, too, for possible inclusion in future editions.

To use the disk that came with this kit, copy the clip art and sample graphics files (everything with a .PCX, .WMF, and .EPS extension) into the Clipart directory in your Word for Windows program directory, which is usually called Winword. Copy the sample documents (all have a .DOC extension) and templates (which have a .DOT extension) into the Word program directory itself. The file KIT_READ.DOC includes instructions for using the disk. It's a regular Word for Windows document that you can open like any other. You should read it before using the clip art, sample documents, or templates.

I use "Word for Windows" and the common abbreviation "Word" interchangeably.

Some of the examples in this book are adapted from actual work I have done for clients. Some were developed for classes I've taught. Still others are taken from my overstuffed notebook— the one in which I keep the ideas I haven't yet found the right time and place to use. If you beat me to it and use them yourself, so much the better.

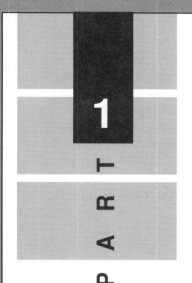

Making Everything You Do Look Like a Designer Did It

You don't have to be a designer to create work that you're proud of and other people appreciate. All you have to do is find some designs you like and start using them. Of course, there are a few rules of thumb to keep in mind, and Chapter 1 explains these rules in common-sense terms.

My students tell me it's helpful to have a sense of what sorts of designs work best with the particular program they're using. Usually, I've found, "best" turns out to be a tasteful compromise between easiest and most attractive. And that's what Chapter 2, *Desktop Designs*, gives you—some of the page designs that work "best" with Word for Windows. I explain the various tricks and techniques that went into each design, and let you know how hard it is (or usually, isn't) to do.

Chapter 3, *Typography Versus Typing,* explains the basics of **typography** (the art of arranging type effectively). And it is an art, though one that is surprisingly easy to learn. The important thing to remember is that you do *not* need to know how to draw, invest your savings in clip art, or hire an artist, in order to get graphics into your documents and publications. What you need is to know how to turn type into graphics. That's what Chapter 3 gives you.

Then comes Chapter 4, *From Start to Print Shop*. A friend told me I should put this chapter first because it explains the whole process of planning a publication and getting it ready for the printer (especially when the printer is a print shop, not just the one on your desk). Although she's right in one sense—it is an important and extremely useful chapter—it's not as much fun as the ones with a lot of designs. Anyway, you have to *start* the process with a design you really like; *then* worry about printing it. ✦

CHAPTER 1

Rules of Thumb

In almost every class I've taught, someone asks the obvious question: "So, what is desktop publishing anyway?" There's more to the answer than first appears. I've discovered that in order to understand what desktop publishing is, you have to know a little about the process it's replacing. The main thing to remember is that desktop publishing is *not* the province of designers. It's the province of people who are simply doing their jobs—jobs that happen to include producing reports, marketing materials, or whatever.

SO, WHAT IS DESKTOP PUBLISHING ANYWAY?

Desktop publishing lets you arrange text and graphics on your computer and produce pages ready to go to the print shop—without ever getting out of your chair. Ten years ago, "publishing" meant a lot of legwork.

For example, it used to be that to publish a four-page brochure you first had to find an artist you felt comfortable with (in terms of both style and fees). Then the artist sketched out a few designs, and you picked the one you liked best. When you were *completely done* writing and editing the text for your brochure, the artist **spec'd** it (pronounced "specked"). In other words, the artist *specified* the typeface and size for the main

Resolution refers to the density of type, with denser being better. A good typewriter produces type at about 90 dots per inch (dpi); most laser printers produce type at 300 dpi; and professional typesetters (and service bureaus) produce type at 1270 to 2450 dpi. For many publications, 300 dpi works fine.

text, the width of the paragraphs, the typeface and size for the various headlines, and so on.

The artist then gave the spec'd copy to a typesetter, who set all the text in the brochure according to the artist's directions, and then produced it at a high-quality **resolution**. (Resolution refers to the density, or blackness, of type, with denser being better.) A typewriter works at about 90 dots per inch (dpi). High-quality resolution is at least 1270 dpi; and it's this level of resolution that's traditionally referred to as "typeset copy."

Ten years ago, the artist you hired also created all the graphic elements for the brochure—the rules, borders, graphs, illustrations, and so on. The artist used pen, ink, markers, and, yes, even clip art to create these graphics. (Books full of copy-right-free art you can just "clip" and use have been around since long before desktop publishing.)

When the typesetter finished with the text, the artist laid out, or arranged, the graphics and typeset text on stiff boards. When everyone was satisfied with how it all looked, the artist pasted it down with rubber cement or hot wax (this process is called **paste-up**). The artist then sent these finished **mechanicals** (also called **camera-ready copy**) to the print shop, where the printer would make the photographic plates used to print the brochure. (Whew!)

With desktop publishing, it's a lot easier. You can publish that brochure right at your desk. You just turn on your computer and "typeset" your copy as you type it in. When you're done typing it in, you "lay it out" on your computer screen. If you want, you can add rules and borders provided by Word for Windows itself, or drawn in Paintbrush or some other drawing program. You can also add clip art, and graphs created with Lotus 1-2-3 or Microsoft Excel. Whenever you want to see how it looks on paper, just print it out on your printer. If you have a laser printer, it prints at a resolution of 300 dots per inch. If you want higher quality resolution, you can send your brochure on diskette or via modem to a commercial "service bureau" that has a really high-quality printer, such as a Linotronic.

That's *desktop* publishing, sometimes called electronic publishing. It's what you do whenever you use your computer to create the camera-ready copy and artwork you send to the print or copy shop. (By the way, the "camera" in camera-ready copy refers to the special cameras that offset printers use to prepare the photographic plates necessary to print a book or brochure. A publication is "camera-ready" when it's ready for a printer to take its picture.)

Desktop publishing recently got a kid sister, **desktop presentation**. Desktop presentation is essentially the same as desktop publishing, except that it focuses on the kind of visual aids used in sales and informational presentations: slides, handouts, and transparencies for overhead projection. (See Chapter 20 for more information on how to do desktop presentations with Word for Windows.)

The trick to successful desktop publishing is to make your publications look as though they were done professionally, when, in fact, you really did them yourself. Step one is to get a sense of the different pieces or "design elements" that make up a page.

Desktop presentation is essentially the same as desktop publishing, except that it focuses on the kind of visual aids used in sales and informational presentations: slides, hand-outs, and transparencies for overhead projection.

BASIC ANATOMY

It's easier to create something you like when you know what your options are, so this section describes the chief "design elements" you can use to make your documents and publications look their best. The diagram entitled *Anatomy of a Page* covers elements common to most brochures, flyers, reports, and so on.

Headers run along the top of every page. They can contain a variety of information, including page number, publication title, date, office or organization that produced the publication, address, phone number, and so on. They can also contain graphics, such as rules (shown in the diagram) and logos. See Chapter 12 for information on using headers in Word for Windows.

Footers run along the bottom of every page and contain the same sorts of information as headers. In this example, even-numbered (left-hand) pages provide both the page number and the title of the document, *Marketing Study, 1991*. Odd-numbered (right-hand) pages give the page number and the chapter title, *Background*. See Chapter 12 for information on using footers in Word for Windows.

Anatomy of a Page

Outquote   **Header**

Double-page spread   **Rule**

Border

Graphic

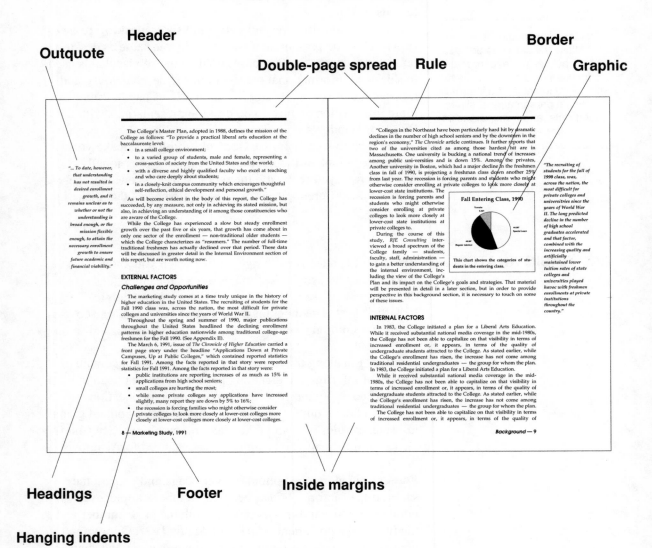

The College's Master Plan, adopted in 1988, defines the mission of the College as follows: "To provide a practical liberal arts education at the baccalaureate level:

- in a small college environment;
- to a varied group of students, male and female, representing a cross-section of society from the United States and the world;
- with a diverse and highly qualified faculty who excel at teaching and who care deeply about students;
- in a closely-knit campus community which encourages thoughtful self-reflection, ethical development and personal growth."

As will become evident in the body of this report, the College has succeeded, by any measure, not only in achieving its stated mission, but also, in achieving an understanding of it among those constituencies who are aware of the College.

While the College has experienced a slow but steady enrollment growth over the past five or six years, that growth has come about in only one sector of the enrollment — non-traditional older students — which the College characterizes as "resumers." The number of full-time traditional freshmen has actually declined over that period. These data will be discussed in greater detail in the Internal Environment section of this report, but are worth noting now.

EXTERNAL FACTORS

Challenges and Opportunities

The marketing study comes at a time truly unique in the history of higher education in the United States. The recruiting of students for the Fall 1990 class was, across the nation, the most difficult for private colleges and universities since the years of World War II.

Throughout the spring and summer of 1990, major publications throughout the United States headlined the declining enrollment patterns in higher education nationwide among traditional college-age freshmen for the Fall 1990. (See Appendix II).

The March 6, 1991, issue of *The Chronicle of Higher Education* carried a front page story under the headline "Applications Down at Private Campuses, Up at Public Colleges," which contained reported statistics for Fall 1991. Among the facts reported in that story were:

- public institutions are reporting increases of as much as 15% in applications from high school seniors;
- small colleges are hurting the most;
- while some private colleges say applications have increased slightly, many report they are down by 5% to 16%;
- the recession is forcing families who might otherwise consider private colleges to look more closely at lower-cost colleges more closely at lower-cost colleges more closely at lower-cost colleges.

"Colleges in the Northeast have been particularly hard hit by dramatic declines in the number of high school seniors and by the downturn in the region's economy," *The Chronicle* article continues. It further reports that two of the universities cited as among those hardest hit are in Massachusetts. One university is bucking a national trend of increases among public uni-versities and is down 15%. Among the privates, Another university in Boston, which had a major decline in the freshmen class in fall of 1990, is projecting a freshman class down another 25% from last year. The recession is forcing parents and students who might otherwise consider enrolling at private colleges to look more closely at lower-cost state institutions. The recession is forcing parents and students who might otherwise consider enrolling at private colleges to look more closely at lower-cost state institutions at private colleges to.

During the course of this study, *RJE Consulting* interviewed a broad spectrum of the College family — students, faculty, staff, administration — to gain a better understanding of the internal environment, including the view of the College's Plan and its impact on the College's goals and strategies. That material will be presented in detail in a later section, but in order to provide perspective in this background section, it is necessary to touch on some of these issues.

Fall Entering Class, 1990

This chart shows the categories of students in the entering class.

INTERNAL FACTORS

In 1983, the College initiated a plan for a Liberal Arts Education. While it received substantial national media coverage in the mid-1980s, the College has not been able to capitalize on that visibility in terms of increased enrollment or, it appears, in terms of the quality of undergraduate students attracted to the College. As stated earlier, while the College's enrollment has risen, the increase has not come among traditional residential undergraduates — the group for whom the plan. In 1983, the College initiated a plan for a Liberal Arts Education.

While it received substantial national media coverage in the mid-1980s, the College has not been able to capitalize on that visibility in terms of increased enrollment or, it appears, in terms of the quality of undergraduate students attracted to the College. As stated earlier, while the College's enrollment has risen, the increase has not come among traditional residential undergraduates — the group for whom the plan.

The College has not been able to capitalize on that visibility in terms of increased enrollment or, it appears, in terms of the quality of

Headings   **Footer**

Inside margins

Hanging indents

Outquotes are literally quotes pulled out of the main text. They're usually set in a typeface, size, and/or style that contrasts with the main text so they catch the reader's eye. In the diagram, the main text is in Palatino, and the outquotes are in Palatino bold, italic. Outquotes are also called pull quotes, callouts, breakouts, or blurbs. They generally contain especially interesting or important information. They are used to convey quickly the gist of the main text, or to entice the reader into it.

Headings, also called headlines or heads, are titles used to organize a document. Long documents especially tend to have several levels of headings—chapter heads, section heads, section subheads, and so on—with each level having its own recognizable style. The diagram shows two levels of headings: section head (*External Factors* and *Internal Factors*) and section subhead (*Challenges and Opportunities*).

Word for Windows provides nine levels of headings (each formatted into a particular style), called **heading 1**, **heading 2**, and so forth. (Usually headings 1 through 3 appear on the style menu; see Chapter 7 for instructions on getting all nine to appear.) Although each of Word's headings has a predefined style, you can easily redefine these styles to suit your taste. You can also use them to generate a table of contents automatically. See Chapter 15 for more information on generating tables of contents.

Graphic usually refers to a picture, graph, scanned image, or artwork of some sort. These are imported (or brought) into Word from another program such as Excel, Designer, or CorelDraw! The term "graphic" can also refer to a photo.

Rules are lines used for design, both vertical and horizontal (as shown in this example). Word offers a wide variety of rules (which it refers to as "borders"). See Chapters 7 and 10 for more information on how to use rules and borders in Word.

Borders are decorative boxes that frame text or graphics. Word has a number of different styles to choose from. Unfortunately, however, because of the way Word handles graphics, you can't create borders in other programs and import them. Instead, you have to create both the border *and* the text or graphic it encloses *outside* of Word, and then import them together as a single picture.

Word does not allow you to place text over, or inside, an imported graphic. However, it does allow you to put a border around imported graphics with its FORMAT, BORDER command. Note that Word uses the term "borders" to refer to rules as well as boxes. See Chapter 7 for more information on using borders in Word; see Chapter 11 for information on placing borders around imported graphics.

Hanging indents are a great way to make lists more interesting. You can dress them up with bullets, dingbats, oversized numbers, and so on to make each point stand out clearly.

A **double-page spread** consists of two pages facing each other that are designed to work together. Such spreads are sometimes called "facing pages"; they are a design opportunity you get whenever you create a double-sided publication. For instance, notice how the outquote on the left-hand page is flush right, and the one on the right-hand page is flush left. This creates a clean line against the main text, leaving the ragged edge to stick into the margins. Notice that a similar technique is used for the footer. You have to turn Word's Facing Pages feature on to make double-sided documents. See Chapter 12 for more information.

The **inside margin** is the space left over for binding the document, whether with a three-ring binder, spiral binding, staples, or some other method. Note that when you're printing a double-sided document, the inside margin is the right margin of even numbered pages and the left margin of odd-numbered pages.

When you are printing a single-sided document, the left margin is used for binding. See Chapter 12 for information on double-sided documents.

RULES OF THUMB FOR BETTER DESIGN

Here are some rules of thumb for better design. These rules are not meant to be "hard and fast." Once you've used them a little and get a feel for what works, you'll know when to break them.

I've divided these rules into two broad categories. The First-Things-First category focuses on some "big picture" issues; Dos & Don'ts gives some specific pointers.

When dealing with design, it's important to *see* whatever's being said. Some of these rules are illustrated in this chapter by three examples, labeled Done, Over Done, and Re-Done. Others, however, are illustrated in later chapters (when this is the case, I indicate where, so you can find them easily).

✦ First Things First

1. Ask yourself: Who is going to read this? What do I want to say to them? The answers to these questions will help you decide what type of document to produce—a brochure or a poster for example—and which ideas or information you want the design to emphasize.

2. Studies show that people are more likely to read headlines, outquotes, and captions than the main text. So, make your headlines "speak" your message; use outquotes whenever it's appropriate; and make sure your captions tell the reader something important. This technique can really pay off, especially in marketing and fund-raising pieces—if your headlines, captions, and outquotes make your pitch, the reader's more likely to hear it.

3. The only reason to bother designing anything is to get across what you want to say. The point is to communicate effectively—*not* to make pretty designs.

4. On the other hand, an appealing presentation makes things easier and more interesting to read.

5. Dress your documents for the occasion. The design (or format) should suit the sort of document you're doing. Don't make the mistake of gussying up your report to the president (or to a client) into a slick marketing piece.

6. If you're going to use a print shop, make sure you talk to the printer early on about the particular publication you're planning. A good printer will be able to help you set things up so that the printing process goes smoothly and *on time.*

✦ Dos & Don'ts

1. Reuse your good ideas. Once you come up with something that works, don't be afraid to use it often. In his book *Ogilvy on Advertising,* David Ogilvy remarks that for years he used one of two "perfect" layouts for all his ads. One layout allowed for a large photo and a relatively small amount of text; the other had a smaller photo and a relatively large amount of text. Both put the photo on top, then the headline, and the text at the bottom of the page. This formula works for flyers, flip sheets, and articles in newsletters, as well as for ads. (See *Good Design Is Just Common Sense* and *Imitate Success* in Chapter 2.)

2. Don't get carried away with all the neat things you can do with Word for Windows. The example labeled Over Done goes overboard. It stuffs half a dozen of Word's best design features onto a single page. Yes, there are all sorts of rules available in Word (note the header and footer); you can copy graphs from Excel; you can use dingbats (see them there, flanking the page number); and, of course, you can put boxes around text and tables and graphics (there's a shadow box around the graph, and there's a box around every single cell of the table).

You can also use expanded letter spacing (see how the letters in the headline "Mutual Funds" and in the heading for the graph are spread out?) and lots of different fonts (this one, short page uses four of them). And it only takes minutes to do! That's the trap. Just because these things are easy to do doesn't mean you should do them.

3. Keep it simple. The example labeled Done does. It uses two typefaces—Times and Helvetica. The headline is the main graphic element, that is, the thing you see first; the table comes in a close second. Both the text and table are easy to read, even when they're reduced to 40% of their original size, as they are here. (See *Keep It Simple* in Chapter 2.)

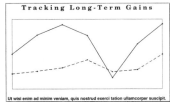

Banking Group Report — Week ending 9/27/91

MUTUAL FUNDS

Orem ipsum dolor sit amet, consectetuer adipiscing elit, sed diam nonummy nibh euismod tincidunt ut laoreet dolore magna aliquam erat volutpat. Ut wisi enim ad minim veniam, quis nostrud exerci tation ullamcorper suscipit lobortis nisl ut aliquip ex ea commodo feugiat consequat. Lorem ipsum dolor sit.

Consectetuer adipiscing elit, sed diam nonummy nibh euismod tincidunt ut laoreet dolore magna aliquam erat volutpat. Ut wisi enim ad minim veniam, quis nostrud exerci tation ullamcorper suscipit lobortis nisl ut aliquip ex ea commodo feugiat consequat. Lorem ipsum dolor sit amet, consectetuer adipiscing elit, sed diam nonummy nibh euismod tincidunt ut laoreet dolore magna aliquam erat volut.

Ut wisi enim ad minim veniam, quis nostrud exerci tation ullamcorper suscipit lobortis nisl ut aliquip ex ea commodo feugiat consequat. Lorem ipsum dolor sit amet, consectetuer adipiscing elit, sed diam nonummy nibh euismod tincidunt ut laoreet dolore magna aliquam erat volutpat. Ut wisi enim ad min. Sum dolor sit amet, consectetuer adipiscing elit, sed diam nonummy nibh euismod tincidunt ut laoreet dolore magna aliquam erat volutpat. Ut wisi enim ad minim veniam.

Nostrud exerci tation ullamcorper suscipit lobortis nisl ut aliquip ex ea commodo feugiat consequat. Lorem ipsum dolor ex ea commodo feugiat consequat. Lorem ipsum dolor.

Sed diam nonummy nibh euismod tincidunt ut laoreet dolore magna aliquam erat volutpat. Ut wisi enim ad minim veniam, quis nostrud exerci tation ullamcorper suscipit lobortis nisl ut aliquip ex ea commodo feugiat consequat. Lorem ipsum dolor sit amet, consectetuer adipiscing elit, sed diam nonummy nibh euismod tincidunt ut laoreet dolore magna aliquam erat volutpat. Feugiat consequat. Lorem ipsum dolor sit amet, consectetuer adipiscing elit, sed diam nonummy nibh euismod tincidunt ut laoreet dolore magna aliquam erat volutpat. feugiat consequat. Lorem ipsum dolor sit amet, consectetuer adipiscing elit, sed diam nonummy nibh euismod tincidunt ut laoreet dolore magna aliquam erat volutpat.

Tracking Long-Term Gains

Ut wisi enim ad minim veniam, quis nostrud exerci tation ullamcorper suscipit.

THE 10 BEST PERFORMERS

	Assets (millions)	Expense Ratio	Total Return		52 Wks	5 Years
			Week	1991		
Fidelity SI Tech	$223.9	2.07%	-0.26%	34.75%	85.01%	138.54%
Fidelity SI Med	37.8	2.16	3.42	32.92	69.52	N/A
Fidelity SI Hlth	373.2	1.71	-0.19	23.35	68.69	154.92
Fidelity Port: Hlth	161.1	1.11	0.12	28.90	65.82	256.96
Oppenheimer Tch	23.3	1.75	2.05	35.33	55.15	N/A
Putnam Hlth Sci	376.1	1.14	-0.98	18.13	45.21	133.69
Vanguard Hlth	163.6	0.32	-0.87	15.12	39.38	141.81
GT Global Health	175.5	2.30	-0.55	18.44	38.62	N/A
Medical Res Inv	4.4	3.40	-1.49	19.58	31.63	74.72
Fidelity SI Comp	24.2	2.58	-2.34	25.67	29.17	42.25

▪ Page 7 ▪

Over Done

4. You don't need a picture to create a graphically appealing page. Compare the examples Done and Re-Done. The example Done doesn't need a graph from Excel to make it interesting. In fact, I like it better without the graph—it's less cluttered and easier to read (the type size for the main text is actually somewhat larger, and there's plenty of space between the lines). However, if you have to use a graph because it conveys important information, Re-Done makes the best of it.

5. It's easier to read a page of text set in a serif face (such as Times) than a sans serif face (such as Helvetica). This is because serif face letters are easier for the eye to recognize.

Note how much simpler it is to read the main text in Done and Re-Done—both are set in Times—than in Over Done, which is set in Helvetica-Narrow. (See Chapter 3.)

6. Don't use lots of typefaces—*ughh*! The problem with using several entirely different typefaces is that every typeface is like a suit of clothes. A typeface conveys character and personality just as plaid trousers do, or a polka-dot shirt. And, just like spotted shirts and plaid pants, they have a tendency to clash—as exhibited in Over Done. (See *Don't Use Lots of Typefaces* in Chapter 2; also, Chapter 3.)

7. Don't be afraid to make things small. A seasoned designer once told me that the most frequent mistake of new

Banking Group Report — Week ending 9/27/91

MUTUAL FUNDS

Orem ipsum dolor sit amet, consectetuer adipiscing elit, sed diam nonummy nibh euismod tincidunt ut laoreet dolore magna aliquam erat volutpat. Ut wisi enim ad minim veniam, quis nostrud exerci tation ullamcorper suscipit lobortis nisl ut aliquip ex ea commodo feugiat consequat. Lorem ipsum dolor sit.

Consectetuer adipiscing elit, sed diam nonummy nibh euismod tincidunt ut laoreet dolore magna aliquam erat volutpat. Ut wisi enim ad minim veniam, quis nostrud exerci tation ullamcorper suscipit lobortis nisl ut aliquip ex ea commodo feugiat consequat. Lorem ipsum dolor sit amet, consectetuer adipiscing elit, sed diam nonummy nibh euismod tincidunt ut laoreet dolore magna aliquam erat volut.

Ut wisi enim ad minim veniam, quis nostrud exerci tation ullamcorper suscipit lobortis nisl ut aliquip ex ea commodo feugiat consequat. Lorem ipsum dolor sit amet, consectetuer adipiscing elit, sed diam nonummy nibh euismod tincidunt ut laoreet dolore magna aliquam erat volutpat. Ut wisi enim ad min. Sum dolor sit amet, consectetuer adipiscing elit, sed diam nonummy nibh euismod tincidunt ut laoreet dolore magna aliquam erat volutpat. Ut wisi enim ad minim veniam.

Nostrud exerci tation ullamcorper suscipit lobortis nisl ut aliquip ex ea commodo feugiat consequat. Lorem ipsum dolor ex ea commodo feugiat consequat. Lorem ipsum dolor.

Sed diam nonummy nibh euismod tincidunt ut laoreet dolore magna aliquam erat volutpat. Ut wisi enim ad minim veniam, quis nostrud exerci tation ullamcorper suscipit lobortis nisl ut aliquip ex ea commodo feugiat consequat. Lorem ipsum dolor sit amet, consectetuer adipiscing elit, sed diam nonummy nibh euismod tincidunt ut laoreet dolore magna aliquam erat volutpat. Lorem ipsum dolor sit amet, consectetuer adipiscing elit, sed diam nonummy nibh euismod tincidunt ut laoreet dolore magna.

THE 10 BEST PERFORMERS

	Assets (millions)	Expense Ratio	Total Return Week	1991	52 Wks	5 Years
Fidelity SI Tech	$223.9	2.07%	-0.26%	34.75%	85.01%	138.54%
Fidelity SI Med	37.8	2.16	3.42	32.92	69.52	N/A
Fidelity SI Hlth	373.2	1.71	-0.19	23.35	68.69	154.92
Fidelity Port: Hlth	161.1	1.11	0.12	28.90	65.82	256.96
Oppenheimer Tch	23.3	1.75	2.05	35.33	55.15	N/A
Putnam Hlth Sci	376.1	1.14	-0.98	18.13	45.21	133.69
Vanguard Hlth	163.6	0.32	-0.87	15.12	39.38	141.81
GT Global Health	175.5	2.30	-0.55	18.44	38.62	N/A
Medical Res Inv	4.4	3.40	-1.49	19.58	31.63	74.72
Fidelity SI Comp	24.2	2.58	-2.34	25.67	29.17	42.25

7

Done: The simplest design often communicates most effectively.

Banking Group Report — Week ending 9/27/91

MUTUAL FUNDS

Orem ipsum dolor sit amet, consectetuer adipiscing elit, sed diam nonummy nibh euismod tincidunt ut laoreet dolore magna aliquam erat volutpat. Ut wisi enim ad minim veniam, quis nostrud exerci tation ullamcorper suscipit lobortis nisl ut aliquip ex ea commodo feugiat consequat. Lorem ipsum dolor sit.

Consectetuer adipiscing elit, sed diam nonummy nibh euismod tincidunt ut laoreet dolore magna aliquam erat volutpat. Ut wisi enim ad minim veniam, quis nostrud exerci tation ullamcorper suscipit lobortis nisl ut aliquip ex ea commodo feugiat consequat. Lorem ipsum dolor sit amet, consectetuer adipiscing elit, sed diam nonummy nibh euismod tincidunt ut laoreet dolore magna aliquam erat volut.

Ut wisi enim ad minim veniam, quis nostrud exerci tation ullamcorper suscipit lobortis nisl ut ea commodo feugiat consequat. Lorem ipsum dolor sit amet, consectetuer adipiscing elit, sed diam nonummy nibh euismod tincidunt ut laoreet dolore magna aliquam erat volutpat. Ut wisi enim ad min. Sum dolor sit amet, consectetuer adipiscing elit, sed diam nonummy nibh euismod tincidunt ut laoreet dolore magna aliquam erat volutpat. Ut wisi enim ad minim veniam.

Nostrud exerci tation ullamcorper suscipit lobortis nisl ut aliquip ex ea commodo feugiat consequat. Lorem ipsum dolor ex ea commodo feugiat consequat. Lorem ipsum dolor.

Sed diam nonummy nibh euismod tincidunt ut laoreet dolore magna aliquam erat volutpat. Ut wisi enim ad minim veniam, quis nostrud exerci tation ullamcorper

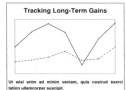

Tracking Long-Term Gains

Ut wisi enim ad minim veniam, quis nostrud exerci tation ullamcorper suscipit.

suscipit lobortis nisl ut aliquip ex ea commodo feugiat consequat. Lorem ipsum dolor sit amet, consectetuer adipiscing elit, sed nonummy nibh euismod tincidunt ut laoreet dolore magna aliquam erat volutpat. Lorem ipsum dolor sit amet, consectetuer adipiscing elit, sed diam nonummy nibh euismod tincidunt ut laoreet dolore magna aliquam erat volutpat euismod tincidunt ut laoreet dolore magna aliquam erat volutpat.

THE 10 BEST PERFORMERS

	Assets (millions)	Expense Ratio	Total Return			
			Week	1991	52 Wks	5 Years
Fidelity SI Tech	$223.9	2.07%	-0.26%	34.75%	85.01%	138.54%
Fidelity SI Med	37.8	2.16	3.42	32.92	69.52	N/A
Fidelity SI Hlth	373.2	1.71	-0.19	23.35	68.69	154.92
Fidelity Port: Hlth	161.1	1.11	0.12	28.90	65.82	256.96
Oppenheimer Tch	23.3	1.75	2.05	35.33	55.15	N/A
Putnam Hlth Sci	376.1	1.14	-0.98	18.13	45.21	133.69
Vanguard Hlth	163.6	0.32	-0.87	15.12	39.38	141.81
GT Global Health	175.5	2.30	-0.55	18.44	38.62	N/A
Medical Res Inv	4.4	3.40	-1.49	19.58	31.63	74.72
Fidelity SI Comp	24.2	2.58	-2.34	25.67	29.17	42.25

7

Re-Done

designers is they make everything too big. Sometimes smaller things look better. Compare the graph in Re-Done with the one in Over Done.

8. On the other hand, don't make things *too* small. It's hard to read anything smaller than 6 points.

9. Be careful with clip art! If you want your work to look serious and professional, don't stick clip art of a phone in the middle of an analysis of the cost of phone service over the past decade. A graph illustrating the change in costs would be much more effective, or perhaps you could use an outquote.

10. Here's one way to decide which design works better: If you think (or someone says) that one of them looks more *artistic,* use the other.

11. Be consistent. Each element should have a recognizable style, and that same style should be used throughout the document. All the chapter heads should look alike; all the section heads should look alike; all the outquotes should look alike. (See *Use Distinctive Headings to Orient the Reader and Organize Your Report* in Chapter 2.)

12. Add "color," even when you're working in black and white. A big, bold head against ample white space is "brighter"—more striking—than a whole page of 12-point text (which looks gray). Note that the Helvetica bold headline in the example Done makes the page more "colorful." (See *You Don't Need Colors to Add Color* in Chapter 2.)

13. Be patient. Sometimes you have to do things fifteen times to get them to look right. Some days it takes even longer.

14. Remember, it's easier to read black letters on a white page than white letters on a black page. When you use color paper for your publications, make sure it's light enough so people can read the text *easily.*

15. The advice Sir Arthur Quiller-Couch gave to writers is just as useful to those of us who try to dress that writing in an appealing presentation: "Murder your darlings." If you think the design you're looking at is the most beautiful—the most clever—you've ever done, chances are you'll be better off if you delete it from your computer immediately and go to lunch.

CHAPTER 2

Desktop Designs

Here's my collection of designs that just about anybody can do with Word for Windows. There are designs suitable for everything from forms to reports to newsletters—in other words, for the kinds of things you might have to do. There's one section on each category of publication. You can use these designs pretty much "as is" or modify them to your particular needs and taste. But remember that these categories are pretty fluid. Sometimes a report layout will strike you as being just right for a brochure, or a catalog layout will seem just right for a newsletter.

The most important thing is to decide which designs you *like*. I always cut pages I like out of magazines and newspapers, stuff them into an old notebook, and think about how to adapt them to the sort of work I do. A lot of those designs have found their way into this book.

All the designs you see in this chapter are very easy to fairly easy to do with Word for Windows. Once you get the text typed in, most of these designs will take the average user only ten minutes or so to finish.

FORMS, CALENDARS, AND NOTICES

You probably wouldn't bother with *forms, calendars,* and *notices* if you didn't have information you needed to get into people's heads (or at least, their hands). Good designs for these sorts of documents are ones that simplify that transfer of information. They should be well organized, easy to read, and just as easy to fill out (usually that means lines long enough for the information requested and boxes for people to make Xs in whenever they need to make a choice).

Although there are almost as many form design programs as page layout programs, in most ways Word for Windows is as good as the best of them. Its table functions (the soul of form design) are easy to use and very much like spreadsheets. It's also easy to dress up your forms with graphics from Microsoft Draw and Word's built-in borders.

This section offers some guidelines for making your standard business communications as successful as possible. The examples all use one of two typefaces, or fonts: Times (also known as Times Roman) and Helvetica (also called "Swiss," which is what "Helvetian" means). These are two of the most widely used typefaces around, and for the best of reasons—they're as pretty to look at as they are easy to read.

✦ Keep it Simple

When you're doing up a notice or memo to explain something in writing—for example, the company's policy regarding reimbursement of travel expenses—keep it clear and simple. But remember, *clear and simple is not an excuse for downright ugly.* Whenever possible, break long paragraphs into shorter paragraphs and break lists into bulleted items. No matter how well written they are, big blocks of text make hard reading.

Headings and bulleted items always provide opportunities to make the page more interesting—don't waste them! In this case, the list is "bulleted" with checkmarks (done in the Zapf Dingbats "picture" font, which comes with PostScript printers). The headings are all done in Helvetica bold. The descriptions of each item on the travel expense form (name, budget, period, and so on) are formatted as hanging indents to make them stand out.

DeZiner Corp. — 8/9/91

Travel Expense Reimbursement

There are 5 things you must do to get your travel expenses reimbursed:

✔ save ALL receipts over $25

✔ fill out form TE-1 for cash expenses (attached)

✔ fill out form TE-2 for credit card expenses (attached)

✔ have your immediate supervisor sign both forms

✔ submit both forms and ALL receipts to Accounts Payable

It generally takes two weeks for Accounts Payable to process your reimbursement. The sooner you get the paperwork in, the sooner you'll get a check reimbursing your expenses. *NO expense over $25 will be reimbursed UNLESS it's accompanied by an original receipt.*

The following explanations cover the information you have to fill out on forms TE-1 and TE-2 in order to get your travel expenses reimbursed.

Form TE-1 Travel Expenses: Cash

Name:	Always fill out your last name first. It's helpful if you print your last name entirely in capital letters.
Budget:	This is a four-digit code for the budget to which your travel expenses are to be charged.
Period:	Fill out a separate form for each travel period. A travel period ends once you arrive back at your home office.
Destination(s):	If you cover more than one destination in a single trip, you can list all of the destinations here. Remember, a travel period ends once you arrive back at your home office. If you need more space than is available here, just attach another sheet of paper to this form.
Purpose:	Write a brief explanation of the nature or your trip, *i.e.*, sales, training, technical assistance, etc.
Cash items:	List everything you spent cash on other than meals, and how much it cost. You must have a valid, original receipt for every purchase over $25. If you need more space than is available here, just attach another sheet of paper to this form.
Credit items:	Include ALL original credit card receipts and a copy of the credit card bill itself. Write a brief explanation of the nature or your trip, *i.e.*, sales, training, technical assistance, etc. Write a brief explanation of the nature or your trip, *i.e.*, sales, training, technical assistance, sales, training, technical assistance, etc.

1 of 4

Don't forget the header and footer (which run along the top and bottom of every page, respectively). They convey important information, such as the page number and date of the notice, so that you can easily determine whether or not the notice you have is the most recent. They also provide a nice design touch. (See Chapter 3 for more information on using dingbats.)

✦ Whenever You Can, Convey Information Visually

It's easier to remember dates marked on a calendar than those listed on a page. The calendar conveys the same information a paragraph would, but more quickly and enjoyably. I understand that Japanese companies often use cartoons to liven up employee newsletters and the like because they have found that people are more likely to read them.

Departmental Calendar — March 1992

SUNDAY	MONDAY	TUESDAY	WEDNESDAY	THURSDAY	FRIDAY	SATURDAY
1	2	3 STAFF MEETING	4	5	6	7
8	9 Blood Drive	10 Blood Drive	11 RG'N MGR Blood Drive	12	13	14
15	16 FEB SALES RPTS DUE	17	18	19 Team Meet New Business	20	21
22	23 TRAINING SIGN UP	24 STAFF MEETING	25	26 COMPUT'R TRAINING	27 COMPUT'R TRAINING	28
29	30 PROJCTNS DUE	31				

REMEMBER:

- All staff meetings start promptly at 9:30 a.m.
- If you have an agenda you want to cover at the staff meeting, you must submit a 1 to 2 page explanatory memo to the director at least three working days prior to the meeting, *e.g.*, agendas for the March 3rd meeting are due February 27th, and agendas for the March 24th meeting are due March 19th. If you don't meet these deadlines, your agenda will be covered at a later staff meeting.
- Computer Training will be on Excel, and will focus on using models for sales projections. It will run from 9:30 to 12:30 both days. Please sign up at the director's office by March 23rd. Guidelines for completing sales reports are available in the director's office. Guidelines for completing sales reports are available in the director's office.
- Guidelines for completing sales reports are available in the director's office.
- Guidelines for completing sales projections are available in the director's office.
- Other guidelines are available in the director's office.

The two calendars shown here were created using Word's table functions. In the top sample, the list below the calendar notes some important procedural points. The next sample adds a few Microsoft Draw graphics and Zapf Dingbats to a very-easy-to-maintain weekly schedule. Some service bureaus can turn calendars like these into poster-sized documents. (See *Settling Down with a Good Service Bureau* in Chapter 4 for more information.)

WEEKLY — **SENIOR CENTER** — SCHEDULE

	SUN.	MON.	TUES.	WED.	THR.	FRI.	SAT.
9:00	☕	Coffee Hour	Coffee Hour	Coffee Hour	Coffee Hour	Coffee Hour	—
10:00		—	*Sewing Club* ✄	*GARDEN Club*	*Chess Club*	—	Coffee Hour
11:00		EXERCISES	—	EXERCISES	—	EXERCISES	—
12:00	*Sunday*	LUNCH	LUNCH	LUNCH	LUNCH	LUNCH	LUNCH
1:30	*Dinner*	MOVIE	Arts & Crafts	MOVIE	Arts & Crafts	*Chess Tournament*	MOVIE
4:00		Afterschool Program	Afterschool Program	Afterschool Program	Afterschool Program	Afterschool Program	Tea
5:00		—	SEMINAR: Phone Assurance	SEMINAR: Healthy Eating	SEMINAR: Handling Emergencies	—	—

✦ Don't Forget the Bottom Line

This is a registration form for members of time dollar programs (a kind of social service barter network) all over the country. Several of its design elements are dictated by the fact that once a member fills a form out, an administrator enters the information into a computer. For instance, although it doesn't make any sense (in terms of the form itself) to number the types of services a person is willing to offer, it makes a lot of sense to the computer operator, who can then use those numbers to enter the information more quickly.

When I was designing this form, I tried to take my own advice and make it as easy as possible to follow and fill out. The boxes where members put Xs next to appropriate answers are done with the Zapf Dingbats font. I drew most of the lines for written answers by underlining **nonbreaking spaces**, which keep words together on the same line and are a fixed width. However, since the lines in the "Comments" section take up the entire paragraph, I was able to make them using Word's FORMAT, BORDER command (much simpler!).

I want to point out two design touches. One is the use of Helvetica to set off the "For Official Use Only" box; all the other text is set in Times. The second is the use of **all caps** (all capital letters) followed by a colon in those cases where a series of choices follows. These touches serve not only to define specific categories of information, but also to make the page a little more appealing.

✦ You Can Even Add!

It used to be that most forms produced on a computer were actually filled out by hand. Now, however, more and more people are creating forms on the computer, filling them out on the computer, and printing them only when they're ready to be proofed and sent off. This is especially true with "recurring forms" such as expense reports.

This two-page expense report is adapted from one I created with employees at Lazard Frères & Co. They had to fill out expense reports every month and wanted the process to be as easy as possible. So we created an expense report **template** similar

NAME:		DeZiner Corp. EXPENSE REPORT					PERIOD From:		To:	
DATE	PLACE VISITED & BUSINESS PURPOSE	AIR/RAIL 21010	BUSINESS MEALS 21011	ENTERTAIN- MENT 21016	HOTELS 21013	TAXIS 21010	AUTO RENTAL 21010	MISC. & TELE 21019	TOTAL: FIRM EXPENSE	CLIENT #

PLEASE NOTE:
- Attach ALL original receipts to this form.
- Call Joyce Bartson in Accounts Payable (x4444) if you have any questions as to how to complete this form.

				TOTAL	
LESS ADVANCES	
EMPLOYEE SIGNATURE	DATE	APPROVED DEPT HEAD	DATE SIGNATURE	BALANCE DUE

DETAILS OF BUSINESS MEALS, ENTERTAINMENT AND MISCELLANEOUS				

BUSINESS MEALS: This expense classification is reserved for meals which have a clear purpose related to revenue-producing business.
BUSINESS ENTERTAINMENT: The IRS requires the name of the people attending, their position and business affiliation (usually company name), and the business purpose of the occasion, in order to justify the expense as business entertainment.

BUSINESS MEALS
(Attach ALL original receipts)

DATE	NAMES	COMPANY & POSITION	PURPOSE OF LUNCH/DINNER	AMOUNT
(Attach additional sheets if necessary)			TOTAL	

BUSINESS ENTERTAINMENT
(Attach ALL original receipts)

DATE	NAMES	COMPANY & POSITION	PURPOSE	NATURE	AMOUNT
(Attach additional sheets if necessary)				TOTAL	

MISCELLANEOUS EXPLANATION: _____
_____
_____

to the pages shown here. (A template is essentially a model document that you can use over and over again.)

Each page of this expense report is a full-page table arranged to print horizontally on the paper (also known as **landscape** mode). The cells that extend over several columns were created using Word's TABLE, MERGE CELLS command.

One of the things people liked best about these forms is that Word can actually *add up* columns of numbers and give you the total. This expense report (adding and all) is used in Chapter 16.

FLYERS

Flyers are one of those things you see every day without really noticing. They are taped on lampposts, tacked on employee bulletin boards, and handed out on street corners and in malls. Usually we don't even bother to read them. But a good flyer can move the reader to do something, to go somewhere, or to buy something as surely as a good fashion ad can make you want that particular striped shirt.

Flyers are usually a single sheet of paper, printed on one side. Their purpose generally is to promote something—whether it's an upcoming lecture, a blood drive, a special sale, or an arts festival—and in this respect they are similar to ads. The key to a good ad, as Alan Swann says in his book *Graphic Design School,* is that "your message has to be conveyed instantly."

✦ Use Space Wisely

If you have a whole page and not a whole lot of words, don't write more text just to fill space. Instead, make the text you have bigger until it fills the page. Although this flyer doesn't have any artwork, it's still artsy—the big-lettered list down the center not only gets the message across; it also invites you to read it. In fact, it insists. One glance and you've got the point.

This flyer is used as an example in Chapter 3 to show how easy it is to turn type into artwork.

The POETRY SOCIETY • CAVEAT EMPTOR UNIVERSITY • SUMMERVILLE, NEW YORK 11111

The POETRY SOCIETY
sponsors a night of...

whimsy
poesy
limericks
rhymes
jingles
jangles
&
vaulting meters

... featuring such greats as Bachelor Burton *by James Thurber,* The Hunting of the Snark *by Lewis Carroll, and T.S. Eliot's* Old Possum's Book of Practical Cats.

APRIL 1ˢᵗ AT 7:00 P.M. IN THE VIRGIL LOUNGE

✦ Get Graphic

Sometimes, a flyer or a brochure looks better if you use artwork or a photo. This flyer for the Winter Arts Fest certainly does. The partridge says "handcrafted," "Christmas," "artistic," and "exquisite" all at the same time, and much more eloquently than the sentence it replaces (see the sample labeled B). The partridge is a folksy image that works well for this crafts fair; if the festival celebrated antiques, you would need an image that said so.

This flyer uses one of the most complex layouts in this book. Yet you can still do it in 15 to 20 minutes *after you've typed in the text*. Which brings us to an important point: Especially when working with complex designs, you should make a habit

OVER 75 REGIONAL ARTISTS & CRAFTSMEN

POTTERY ▪ PAINTINGS ▪ WOODWORK ▪ SCULPTURE

HAVERFORD COUNTY'S THIRD ANNUAL
WINTER ARTS FEST

VASES ▪ JEWELRY ▪ MUGS ▪
HAND-WOVEN RUGS ▪ SILVER-
WARE ▪ CUPS ▪ PLATES ▪ BOWLS
▪ MUGS ▪ JEWELRY ▪ FURNITURE
▪ PAINTINGS ▪ CUPS ▪ PORTRAITS
▪ SCULPTURE ▪ MUGS ▪ JEWELS ▪
SILVERWARE ▪ CUPS ▪ PLATES ▪
BOWLS ▪ MUGS ▪ JEWELRY ▪
FURNITURE ▪ PAINTINGS ▪ CUPS
PORTRAITS ▪ SCULPTURE ▪ RUGS
▪ ETCHINGS ▪ CANDLESTICKS ▪
VASES ▪ JEWELRY ▪ BOWLS
SILVERWARE ▪ CUPS ▪ PLATES ▪
BOWLS ▪ MUGS ▪ CUPS ▪ RINGS
FURNITURE ▪ PAINTINGS ▪ CUPS ▪
RINGS ▪ MUGS ▪ CUPS ▪ FURNI-
TURE ▪ PLATTERS ▪ CUPS ▪ MUGS

VISIT THE NEWLY RENOVATED
HOMESPUN MUSEUM
11 Main Street ▪ Haverford, CT ▪ (203) 222-2222

DECEMBER 1st - 22nd
Monday-Saturday 10:00-7:00 ▪ Sunday 12:00-5:00

A

23

OVER 75 REGIONAL ARTISTS & CRAFTSMEN

POTTERY ▪ PAINTINGS ▪ WOODWORK ▪ SCULPTURE

HAVERFORD COUNTY'S THIRD ANNUAL

WINTER ARTS FEST

Choose your Christmas gifts from among the
largest selection of hand-crafted items available.
Each item is exquisitely designed
and signed by the artist.

VASES ▪ JEWELRY ▪ MUGS ▪ HAND-WOVEN RUGS ▪ SILVERWARE ▪
CUPS ▪ PLATES ▪ BOWLS ▪ MUGS ▪ JEWELRY ▪ FURNITURE ▪
PAINTINGS ▪ CUPS ▪ PORTRAITS ▪ SCULPTURE ▪ MUGS ▪ JEWELS ▪
SILVERWARE ▪ CUPS ▪ PLATES ▪ BOWLS ▪ MUGS ▪ JEWELRY ▪
FURNITURE ▪ PAINTINGS ▪ CUPS ▪ PORTRAITS ▪ SCULPTURE ▪ RUGS ▪
ETCHINGS ▪ CANDLESTICKS ▪ VASES ▪ JEWELRY ▪ BOWLS ▪
SILVERWARE ▪ CUPS ▪ PLATES ▪ BOWLS ▪ MUGS ▪ CUPS ▪ RINGS ▪
FURNITURE ▪ PAINTINGS ▪ CUPS ▪ RINGS ▪ MUGS ▪ CUPS ▪ FURNI-
TURE ▪ PLATTERS ▪ CUPS ▪ MUGS ▪ VASES ▪ JEWELRY ▪ MUGS ▪ HAND-
WOVEN RUGS ▪ SILVERWARE ▪ CUPS ▪ PLATES ▪ BOWLS ▪ MUGS ▪
JEWELRY ▪ FURNITURE ▪ PAINTINGS ▪ CUPS ▪ PORTRAITS ▪ RUGS ▪

VISIT THE NEWLY RENOVATED

HOMESPUN MUSEUM

11 Main Street ▪ Haverford, CT ▪ (203) 222-2222

DECEMBER 1st - 22nd
Monday-Saturday 10:00-7:00 ▪ Sunday 12:00-5:00

B

of finalizing your text *before* formatting it. You'll save a lot of time because you won't have to *reformat* your work every time the text changes. For instance, if you added text to the flyer at this point, you would have to reduce the image of the partridge, the list of items available at the festival, and the spacing between lines to make it all fit. If you decided later to cut some text, you'd have to enlarge and expand everything again.

Whenever you're working with graphics positioned with the FORMAT, FRAME command (this flyer, for example), you need to use the VIEW, PAGE LAYOUT option when finishing up. This mode basically gives you **WYSIWYG** (an acronym for "What You See Is What You Get" and pronounced "wizzy-wig") for page layout, so you can see—while you are still formatting—the graphics and text positioned just as they'll print. Unfortunately this option slows things down considerably, and it can be excruciating to sit and watch the screen redraw whenever you change a word. Although you'll probably need to tweak the publication into its final form using this mode, be forewarned—it's *slow.*

One more thing about working in the VIEW, PAGE LAYOUT mode: it is not one hundred percent accurate. You'll sometimes notice that when you use Word's Print Preview feature, things line up differently. Although Print Preview isn't one hundred percent either, it's usually the better bet.

ADS

Although I would never suggest using Word for Windows to lay out a flashy fashion ad for *Vogue,* it's all you need for most newspaper ads—from help-wanted ads to appeals for good causes. Since such ads are usually **text based** (as opposed to photos and frills), their graphic interest relies largely on how you handle that text, especially the headline.

"On the average, five times as many people read the headlines as read the body copy," David Ogilvy observed in his book, *Ogilvy on Advertising.* "It follows that unless your headline sells your product, you have wasted 90% of your money. . . . Headlines, more than anything else, decide the success or failure of an advertisement."

So make sure your headline has a clear message and graphic appeal. An effective ad, like any effective promotional piece, needs to capture your readers' eye and interest when they glance at the page.

The ads shown here are standard sizes for *The New York Times.* When you're developing an ad, get the **rate cards** (which list the ad sizes available and the prices) from all the different publications you're considering. This helps you decide the general size and shape you want the ad to be. You can enlarge or reduce the ad to fit different-sized slots by having **stats** made to the correct size (a stat, or photostat, is a fairly inexpensive but high-quality copy made at most quick-print shops).

Remember that when you enlarge a document, you enlarge its flaws as well. By the same token, when you reduce it, you can lose detail, especially if it has fine lines or fine print. Generally speaking, however, you can improve the quality of a document slightly by reducing it slightly.

The 5-Minute Makeover

This makeover took only 5 minutes—literally. That was all the time I had when the man who created this flyer asked me to put the finishing touches on it. He thought it looked all right, but wasn't quite satisfied. I made only two text changes. I added "A one-day seminar" and the actual date of the course. The layout changes were based on the simplest principles of design. Once you know them, you will have the bulk of the literature on design under your belt.

- I reduced the size of the body copy from 12-point to 11-point Times. This gave me a little more space to work with, without sacrificing readability.

- I got rid of the ragged look by justifying the body copy. I also eliminated the indents that started each paragraph and preceded each bullet point.

Windows & OS/2 Conference
Application Integration with Windows:
A new methodology for Leveraging Systems Development in the 90's
August 1991, Boston MA

Overview:

Powerful windows products and their macro languages enable corporate developers to build integrated business systems faster and at a lower cost. The resultant applications are more useful to business users, enhancing business decision making capabilities. End users are empowered with tools to perform their own customized "what-if" scenario analysis and modeling. We will explore how integrated applications can be created with a combination of macro languages, DDE and DLLs. We will review case studies of strategic success solutions implemented by leading Wall Street institutions.

What you will learn:

- Dramatically reduce your organizations application development backlog.
- Choosing successful integration tools for your organization's application needs.
- Provide a dynamic framework for analysis. Discuss when to use the client server model, when to use dynamic and extensible spreadsheet models.
- Fast prototyping and development and their impact on application roll-out, support and end-user acceptance.
- How business units can work closely with development groups to reduce the time spent in design and development -- and deliver systems at a lower cost. Eliminate the "designed in a vacuum syndrome."
- The "build vs. buy" decision -- how the rules have change under Windows.
- The changing skills used to successfully implementing the integrated environment.
- How to effectively use Excel and Word for Windows and their macro languages. What tasks are better left for other development tools.
- Provide user with information and tools empowering them to more effectively analyze their business problems.

Who should attend:

This course is valuable for managers, developers, and application integrators involved in designing, building and customizing an integrated corporate Windows environment.

Instructor:

Andrew Mehring is a co-founder and managing partner of Micro Modeling Associates, which provides Windows software development and integration services to Fortune 1000 companies including Merrill Lynch, Donaldson Lufkin & Jenrette, and the New York Stock Exchange. Micro Modeling has used the methods described above to dramatically reduce development costs, and delivery times, while delivering more applications that are successful corporate solutions.

Before

Windows & OS/2 Conference
Application Integration with Windows:
A New Methodology for Leveraging Systems Development in the 90's

A one-day seminar • August 24, 1991 • Boston, MA

Overview:
Powerful windows products and their macro languages enable corporate developers to build integrated business systems faster and at a lower cost. The resultant applications are more useful to business users, enhancing business decision making capabilities. End users are empowered with tools to perform their own customized "what-if" scenario analysis and modeling. We will explore how integrated applications can be created with a combination of macro languages, DDE and DLLs. We will review case studies of strategic success solutions implemented by leading Wall Street institutions.

What you will learn:
- Dramatically reduce your organizations application development backlog.
- Choosing successful integration tools for your organization's application needs.
- Provide a dynamic framework for analysis. Discuss when to use the client server model, when to use dynamic and extensible spreadsheet models.
- Fast prototyping and development and their impact on application roll-out, support and end-user acceptance.
- How business units can work closely with development groups to reduce the time spent in design and development -- and deliver systems at a lower cost. Eliminate the "designed in a vacuum syndrome."
- The "build vs. buy" decision — how the rules have change under Windows.
- The changing skills used to successfully implementing the integrated environment.
- How to effectively use Excel and Word for Windows and their macro languages. What tasks are better left for other development tools.
- Provide user with information and tools empowering them to more effectively analyze their business problems.

Who should attend:
This course is valuable for managers, developers, and application integrators involved in designing, building and customizing an integrated corporate Windows environment.

Instructor:
Andrew Mehring is a co-founder and managing partner of Micro Modeling Associates, which provides Windows software development and integration services to Fortune 1000 companies including Merrill Lynch, Donaldson Lufkin & Jenrette, and the New York Stock Exchange. Micro Modeling has used the methods described above to dramatically reduce development costs, and delivery times, while delivering more applications that are successful corporate solutions.

After

- **Typesetting characters** such as em dashes and curved quotation marks are easy graphic touches, and they assure your readers that they are reading a professionally produced document. I went through this flyer changing the "--" to "—" (known as em dashes because they're about the width of the letter "m"), and the straight apostrophes and quotation marks (' ") to curved apostrophes and quotation marks (' " "). For more information on this point, refer to Chapter 6.

- Spacing is really important. In the first draft, the text is too close to the top and bottom of the page. The originator put too much space between the heading and the main text. He also left too much space between each of the subheads and the text. The result? He didn't have enough space left to leave respectable top and bottom margins.

  Note that you don't need *any* space between the subhead and the text. What you do need is contrast between the weight and size of the type. In this case, I boosted the size of the subheads to 13 points and bolded them.

- I eliminated the underlines, which you should use sparingly; they generally look amateurish. You don't need underlines to separate things—size, space, bolding, and italics do a much better job.

- After I eliminated the space between the subhead and the text and the extra space between the heading and the main body of text, I increased the margins at the top and bottom of the page. Since lots of space was still left over . . .

- I increased the space *above* each of the subheads (this made the four sections of the flyer stand out clearly) and . . .

- I increased the space between each bullet point (making each item more distinct and easier to read) and . . .

- I spent the rest of my 5 minutes working on the heading. Because people glance at the heading and decide whether they should read any further, it needs to be as inviting as possible.

  I added a little space *after* the first line of the heading. Then I added nearly double that amount between the second section of the heading ("Application Integration . . .") and the last line ("A one-day seminar . . ."). Then I inserted a rule between them. In this case, the rule serves to draw attention to the heading.

- I inserted bullets between each of the items in the last line of the heading. This not only separates somewhat unrelated elements, it also has the advantage of recalling the bulleted items in the text.

A final word about this makeover. Like everyone else, and even when I don't have much time, I work primarily by the time-honored technique of trial and error. There is no other way. It's relatively easy to decide that space is required before a subhead rather than after it, but you'll only know *how much* space by fiddling with it.

✦ Don't Use Lots of Typefaces

A famous designer, Colin McHenry, likes to ask design students how many typefaces they think are used in an expensively designed magazine such as *Elle*. "The usual response is that a number of typefaces must be used to create the varied and interesting design layouts," McHenry writes. "In this they would probably be wrong. I believe that only two typefaces are used—one for text and one for headlines, subheads, and quotes." (From Alan Swann, *Graphic Design School*.)

The main problem with using several entirely different typefaces is that every typeface—like a suit of clothes—conveys character and personality (see Dos and Don'ts #6). To avoid a personality clash, you have to decide the character you want to convey, and then use the typeface or two that conveys it. (See Chapter 3 for more information.)

This ad is just a little over 2 inches wide by approximately 3.25 inches high and uses only one typeface—Times. However, it uses three styles of Times—regular, bold, and all caps. First-time designers tend to resort to entirely different typefaces to catch the reader's eye, forgetting that any one face contains a whole family of styles, sizes, weights, and widths.

In this case, the headline is the job position being advertised. It tries to attract the attention of people looking for that sort of high-level position. The relatively large bottom line of text defines the type of person you're looking for, one who is also dedicated to improving the lives of children. However, your strategy might be to headline the name of the company, or the salary, or the flexible working hours—whatever you think will attract the people you want to employ.

CHELSEA WEE CARE, INC.

Executive Director

Lorem ipsum dolor sit amet, consectetuer adipiscing elit, sed diam nonummy nibh euismod tincidunt ut laoreet dolore.

Ut wisi enim ad minim veniam. Send your résumé and to Susan Briche at 111 Truro Rd., Jamestown, LA 11111.

DEDICATED TO IMPROVING THE LIVES OF CHILDREN

✦ If You Have Only One Thing to Say, Say It BIG

Next time you look through a newspaper or magazine, notice how many ads blare a single message. Don't be afraid to do the same. The message takes up almost a half of the ad labeled A (originally sized at 4.25 × 5.25 inches).

Notice that the holly says "Christmas" before the reader reads a word. It also serves as a border to separate this ad from the others on the crowded page.

A

TOYS
FOR
TOTS

This Christmas, give a gift
to *all* the children of our city.

Donate toys to the
Chelsea WEE CARE Center.

Gifts are tax-deductible. Chelsea Wee Care Center is a non-profit organization.

111 Mockingbird Lane
Our Town, Louisiana 11111
111-222-2121

B

TOYS
FOR
TOTS

This Christmas, give a gift to
all the children of our city.

Donate toys to the **Chelsea
WEE CARE Center.**

Gifts are tax-deductible. Chelsea Wee Care
Center is a non-profit organization.

111 Mockingbird Lane
Our Town, Louisiana 11111
111-222-2121

*Come to our
open house!
December 18,
10 am - 6 pm.*
Lorem ipsum
dolor sit amet,
consectetuer
adipiscing elit,
sed diam
nonummy nibh
euismod tincidunt
ut laoreet dolore
magna aliquam
erat volutpat. Ut
wisi enim ad.
*Supervised games
for kids.*

*Refreshments
will be served.*

✦ If You're Talking About Two Different Things, Make Them Look Like Two Different Things

The easiest way to separate two ideas is to draw a line. Unfortunately lines used as dividers usually look amateurish. In the ad labeled B, the organization is advertising their donations drive in conjunction with an open house, so that donors can see their donations going to good use. The original ad, which was written for the donations drive alone, was resized to accommodate the open house information in the same-sized space (4.25 × 5.25 inches).

The two ads are set apart by the different *shapes* of the text; they're held together by the use of the same typeface and by the placement of the holly. Note that the two distinct shapes in the ad—the big, broad shape of the main ad, and the long, narrow shape of the open house ad—are graphic elements in their own right, just as rules and photographs are. This ad is used as an example in Chapter 8.

✦ Small Is Beautiful

This small ad (2 × 1.5 inches) for a nursing college speaks to anyone interested in nursing. The key to items this small is to focus on one thing—even one word. The title "Nursing" is as big as the ad's 2-inch width allows. The phone number is bolded and put at the end, where it stands out more.

Nursing

Lorem ipsum dolor sit amet, consectetuer adipiscing elit, sed diam nonummy nibh euismod tincidunt ut laoreet dolore magna. Call Susan Briche at **413-444-4321**.

FLIP SHEETS

The two **flip sheets** (sometimes called data sheets or, more generically, marketing pieces) shown in this section mix elements of very different types of publications.

They are similar to flyers in that they're done on letter-sized (8.5 × 11-inch) sheets. They are similar to ads because they're designed to *sell* the product. In some cases, flip sheets serve as substitutes for brochures. They are painstakingly written and designed; and, in the cases shown here, they served as the product's main marketing piece. They were photocopied, mailed, faxed, and handed out at conferences. Although flip sheets are great for all sorts of *products,* they're a little too informal for professional or nonprofit services, or for big-ticket items like education—you'd better stick with brochures for those.

The first page of the Cicero piece shown in the following section was designed to fit on **preprinted** color paper—the left rule is preprinted in navy, and the bottom rule in burgundy (both shown in gray here). Preprinted paper is most often used for stationery and newsletter mastheads. However, it also provides a relatively inexpensive way for any office that prepares a lot of reports and presentations to add color to them. You can use it for report covers, hand-outs, flyers, flip sheets, and so on.

The most versatile preprinted designs let you use the paper two ways: vertically (also known as **portrait** orientation), as it appears in the Cicero marketing piece, and horizontally (or **landscape** orientation), which is especially good for presenting graphs and tables. (In this case, the navy rule would then be on the top and the burgundy rule on the left.) Using preprinted paper has another advantage: it gives your work a recognizable "look," a little like a logo.

✦ If You Have a Lot of Relevant Graphics, Don't Be Afraid to Use Them

The key word here is "relevant." As long as the graphics you use fit logically into your publication, use them. As many as you can. But be careful not to use a graphic that doesn't fit logically just because you have it. And don't crowd in graphics that you don't have room for.

Each of the graphics that appear in the Cicero marketing piece illustrates important features of the product. They all have meaningful, sales-oriented captions. If you read only the sub-heads and the captions (the two things research shows that people are most likely to read), you will get *every* important point made in the text.

This marketing piece is for a computer program developed by Merrill Lynch. It was originally done on letter-sized paper, double-sided, and stapled in the corner. It eventually became a three-color, four-page brochure. Note that pages 2 and 3 were designed to convert easily into a center spread.

The one-word headline "Cicero" (set in Palatino bold) was reshaped in Micrografx Designer to appear somewhat shorter and wider than normal; the diagram on the back page was put together in Microsoft PowerPoint; and the "snaps" of the program's computer screens were taken with Tiffany. This layout is surprisingly easy to do with Word. I used the FORMAT, FRAME function to arrange the graphics and captions in columns. Note that the footer serves double duty—it's a nice design touch as well as insurance that the reader will be able to contact the seller even if the two pages become separated from each other.

Only two typefaces are used—Palatino (regular, bold, and italic) and Helvetica (only the bold style, which is used for captions and footers). The large block of tiny text at the bottom of the back page is the lengthy legal notification of registered product names and trademarks.

CICERO

For the intelligent analysis of financial data. And the ability to present it persuasively.

What is Cicero?

Cicero is a tool that lets you easily **retrieve** data from databases such as Lotus One Source U.S. Equities and bring that data directly into an Excel spreadsheet; **analyze** it; and **present** it in polished reports that can include tables and color charts.

To find information on a company, prospect new clients, analyze investments, determine merger and acquisition potential, and perform other sophisticated data queries, you simply point and click on a series of dialog boxes. Cicero does not require any programming, knowledge of database query languages, or extensive training.

Cicero works in conjunction with Microsoft Excel, and takes full advantage of the Windows graphical environment. It can be based on a stand-alone PC, or on a LAN serving any number of users.

In addition to providing several built-in financial models, charts, and report templates, Cicero gives you the ability to easily create complex analytic models and sophisticated presentations.

Who Should Use Cicero?

Cicero was created for business professionals who use databases to analyze information on public and private companies. Professionals in the following areas will be able to use Cicero to its fullest advantage:

- investment banking
- commercial banking
- investment research
- money management
- insurance
- business planning and analysis

Cicero can retrieve financial information from databases such as Lotus One Source. You never have to leave your Excel spreadsheet.

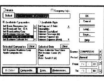

Cicero's dialog boxes lead you through the process of designing your own queries.

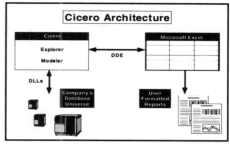

Cicero Architecture

Unlike other programs, Cicero does *not* require a multi-step process to download and report data. All queries, scanning, and reporting is performed in Excel. Because Cicero's Dynamic Link Libraries (DLLs) and Dynamic Data Exchange (DDE) calls perform these tasks in the background, you no longer have to switch between database and spreadsheet applications.

Other services available through Micro Modeling Associates:

- on-site training
- customized financial applications using *Cicero Modeler*
- DLLs that link your databases to Cicero
- integration of Cicero with other Windows programs to provide enhanced analytic and presentation capabilities
- consulting on custom and commercial programs operating under Windows
- consulting on the migration of character-based to Windows-based applications
- downsizing mainframe applications to the distributed PC environment

FOR MORE INFORMATION CONTACT:
Micro Modeling Associates, Inc.
World Financial Center
North Tower, 18th Floor
New York, NY 10281-1318
Telephone: (212) 432-4245
FAX: (212) 432-4246

Cicero's scan feature allows you to narrow the universe of companies according to specific criteria.

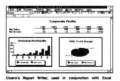

Cicero's composite feature allows you to use Excel's extensive set of mathematical and statistical functions to perform analyses on data for a group of companies.

Cicero's Report Writer, used in conjunction with Excel templates, allows you to format sophisticated reports simply by pointing and clicking.

Why You Need Cicero

Cicero provides simultaneous access to multiple **external** databases (such as Lotus One Source U.S. Equities), and your own **in-house** and **SQL** databases. Cicero also makes it easy to **add new** databases as they become available, or as your informational needs expand.

Because Cicero bypasses the complexities of traditional database searches, you can *easily:*

- construct *queries* to retrieve financial data from a database and bring it into an Excel spreadsheet in a *single step*
- use *scans* to narrow the universe of companies according to specific criteria
- create your own composites to sum, average, index, or perform other types of analysis on data for a group of companies
- edit and save queries, scans, and composites for future use
- use Cicero's built-in financial models to analyze data
- create your own sophisticated financial and statistical models with Cicero's *Modeler*
- graph the data automatically by selecting one of Cicero's built-in chart types, or create your own charts through Microsoft Excel's extensive charting capability
- format the data into a quality report integrating text, tables, and color charts with one of Cicero's built-in templates, or create your own reporting format with Cicero's *Report Writer*
- use the data with other Windows programs, including word processing, graphics, desktop publishing, spreadsheets, and databases
- train your staff *at one sitting* to use all databases supported by Cicero

---

What You Get With Cicero

Cicero is a Windows-based interface composed of two modules. These modules can be used together or independently, depending on the type of analysis you want to perform. Both are completely interactive with Excel, so that you can use all of Excel's standard features, in addition to Cicero's specialized capabilities.

- One module, *Cicero Explorer*, allows you to retrieve financial data from a database and bring it into an Excel spreadsheet in a single step. It also allows you to create sophisticated reports simply by pointing and clicking with your mouse.
- *Cicero Modeler* (the second module) is an extension of the Excel macro language. It provides access to the full functionality of *Cicero Explorer* for use in building customized financial applications.

Purchasers of Cicero also receive:

- on-site installation of Cicero's two modules
- on-site introductory training on how to use
- complete documentation
- a set of financial applications developed with *Cicero Modeler*, including *Stock Analysis, Financial Statement Analysis*

Cicero Modeler makes it easy to create your own complex financial applications. The chart and screen pictured above are from applications that are shipped with Cicero. These models were created using Cicero Modeler in conjunction with the Excel macro language.

NOTE: Cicero is currently shipping with a link for Lotus On Source U.S. Equities database. A link to your company' databases can be added through creation of Dynamic Lin Libraries (DLLs). Additional DLLs (C subroutines) can b provided by Micro Modeling Associates, Inc.

System requirements:
- PC using a 80286, 386, or 486 processor
- 2MB memory recommended
- Hard disk
- MS-DOS or PC-DOS operating system version 3.1 or higher
- Microsoft Windows version 3.0 or higher
- Mouse recommended
- EGA, VGA, 8514/A, Hercules graphics card, or compatible
- Microsoft Excel version 2.1c
- 8087, 80287, or 80387 math coprocessors optional

Compatible networks:
- AT&T Star LAN
- Banyan Vines
- IBM PC Network
- IBM Token-Ring Network
- Microsoft LAN Manager
- Novell Netware
- PC-NFS
- 3Com 3+
- 3Com EtherSeries
- Ungermann-Bass Net/One

or any other networks compatible with Microsoft Windows 3.0 or higher

✦ Good Design Is Just Common Sense

"Rationality," wrote the noted typographer Eric Gill, "remains the chief ingredient in the recipe for the making of things of beauty." (Eric Gill, *An Essay on Typography*.) In this case, the diagram of Power Tools' main menu works because it makes sense—it illustrates the points in the text about how easy it is to use the program's powerful features. The diagram was created using Micrografx Designer, saved as an EPS file, and then imported into Word for Windows.

There's another "rational" aspect to this design—the use of the Machine typeface for the main headline, "Power Tools," on the front page. Because of the way Machine overpowers everything around it, however, I couldn't use it for subheads. As a result, I used it only three times—for the main headline, for the

Back

It's easy to switch to Excel with

POWER TOOLS

What is Power Tools?
Power Tools is a time-saving conversion, formatting, and print utility for Excel. It reformats your Lotus 1-2-3 spreadsheets as they're converted into Excel worksheets, so you don't waste time doing it manually. It provides print tools so powerful you can print things just the way you want them — without fiddling with frustrating print macros. Plus, Power Tools gives you advanced formatting features you just can't get anywhere else.

Power Tools Makes Your Converted 1-2-3 Spreadsheets Look as Good as the Originals... Right Off the Bat
Excel includes a built-in utility capable of converting even the most complex 1-2-3 spreadsheet into an Excel worksheet. Unfortunately, this conversion utility has some holes. It doesn't convert your fonts, formatting, or print ranges, so you get an unpaginated worksheet set in courier and pockmarked with #VALUE! errors.

This means that once you've converted your 1-2-3 spreadsheet into Excel, you still have a job on your hands. You have to reformat it, repaginate it, and correct all the #VALUE! errors caused by formula-handling differences between 1-2-3 and Excel.

You have to make these changes for *every* spreadsheet. Unless you have Power Tools.

Power Tools reformats your 1-2-3 spreadsheets as they're converted into Excel worksheets. Because Power Tools lets you specify how you want Excel to handle common formatting features (such as underscores) your converted spreadsheets look as good as the original without time-consuming manual formatting.

If your spreadsheet has #VALUE! errors, you can eliminate them quickly and easily with Power Tools' circular reference commands. And since Power Tools lets you save your conversion parameters, you can convert whole batches of similar spreadsheets in a fraction of the time it takes now.

Power Tools' Print Functions are So Sophisticated You Can Stop Fiddling with Print Macros and Get Some Work Done
Computer industry experts estimate that over 90% of macros are written to make it easier to set up and print documents. But since Power Tools gives you the most sophisticated printing capability available, you can forget about those frustrating macros, and still print things just the way you want them.

Power Tools allows you to define and save *entirely different* specifications for each page of your worksheet. This includes

Power Tools is as easy to use as it is powerful. All its features are accessible through the menu it adds to Excel's main screen.

A 1-2-3 spreadsheet converted using Excel's built-in conversion utility...

... and a 1-2-3 spreadsheet converted using Power Tools. Which would you rather see on your screen?

Micro Modeling Associates, Inc. · World Financial Center, North Tower, 18th Floor · NY, NY 10281-1318
PHONE (212) 432-4245 · FAX (212) 432-4246

Front

running head at the top of the back page, and for the "For more information" line at the bottom of the back page.

Note that the design for the first page of the Power Tools marketing piece is extremely similar to the design for the Cicero piece. Because it's a good design, I use it fairly often. It allows for plenty of graphics, captions, a large headline, and a respectable amount of copy. Don't hesitate to reuse ideas, layouts, and styles *that work*.

BROCHURES

All brochures have one thing in common: a cover. The cover designs shown here were done in Word for Windows in a matter of minutes. When you're working on a brochure, remember that the point isn't to create a clever design; it's to communicate what you have to say effectively. The ideas you want to get across should dictate the design, just as they dictate your choice of words. If you're trying to portray an organization as giving every client the personal touch, for example, steer clear of bold, angular, impersonal graphics, no matter how exquisitely rendered.

David Ogilvy's advice to advertising art directors applies equally to people who design brochures. "Advertising suffers from sporadic epidemics of Artdirectoritis," Ogilvy wrote. "Those afflicted with this disease speak in hushed voices of 'cool gray bands of type,' as if . . . copy . . . were a mere *design* element. They extol the virtues of 'movement,' 'balance,' and other mysterious principles of design. I tell them KISS—an acronym for Keep It Simple Stupid." (From *Ogilvy on Advertising*.)

✦ The All-Purpose Letter-Fold Brochure Still Serves Well

The reason letter-fold brochures are so common is that they serve their purpose so well. You can stick them in display racks, pile them on tables, mail them, and even fax them. They give you six different pages (or panels), without expensive stapling or binding. They're almost always printed on coated (glossy) paper and often use at least one colored ink in addition to black. Printers refer to the use of black ink plus one color ink, such as green, as a **two-color job**; they refer to black plus two color inks as a **three-color job**. You need the four standard process colors (yellow, magenta, cyan, and black) to print full-color photographs.

Letter-fold brochures come in a variety of sizes. The ones designed to be displayed in standard display racks are usually 4 × 9 inches; the ones I get from my bank are 3.5 × 7.25 inches; and this brochure for the fictitious Little Bank is 3.6 × 8.5 inches. The Little Bank brochure is the most economical size because you can make it from letter-sized paper, and the printer doesn't have to trim it. (See *Folding Paper into Publications* in Chapter 4 for more information.)

I created this easy-to-do brochure using Word for Windows' table and column functions. Each panel on the *outside* of the brochure—including the front cover, the back cover, and the fold-out panel (see the sample)—is a single cell of a table. I formatted the *inside* of the brochure in three columns. This brochure is used as an example in Chapter 17.

Note that every time Little Bank's full name is used, it's set in small caps. This makes the bank's name stand out, almost like a logo, and adds a little "typographic interest" to the text.

To prepare a letter-fold brochure for printing, you need to arrange it on two sheets (called mechanicals), as shown on the

The LITTLE SUPER SAVINGS ACCOUNT

Five great ways of ensuring that *everybody* can get richer.
Not just the rich.

1. A minimum balance of $1,000.

2. Free checking.

3. Bounce protection.

4. Free Visa Card (if you qualify).

5. Preferred interest rates linked to how long you've been a customer... *not* to how much money you have in the bank.

Fold-out panel

LITTLE BANK
We're the little bank on your corner...

... wherever you are.

Back cover

We all need to save for the future. But who can afford to?

At LITTLE BANK, who can afford *not* to?

LITTLE BANK is an insured bank

Front cover

How do I open a Little Super Savings Account?

Ipsum dolor sit amet, consectetuer adipiscing elit, sed diam nonummy nibh euismod tincidunt ut laoreet dolore magna aliquam erat volutpat. Ut wisi enim ad minim veniam.

Quis nostrud exerci tation ullamcorper suscipit lobortis nisl ut aliquip ex ea commodo feugiat consequat.

Lorem ipsum dolor sit amet, consectetuer adipiscing elit, sed diam nonummy nibh euismod tincidunt ut laoreet dolore magna aliquam erat volutpat dolore magna aliquam erat volutpat dolore magna aliquam erat.

How is the Little Super Savings Account better than similar accounts at other banks?

Lorem ipsum dolor sit amet, consectetuer adipiscing elit, sed diam nonummy nibh euismod tincidunt ut laoreet dolore magna aliquam erat volutpat.

Ut wisi enim ad minim veniam, quis nostrud exerci tation ullamcorper suscipit lobortis nisl ut aliquip ex ea commodo feugiat consequat.

Dolor sit amet, consectetuer adipiscing elit, sed diam nonummy nibh euismod tincidunt ut laoreet dolore magna aliquam erat volutpat volutpat.

Wisi enim ad minim veniam, quis nostrud exerci tation ullamcorper suscipit lobortis nisl ut aliquip ex ea commodo feugiat consequat. Wisi enim ad minim veniam, quis nostrud.

Inner left panel

Quis nostrud exerci tation ullamcorper suscipit lobortis nisl ut aliquip ex ea commodo feugiat consequat aliquip ex ea commodo feugiat consequat.

What kind of benefits do long-time customers get?

Dolor sit amet, consectetuer adipiscing elit, sed diam nonummy nibh euismod tincidunt ut laoreet dolore magna aliquam erat volutpat. Ut wisi enim ad minim veniam.

Quis nostrud exerci tation ullamcorper suscipit lobortis nisl ut aliquip ex ea commodo feugiat consequat. Lorem ipsum dolor sit amet, consectetuer adipiscing elit, sed diam nonummy nibh.

- lobortis nisl ut aliquip ex ea commodo feugiat consequat
- exerci tation ullamcorper suscipit lobortis nisl ut aliquip ex ea commodo feugiat
- suscipit lobortis nisl ut aliquip ex ea commodo feugiat consequat
- enim ad minim veniam, quis nostrud exerci tation ullamcorper suscipit lobortis
- nisl ut aliquip ex ea commodo feugiat
- nostrud exerci tation ullamcorper suscipit lobortis nisl
- tation ullamcorper suscipit lobortis nisl ut aliquip ex ea commodo
- ut wisi enim ad minim veniam, quis nostrud exerci tation
- ullamcorper suscipit lobortis nisl ut aliquip ex ea commodo suscipit lobortis nisl ut aliquip ex ea commodo

Center

Lorem ipsum dolor sit amet, consectetuer adipiscing elit, sed diam nonummy nibh euismod tincidunt ut laoreet dolore magna aliquam erat volutpat.

Ut wisi enim ad minim veniam, quis nostrud exerci tation ullamcorper suscipit lobortis nisl ut aliquip ex ea commodo feugiat consequat. Wisi enim ad minim veniam, quis nostrud exerci tation ullamcorper suscipit lobortis nisl ut aliquip ex ea commodo feugiat consequat.

What other advantages does LITTLE BANK give its customers?

Consectetuer adipiscing elit, sed diam nonummy nibh euismod tincidunt ut laoreet dolore magna aliquam erat volutpat. Ad minim veniam, quis nostrud exerci tation ullamcorper suscipit lobortis nisl ut aliquip ex ea commodo feugiat consequat.

Lorem ipsum dolor sit amet, consectetuer adipiscing elit, sed diam nonummy nibh euismod tincidunt ut laoreet dolore magna aliquam erat volutpat.

Ut wisi enim ad minim veniam, quis nostrud exerci tation ullamcorper suscipit lobortis nisl ut aliquip ex ea commodo feugiat consequat.

How do I get more information?

Ut wisi enim ad minim veniam, quis nostrud exerci tation ullamcorper suscipit lobortis nisl ut aliquip ex ea commodo feugiat consequat.

Enim ad minim veniam, quis nostrud exerci tation ullamcorper Enim ad minim veniam, quis nostrud exerci tation ullamcorper.

Right

preceding page. One sheet is for the outside of the brochure, and the other is for the inside. (See *Getting It to the Printer* in Chapter 4 for more on this.)

✦ Color Paper Costs Less Than Color Ink

This mock-up of a membership brochure for service credit (or time dollar) programs illustrates the simplest, most inexpensive brochure layout going. It's made by folding a letter-sized sheet in two, so that each page is 5.5×8.5 inches. It can be printed on either coated or uncoated (text) paper, with or without color ink. In fact, a nice feature of such single-fold brochures is that they're often done on **color paper**, which avoids the expense of a two-color print job.

I used large margins in this brochure for two reasons: 1) They make it a little quicker to read because the lines of type are shorter, and 2) they *lengthen* the relatively short text. I used two other techniques to lengthen this text so that it filled the brochure. Instead of indenting paragraphs, I added a line of space between them. I also used extra leading. (**Leading** describes the amount of space between lines. In the days of hand typesetting, the printer would actually insert a strip of lead between lines of type to separate them. See Chapter 3 for more information.)

A word about the cover. The title of the brochure, "What Membership Means," was consciously given second billing to the program's name, "Service Credits." The idea here was that Service Credits themselves would pique the reader's attention and would *make* membership interesting. This brochure is used as the basis for examples in both Chapters 12 and 21.

dolore magna aliquam erat volutpat. Ut wisi enim ad minim veniam, quis nostrud exerci tation ullamcorper suscipit.

Lobortis nisl ut aliquip ex ea commodo feugiat consequat. Ut wisi enim ad minim veniam, quis nostrud exerci tation ullamcorper.bestia, per la qual tu gride, non lascia altrui passar per la. A te convien tenere altro viaggio se vuo' campar d'esto loco sel vaggio: che questa bestia, per la qual tu gride.

So what's the next step?

Magna aliquam erat volutpat. Ut wisi enim ad minim veniam, quis nostrud exerci tation ullamcorper suscipit.

Nisl ut aliquip ex ea commodo feugiat consequat. Ut wisi enim ad minim veniam, quis nostrud exerci tation ullamcorper. Nisl ut aliquip ex ea commodo feugiat consequat. Ut wisi enim ad minim veniam, quis nostrud exerci tation ullamcorper.

Magna aliquam erat volutpat. Ut wisi enim ad minim veniam, quis nostrud exerci tation ullamcorper suscipit.

The Greater New York Consortium
1111 Broadway, Suite 222
New York City, New York 11111
(212)111-1111

THE GREATER NEW YORK CONSORTIUM

SERVICE

What Membership Means

CREDITS

Back cover

What are service credits and how do they work?

Lorem ipsum dolor sit amet, consectetuer adipiscing elit, sed diam nonummy nibh euismod tincidunt ut laoreet dolore magna aliquam erat volutpat. Ut wisi enim ad minim veniam, quis nostrud exerci tation ullamcorper suscipit lobortis nisl ut aliquip ex ea commodo feugiat consequat.

Sum dolor sit amet, consectetuer adipiscing elit, sed diam nonummy nibh euismod tincidunt ut laoreet dolore magna aliquam erat volutpat. Ut wisi enim ad minim veniam, quis nostrud exerci tation ullamcorper.

Ut wisi enim ad minim veniam, quis nostrud exerci tation ullamcorper suscipit lobortis nisl ut aliquip ex ea commodo feugiat consequat.

What do service credits volunteers do?

Dolor sit amet, consectetuer adipiscing elit, sed diam nonummy nibh euismod tincidunt ut laoreet dolore magna aliquam erat volutpat.

Wisi enim ad minim veniam, quis nostrud exerci tation ullamcorper suscipit lobortis nisl ut aliquip ex ea commodo feugiat consequat. Sum dolor sit amet, consectetuer adipiscing elit, sed diam nonummy nibh euismod tincidunt ut laoreet dolore magna aliquam erat volutpat.

Ut wisi enim ad minim veniam, quis nostrud exerci tation ullamcorper suscipit lobortis su.

Sum dolor sit amet, consectetuer adipiscing elit, sed diam nonummy nibh euismod tincidunt ut laoreet dolore magna aliquam erat volutpat. Ut wisi enim ad minim veniam, quis nostrud exerci tation ullamcorper.

What sort of people are members of this program?

Amet, consectetuer adipiscing elit, sed diam nonummy nibh euismod tincidunt ut laoreet dolore magna aliquam erat volutpat.

Enim ad minim veniam, quis nostrud exerci tation ullamcorper suscipit lobortis nisl ut aliquip ex ea commodo feugiat consequat. Sum dolor sit amet, consectetuer adipiscing elit, sed diam nonummy nibh euismod tincidunt ut laoreet dolore magna aliquam erat volutpat.

Minim veniam, quis nostrud exerci tation ullamcorper suscipit lobortis nisl ut aliquip ex ea commodo feugiat consequat. Ut wisi enim ad minim veniam, quis nostrud exerci tation ullamcorper.

Why you should become a member of the service credits program

Dolor sit amet, consectetuer adipiscing elit, sed diam nonummy nibh euismod tincidunt ut laoreet dolore magna aliquam erat volutpat.

Wisi enim ad minim veniam, quis nostrud exerci tation ullamcorper suscipit lobortis nisl

Inside spread

✦ Color It Gray

Here are two more cover samples for the Service Credits brochure. The only difference between them is that the one labeled B uses gray type. Although gray can be tricky to use, it can also be an inexpensive way of getting "color" into your publications. Since it's essentially a muted black, the printer still considers it a black ink, or **one-color job** (the most inexpensive kind).

Note that the gray type lightens the cover and makes the publication's title, "What Membership Means," stand out more forcefully. (See Chapter 12 for instructions on laying out a single-fold brochure; see Chapter 21 to learn how to use PostScript to turn black type gray.)

SERVICE
What Membership Means
CREDITS

The Greater New York Consortium

A

SERVICE
What Membership Means
CREDITS

The Greater New York Consortium

B

✦ What Do You *Really* Want to Say?

The sample cover labeled A focuses the reader's attention on the membership information in the brochure—period. That it concerns membership in a Service Credits program is incidental. The message is completely different from that of the preceding covers, yet the words are *exactly* the same. Design *does* affect the message; so ask yourself, "Is this what I *really* want to say?"

✦ Try Setting Text Vertically on the Page

It's generally harder to read things printed vertically than horizontally. However, if the text is very short and the type relatively large (as in the sample labeled B), it can work. Note how the vertical type at the left and the line of informational text at the top become a half-border. Unfortunately the overall effect is rather angular—not necessarily the best image for a friendly, community social service program.

SERVICE CREDITS

What Membership Means

THE GREATER NEW YORK CONSORTIUM

A

THE GREATER NEW YORK CONSORTIUM

S
E
R
V
I
C
E
C
R
E
D
I
T
S

What Membership Means

B

Turn Your Title Into a Cover

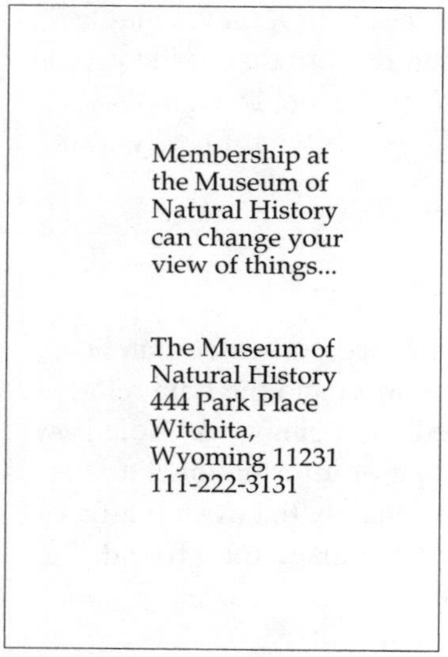

Membership at
the Museum of
Natural History
can change your
view of things...

The Museum of
Natural History
444 Park Place
Witchita,
Wyoming 11231
111-222-3131

Step 1

Start with your title, and the size you want the cover to be. In this example, the cover is 5.5 × 8.5 inches. The text is set in Palatino at 24 **points**. (Points are used to measure the size of type; see *Type Sizes* in Chapter 3.)

M embership at the
Museum of
Natural History
can change your
view of things...

The Museum of Natural History
444 Park Place Witchita, Wyoming 11231 111-222-3131

Step 2

Add your main graphic elements. In this case, I added two: the oversized "M" (set in Palatino at 94 points—almost four times the size of the title itself); and the footer (set at 12 points).

Note: *This design uses Word's Table function. The "M" is in one cell of the table; the rest of the title is in the other cell.*

M embership at the
MUSEUM OF
NATURAL HISTORY
can change your
view of things...

The MUSEUM OF NATURAL HISTORY
444 Park Place ▪ Witchita, Wyoming 11231 ▪ 111-222-3131

Step 3

Pay attention to details. In this case, I decided to use small caps to make the name of the museum stand out. Whenever you make such a decision, apply it consistently—for instance, in both the title and the footer, as shown here.

M embership
at the
MUSEUM OF
NATURAL
HISTORY can
change
your view
of things...

The MUSEUM OF NATURAL HISTORY
444 Park Place ▪ Witchita, Wyoming 11231 ▪ 111-222-3131

Step 4

Make the title fit the page. I boosted the type size from 24 points to 36 points. Although some people would stop designing right about now, I went one step further.

M embership
at the
MUSEUM OF
NATURAL
HISTORY can
change
your view
of things...

The MUSEUM OF NATURAL HISTORY
444 Park Place ▪ Witchita, Wyoming 11231 ▪ 111-222-3131

Step 5

I like the look of having the title hang from a heavy rule (which, by the way, was created using Word's FORMAT, BORDER command). The rule gives the cover a certain symmetry—a finished line at the top to square off the footer at the bottom. However, a friend indicated he would probably have stopped at Step 4. In practice, the only real rule is that the boss's taste wins.

✦ Get as Much Mileage out of a Publication as You Can

This fund-raising brochure was originally done in PageMaker for the Macintosh. It was extremely easy to redo in Word for Windows and it looks as good as the original.

This spread was created using Word's column function. Note that the thin rule (created in Microsoft Draw and placed in the document's header) runs across the entire inside spread without being interrupted by a margin. The thick rectangle at the left serves to emphasize the drop cap. All the text is set in Palatino with extra leading. Note that the brochure's two distinct sections each begin with a drop cap instead of a title.

THE GRADUATE SCHOOL OF POLITICAL MANAGEMENT is the nation's first school of professional politics. The Trustees have established The GSPM to contribute to the advancement of professional politics in the following ways:

To Reaffirm the Importance of Politics in a Democratic Society. Unlike schools of public administration or public policy — programs which train students for careers in government — The Graduate School of Political Management trains its students in the modern political skills required to organize, manage, and give expression to the interests and constituencies by whose authority, and in whose name, government officials are empowered to act. These skills include polling and statistical analysis, lobbying, campaign management, campaign finance, grass roots organizing, advertising, fund raising, press relations, and computer and communication skills.

In organizing a faculty whose careers reflect the highest standards of professional practice, and in attracting a diverse and excellent student body, The GSPM intends to establish itself as an important center for teaching and research in professional politics.

To Strengthen Professional Standards of Competence and Ethics. The word "professional" itself suggests something more than the acquisition of technical skills. It implies a system of values which governs the conduct of the practitioner, and contributes to the public interest.

Unlike the professions of law or medicine, entry into or continued practice of professional politics cannot be conditioned on the attainment of a professional degree or on the approval of a licensing agency. Politics must remain an unlicensed activity with only such regulation as may be required to avoid obvious abuses and to ensure access and equity in the exercise of political rights.

However, it is important to the consensus on which our political system is based that standards of ethics and competence be established and accepted as governing imperatives. Historically in the development of professions, the establishment of a degree-granting professional school is the critical first step.

THOSE WHO HAVE BEEN ASSOCIATED with The Graduate School of Political Management's development regard politics as a high calling. In the words of the English philosopher Bernard Crick, we hope to contribute "to the task of restoring confidence in the virtues of politics as a great and civilizing human activity."

The Graduate
School of
Political Management
17 Lexington Avenue
New York, NY 10010
212-725-4400

Main fund-raising piece

This brochure was printed on heavy, textured paper with a delicate, pinkish-gray hue. I have always liked this "pearls and jeans" look—the elegance of the drop caps, the thin rule, the open leading versus the ragged-right type and cottony paper. Like the Service Credits brochures shown earlier, this one folds to a 5.5 × 8.5-inch page size.

When I produced this brochure, The Graduate School of Political Management was raising money for several different programs. Rather than creating a separate brochure for each one or mixing them together in a single piece, we decided to use the spread shown in this example as the main text. We then produced a one-page insert for each of the different programs. When we contacted prospective donors, we gave them the fundraising piece with the appropriate insert. The inserts were produced on white paper of a similar texture to the main piece, but much lighter in weight.

The SCHOLARSHIP PROGRAM

Ipsum dolor sit amet, consectetuer adipiscing elit, sed diam nonummy nibh euismod tincidunt ut laoreet dolore magna aliquam erat volutpat. Ut wisi enim ad minim veniam, quis nostrud exerci tation ullamcorper suscipit lobortis nisl ut aliquip ex ea commodo feugiat.

Dolor sit amet, consectetuer adipiscing elit, sed diam nonummy nibh euismod tincidunt ut laoreet dolore magna aliquam erat volutpat. Ut wisi enim ad minim veniam, quis nostrud exerci tation ullamcorper suscipit lobortis nisl ut aliquip ex ea commodo feugiat ex ea commodo.

Consectetuer adipiscing elit, sed diam nonummy nibh euismod tincidunt ut laoreet dolore magna aliquam erat volutpat. Dolor sit amet, consectetuer adipiscing elit, sed diam nonumm.

Nonummy nibh euismod tincidunt ut laoreet dolore magna aliquam erat volutpat. Ut wisi enim ad minim veniam, quis nostrud exerci tation ullamcorper suscipit lobortis nisl ut aliquip ex ea commodo feugiat ex ea commodo sed diam.

Adipiscing elit, sed diam nonummy nibh euismod tincidunt ut laoreet dolore magna aliquam erat volutpat. Dolor sit amet, consectetuer adipiscing elit, sed diam nonumm. Dolor sit amet, consectetuer adipiscing elit, sed diam nonummy nibh euismod tincidunt ut laoreet dolore magna aliquam erat erat

Insert

45

BOOKLETS, DIRECTORIES, AND CATALOGS

I lump booklets, catalogs, and directories together because they're generally bigger than a brochure but smaller than a book, and their covers are usually printed on paper different from that used for the inside pages. They range from the standard employee phone directory to election guides and direct mail catalogs. They come in all sizes and price ranges. The samples shown here are geared toward people who have to produce appealing, professional-looking publications on a low to medium budget, with minimal hassles.

✦ Keep Things Interesting

This catalog is the most difficult piece in this book. It's a scaled-down version of one I did for the Audio-Language Knowledge Institute using PageMaker on the Macintosh. The original was a tabloid-sized, newspaper-style, direct mail catalog. This layout retains a lot of that style; in many ways, it could serve just as well for a newsletter.

The thing I like best about this design is that it follows the trusty tabloid formula of having so much going on that its readers are bound to find something that interests them. The tabloid design reinforces the catalog's "busy-busy" theme, as do the dotted rules and the way the text and photos are arranged in a variety of shapes—big blocks, long blocks, wide blocks, and small blocks.

Cover

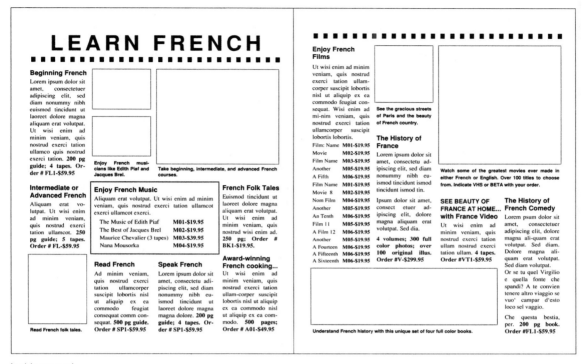

LEARN FRENCH

Beginning French

Lorem ipsum dolor sit amet, consectetuer adipiscing elit, sed diam nonummy nibh euismod tincidunt ut laoreet dolore magna aliquam erat volutpat. Ut wisi enim ad minim veniam, quis nostrud exerci tation ullamco quis nostrud exerci tation. **200 pg guide; 4 tapes. Order # FL1-$59.95**

Enjoy French musicians like Edith Piaf and Jacques Brel.

Take beginning, intermediate, and advanced French courses.

Intermediate or Advanced French

Aliquam erat volutpat. Ut wisi enim ad minim veniam, quis nostrud exerci tation ullamcot. **250 pg guide; 5 tapes. Order # FL-$59.95**

Read French folk tales.

Enjoy French Music

Aliquam erat volutpat. Ut wisi enim ad minim veniam, quis nostrud exerci tation ullamcot exerci ullamcot exerci.

The Music of Edith Piaf	M01-$19.95
The Best of Jacques Brel	M02-$19.95
Maurice Chevalier (3 tapes)	M03-$39.95
Nana Mousorka	M04-$19.95

Read French

Ad minim veniam, quis nostrud exerci tation ullamcorper suscipit lobortis nisl ut aliquip ex ea commodo feugiat consequat comm consequat. **500 pg guide. Order # SP1-$59.95**

Speak French

Lorem ipsum dolor sit amet, consectetu adipiscing elit, sed diam nonummy nibh euismod tincidunt ut laoreet dolore magna magna dolore. **200 pg guide; 4 tapes. Order # SP1-$59.95**

French Folk Tales

Euismod tincidunt ut laoreet dolore magna aliquam erat volutpat. Ut wisi enim ad minim veniam, quis nostrud wisi enim ad. **250 pg; Order # BK1-$19.95.**

Award-winning French cooking...

Ut wisi enim ad minim veniam, quis nostrud exerci tation ullam-corper suscipit lobortis nisl ut aliquip ex ea commodo nisl ut aliquip ex ea commodo. **500 pages; Order # A01-$49.95**

Enjoy French Films

Ut wisi enim ad minim veniam, quis nostrud exerci tation ullam-corper suscipit lobortis nisl ut aliquip ex ea commodo feugiat consequat. Wisi enim ad mi-nim veniam, quis nostrud exerci tation ullamcorper suscipit lobortis lobortis.

Film: Name	M01-$19.95
Movie	M02-$19.95
Film Name	M03-$19.95
Another	M05-$19.95
A Fifth	M06-$19.95
Film Name	M01-$19.95
Movie 8	M02-$19.95
Nom Film	M04-$19.95
Another	M05-$19.95
An Tenth	M06-$19.95
Film 11	M05-$19.95
A Film 12	M06-$19.95
Another	M05-$19.95
A Fourteen	M06-$19.95
A Fifteenth	M06-$19.95
A Sixteenth	M06-$19.95

See the gracious streets of Paris and the beauty of French country.

The History of France

Lorem ipsum dolor sit amet, consectetu ad-ipiscing elit, sed diam nonummy nibh eu-ismod tincidunt ismod tincidunt tin.

Ipsum dolor sit amet, consect etuer ad-ipiscing elit, dolore magna aliquam erat volutpat. Sed dia.

4 volumes; 300 full color photos; over 100 original illus. Order #V-$299.95

Watch some of the greatest movies ever made in either French or English. Over 100 titles to choose from. Indicate VHS or BETA with your order.

SEE BEAUTY OF FRANCE AT HOME... with France Video

Ut wisi enim ad minim veniam, quis nostrud exerci tation ullam nostrud exerci tation ullam. **4 tapes. Order #VT1-$59.95**

The History of French Comedy

Lorem psum dolor sit amet, consectetuer adipiscing elit, dolore magna ali-quam erat volutpat. Sed diam. Dolore magna ali-quam erat volutpat. Or se tu quel Virgilio e quella fonte che spandi? A te convien tenere altro viaggio se vuo' campar d'esto loco sel vaggio.

Che questa bestia, per. **200 pg book. Order #FL1-$59.95**

Understand French history with this unique set of four full color books.

Inside spread

I created this catalog in four columns using tables. Wherever an element spills over into more than one column, I used Word's TABLE, MERGE CELLS command. I created the empty boxes called **picture windows**, which indicate where photos go, by bordering a series of carriage returns with Word's FORMAT, BORDER command.

This catalog is meant to be printed on 11 × 17-inch paper. The "Busy People" graphic was created from clip art that comes with Micrografx Designer. It was saved as an EPS (Encapsulated PostScript) file and imported into Word. Once again, only two typefaces were used: Helvetica for the captions and head, and Times for the text.

✦ Don't Waste the Best Selling Space You Have

Sales catalogs take their cue from the old adage that the best way to sell a product is to show it—which is what this very simple layout does. You can easily substitute photos for the clip art images shown here, and you can use more but smaller pictures when you need to. Note that the pictures themselves largely set the tone—the cartoons spice up the catalog a bit (see sample B) and the hardware illustrations tone it down (see sample A).

If you look at the catalogs you get in the mail, you'll notice that a lot of them (especially those for office supplies) turn their first page into the cover and put their best-selling products on it. This tried-and-true selling device is an answer to the ad man's question, "Why waste the best selling space you have?"

This layout was created using tables; in those cases where the graphics and text are side by side, each is placed in its own

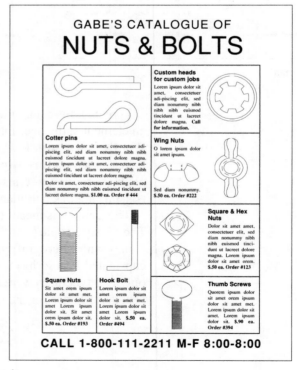

A

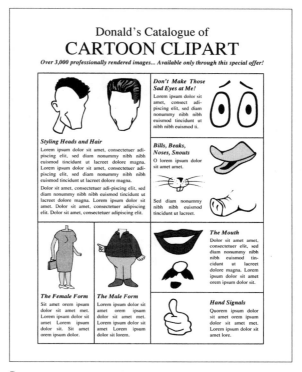

B

cell. The clip art is by Micrografx: the cartoons come with Designer, and the nuts and bolts are included in the technical clip art collection.

✦ Always Number the Pages Correctly (and Spell Your Name Right)

Since the spread of the printing press in the sixteenth century, booklets (also called pamphlets or leaflets) have been one of the most popular forms of publication. "The pamphlet's greatest asset was perhaps its flexibility in size," Bernard Bailyn wrote in his book *Pamphlets of the American Revolution*. "For while it could contain only a few pages and hence be used for publishing short squibs . . . it could also accommodate much longer, more serious and permanent writing as well."

Most of the booklets I pick up these days are computer and office procedures manuals, studies by nonprofit groups, or direct mail catalogs. However, I do run into an occasional voters' guide, and one of them inspired the sample design shown here. Since its publishers didn't seem to realize that inexpensive publications don't *have* to be ugly, I decided to prove it by designing one myself.

This booklet can be printed on letter-sized paper folded in two—each page is 5.5 × 8.5 inches. Once the text is typed in, it takes only a few minutes to format. I used the FORMAT, BORDER command to create the border on the cover and the INSERT, TABLE OF CONTENTS command to generate the table of contents automatically.

Now, here's where the "book-ish" qualities of booklets show through. Open any book and notice four things:

1. It's double-sided; that is, it's printed on both sides of the page. This is very easy to do with Word; just turn mirror-margins "on."

2. The left-hand pages are all even numbers.

3. The right-hand pages are all odd numbers.

4. The table of contents and new chapters almost always start on a right-hand (odd-numbered) page. To do this, you sometimes need to insert a blank page by adding a page break. Note that this blank page turns up as a left-hand (even-numbered) page.

SPEAK UP.

Tell the government what you think.

THE INSTITUTE FOR ACTIVE CITIZENS
444 Park Place ▪ Witchita, WY 11232 ▪ (222)111-3131

Cover

Table of Contents

Register to Vote 5

Vote 5

Phone...6

Write...7

Fax 7

Telegram 8

Petition 8

Demonstrate 10

Run for Office 11

Requirements of Running for Office 13

Who to Contact in Your State.......................................15

Making Elected Officials Accountable.....................19

Directory of State Congressional Delegations 25

3

Table of contents

REGISTER TO VOTE

Lorem ipsum dolor sit amet, consectetuer adipiscing elit, sed diam nonummy nibh euismod tincidunt ut laoreet dolore magna aliquam erat volutpat. Ut wisi enim ad minim veniam, quis nostrud exerci tation ullamcorper suscipit lobortis nisl ut aliquip ex ea commodo feugiat consequat.

Ut wisi enim ad minim veniam, quis nostrud exerci tation ullamcorper suscipit lobortis nisl ut aliquip ex ea commodo feugiat consequat.

Wisi enim ad minim veniam, quis nostrud exerci tation ullamcorper suscipit lobortis nisl ut aliquip ex ea commodo feugiat consequat.

Enim ad minim veniam, quis nostrud exerci tation ullamcorper suscipit lobortis nisl ut aliquip ex ea commodo feugiat consequat. Ut wisi enim ad minim veniam, quis nostrud exerci tation ullamcorper suscipit lobortis nisl ut aliquip ex ea commodo feugiat consequat.

Ad minim veniam, quis nostrud exerci tation ullamcorper suscipit lobortis nisl ut aliquip ex ea commodo feugiat.

VOTE

Minim veniam, quis nostrud exerci tation ullamcorper suscipit lobortis nisl ut aliquip ex ea commodo feugiat consequat. Ut wisi enim ad minim veniam, quis nostrud exerci tation ullamcorper suscipit lobortis nisl ut aliquip ex ea commodo feugiat consequat. Nisl ut aliquip ex ea commodo feugiat consequat nisl.

5

First page of text

Veniam, quis nostrud exerci tation ullamcorper suscipit lobortis nisl ut aliquip ex ea commodo feugiat consequat. Ut wisi enim ad minim veniam, quis nostrud exerci tation ullamcorper suscipit lobortis nisl ut aliquip ex ea commodo feugiat consequat. Nisl ut aliquip ex ea commodo feugiat consequat.

- orem ipsum dolor sit amet, consectetuer adipiscing elit
- sed diam nonummy nibh euismod tincidunt ut
- dolore magna aliquam erat volutpat commodo feugiat
- minim veniam, quis nostrud exerci tation
- aliquam erat volutpat ut wisi enim ad minim veniam
- veniam quis nostrud exerci tation ullamcorper suscipit lobortis nisl ut aliquip ex ea commodo feugiat consequat

Lorem ipsum dolor sit amet, consectetuer adipiscing elit, sed diam nonummy nibh euismod tincidunt ut laoreet dolore magna aliquam erat volutpat. Ut wisi enim ad minim veniam, quis nostrud exerci tation ullamcorper suscipit lobortis.

Consectetuer adipiscing elit, sed diam nonummy nibh euismod tincidunt ut laoreet dolore magna aliquam erat volutpat. Ut wisi enim ad minim veniam, quis nostrud exerci tation ullamcorper suscipit lobortis nisl.

PHONE

Dolor sit amet, consectetuer adipiscing elit, sed diam nonummy nibh euismod tincidunt ut laoreet dolore magna aliquam erat volutpat. Ut wisi enim ad minim veniam. Aadipiscing elit, sed diam nonummy nibh euismod tincidunt nibh wisi enim ad minim veniam ullamcorper suscipit

6

lobortis nisl Lorem ipsum dolor sit amet, consectetuer adipiscing elit, sed diam nonummy nibh euismod tincidunt ut laoreet dolore magna aliquam erat volutpat. Ut wisi enim ad minim veniam, quis nostrud exerci tation ullamcorper.

Ladipiscing elit, sed diam nonummy nibh euismod tincidunt ut laoreet dolore magna aliquam erat volutpat. Ut wisi enim ad minim veniam, quis nostrud exerci tation ullamcorper suscipit lobortis nisl ut aliquip ex ea commodo feugiat consequat.

WRITE

Lorem ipsum dolor sit amet, consectetuer adipiscing elit, sed diam nonummy nibh euismod tincidunt ut laoreet dolore magna aliquam erat volutpat.

Wut wisi enim ad minim veniam, quis nostrud exerci tation ullamcorper suscipit lobortis nisl ut aliquip ex ea commodo feugiat consequat. Wisi enim ad minim veniam, quis nostrud exerci tation ullamcorper suscipit lobortis nisl.

FAX

Sed diam nonummy nibh euismod tincidunt ut laoreet dolore magna aliquam erat volutpat. Ut wisi enim ad minim veniam, quis nostrud exerci tation ullamcorper suscipit lobortis nisl ut aliquip ex ea commodo feugiat consequat. Ullamcorper suscipit lobortis nisl ut aliquip ex ea commodo.

Ut wisi enim ad minim veniam, quis nostrud exerci tation ullamcorper suscipit lobortis nisl ut aliquip ex ea commodo feugiat consequat ea commodo feugiat consequat.

7

Facing pages

✦ Directories Should *Direct* Readers to the Information They're Seeking

---
A

ALABAMA: A te convien tenere altro viaggio se vuo' campar d'esto loco sel gride, non lascia altrui passar per la tua.
ALASKA: Or se tu quel Virgilio e quella fonte che spandi di parlar si largo fiume.
Arizona: Tu se' lo mio maestro e 'l mio autore; tu se' solo colui da cu' io mi tolsi lo bello stilo che m' ha fatto onore.
ARKANSAS: O delli altri poeti onore e lume, vagliami 'l lungo studio e 'l grande amore che m' ha fatto cercar lo tuo volume.
ARIZONA: Vedi la bestia per cu' io mi volsi: aiutami da lei, famoso saggio, ch'ella mi fa tremar le vene e i polsi.

B

BANGOR, ME: Or se tu quel Virgilio e quella fonte che spandi di parlar si largo fiume. O delli altri poeti onore e lume.
BINGHAMTON, NY: A te convien tenere altro viaggio se vuo' campar d'esto loco sel vaggio: che questa bestia, per la qual tu gride, non lascia altrui passar per la sua. Florida: per la qual tu gride, non lascia altrui passar per la sua.
BOSTON, MA: A te convien tenere altro viaggio se vuo campar d'esto loco sel vaggio campar d'esto loco sel vaggio d'esto loco sel vaggio.
BUFFALO, NY: O delli altri poeti onore e lume, vagliami 'l lungo studio e 'l grande amore che m' ha fatto cercar lo tuo volume.

C

CALCUTTA, INDIA: O delli altri poeti onore e lume, vagliami 'l lungo studio el grande amore che lo tuo volume.
CALIFORNIA: Te convien tenere altro viaggio se vuo' campar d'esto loco sel vaggio: che questa bestia, per la qual tu gride, non lascia altrui passar per la sua.
CHARLOTTE, NC: A te convien tenere altro viaggio se vuo' campar d'esto loco sel vaggio: che questa bestia, per la qual tu gride, non lascia altrui passar per la sua.
CHICAGO, IL: Delli altri poeti onore e lume, vagliami 'l lungo studio e 'l grande amore che m' ha fatto cercar lo tuo volume.
COLORADO: Se tu quel Virgilio e quella fonte che spandi di parlar si largo fiume? O delli altri poeti onore e lume, vagliami 'l

lungo studio el grande amore che m' ha fatto cercar lo tuo volume.
CONNECTICUT: Tu quel Virgilio e quella fonte che spandi di parlar si largo fiume or.
CORPUS CHRISTI, TX: A te convien ten altro viaggio se vuo' campar d'esto loco sel vaggio: che questa bestia, per la qual tu gride, non lascia altrui passar per la sua.

D

DALLAS, TX: O delli altri poeti onore e lume, vagliami 'l lungo studio e lo tuo. O delli altri poeti onore e lume, vagliami 'l lungo studio e 'l grande amore che m' ha fatto cercar lo grande amore che.
DELAWARE: Delli altri poeti onore e lume, vagliami 'l lungo studio e 'l grande amore che m' ha fatto cercar lo tuo.
DETROIT: Te convien tenere altro viaggio se vuo' campar d'esto loco sel vaggio.
DISTRICT OF COLUMBIA: A te convien tenere altro viaggio se vuo' campar d'esto loco sel vaggio: che questa bestia, per la qual tu gride, non lascia altrui passar per la.

E

ELMIRA, NY: Via se vuo' campar d'esto loco sel vaggio: che questa bestia, per la qual tu gride, non lascia altrui passar per la sua. Altro via se vuo' campar d'esto loco sel.
EMMAUS, PA: Altro via se vuo' campar d'esto loco sel vaggio: che questa bestia, per la qual tu gride, non lascia altrui passar per la sua. Altro via se vuo' campar d'esto loco sel vaggio: che questa bestia, per la qual tu gride, non lascia altrui passar per la sua.
EVANSVILLE, IN: Convien tenere altro via se vuo' campar d'esto loco sel vaggio: che questa bestia, per la qual tu gride, non lascia altrui passar per la sua.

F

FALMOUTH, MA: O delli altri poeti onore e lume, vagliami el lungo studio el grande amore che lo tuo volume.
FOREST HILLS, QUEENS: Te convien tenere altro viaggio se vuo' campar d'esto loco sel vaggio: che questa bestia, per la qual tu gride, non lascia altrui passar per la sua. Che questa bestia, per la qual tu gride. Che questa bestia, per la qual tu gride, non lascia Se tu quel Virgilio e quella fonte che.

1

The two samples shown here do just that. They make the major categories clear to even the most casual reader—the design at left says "look up information alphabetically" and the one below says "look it up by state." I'm always surprised at how many directories substitute long explanations on how to use the directory for such obvious visual pointers.

Note that the information shown in these samples is also organized clearly within each category. The types of information available are in bold in the sample below and are in bold and capitalized in the left sample's more cramped design. Sometimes, when there's a great deal of information, "cramped" can't be avoided; however, "confused" can.

Alabama

Last Name, First Name
Congressional District: 10th
Address: US Congress, Washington, DC 20510
Telephone: 202-224-3121
Fax: 202-222-2222
Legislative Assistant: First and Last Name

Last Name, First Name
Congressional District: 10th
Address: US Congress, Washington, DC 20510
Telephone: 202-224-3121
Fax: 202-222-2222
Legislative Assistant: First and Last Name

Alaska

Last Name, First Name
Congressional District: 10th
Address: US Congress, Washington, DC 20510
Telephone: 202-224-3121
Fax: 202-222-2222
Legislative Assistant: First and Last Name

Last Name, First Name
Congressional District: 10th
Address: US Congress, Washington, DC 20510
Telephone: 202-224-3121
Fax: 202-222-2222

Legislative Assistant: First and Last Name
Last Name, First Name
Congressional District: 10th
Address: US Congress, Washington, DC 20510
Telephone: 202-224-3121
Fax: 202-222-2222
Legislative Assistant: First and Last Name

Arizona

Last Name, First Name
Congressional District: 10th
Address: US Congress, Washington, DC 20510
Telephone: 202-224-3121
Fax: 202-222-2222
Legislative Assistant: First and Last Name

Last Name, First Name
Congressional District: 10th
Address: US Congress, Washington, DC 20510
Telephone: 202-224-3121
Fax: 202-222-2222
Legislative Assistant: First and Last Name

California

Last Name, First Name
Congressional District: 10th
Address: US Congress, Washington, DC 20510
Telephone: 202-224-3121

NEWSLETTERS AND OTHER PERIODICALS

Whenever someone asks me why I prefer one design over another, I think of an observation made in *Newspaper Design Today, A Manual for Professionals* by Allen Hutt and Bob James. "Beauty, they say, is in the eye of the beholder, and you can be sure that some of the things that send us into raptures will dispatch others in a different direction altogether. There can be no unanimity about what makes the perfect page; there will always be those who know they can improve it. And anyway . . . design is not a thing that can be judged on its own . . . the most important criteria is that of appropriateness."

So I always try to use "appropriateness" as my yardstick. Is it easy to read? Is it clear where articles begin, and continue, and end? Could it use a few graphic images or photos? Do the images that are used, fit? Are the graphs and photos meaningfully captioned? Is it interesting without being confusing? Do the headlines stand out? Does the format fit the content? Does the design convey the tone or the impression that you want to convey?

When you're thinking about putting together your publication, ask yourself the same questions. The process of thinking through the answers is what "design" really means.

✦ Let the Content Decide the Format

When you're putting together your newsletter, the most important question is "What sorts of stories will it contain?" Many *news*letters contain no real news at all; they're essentially a series of updates and anecdotes targeted at a specific audience—employees, members, Republicans, parents, and so on. Even newspapers aren't all news; they contain feature stories, reviews, personality profiles, and the like. When magazines cover news items, they tend to present them in a narrow-column format, much as newspapers do. When newspapers handle feature stories, they tend to use wider columns, more like magazines.

This is not entirely a matter of habit. I understand that it's actually faster to read narrow columns than wide ones—readers can take the whole line in with one gulp, so to speak. However, it's tiring to read fast for long; so feature stories, which are

Trumans'
FINANCIAL *news*

Volume 3, Number 7 *June 14, 1991*

Market Analysis

Tu se' lo mio maestro e 'l mio autore; tu se' solo colui da cu' io mi tolsi lo bello stilo che m' ha fatto onore. Vedi la bestia per cu' io mi volsi: aiutami da lei, famoso saggio, ch'ella mi fa tremar le vene e i polsi le vene e i polsi.

A te convien tenere altro viaggio se vuo' campar d'esto loco sel vaggio: che questa bestia, per la qual tu gride, non lascia altrui passar per la sua. Or se tu quel Virgilio e quella fonte che spandi di parlar si largo fiume.

O delli altri poeti onore e lume, vagliami 'l lungo studio e 'l grande amore che m' ha fatto cercar lo tuo volume. O delli altri poeti onore e lume, vagliami 'l lungo studio. O delli altri poeti onore.

Continued on page 4

This Week's Numbers

A te convien tenere altro viaggio se.

Who's Down on the Dollar Now?

O delli altri poeti onore e lume, vagliami 'l lungo studio e 'l grande amore che m' ha fatto cercar lo tuo volume. O delli altri poeti onore e lume.

Or se tu quel Virgilio e quella fonte che spandi di parlar si largo fiume. O delli altri poeti onore e lume, vagliami 'l lungo studio e 'l grande. Or se tu quel Virgilio or se tu quel or se tu quel or se tu quel or se tu qaltri poeti onore e lume, vagliami 'l uel se altri poeti onore e lume, vagliami 'l tu quel se tu quel or se tu quel altri poeti onore e lume, vagliami..

A te convien tenere altro viag-gio se vuo' campar d'esto loco sel vaggio. Non lascia altrui passar per la sua passar per la sua.

Tu se' lo mio maestro e 'l mio autore; tu se' solo colui da cu' io mi tolsi lo bello stilo che m' ha fatto onore. Vedi la bestia per cu' io mi volsi: aiutami da lei, famoso saggio, se tu quel or se tu quel se tu quel se tu quel or se tu quel se tu quel ch'ella mi fa tremar.

A te convien tenere altro viag-gio se vuo' campar d'esto loco sel vaggio: che questa bestia, per la qual tu altr altri poeti onore e lume, vagliami 'l i poeti onore e .▲▼

INDUSTRY ANALYSIS

Outperforming the Dow 30... Again & Again

Or se tu quel Virgilio e quella fonte che spandi di parlar si largo fiume? O delli altri poeti onore e lume, vagliami 'l lungo studio e 'l grande amore che m' ha fatto cercar lo tuo volume.

Tu se' lo mio maestro e 'l mio autore; tu se' solo colui da cu' io mi tolsi lo bello stilo che m' ha fatto onore. Vedi la bestia per cu' io mi volsi: aiutami da lei, famoso saggio, ch'ella mi fa tremar le vene e i polsi.

A te convien tenere altro viaggio se vuo' campar d'esto loco sel vaggio: che questa bestia, per la qual tu gride, non lascia altrui passar per la sua.

Or se tu quel Virgilio e quella fonte che spandi di parlar si largo fiume? O delli altri poeti onore e lume, vagliami 'l lungo studio e 'l grande amore che m' ha fatto cercar lo tuo volume. O delli altri poeti onore e lume, vagliami 'l lungo studio e 'l grande amore.

A te convien tenere altro viaggio se vuo' campar d'esto loco sel vaggio: che questa bestia, per la qual tu gride, non lascia altrui passar per la sua via, ma tanto lo 'mpedisce che l'uccide; e ha natura si malvagia e ria, che mai non empie la bramosa voglia, e dopo 'l pasto ha piu fame che pria pasto ha pui fame che pria.

E dopo 'l pasto ha piu fame che pria pasto ha pui fame che e dopo 'l pasto ha piu fame che priapria e dopo 'l pasto ha piu fame che pria pasto ha pui fame che pria. ▲▼

Front cover

PETE MICHAELS

The Low-Down on Consumer Interest Rates

Or se tu quel Virgilio e quella fonte che spandi di pa-rlar si largo fiume? O delli altri poeti onore e lume, vagliami 'l lungo studio e 'l grande amore che m' ha fatto cercar lo tuo volume.

Tu se' lo mio maestro e 'l mio autore; tu se' solo colui da cu' io mi tolsi lo bello stilo che m' ha fatto onore. Vedi la bestia per cu' io mi volsi: aiutami da lei, famoso saggio, ch'ella mi fa tremar le vene e i po.

How Low is Low?

Or se tu quel Virgilio e quella fonte che spandi di parlar si largo fiume? O delli altri poeti onore e lume, vagliami 'l lungo studio e 'l grande amore che m' ha fa-tto cercar lo tuo volume. O delli altri poeti onore e lume, vagliami 'l lungo studio e 'l grande amore.

A te convien tenere altro viaggio se vuo' campar d'esto loco sel vaggio: che questa bestia, per la qual tu gride, non lascia altrui passar per la sua via, ma tanto lo 'mpedisce che l'uccide; e ha natura si malvagia e ria, che mai non empie la bramosa voglia, e dopo 'l pasto ha piu fame che pria pasto ha pui fame che pria.

A te convien tenere altro viaggio se vuo' campar d'esto loco sel vaggio: che questa bestia, per la qual tu gride, non lascia altrui passar per la sua non lascia altrui passar per la sua non lascia.

Let's Hope It Gets Better Before It Gets Worse

Sel vaggio: che questa bestia, per la qual tu gride, non lascia altrui passar per la sua via, ma tanto lo 'mpedisce che l'uccide; e ha natura si malvagia e ria, che mai non empie la bramosa voglia, e dopo 'l pasto ha piu fame che pria pasto ha pui fame che pria.

A te convien tenere altro viaggio se vuo' campar d'esto loco sel vaggio: che questa bestia, per la qual tu gride, non lascia altrui passar per la sua non lascia altrui passar per la sua non lascia altrui passar per.

Or se tu quel Virgilio e quella fonte che spandi di pa-rlar si largo fiume? O delli altri poeti onore e lume, vagliami 'l lungo studio e 'l grande amore che m' ha fatto cercar lo tuo volume.

Vedi la bestia per cu' io mi volsi: aiutami da lei, famoso saggio, ch'ella mi fa tremar le vene.

Interest Rates

1/1/91	A.B.P. Bank	9.00
1/5/91	Ace Light Bank	9.25
1/5/91	Wheelin's Bank	9.13
1/5/91	Rayson's Bank	9.00
1/5/91	City of Franklin Savings	9.25
1/6/91	SW Regional	9.13
1/6/91	Trader's Bank	9.30
1/6/91	Farmer's Bank	9.40
1/15/91	Bank of J Town	9.00
1/15/91	Jone's Bank	9.20
1/31/91	A.B. Savings & Loan	9.25
1/31/91	SW Bank	9.13
2/1/91	A.B.P. Bank	9.00
2/5/91	Ace Light Bank	9.25
2/5/91	Wheelin's Bank	9.13
2/5/91	Rayson's Bank	9.00
2/5/91	City of Franklin Savings	9.25
2/6/91	SW Regional	9.13
2/6/91	Trader's Bank	9.30
2/6/91	Farmer's Bank	9.40
2/15/91	Bank of J Town	9.00
2/15/91	Jone's Bank	9.20
2/31/91	A.B. Savings & Loan	9.25
2/31/91	SW Bank	9.13

A te convien tenere altro viaggio se vuo' campar d'esto loco sel vaggio: che questa bestia, per la qual tu gride, non lascia altrui passar per la sua non lascia.

Or se tu quel Virgilio e quella fonte che spandi di pa-rlar si largo fiume? O delli altri poeti onore e lume, vagliami 'l lungo studio. ▲▼

Market Analysis ***(continued from page 1)***

A te convien tenere altro viaggio se vuo' campar d'esto loco sel vaggio: che questa bestia, per la qual tu gride, non lascia altrui passar per la sua.

O delli altri poeti onore e lume, vagliami 'l lungo studio e 'l grande amore che m' ha fatto cercar lo tuo volume che m' ha fatto.

Tu se' lo mio maestro e 'l mio autore; tu se' solo colui da cu' io mi tolsi lo bello stilo che m' ha fatto onore. Vedi la bestia per cu' io mi volsi: aiutami da lei, famoso saggio, ch'ella mi fa tremar le vene e i polsi volume contient.

O delli altri poeti onore e lume, vagliami 'l lungo studio e 'l grande amore che m' ha fatto cercar lo tuo volume che m' ha fatto.

Tu se' lo mio maestro e 'l mio autore; tu se' solo colui da cu' io mi tolsi lo bello stilo che m' ha fatto onore. Vedi la bestia per cu' io mi volsi: aiutami da lei, famoso saggio, ch'ella mi fa tremar le vene e i polsi vene soutien.

O delli altri poeti onore e lume, vagliami 'l lungo studio e 'l grande amore che m' ha fatto cercar lo tuo volume che m' ha fatto.

Tu se' lo mio maestro e 'l mio autore; tu se' solo colui da cu' io mi tolsi lo bello stilo che m' ha fatto onore. Vedi la bestia per cu' io mi volsi: aiutami da lei, famoso saggio, ch'ella mi fa tremar le vene e i polsi dent fume per suo.

A te convien tenere altro viaggio se vuo' campar d'esto loco sel vaggio: campar d'esto loco sel vaggioche questa bestia, per la qual tu gride. ▲▼

Truman's Financial News is published weekly by Truman's Financial News, Inc. The cost is $150.00/year or $3.00/issue.
Publisher: Joseph Truman
Editor: Sally Truman
Production Mgr: JJ Truman
111 Newby St., Villa, MA 1111

4 — Financial News

Back cover

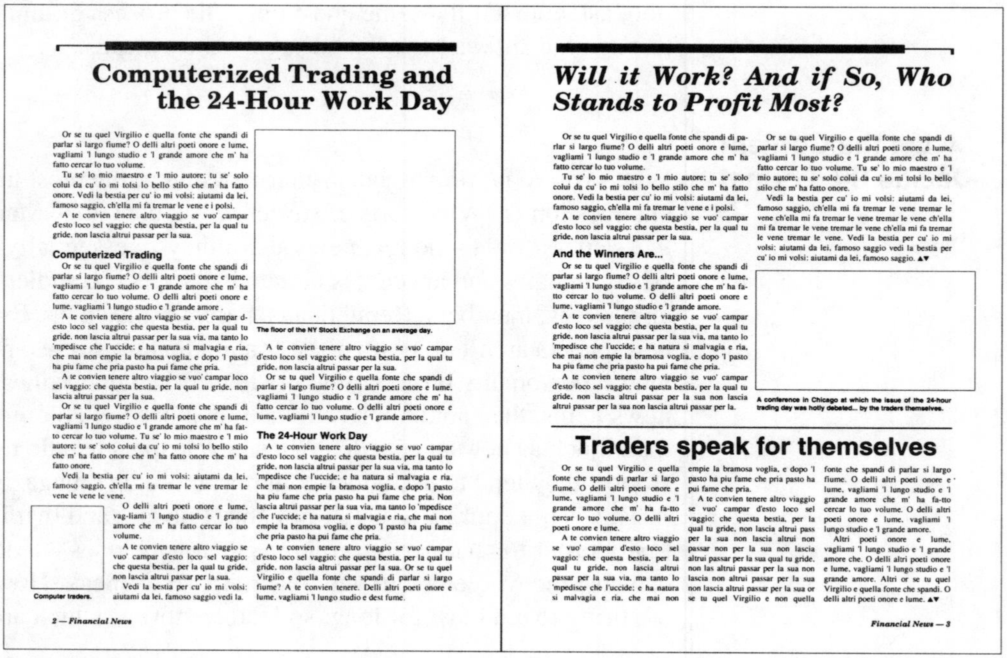

Computerized Trading and the 24-Hour Work Day

Or se tu quel Virgilio e quella fonte che spandi di parlar si largo fiume? O delli altri poeti onore e lume, vagliami 'l lungo studio e 'l grande amore che m' ha fatto cercar lo tuo volume.

Tu se' lo mio maestro e 'l mio autore; tu se' solo colui da cu' io mi tolsi lo bello stilo che m' ha fatto onore. Vedi la bestia per cu' io mi volsi: aiutami da lei, famoso saggio, ch'ella mi fa tremar le vene e i polsi.

A te convien tenere altro viaggio se vuo' campar d'esto loco sel vaggio: che questa bestia, per la qual tu gride, non lascia altrui passar per la sua.

Computerized Trading

Or se tu quel Virgilio e quella fonte che spandi di parlar si largo fiume? O delli altri poeti onore e lume, vagliami 'l lungo studio e 'l grande amore che m' ha fatto cercar lo tuo volume. O delli altri poeti onore e lume, vagliami 'l lungo studio e 'l grande amore .

A te convien tenere altro viaggio se vuo' campar d-esto loco sel vaggio: che questa bestia, per la qual tu gride, non lascia altrui passar per la sua via, ma tanto lo 'mpedisce che l'uccide: e ha natura si malvagia e ria, che mai non empie la bramosa voglia, e dopo 'l pasto ha piu fame che pria pasto ha pui fame che pria.

A te convien tenere altro viaggio se vuo' campar loco sel vaggio: che questa bestia, per la qual tu gride, non lascia altrui passar per la sua.

Or se tu quel Virgilio e quella fonte che spandi di parlar si largo fiume? O delli altri poeti onore e lume, vagliami 'l lungo studio e 'l grande amore che m' ha fat-to cercar lo tuo volume. Tu se' lo mio maestro e 'l mio autore: tu se' solo colui da cu' io mi tolsi lo bello stilo che m' ha fatto onore che m' ha fatto onore che m' ha fatto onore.

Vedi la bestia per cu' io mi volsi: aiutami da lei, famoso saggio, ch'ella mi fa tremar le vene tremar le vene le vene le vene.

O delli altri poeti onore e lume, vag-liami 'l lungo studio e 'l grande amore che m' ha fatto cercar lo tuo volume.

A te convien tenere altro viaggio se vuo' campar d'esto loco sel vaggio: che questa bestia, per la qual tu gride, non lascia altrui passar per la sua.

Vedi la bestia per cu' io mi volsi: aiutami da lei, famoso saggio vedi la.

Computer traders.

The floor of the NY Stock Exchange on an average day.

A te convien tenere altro viaggio se vuo' campar d'esto loco sel vaggio: che questa bestia, per la qual tu gride, non lascia altrui passar per la sua.

Or se tu quel Virgilio e quella fonte che spandi di parlar si largo fiume? O delli altri poeti onore e lume, vagliami 'l lungo studio e 'l grande amore che m' ha fatto cercar lo tuo volume. O delli altri poeti onore e lume, vagliami 'l lungo studio e 'l grande amore .

The 24-Hour Work Day

A te convien tenere altro viaggio se vuo' campar d'esto loco sel vaggio: che questa bestia, per la qual tu gride, non lascia altrui passar per la sua via, ma tanto lo 'mpedisce che l'uccide: e ha natura si malvagia e ria, che mai non empie la bramosa voglia, e dopo 'l pasto ha piu fame che pria pasto ha pui fame che pria. Non lascia altrui passar per la sua via, ma tanto lo 'mpedisce che l'uccide: e ha natura si malvagia e ria, che mai non empie la bramosa voglia, e dopo 'l pasto ha piu fame che pria pasto ha pui fame che pria.

A te convien tenere altro viaggio se vuo' campar d'esto loco sel vaggio: che questa bestia, per la qual tu gride, non lascia altrui passar per la sua. Or se tu quel Virgilio e quella fonte che spandi di parlar si largo fiume? A te convien tenere. Delli altri poeti onore e lume, vagliami 'l lungo studio e dest fume.

2 — Financial News

Will it Work? And if So, Who Stands to Profit Most?

Or se tu quel Virgilio e quella fonte che spandi di pa-rlar si largo fiume? O delli altri poeti onore e lume, vagliami 'l lungo studio e 'l grande amore che m' ha fatto cercar lo tuo volume.

Tu se' lo mio maestro e 'l mio autore; tu se' solo colui da cu' io mi tolsi lo bello stilo che m' ha fatto onore. Vedi la bestia per cu' io mi volsi: aiutami da lei, famoso saggio, ch'ella mi fa tremar le vene e i polsi.

A te convien tenere altro viaggio se vuo' campar d'esto loco sel vaggio: che questa bestia, per la qual tu gride, non lascia altrui passar per la sua.

And the Winners Are...

Or se tu quel Virgilio e quella fonte che spandi di parlar si largo fiume? O delli altri poeti onore e lume, vagliami 'l lungo studio e 'l grande amore che m' ha fa-tto cercar lo tuo volume. O delli altri poeti onore e lume, vagliami 'l lungo studio e 'l grande amore.

A te convien tenere altro viaggio se vuo' campar d'esto loco sel vaggio: che questa bestia, per la qual tu gride, non lascia altrui passar per la sua via, ma tanto lo 'mpedisce che l'uccide; e ha natura si malvagia e ria, che mai non empie la bramosa voglia, e dopo 'l pasto ha piu fame che pria pasto ha pui fame che pria.

A te convien tenere altro viaggio se vuo' campar d'esto loco sel vaggio: che questa bestia, per la qual tu gride, non lascia altrui passar per la sua non lascia altrui passar per la sua non lascia altrui passar per la.

Or se tu quel Virgilio e quella fonte che spandi di parlar si largo fiume? O delli altri poeti onore e lume, vagliami 'l lungo studio e 'l grande amore che m' ha fatto cercar lo tuo volume. Tu se' lo mio maestro e 'l mio autore; tu se' solo colui da cu' io mi tolsi lo bello stilo che m' ha fatto onore.

Vedi la bestia per cu' io mi volsi: aiutami da lei, famoso saggio, ch'ella mi fa tremar le vene tremar le vene ch'ella mi fa tremar le vene tremar le vene ch'ella mi fa tremar le vene tremar le vene ch'ella mi fa tremar le vene tremar le vene. Vedi la bestia per cu' io mi volsi: aiutami da lei, famoso saggio vedi la bestia per cu' io mi volsi: aiutami da lei, famoso saggio. ▲▼

A conference in Chicago at which the issue of the 24-hour trading day was hotly debated... by the traders themselves.

Traders speak for themselves

Or se tu quel Virgilio e quella fonte che spandi di parlar si largo fiume. O delli altri poeti onore e lume, vagliami 'l lungo studio e 'l grande amore che m' ha fa-tto cercar lo tuo volume. O delli altri poeti onore e lume.

A te convien tenere altro viaggio se vuo' campar d'esto loco sel vaggio: che questa bestia, per la qual tu gride, non lascia altrui passar per la sua via, ma tanto lo 'mpedisce che l'uccide; e ha natura si malvagia e ria, che mai non empie la bramosa voglia, e dopo 'l pasto ha piu fame che pria pasto ha pui fame che pria.

A te convien tenere altro viaggio se vuo' campar d'esto loco sel vaggio: che questa bestia, per la qual tu gride, non lascia altrui pass per la sua non lascia altrui non passar non per la sua non lascia altrui passar per la sua qual tu gride, non las altrui passar per la sua non lascia non altrui passar per la sua non lascia altrui passar per la sua or se tu quel Virgilio e non quella fonte che spandi di parlar si largo fiume. O delli altri poeti onore e lume, vagliami 'l lungo studio e 'l grande amore che m' ha fa-tto cercar lo tuo volume. O delli altri poeti onore e lume, vagliami 'l lungo studio e 'l grande amore.

Altri poeti onore e lume, vagliami 'l lungo studio e 'l grande amore che. O delli altri poeti onore e lume, vagliami 'l lungo studio e 'l grande amore. Altri or se tu quel Virgilio e quella fonte che spandi. O delli altri poeti onore e lume. ▲▼

Financial News — 3

Center spread

meant to be read at a more leisurely pace, often have the wider columns to slow us down.

The cover and back of this four-page mock-up of the fictitious *Financial News* contain news stories; that's why they're formatted in narrow columns. Compare this to the center spread—a feature story formatted with a distinctly "magazine" flavor. This is what is meant by letting the *content* decide the format.

Note that the magazine format for the center spread has the same look and feel as the news pages. This consistency is maintained largely through the headline typefaces and the rules.

This newsletter is used as the basis of Chapter 19.

✦ Imitate Success

These popular designs are *very* easy to do with Word for Windows. Sample A was created using Word's FORMAT, SECTION and

Ipsum dolor sit amet, consectetuer adipiscing elit, sed diam nonummy nibh euismod tincidunt ut laoreet dolore magna aliquam erat volutpat. Ut wisi enim ad minim veniam.

Quis nostrud exerci tation ullamcorper suscipit lobortis nisl ut aliquip ex ea commodo feugiat consequat.

Lorem ipsum dolor sit sit amet, consectetuer adi-piscing elit, sed diam nonummy nibh euismod tincidunt ut laoreet dolore magna aliquam

Ipsum dolor sit amet, consectetuer adipiscing elit, sed diam nonummy nibh euismod tincidunt ut laoreet dolore magna aliquam erat volutpat. Ut wisi enim ad minim veniam minim veniam minim ven.

Quis nostrud exerci tation ullamcorper suscipit lobortis nisl ut aliquip ex ea commodo feugiat consequat.

Lorem ipsum dolor sit amet, consectetuer adipiscing elit, sed diam nonummy nibh euismod tincidunt ut laoreet dolore magna aliquam.

Ipsum dolor sit amet, consectetuer adipiscing elit, sed diam nonummy nibh euismod tincidunt ut laoreet dolore magna aliquam erat volutpat. Ut wisi enim ad minim veniam.

Quis nostrud exerci tation ullam.

A Letter from the Editor

Corper suscipit lobortis nisl ut aliquip ex ea commodo feugiat consequat.

Lorem ipsum dolor sit amet, consectetuer adipiscing elit, sed diam nonummy nibh euismod tincidunt ut laoreet dolore magna aliquam.

Ipsum dolor sit amet, consectetuer adipiscing elit, sed diam nonummy nibh euismod tincidunt ut laoreet dolore magna aliquam erat vo-lutpat. Ut wisi enim ad minim veniam.

Quis nostrud exerci tation ullam-corper suscipit lobortis nisl ut aliquip ex ea commodo feugiat consequat.

Lorem ipsum dolor sit amet, consectetuer adi-piscing elit, sed diam nonummy nibh euismod tincidunt ut laoreet dolore magna aliquam minim veniam.

Ipsum dolor sit amet, consectetuer adipiscing elit, sed diam nonummy nibh euismod tincidunt ut laoreet dolore magna aliquam erat volutpat. Ut wisi enim ad minim veniam.

Quis nostrud exerci tation ullam-corper suscipit lobortis nisl ut aliquip ex ea commodo feugiat consequat.

Lorem ipsum dolor sit amet, consectetuer adipiscing elit, sed diam nonummy nibh euismod tincidunt ut

A

THE Mackintosh House

THE CHARLES MACKINTOSH House at the Hunterian Art Gallery lorem ipsum dolor sit amet, consectetuer adipiscing elit, sed diam nonummy nibh euismod tincidunt ut laoreet dolore magna aliquam erat volutpat.

Ut wisi enim ad minim veniam, quis nostrud exerci tation ullamcorper suscipit lobortis nisl ut aliquip ex ea commodo feugiat consequat.

Lorem ipsum dolor sit amet, consectetuer adipiscing elit, sed diam nonummy nibh euismod tincidunt ut laoreet. Tincidunt ut laoreet.

Dolore magna aliquam erat volutpat ut wisi enim ad minim veniam, quis nostrud exerci tation ullamcorper suscipit lobortis nisl ut aliquip ex ea commodo feugiat consequat.

Lorem ipsum dolor sit amet, consectetuer adipiscing elit, sed diam nonummy nibh euismod tincidunt ut laoreet dolore magna aliquam erat volutpat. Ut wisi enim ad minim veniam tincidunt ut laoreet. Ut wisi enim ad minim veniam tincidunt ut laoreet. Ut wisi enim ad minim veni.

Lorem ipsum dolor sit amet, consectetuer adipiscing elit, sed diam nonummy nibh euismod tincidunt ut laoreet dolore magna aliquam erat volutpat.

Ut wisi enim ad minim veniam, quis nostrud exerci tation ullamcorper suscipit lobortis nisl ut aliquip ex ea commodo feugiat consequat. Lorem ipsum dolor sit amet, consectetuer adipiscing elit, sed diam nonummy nibh euismod tincidunt ut laoreet.

Lorem ipsum dolor sit amet, consectetuer adipiscing elit, sed diam nonummy nibh euismod tincidunt ut laoreet dolore magna aliquam erat volutpat. Ut wisi enim ad minim veniam minim veniam.

Dolore magna aliquam erat volutpat ut wisi enim ad minim veniam, quis nostrud exerci tation ullamcorper suscipit lobortis nisl ut aliquip ex ea commodo feugiat consequat.

Lorem ipsum dolor sit amet, consectetuer adipiscing elit, sed diam nonummy nibh euismo. Elit, sed diam nonummy nibh euismo

B

FORMAT, FRAME commands. I present it here as the starting page for an article, with the headline boxed in the center. However, it could just as easily be a continuing page—in which case you would eliminate the stick-up cap at the beginning and use the center box for an outquote.

Sample B is one of the most popular and versatile layouts around—variations on it are widely used in journals, magazines, booklets, and ads. The large headline is placed at the top of the page, and the text is set in two columns of a three-column table. In this case, the graphic in the thin center column adds "bang." However, this line of blocks is not gratuitous—it's the fundamental design Mackintosh popularized in the early 1900s. The vertical "THE" (done in Microsoft WordArt) mirrors the vertical arrangement of the blocks.

✦ You Don't Need Colors to Add Color

You don't need to spend lots of money on colored inks to add color to your publications. The three samples shown here are magazine-type **spreads** (two facing pages designed as a unit) giving nuggets of travel information on the major areas of Scotland. Although the samples are essentially the same, each one is *colored* differently. Sample A is colored gray and dingy. There's little contrast between the text, the subheads, and even the headline itself. A reader scanning this page to pick out something of interest would probably turn the page instead.

Sample B is more colorful. It provides enough contrast among the text, subheads, borders, and headline to define each element clearly. This makes it easier for readers to find what they're looking for.

Sample C is brightly colored. Although (like the others) it's done entirely in black and white, the high contrast between the different elements makes them shout—somewhat the way red would.

MODERN SCOTLAND

ABERDEENSHIRE

Or se tu quel Virgilio e quella fonte che spandi di parlar si largo fiume? O delli altri poeti onore e lume, vagliami 'l lungo studio e 'l grande amore che m' ha fatto cercar lo tuo volume volume.

Tu se' lo mio maestro e 'l mio autore; tu se' solo colui da cu' io mi tolsi lo bello stilo che m' ha fatto onore. Vedi la bestia per cu' io mi volsi: aiutami da lei, famoso saggio, ch'ella mi fa tremar le vene e i polsi.

A te convien tenere altro viaggio se vuo' campar d'esto loco sel vaggio: che questa bestia, per la qual tu gride, non lascia altrui passar per la sua.

ANGUS

Or se tu quel Virgilio e quella fonte che spandi di parlar si largo fiume? O delli altri poeti onore e lume, vagliami 'l lungo studio e 'l grande amore che m' ha fatto cercar lo tuo lume, vagliami 'l lungo studio e 'l grande amore 'l grande amore 'l grande amore 'l grande amore.

A te convien tenere altro viaggio se vuo' campar d'esto loco sel vaggio: che questa bestia, per la qual tu gride, non lascia altrui passar per la sua via, ma tanto lo 'mpedisce che l'uccide; e ha natura si malvagia e ria e ha natura si malvagia e ria.

CLACKMANNANSHIRE

Or se tu quel Virgilio e quella fonte che spandi di parlar si largo fiume? O delli altri poeti onore e lume, vagliami 'l lungo studio e 'l grande amore che m' ha fatto cercar lo tuo

pria pasto a pui fame che che pria che che pria che che pria.

Or seta quel Virgilio e quella fonte he spandi di parlar si largo fiume? O delli altri poeti onore lume, vagliami 'l lungo studio 'l grande amore che m' ha fatto cercar lo tuo volume. Odelli altri poeti onore e lume, vagliami 'l lungo studio e 'l grande amore amore amore.

ARGYLL and AYRSHIRE

Or se tu quel Virgilio e quella fonte che spandi di parlar si largo fiume? O delli altri poeti onore e lume, vagliami 'l lungo studio e 'l grande amore che m' ha fatto cercar lo tuo volume cercar lo tuo volume.

O delli altri poeti onore e lume, vagliami 'l lungo studio e 'l grande amore e 'l grande amore.

A te convien tenere altro viaggio se vuo' campar d'esto loco sel vaggio: che questa bestia, per la qual tu gride, non lascia altrui passar per la sua via, ma tanto lo 'mpedisce che l'uccide; e ha natura si malvagia e ria e ha natura si malvagia e ria.

Che mai non empie la bramosa voglia, e dopo 'l pasto ha piu fame che pria pasto ha pui fame che.

DUMFRIESSHIRE

Or se tu quel Virgilio e quella fonte che spandi di parlar si largo fiume? O delli altri poeti onore e lume, vagliami 'l lungo studio e 'l grande amore che m' ha fatto cercar lo tuo volungo studio e 'l grande amore.

A te convien tenere altro viaggio se vuo' campar d'esto loco sel vaggio: che questa bestia, per la qual tu gride, non lascia altrui passar per la sua via, ma tanto lo 'mpedisce che l'uccide; e ha natura si malvagia e ria, che mai non empie la bramosa voglia, e dopo 'l pasto ha piu fame che pria pasto ha pui fame che pria.

Or se tu quel Virgilio e quella fonte che spandi di parlar si largo fiume? O delli altri poeti.

EDINBURGH and the LOTHIANS

Or se tu quel Virgilio e quella fonte che spandi di parlar si largo fiume?

volume. O delli altri poeti onore e lume, vagliami 'l lungo studio e 'l grande amore.

A te convien tenere altro viaggio se vuo' campar d'esto loco sel vaggio: che questa bestia, per la qual tu gride, non lascia altrui passar per la sua via, ma tanto lo 'mpedisce che l'uccide; e ha natura si malvagia e ria, che mai non empie la bramosa voglia, e dopo 'l pasto ha piu fame che pria pasto ha pui fame che pria.

Or se tu quel Virgilio e quella fonte che spandi di parlar si largo fiume? O delli altri poeti.

O delli altri poeti onore e lume, vagliami 'l lungo studio e 'l grande amore che m' ha fatto cercar lo tuo volume, vagliami 'l lungo studio e 'l grande amore.

A te convien tenere altro viaggio se vuo' campar d'esto loco sel vaggio: che questa bestia, per la qual tu gride, non lascia altrui passar per la sua via, ma tanto lo 'mpedisce che l'uccide; e ha natura si malvagia e ria, che mai non empie la bramosa voglia, e dopo 'l pasto ha piu fame che pria pasto ha pui fame che pria.

Or se tu quel Virgilio e quella fonte che spandi di parlar si largo fiume? O delli altri poeti onore e lume, vagliami 'l lungo studio e 'l grande amore.

GLASGOW

Or se tu quel Virgilio e quella fonte che spandi di parlar si largo fiume? O delli altri poeti onore e lume, vagliami 'l lungo studio e 'l grande

amore che m' ha fatto cercar lo tuo volume. O delli altri poeti onore e lume, vagliami 'l lungo studio e 'l grande amore.

A te convien tenere altro viaggio se vuo' campar d'esto loco sel vaggio: che questa bestia, per la qual tu gride, non lascia altrui passar per la sua via, ma tanto lo 'mpedisce che l'uccide; e ha natura si malvagia e ria non lascia altrui passar per la sua via, ma tanto.

Ce mai non empie la bramosa voglia, e dopo 'l pasto ha piu fame che pria pasto ha pui fame che.

Or se tu quel Virgilio e quella fonte che spandi di parlar si largo fiume? O delli altri poeti onore e lume, vagliami 'l lungo studio e 'l grande amore che m' ha fatto cercar lo tuo volume. O delli altri poeti onore e lume, vagliami 'l lungo studio e 'l grande amore. A te convien tenere altro viaggio se vuo' campar d'esto loco sel vaggio: che questa bestia, per la qual tu gride, non lascia altrui passar per la sua via, ma tanto.

PEEBLESSHIRE

Or se tu quel Virgilio e quella fonte che spandi di parlar si largo fiume? O delli altri poeti onore e lume, vagliami 'l lungo studio e 'l grande amore che m' ha fatto cercar lo tuo volume. O delli altri poeti onore e lume, vagliami 'l lungo studio e 'l grande amore.

A te convien tenere altro viaggio se vuo' campar d'esto loco sel vaggio: che questa bestia, per la qual tu gride, non lascia altrui passar per la sua via, ma tanto lo 'mpedisce che l'uccide; e ha natura si malvagia e ria, che mai non empie la bramosa voglia, e dopo 'l pasto ha piu fame che pria pasto ha pui fame che pria. pasto ha piu fame che pria pasto.

The ORKNEY and SHETLAND Islands

Or se tu quel Virgilio e quella fonte che spandi di parlar si largo fiume?

O delli altri poeti onore e lume, vagliami 'l lungo studio e 'l grande amore che m' ha fatto cercar lo tuo volume. O delli altri poeti onore e lume, vagliami 'l lungo studio e 'l grande amore.

A te convien tenere altro viaggio se vuo' campar d'esto loco sel vaggio: che questa bestia, per la qual tu gride, non lascia altrui passar per la sua via, ma tanto lo 'mpedisce che l'uccide; e ha natura si malvagia e ria, che mai non empie la bramosa voglia, c dopo 'l pasto ha piu fame che pria pasto ha pui fame che pria.

Or se tu quel Virgilio e quella fonte che spandi di parlar si largo fiume? O delli altri poeti onore e lume, vagliami 'l lungo studio e 'l grande amore che m' ha fatto cercar lo tuo volume. O delli altri poeti onore e lume, vagliami 'l lungo studio e 'l grande amore che m' ha fatto cercar lo tuo volume. O delli altri poeti onore e lume, vagliami 'l lungo studio.

TRAVEL TIPS

Or se tu quel Virgilio e quella fonte che spandi di parlar si largo fiume?

O delli altri poeti onore e lume, vagliami 'l lungo studio e 'l grande amore che m' ha fatto cercar lo tuo volume. O delli altri poeti onore e lume, vagliami 'l lungo studio.

A te convien tenere altro viaggio se vuo' campar d'esto loco sel vaggio: che questa bestia, per la qual tu gride, non lascia altrui passar per la sua via, ma tanto lo 'mpedisce che l'uccide; e ha natura si malvagia e ria, che mai non empie la bramosa voglia, e dopo 'l pasto ha piu fame che pria pasto ha pui fame che. ■

A

MODERN SCOTLAND

▪▪▪▪
ABERDEENSHIRE

Or se tu quel Virgilio e quella fonte che spandi di parlar sì largo fiume? O delli altri poeti onore e lume, vagliami 'l lungo studio e 'l grande amore che m' ha fatto cercar lo tuo volume volume.

Tu se' lo mio maestro e 'l mio autore; tu se' solo colui da cu' io mi tolsi lo bello stilo che m' ha fatto onore. Vedi la bestia per cu' io mi volsi: aiutami da lei, famoso saggio, ch'ella mi fa tremar le vene e i polsi.

A te convien tenere altro viaggio se vuo' campar d'esto loco sel vaggio: che questa bestia, per la qual tu gride, non lascia altrui passar per la sua.

▪▪▪▪
ANGUS

Or se tu quel Virgilio e quella fonte che spandi di parlar sì largo fiume? O delli altri poeti onore e lume, vagliami 'l lungo studio e 'l grande amore che m' ha fatto cercar lo tuo volume. O delli altri poeti onore e lume, vagliami 'l lungo studio e 'l grande amore 'l grande amore 'l grande amore.

A te convien tenere altro viaggio se vuo' campar d'esto loco sel vaggio: che questa bestia, per la qual tu gride, non lascia altrui passar per la sua via, ma tanto lo 'mpedisce che l'uccide; e ha natura sì malvagia e

ria, che mai non empie la bramosa voglia, e dopo sto ha piu fame che pria pasto a pui fame che che pria che che pria che pria.

Or setu quel Virgilio e quella fonte he spandi di parlar sì largo fiume? O delli altri poeti onore lume, vagliami 'l lungo studio 'l grande amore che m' ha fatto cercar lo tuo volume. Odelli altri poeti onore e lume, vagliami 'l lungo studio e 'l grande amore amore.

▪▪▪▪
ARGYLL and AYRSHIRE

Or se tu quel Virgilio e quella fonte che spandi di parlar sì largo fiume? O delli altri poeti onore e lume, vagliami 'l lungo studio e 'l grande amore che m' ha fatto cercar lo tuo volume cercar lo tuo volume.

O delli altri poeti onore e lume, vagliami 'l lungo studio e 'l grande amore e natura sì malvagia e ria.

A te convien tenere altro viaggio se vuo' campar d'esto loco sel vaggio: che questa bestia, per la qual tu gride, non lascia altrui passar per la sua via, ma tanto lo 'mpedisce che l'uccide; e ha natura sì malvagia e ria e ha natura sì malvagia e ria.

▪▪▪▪
CLACKMANNANSHIRE

Or se tu quel Virgilio e quella fonte che spandi di parlar sì largo fiume? O delli altri poeti onore e lume, vagliami 'l lungo studio e 'l grande

A te convien tenere altro viaggio se vuo' campar d'esto loco sel vaggio: che questa bestia, per la qual tu gride, non lascia altrui passar per la sua via, ma tanto lo 'mpedisce che l'uccide; e ha natura sì malvagia e ria, che mai non empie la bramosa voglia. O delli altri poeti onore e lume, vagliami 'l lungo studio e 'l grande amore.

▪▪▪▪
DUMFRIESSHIRE

Or se tu quel Virgilio e quella fonte che spandi di parlar sì largo fiume? O delli altri poeti onore e lume, vagliami 'l lungo studio e 'l grande amore che m' ha fatto cercar lo tuo volungo studio e 'l grande amore.

A te convien tenere altro viaggio se vuo' campar d'esto loco sel vaggio: che questa bestia, per la qual tu gride, non lascia altrui passar per la sua via, ma tanto lo 'mpedisce che l'uccide; e ha natura sì malvagia e ria, che mai non empie la bramosa voglia, e dopo 'l pasto ha piu fame che pria pasto ha pui fame che pria e dopo 'l pasto ha piu fame che pria.

▪▪▪▪
EDINBURGH and the LOTHIANS

Or se tu quel Virgilio e quella fonte che spandi di parlar sì largo fiume? O delli altri poeti onore e lume, vagliami 'l lungo studio e 'l grande amore che m' ha fatto cercar lo tuo volume. O delli altri poeti onore e lume, vagliami 'l lungo studio e 'l O delli altri poeti onore e lume.

▪▪▪▪
GLASGOW

Or se tu quel Virgilio e quella fonte che spandi di parlar sì largo fiume? O delli altri poeti onore e lume, vagliami 'l lungo studio e 'l grande amore che m' ha fatto cercar lo tuo O delli altri poeti onore e lume.

A te convien tenere altro viaggio se vuo' campar d'esto loco sel vaggio: che questa bestia, per la qual tu gride, non lascia altrui passar per la sua via, ma tanto lo 'mpedisce che l'uccide; e ha natura sì malvagia e ria, che mai non empie la bramosa voglia, e dopo 'l pasto a pui fame che pria pasto a pui fame che che pria.

Or se tu quel Virgilio e quella fonte che spandi di parlar sì largo fiume?

O delli altri poeti onore e lume, vagliami 'l lungo studio e 'l grande amore che m' ha fatto cercar lo tuo volume. O delli altri poeti onore e lume, vagliami 'l lungo studio e 'l grande amore. A te convien tenere altro viaggio se vuo' campar d'esto loco sel vaggio: che questa bestia, per la qual tu gride.

Non lascia altrui passar per la sua via, ma tanto lo 'mpedisce che l'uccide; e ha natura sì malvagia e ria, che mai non empie la bramosa voglia, e dopo 'l pasto ha piu fame pui fame che pria.

O delli altri poeti onore e lume, vagliami 'l lungo studio e 'l grande amore che m' ha fatto cercar lo tuo volume. O delli altri poeti onore e lume, vagliami o delli altri poeti onore e lume, vagliami o delli altri poeti onore e lume, vagliami. O delli altri poeti onore e lume, vagliami.

El grande amore vagliami 'l lungo studio e 'l grande amore amore.

A te convien tenere altro viaggio se vuo' campar d'esto loco sel vaggio: che questa bestia, per la qual tu gride, non lascia altrui passar per la sua, ma tanto lo 'mpedisce che l'uccide; e ha natura sì malvagia e ria, che mai non empie la bramosa voglia, e dopo 'l pasto ha piu fame che pria pasto a pui fame che pria.

O delli altri poeti onore e lume, vagliami 'l lungo studio e 'l grande amore che m' ha fatto cercar lo tuo volume, vagliami 'l lungo studio.

El grande amore che m' ha fatto cercar lo tuo volume che m' ha fatto cercar lo tuo volume.

▪▪▪▪
PEEBLESSHIRE

Or se tu quel Virgilio e quella fonte che spandi di parlar sì largo fiume? O delli altri poeti onore e lume, vagliami 'l lungo studio e 'l grande amore che m' ha fatto cercar lo tuo volume. O delli altri poeti onore e lume, vagliami 'l lungo studio e 'l grande amore.

A te convien tenere altro viaggio se vuo' campar d'esto loco sel vaggio: che questa bestia, per la qual tu gride, non lascia altrui passar per la sua via, ma tanto lo 'mpedisce che l'uccide; e ha natura sì malvagia e ria, che mai non empie la bramosa voglia, e dopo 'l pasto ha piu fame che pria pasto ha piu fame che pria pasto ha piu fame che pria pasto.

▪▪▪▪
The ORKNEY and SHETLAND Islands

Or se tu quel Virgilio e quella fonte che spandi di parlar sì largo fiume?

O delli altri poeti onore e lume, vagliami 'l lungo studio e 'l grande amore che m' ha fatto cercar lo tuo volume. O delli altri poeti onore e lume, vagliami 'l lungo studio e 'l grande amore vagliami 'l lungo studio e 'l grande amore.

A te convien tenere altro viaggio se vuo' campar d'esto loco sel vaggio: che questa bestia, per la qual tu gride, non lascia altrui passar per la sua via, ma tanto lo 'mpedisce che l'uccide; e ha natura sì malvagia e ria natura sì malvagia e ria.

O delli altri poeti onore e lume, vagliami 'l lungo studio e 'l grande amore che m' ha fatto cercar lo tuo volume che m' ha fatto cercar lo tuo volume o delli altri poeti onore e lume, vagliami 'l lungo studio.

El grande amore che m' ha fatto cercar lo tuo volume che m' ha fatto cercar lo tuo volume.

▪▪▪▪
TRAVEL TIPS

Or se tu quel Virgilio e quella fonte che spandi di parlar sì largo fiume?

O delli altri poeti onore e lume, vagliami 'l lungo studio e 'l grande amore che m' ha fatto cercar lo tuo volume. O delli altri poeti onore e lume, vagliami 'l lungo studio. ∎

B

MOD SCOTLAND

Aberdeenshire

Or se tu quel Virgilio e quella fonte che spandi di parlar sì largo fiume? O delli altri poeti onore e lume, vagliami 'l lungo studio e 'l grande amore che m' ha fatto cercar lo tuo volume volume volume.

Tu se' lo mio maestro e 'l mio autore; tu se' solo colui da cu' io mi tolsi lo bello stilo che m' ha fatto onore. Vedi la bestia per cu' io mi volsi: aiutami da lei, famoso saggio, ch'ella mi fa tremar le vene e i polsi.

A te convien tenere altro viaggio se vuo' campar d'esto loco sel vaggio: che questa bestia, per la qual tu gride, non lascia altrui passar per la sua.

Angus

Or se tu quel Virgilio e quella fonte che spandi di parlar sì largo fiume? O delli altri poeti onore e lume, vagliami 'l lungo studio e 'l grande amore che m' ha fatto cercar lo tuo volume. O delli altri poeti onore e lume, vagliami 'l lungo studio e.

A te convien tenere altro viaggio se vuo' campar d'esto loco sel vaggio: che questa bestia, per la qual tu gride, non lascia altrui passar per la sua via, ma tanto lo 'mpedisce che l'uccide; e ha natura sì malvagia e

ria, che mai non empie la bramosa voglia, e dopo sto ha piu fame che pria pasto a pui fame che che pria che che pria.

Or setu quel Virgilio e quella fonte he spandi di parlar sì largo fiume? O delli altri poeti onore e lume, vagliami 'l lungo studio e 'l grande amore che m' ha fatto cercar lo tuo volume. Odelli altri poeti onore e lume, vagliami 'l lungo studio e 'l grande amore amore.

Argyll and Ayrshire

Or se tu quel Virgilio e quella fonte che spandi di parlar sì largo fiume? O delli altri poeti onore e lume, vagliami 'l lungo studio e 'l grande amore che m' ha fatto cercar lo tuo volume e ha natura sì malvagia.

O delli altri poeti onore e lume, vagliami 'l lungo studio e 'l grande amore e natura sì malvagia e ria.

A te convien tenere altro viaggio se vuo' campar d'esto loco sel vaggio: che questa bestia, per la qual tu gride, non lascia altrui passar per la sua via, ma tanto lo 'mpedisce che l'uccide; e ha natura sì malvagia e ria, che mai non empie la bramosa voglia, e dopo 'l pasto ha piu fame che pria pasto ha piu fame che pria.

Che mai non empie la bramosa voglia, e dopo 'l pasto ha piu fame che pria pasto ha pui fame che che. A te convien tenere altro viaggio se vuo'

campar d'esto loco sel vaggio: che questa bestia, per la qual tu gride, non lascia altrui passar per la sua via, ma tanto lo 'mpedisce che l'uccide; e ha natura sì malvagia e.

Clackmannanshire

Or se tu quel Virgilio e quella fonte che spandi di parlar sì largo fiume? O delli altri poeti onore e lume, vagliami 'l lungo studio e 'l grande amore che m' ha fatto cercar lo tuo volume. O delli altri poeti onore e lume, vagliami 'l lungo studio e 'l grande amore.

A te convien tenere altro viaggio se vuo' campar d'esto loco sel vaggio: che questa bestia, per la qual tu gride, non lascia altrui passar per la sua via, ma tanto lo 'mpedisce che l'uccide; e ha natura sì malvagia e ria, che mai non empie la bramosa voglia, e dopo 'l pasto ha piu fame che pria pasto ha piu fame che pria.

Dumfriesshire

Or se tu quel Virgilio e quella fonte che spandi di parlar sì largo fiume? O delli altri poeti onore e lume, vagliami 'l lungo studio e 'l grande amore che m' ha fatto cercar lo tuo volungo studio e 'l grande amore lo tuo volungo studio e 'l grande.

A te convien tenere altro viaggio se vuo' campar d'esto loco sel vaggio: che questa bestia, per la qual tu gride, non lascia altrui passar per la sua via, ma tanto lo 'mpedisce che l'uccide; e ha natura sì malvagia e ria, che mai non empie la bramosa voglia, e dopo 'l pasto ha piu fame che pria pasto ha pui fame che pria.

Or se tu quel Virgilio e quella fonte che spandi di parlar sì largo fiume? O delli altri poeti.

Edinburgh and the Lothians

Or se tu quel Virgilio e quella fonte che spandi di parlar sì largo fiume? O delli altri poeti onore e lume, vagliami 'l lungo studio e 'l grande amore che m' ha fatto cercar lo tuo volume. O delli altri poeti onore e 'l grande amore.

A te convien tenere altro viaggio se vuo' campar d'esto loco sel vaggio: che questa bestia, per la qual tu gride, non lascia altrui passar per la sua via, ma tanto lo 'mpedisce che l'uccide; e ha natura sì malvagia e ria, che mai non empie la bramosa voglia, e dopo 'l pasto ha piu fame che pria pasto ha piu fame che pria.

Or se tu quel Virgilio e quella fonte che spandi di parlar sì largo fiume? O delli altri poeti onore e lume, vagliami 'l lungo studio e 'l grande amore che m' ha fatto cercar lo tuo volume. O delli altri poeti onore e lume, vagliami 'l lungo studio e 'l grande amore viaggio se vuo' campar d'esto loco sel vaggio sel vaggio.

Glasgow

Or se tu quel Virgilio e quella fonte che spandi di parlar sì largo fiume? O delli altri poeti onore e lume, vagliami 'l lungo studio e 'l grande amore che m' ha fatto cercar lo tuo volume. O delli altri poeti onore e lume, vagliami cel lungo studio e 'l grande amore.

A te convien tenere altro viaggio se vuol campar d'esto loco sel vaggio: che questa bestia, per la qual tu gride, non lascia altrui passar per la sua via, ma tanto lo 'mpedisce che l'uccide; e ha natura sì malvagia.

Ce mai non empie la bramosa voglia, e dopo al pasto ha piu fame che. Ce mai non empie la bramosa voglia, e dopo al pasto ha piu fame che pria pasto ha pui fame che che pria pasto ha pui fame che.

Tenere altro viaggio se vuo' campar d'esto loco sel vaggio: che questa bestia, per la qual tu gride gride.

Non lascia altrui passar per la sua via, ma tanto lo 'mpedisce che l'uccide; e ha natura sì malvagia e ria, che mai non empie la bramosa voglia, e dopo 'l pasto ha piu fame che pria pasto ha pui fame che pria pui fame che pria.

O delli altri poeti onore e lume, vagliami 'l lungo studio e 'l grande amore che m' ha fatto cercar lo tuo volume. O delli altri poeti onore e lume, vagliami.

Peeblesshire

Or se tu quel Virgilio e quella fonte che spandi di parlar sì largo fiume? O delli altri poeti onore e lume, vagliami 'l lungo studio e 'l grande amore che m' ha fatto cercar lo tuo volume. O delli altri poeti onore e lume, vagliami lungo grande amore lungo grande amore.

A te convien tenere altro viaggio se vuo' campar d'esto loco sel vaggio: che questa bestia, per la qual tu gride, non lascia altrui passar per la sua via, ma tanto lo 'mpedisce che l'uccide; e ha natura sì malvagia e ria, che mai non empie la bramosa voglia, e dopo 'l pasto ha piu fame che pria pasto ha piu fame che che pria pasto ha piu fame che pria pasto.

The ORKNEY and SHETLAND Islands

Or se tu quel Virgilio e quella fonte che spandi di parlar sì largo fiume?

O delli altri poeti onore e lume, vagliami aal lungo studio e al grande amore che m' ha fatto cercar lo tuo volume. O delli altri poeti onore e lume, vagliami cel lungo studio e el grande amore.

A te convien tenere altro viaggio se vuo' campar d'esto loco sel vaggio: che questa bestia, per la qual tu gride, non lascia altrui passar per la sua via. ▣

C

These samples illustrate the use of both color and of *style*. Spread C is about *Mod* Scotland. Its typeface (Bookman bold) says "mod." Its borders (drawn in Microsoft Draw) say "mod." The **dingbat** (decorative symbol) at the very end of the piece says "mod." Its color says "mod." If you don't want to say "mod," you want another design. (Spread C is used as an example in Chapter 13.)

Sample B is about *Modern* Scotland—new, simple, and clean. This less colorful design conveys an entirely different image, not only of the Scotland described in the text, but of your publication.

REPORTS, PROPOSALS, AND PRESENTATIONS

Whenever I'm producing a report or a proposal for a client, I feel a little like I'm balancing on a tightrope. On the one hand, I want to make it look as appealing as possible. On the other, I don't want it to look like a glitzy marketing piece. The reports, proposals, and presentations shown here walk that tightrope well. Reports need to *look* as though they contain real information as much as they need to contain it.

This section also includes several samples that present tabular data in attractive, easy-to-follow formats. I explain how to turn this sort of data into visual presentations (slides, overhead transparencies, and hand-outs) in Chapter 20.

All the graphs in these samples were done in Excel for Windows, and their headlines and captions were done in Word for Windows.

✦ Use Distinctive Headings to Orient the Reader and Organize Your Report

This report layout was originally designed using PageMaker for the Macintosh. Although different techniques are required to replicate the design in Word for Windows, it's by no means any harder. The format is carefully organized, rather like an outline. It uses four orders of headings—chapter headings (labeled A, B, C), section headings (labeled I, II, III), and first- and second-level subheads within sections (labeled a, b, c and 1, 2, 3, respectively).

Although each heading has its own distinct style, the use of letters and numerals makes it easier for the reader to follow. Most people don't remember things like "Helvetica-bold-italic-upper-lower-case means second level subhead"; it's a lot easier to remember what A, B, and C mean.

I want to point out three other details:

1. The report is printed single sided.

2. Unlike most of the page layouts in this book, the body text is set in Helvetica, as are three of the four headings. (This is simply because the company's owner likes Helvetica.)

3. Each new chapter starts with a centered headline and features a rather long outquote set in Times italic. This design makes a clear break with the previous chapter and starts the reader off on a new train of thought.

When the company's owner was finalizing this format (he uses it for all his reports), two advisors urged him to consider various "folio treatments" to spice it up a little. After they explained that a **folio treatment** is a fancy way of handling the page number—for instance, with little dashes on each side, a dingbat, a rule, or the company's name—he nixed it right away. That kind of "silliness" around page numbers always bugged him, he said. He just wanted it in Helvetica, centered. (See Chapter 12 for more on folio treatments.)

This report is used as the example in Chapter 18.

B. BACKGROUND

The College's Master Plan, adopted in 1988, defines the mission of the College as follows: "To provide a practical liberal arts education at the baccalaureate level:

- in a small college environment;
- to a varied group of students, male and female, representing a cross-section of society from the United States and the world;
- with a diverse and highly qualified faculty who excel at teaching and who care deeply about students;
- in a closely-knit campus community which encourages thoughtful self-reflection, ethical development and personal growth."

As will become evident in the body of this report, the College has succeeded, by any measure, not only in achieving its stated mission, but also, in achieving an understanding of it among those constituencies who are aware of the College. To date, however, that understanding has not resulted in desired enrollment growth, and it remains unclear as to whether or not the understanding is broad enough or the mission flexible enough to attain the necessary enrollment growth to ensure future academic and financial viability.

A 1987 financial analysis done for the College indicates that it should have a full-time enrollment of about 600 to remain financially viable. A 1987 financial analysis done for the College indicates that it should have a full-time enrollment of about 600 to remain financially viable. A 1987 financial analysis done for the College indicates that it should have a full-time enrollment of about 600 to remain financially viable. A 1987 financial analysis done for the College indicates that it should have a full-time enrollment of about 600.

While the College has experienced a slow but steady enrollment growth over the past five or six years, that growth has come about in only one sector of the enrollment — non-traditional older students — which the College characterizes as "resumers." The number of full-time traditional freshmen has actually declined over that period. These data will be discussed in greater detail in

"... To date, however, that understanding has not resulted in desired enrollment growth, and it remains unclear as to whether or not the understanding is broad enough, or the mission flexible enough, to attain the necessary enrollment growth to ensure future academic and financial viability."

3

---

since the years of World War II universities since the years of World War II universities since the years of World War II.

I. EXTERNAL FACTORS

Throughout the spring and summer of 1990, major publications throughout the United States headlined the declining enrollment patterns in higher education nationwide among traditional college-age freshmen for the Fall 1990. (See Appendix II).

The March 6, 1991, issue of *The Chronicle of Higher Education* carried a front page story under the headline "Applications Down at Private Campuses, Up at Public Colleges," which contained reported statistics for Fall 1991. Among the facts reported in that story were:

- public institutions are reporting increases of as much as 15% in applications from high school seniors;
- while some private colleges say applications have increased slightly, many report they are down by 5% to 16%;
- small colleges are hurting the most;
- the recession is forcing parents and students who might otherwise consider enrolling at private colleges to look more closely at lower-cost state institutions.

"Colleges in the Northeast have been particularly hard hit by dramatic declines in the number of high school seniors and by the downturn in the region's economy," *The Chronicle* article continues. It further reports that two of the universities cited as among those hardest hit are in Massachusetts.

II. INTERNAL FACTORS

a. Academic Challenges and Opportunities

During the course of this study, *RJE Consulting* interviewed a broad spectrum of the College family — students, faculty, staff, administration — to gain a better understanding of the internal environment, including the view of the College's Plan and its impact on the College's goals and strategies. That material will be presented in detail in a later section, but in order to provide perspective in this background section, it is necessary to touch on some of these issues.

In 1983, the College initiated a plan for a Liberal Arts Education. While it received substantial national media coverage in the mid-1980s, the College has not been able to capitalize on that visibility in terms of increased enrollment or, it appears, in terms of the quality of undergraduate students attracted to the College.

As stated earlier, while the College's enrollment has risen, the increase has not come among traditional residential undergraduates — the group for whom the plan

4

was initially designed. Instead, it has come in the transfer population, especially among non-traditional transfer students (see graph below). While that trend has caused great concern among some at the College relative to its impact on the goals of the plan, it clearly offers some important opportunities.

b. Administrative Challenges and Opportunities

1. New Leadership and Physical Facilities

Within the past two years, the College has put almost an entirely new senior administrative team in place. The vice president for finance was hired in 1989 and the vice president for institutional advancement in 1990. This new team has the distinct advantage of being able to build on a sound foundation, but it faces some major challenges in the immediate future which must be dealt with if the College is to deliver on its promise. Given those factors, a healthy discussion is now taking place within the academic community regarding the right student "mix".

New Enrollment, Fall 1985 through Fall 1990

Within the past two years, the College has put almost an entirely new senior administrative team in place. The vice president for finance was hired in 1989 and the vice president for institutional advancement in 1990. This new team has the distinct advantage of being able to build on a sound foundation, but it faces some major challenges in the immediate future which must be dealt with if the College is to deliver on its promise. Given those factors, a healthy discussion is now taking place within the academic community regarding the right student "mix".

Within the past two years, the College has put almost an entirely new senior administrative team in place. The vice president for finance was hired in 1989 and the vice president for institutional advancement in 1990. This new team has the distinct advantage of being able to build on a sound foundation, but it faces some major challenges in the immediate future which must be dealt with if the College is

5

✦ If You Summarize Important Points in Captions and Outquotes, More People Will Read Them

Although the previous format only used outquotes on the first page of each chapter, this one uses outquotes on every page. They summarize all the important points. If you flip through and read just the outquotes and captions, you'll get the gist of the whole report.

This is a great format for the booklet-type, informational reports often published by nonprofit organizations—it gets your information across to even the most casual reader. It's probably a little pretentious, however, for a report to the board.

This report is printed double sided. Note how the outquote on the left-hand page is flush right, and the outquote on the right-hand page is flush left. This little design touch confines the raggedness to the margin of the page.

The College's Master Plan, adopted in 1988, defines the mission of the College as follows: "To provide a practical liberal arts education at the baccalaureate level:

- in a small college environment;
- to a varied group of students, male and female, representing a cross-section of society from the United States and the world;
- with a diverse and highly qualified faculty who excel at teaching and who care deeply about students;
- in a closely-knit campus community which encourages thoughtful self-reflection, ethical development and personal growth."

As will become evident in the body of this report, the College has succeeded, by any measure, not only in achieving its stated mission, but also, in achieving an understanding of it among those constituencies who are aware of the College.

A 1987 financial analysis done for the College indicates that it should have a full-time enrollment of about 600 to remain financially viable.

While the College has experienced a slow but steady enrollment growth over the past five or six years, that growth has come about in only one sector of the enrollment — non-traditional older students — which the College characterizes as "resumers." The number of full-time traditional freshmen has actually declined over that period. These data will be discussed in greater detail in the Internal Environment section of this report, but are worth noting now.

The marketing study comes at a time truly unique in the history of higher education in the United States. The recruiting of students for the Fall 1990 class was, across the nation, the most difficult for private colleges and universities since the years of World War II.

I. External Factors

Throughout the spring and summer of 1990, major publications throughout the United States headlined the declining enrollment patterns in higher education nationwide among traditional college-age freshmen for the Fall 1990. (See Appendix II).

The March 6, 1991, issue of *The Chronicle of Higher Education* carried a front page story under the headline "Applications Down at Private Campuses, Up at Public Colleges," which contained reported statistics for Fall 1991. Among the facts reported in that story were:

- public institutions are reporting increases of as much as 15% in applications from high school seniors;
- while some private colleges say applications have increased slightly, many report they are down by 5% to 16%;
- public institutions are reporting increases of as much as 15% in applications from high school seniors;
- while some private colleges say applications have increased;

"... To date, however, that understanding has not resulted in desired enrollment growth, and it remains unclear as to whether or not the understanding is broad enough, or the mission flexible enough, to attain the necessary enrollment growth to ensure future academic and financial viability."

- small colleges are hurting the most;
- the recession is forcing parents and students who might otherwise consider enrolling at private colleges to look more closely at lower-cost state institutions at private colleges to.

"Colleges in the Northeast have been particularly hard hit by dramatic declines in the number of high school seniors and by the downturn in the region's economy," *The Chronicle* article continues. It further reports that two of the universities cited as among those hardest hit are in Massachusetts. One university is bucking a national trend of increases among public uni-versities and is down 15%. Among the privates, Another university in Boston, which had a major decline in the freshmen class in fall of 1990, is projecting a freshman class down another 25% from last year. The recession is forcing parents and students who might otherwise consider enrolling at private colleges to look more closely at lower-cost state institutions. The recession is forcing parents and students who might otherwise consider enrolling at private colleges to look more closely at lower-cost state institutions at private colleges to.

Fall Entering Class, 1990

This chart shows the categories of students in the entering class.

II. Internal Factors

a. Academic Challenges and Opportunities

During the course of this study, *RJE Consulting* interviewed a broad spectrum of the College family — students, faculty, staff, administration — to gain a better understanding of the internal environment, including the view of the College's Plan and its impact on the College's goals and strategies. That material will be presented in detail in a later section, but in order to provide perspective in this background section, it is necessary to touch on some of these issues.

In 1983, the College initiated a plan for a Liberal Arts Education. While it received substantial national media coverage in the mid-1980s, the College has not been able to capitalize on that visibility in terms of increased enrollment or, it appears, in terms of the quality of undergraduate students attracted to the College.

As stated earlier, while the College's enrollment has risen, the increase has not come among traditional residential undergraduates — the group As stated earlier, while the College's enrollment has risen, the increase has not come among traditional residential undergraduates — the group As stated earlier, while the College's enrollment has risen, the increase.

"The recruiting of students for the fall of 1990 class, was, across the nation, the most difficult for private colleges and universities since the years of World War II. The long predicted decline in the number of high school graduates accelerated and that factor, combined with the increasing quality and artificially maintained lower tuition rates of state colleges and universities played havoc with freshmen enrollments at private institutions throughout the country. There is little to suggest any real changes in these factors..."

8

9

✦ Add a Little Panache with Practical Headers and Footers

This format is especially good for long reports because it helps readers know where they are—the headers identify the chapter and the footers identify the page number and source of the report. You could also include such information as the date and title of the report or the name of the company that prepared it.

Do you see how the header and footer on the left-hand page are flush left, whereas the header and footer on the right-hand page are flush right? This is a common, professional-looking way of handling page numbers on double-sided spreads. It's done using Word's Different Odd and Even Pages option under the VIEW, HEADER/FOOTER command.

This example is used again in Chapter 10.

Background

The College's Master Plan, adopted in 1988, defines the mission of the College as follows: "To provide a practical liberal arts education at the baccalaureate level:

- in a small college environment;
- to a varied group of students, male and female, representing a cross-section of society from the United States and the world;
- with a diverse and highly qualified faculty who excel at teaching and who care deeply about students;
- in a closely-knit campus community which encourages thoughtful self-reflection, ethical development and personal growth."

As will become evident in the body of this report, the College has succeeded, by any measure, not only in achieving its stated mission, but also, in achieving an understanding of it among those constituencies who are aware of the College.

Enrollment Mix: Changes 1985 through 1989

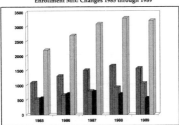

While the College has experienced a slow but steady enrollment growth over the past five or six years, that growth has come about in only one sector of the enrollment — non-traditional older students — which the College characterizes as "resumers." The number of full-time traditional freshmen has actually declined over that period. These data will be discussed in greater detail in the Internal Environment section of this report, but are worth noting now.

The marketing study comes at a time truly unique in the history of higher education in the United States. The recruiting of students for the Fall 1990 class was, across the nation, the most difficult for private colleges and universities since the years of World War II. The long predicted decline in the number of high school graduates accelerated.

The marketing study comes at a time truly unique in the history of higher education in the United States. The recruiting of students for the Fall 1990 class was, across the nation, the most difficult for private colleges and universities since the years of World

---

Background

And that factor, combined with the increasing quality and artificially maintained lower tuition rates of state colleges and universities, played havoc with freshmen enrollments at private institutions throughout the country. There is little to suggest any real changes in these factors over the next decade.

So it, like private colleges and universities throughout the United States, and especially those in the Northeast, faces major challenges in attracting and retaining adequate numbers of good quality traditional undergraduates from a declining pool. The challenge is great, but so is the opportunity.

I. EXTERNAL FACTORS

Throughout the spring and summer of 1990, major publications throughout the United States headlined the declining enrollment patterns in higher education nationwide among traditional college-age freshmen for the Fall 1990.

The March 6, 1991, issue of *The Chronicle of Higher Education* carried a front page story under the headline "Applications Down at Private Campuses, Up at Public Colleges," which contained reported statistics for Fall 1991. Among the facts reported in that story were:

- public institutions are reporting increases of as much as 15% in applications from high school seniors;
- while some private colleges say applications have increased slightly, many report they are down by 5% to 16%;
- small colleges are hurting the most;
- the recession is forcing parents and students who might otherwise consider enrolling at private colleges to look more closely at lower-cost state institutions.

"Colleges in the Northeast have been particularly hard hit by dramatic declines in the number of high school seniors and by the downturn in the region's economy," The Chronicle article continues. It further reports that two of the universities cited as among those hardest hit are in Massachusetts. One university is bucking a national trend of increases among public universities and is down 15%.

Clearly these major demographic shifts — combined with the increasing tuition gap between public and private institutions — require whole new approaches and perhaps major changes in the way colleges like the College market their educational experience.

II. INTERNAL FACTORS

a. Academic Challenges and Opportunities

During the course of this study, *RJE Consulting* interviewed a broad spectrum of the College family — students, faculty, staff, administration — to gain a better understanding of the internal environment, including the view of the College's Plan and its impact on the College's goals and strategies. That material will be presented in detail in a later section, but in order to provide perspective.

During the course of this study, *RJE Consulting* interviewed a broad spectrum of the College family — students, faculty, staff, administration — to gain a better understanding of the internal environment, including the view of the College's Plan and its impact on the College's goals and strategies. That material will be presented in detail in a later section, but in order to provide perspective. During the course of this

---

63

✦ Don't Be Afraid to Try Something a Little Different

Different designs do more than make things look nice. They emphasize different features. Sample A has headings in the left-hand margin to make them stand out so that readers can find the topic they want quickly. Because of this, it's an especially good format for manuals, data-oriented reports, or proposals that people are likely to scan for specific information. It's used as an example in Chapter 13.

This format tends to work best when you limit yourself to two or three short headlines per page, or one long headline. More than that and the left-hand margin gets too cluttered.

Sample B emphasizes the chapter and section heads by making them hang over the edge of the text. It also emphasizes section subheads (for example, "Approvals") by *not* making them hang. This gives the report an "outline" quality, much as the use of A, B, C, I, II, III, and so on does.

Accounts Payable Manual, 1991/92 — Office Procedures

OFFICE PROCEDURES

Lorem ipsum dolor sit amet, consectetuer adipiscing elit, sed diam nonummy nibh euismod tincidunt ut laoreet dolore magna aliquam erat volutpat. Ut wisi enim ad minim veniam, quis nostrud exerci tation ullamcorper suscipit lobortis nisl ut aliquip ex ea commodo feugiat consequat.

Lorem ipsum dolor sit amet, consectetuer adipiscing elit, sed diam nonummy nibh euismod tincidunt ut laoreet dolore magna aliquam erat volutpat. Ut wisi enim ad minim veniam, quis nostrud exerci tation ullamcorper suscipit lobortis nisl ut aliquip ex ea commodo feugiat consequat.

- lorem ipsum dolor sit amet lorem ipsum dolor sit amet lorem ipsum dolor sit amet
- ipsum dolor sit amet nonummy nibh euismod
- magna aliquam erat volutpat
- quis nostrud exerci tation ullamcorper suscipit
- magna aliquam erat volutpat ut wisi enim ad mini
- nonummy nibh euismod tincidunt ut
- diam nonummy nibh euismod tincidunt ut laoreet dolore magna

Internal Control Procedures

Lorem ipsum dolor sit amet, consectetuer adipiscing elit, sed diam nonummy nibh euismod tincidunt ut laoreet dolore magna aliquam erat volutpat. Ut wisi enim ad minim veniam, quis nostrud exerci tation ullamcorper suscipit lobortis nisl ut aliquip ex ea commodo feugiat consequat.

Dolor sit amet, consectetuer adipiscing elit, sed diam nonummy nibh euismod tincidunt ut laoreet. Ipsum dolor sit amet, consectetuer adipiscing elit, sed diam nonummy nibh euismod tincidunt ut laoreet dolore magna aliquam erat volutpat. Ut wisi enim ad minim veniam, quis nostrud exerci tation ullamcorper suscipit lobortis nisl ut aliquip ex ea commodo feugiat consequat.

Approvals

Lorem ipsum dolor sit amet, consectetuer adipiscing elit, sed diam nonummy nibh euismod tincidunt ut laoreet. Magna aliquam erat volutpat. Ut wisi enim ad minim veniam, quis nostrud exerci tation ullamcorper suscipit lobortis nisl ut aliquip ex ea commodo feugiat. Nonummy nibh euismod tincidunt ut laoreet dolore magna aliquam erat volutpat. Ut wisi enim ad minim veniam onummy nibh euismod tincidunt.

Ut wisi enim ad minim veniam, quis nostrud exerci tation ullamcorper suscipit lobortis nisl ut aliquip ex ea commodo feugiat. Nonummy nibh euismod tincidunt ut laoreet dolore

OWR Plastic Products, Inc. — Office of Accounting   Page 3

A

Accounts Payable Manual, 1991/92 — Office Procedures

OFFICE PROCEDURES

Tipsum dolor sit amet, consectetuer adipiscing elit, sed diam nonummy nibh euismod tincidunt ut laoreet dolore magna aliquam erat volutpat. Ut wisi enim ad minim veniam, quis nostrud exerci tation ullamcorper suscipit lobortis nisl ut aliquip ex ea commodo feugiat consequat:

- lorem ipsum dolor sit amet lorem ipsum dolor sit amet
- ipsum dolor sit amet nonummy nibh euismod
- magna aliquam erat volutpat
- quis nostrud exerci tation ullamcorper suscipit
- lorem ipsum dolor sit amet lorem ipsum dolor sit amet
- dolor sit amet lorem ipsum dolor sit amet lorem ipsum dolor sit amet quis nostrud exerci tation ullamcorper suscipit

Internal Control Procedures

Tipsum dolor sit amet, consectetuer adipiscing elit, sed diam nonummy nibh euismod tincidunt ut laoreet dolore magna aliquam erat volutpat. Ut wisi enim ad minim veniam, quis nostrud exerci tation ullamcorper suscipit lobortis nisl ut aliquip ex ea commodo feugiat consequat.

Consectetuer adipiscing elit, sed diam nonummy nibh euismod tincidunt ut laoreet dolore magna aliquam erat volutpat. Ut wisi enim. Lorem ipsum dolor sit amet, consectetuer adipiscing elit, sed diam nonummy nibh euismod tincidunt ut laoreet dolore magna aliquam erat volutpat. Ut wisi enim ad minim veniam, quis nostrud exerci tation ullamcorper suscipit lobortis nisl ut aliquip ex ea commodo feugiat consequat.

Approvals

Dolor sit amet, consectetuer adipiscing elit, sed diam nonummy nibh euismod tincidunt ut laoreet dolore magna aliquam erat volutpat. Ut wisi enim ad minim veniam, quis nostrud exerci tation ullamcorper suscipit lobortis nisl ut aliquip ex ea commodo feugiat consequat. Dlore ipsum dolor sit amet, consectetuer adipiscing elit, sed diam nonummy nibh euismod tincidunt ut laoreet dolore magna aliquam erat volutpat.

Tipsum dolor sit amet, consectetuer adipiscing elit, sed diam nonummy nibh euismod tincidunt ut laoreet dolore magna aliquam erat volutpat. Ut wisi enim ad minim veniam, quis nostrud exerci. Lorem ipsum dolor sit amet, consectetuer adipiscing elit, sed diam.

Dolor sit amet, consectetuer adipiscing elit, sed diam nonummy nibh euismod tincidunt ut laoreet dolore magna aliquam erat volutpat. Ut wisi enim ad minim veniam, quis nostrud exerci tation ullamcorper suscipit lobortis nisl ut aliquip ex ea commodo feugiat.

OWR Plastic Products, Inc. — Office of Accounting   Page 3

B

◆ Data Doesn't Have to Be Ugly to Be Useful

Here are three formats that prove it. They all present large amounts of data in formats that are easy on the eyes. All were done using Word for Windows' Table function. The first design is used as an example in Chapter 14.

Banking Group Report

MUTUAL FUNDS

Orem ipsum dolor sit amet, consectetuer adipiscing elit, sed diam nonummy nibh euismod tincidunt ut laoreet dolore magna aliquam erat volutpat. Ut wisi enim ad minim veniam, quis nostrud exerci tation ullamcorper suscipit lobortis nisl ut aliquip ex ea commodo feugiat consequat. Lorem ipsum dolor sit. Orem ipsum dolor sit amet, consectetuer adipiscing elit, sed diam nonummy nibh euismod tincidunt ut laoreet dolore magna aliquam erat volutpat. Ut wisi enim ad minim veniam, quis nostrud exerci tation ullamcorper suscipit lobortis nisl ut aliquip ex ea commodo feugiat consequat. Lorem ipsum dolor sit.

Consectetuer adipiscing elit, sed diam nonummy nibh euismod tincidunt ut laoreet dolore magna aliquam erat volutpat. Ut wisi enim ad minim veniam, quis nostrud exerci tation ullamcorper suscipit lobortis nisl ut aliquip ex ea commodo feugiat consequat. Lorem ipsum dolor sit amet, consectetuer adipiscing elit, sed diam nonummy nibh euismod tincidunt ut laoreet dolore magna aliquam erat volut.

Ut wisi enim ad minim veniam, quis nostrud exerci tation ullamcorper suscipit lobortis nisl ut aliquip ex ea commodo feugiat consequat. Lorem ipsum dolor sit amet, consectetuer adipiscing elit, sed diam nonummy nibh euismod tincidunt ut laoreet dolore magna aliquam erat volutpat. Ut wisi enim ad min. Sum dolor sit amet, consectetuer adipiscing elit, sed diam nonummy nibh euismod tincidunt ut laoreet dolore magna aliquam erat volutpat. Ut wisi enim ad minim veniam.

Nostrud exerci tation ullamcorper suscipit lobortis nisl ut aliquip ex ea commodo feugiat consequat. Lorem ipsum dolor ex ea commodo feugiat consequat. Lorem ipsum dolor. Nostrud exerci tation ullamcorper suscipit lobortis nisl ut aliquip ex ea commodo feugiat consequat. Lorem ipsum dolor ex ea commodo feugiat consequat. Lorem ipsum dolor.

Sed diam nonummy nibh euismod tincidunt ut laoreet dolore magna aliquam erat volutpat. Ut wisi enim ad minim veniam, quis nostrud exerci tation ullamcorper suscipit lobortis nisl ut aliquip ex ea commodo feugiat consequat. Lorem ipsum dolor sit amet, consectetuer adipiscing elit, sed diam nonummy nibh euismod tincidunt ut laoreet dolore magna aliquam erat volutpat. Orem ipsum dolor sit amet, consectetuer adipiscing elit, sed diam nonummy nibh euismod tincidunt ut laoreet dolore magna.

Ut wisi enim ad minim veniam, quis nostrud exerci tation ullamcorper suscipit lobortis nisl ut aliquip ex ea commodo feugiat consequat. Lorem ipsum dolor sit.

The 10 Best Performers

	Assets (millions)	Expense Ratio	Total Return		52 Wks	5 Years
			Week	1991		
Fidelity SI Tech	$223.9	2.07%	-0.26%	34.75%	85.01%	138.54%
Fidelity SI Med	37.8	2.16	3.42	32.92	69.52	N/A
Fidelity SI Hlth	373.2	1.71	-0.19	23.35	68.69	154.92
Fidelity Port: Hlth	161.1	1.11	0.12	28.90	65.82	256.96
Oppenheimer Tch	23.3	1.75	2.05	35.33	55.15	N/A
Putnam Hlth Sci	376.1	1.14	-0.98	18.13	45.21	133.69
Vanguard Hlth	163.6	0.32	-0.87	15.12	39.38	141.81
GT Global Health	175.5	2.30	-0.55	18.44	38.62	N/A
Medical Res Inv	4.4	3.40	-1.49	19.58	31.63	74.72

7

OWR PLASTIC PRODUCTS

Income Statement (Unaudited)
($ in millions)

	Year Ended December 31,			Six Months Ended June 31,		Year Ended December 31,		
	1988	1989	1990	1989	1990	1991[1]	1992[1]	1993[1]
Net Sales:								
U.S.	$37,482	$45,377	$46,753	$22,814	$22,234	$44,468	$48,900	$51,200
Canada & Foreign	1,980	1,697	2,379	1,456	2,032	2,817	2,600	2,800
Total Net Sales	39,462	47,074	49,132	24,270	24,266	47,285	51,500	54,000
Cost of Goods Sold (FIFO)	27,051	33,594	35,715	16,956	17,649	34,907	37,600	39,500
Gross Profit	12,411	13,480	13,417	7,314	6,617	12,378	13,900	14,500
S,G&A before Corporate Charges	3,880	3,943	3,685	2,126	2,127	3,762	4,300	4,500
Operating Profit	8,531	9,537	9,732	5,188	4,490	8,616	9,600	10,000
Corporate Charges [2]	10	20	245	122	126	252	252	252
Plus: Extraordinary Expense [3]	500	250	100	60	-	-	-	-
Adjusted Operating Profit	$9,021	$9,767	$9,587	$5,126	$4,364	$8,364	$9,348	$9,748

(1) Management projection as of September 14, 1990. Refer to the appendix for detailed information.
(2) As described previously under *Section V. Corporate Charges*, pages 58-59.
(3) As described previously under *Section VII. Extraordinary Expenses*, page 64.

DRAFT 9/30/91 — pg 89

Frey Banking - Mergers & Acquisitions Group

PRELIMINARY LIST: POTENTIAL PURCHASERS OF JENRET'S PLASTICS CO.

Company Name	Sales/Market Value *(millions)*	Activities	Comments
Denton-James Ltd. (UK)	£4,504.0 3,486.8	Or se tu quel Virgilio e quella fonte che spandi di parlar si largo fiume? O delli altri poeti onore e lume, vagliami 'l lungo studio e 'l grande amore che m' ha fatto cercar lo tuo volume. Tu se' lo mio maestro e 'l mio autore; tu se' solo colui da cu' io mi tolsi lo bello stilo che m' ha fatto onore. Vedi la bestia per cu' io mi volsi: aiutami da lei, famoso saggio, ch'ella mi fa tremar le vene e i polsi le vene e i polsi ch'ella mi fa tremar le vene e i polsi le vene e i polsi le vene e i polsi le vene.	• Does not have any commercial plastic products. Should have **great interest in the commercial plastics division.** Not likely to bid high for fear of market criticism. Viewed as a takeover target due to perceived poor management. • Has some very strong industrial plastic products so **not likely to be interested in industrial division.** • **May offer for entire package** in conjunction with its joint venture partner.
Dinfeld Plastics, Inc. (US)	$11,980.00 3,975.90	A te convien tenere altro viaggio se vuo' campar d'esto loco sel vaggio: che questa bestia, per la qual tu gride, non lascia altrui passar per la sua via, ma tanto lo 'mpedisce che l'uccide; e ha natura si malvagia e ria, che mai non empie la bramosa voglia, e dopo 'l pasto ha piu fame che.	• **May bid for whole or just industrial division.** Looking to acquire brands and increase market share and international presence. • Has metal products portfolio. **May have an interest in plastics** to bolster portfolio, particularly in its European operations.
Kraft & Kelly, Ltd. (UK)	£6,028.7 5,222.6	Or se tu quel Virgilio e quella fonte che spandi di parlar si largo fiume. O delli altri poeti onore e lume, vagliami 'l lungo studio e 'l grande amore che m' ha fatto cercar lo tuo volume. O delli altri poeti onore e lume, vagliami 'l lungo studio e 'l grande amore che m' ha fatto cercar lo.	• Already has strong industrial plastic products. **Not likely to want industrial division.** • Already has strong commercial products. **Not likely to want commercial division.** • **May bid for entire package** to gain critical mass.

Page ii

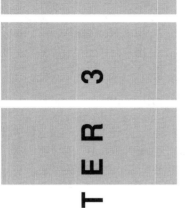

CHAPTER 3

Typography Versus Typing

Typography is the art of arranging type effectively. Though it is an art, it is one that is surprisingly easy to learn. The great thing about typography is that it lets you give your pages a graphic appeal, even if you don't know how to draw or have the money to invest in clip art.

Typography has two chief purposes: to *catch* the reader's attention, and to help *hold* that attention by making the reading easy. To the extent that we communicate in *words*, typography, unlike other sorts of graphics, does double-duty. It dresses the words themselves in a design and creates a graphic impression by their arrangement on the page.

Two words you'll see a lot are "typeface" and "font." "Typeface" was originally two separate words. "Type" referred to the particular design of each letter of the alphabet, each number, each punctuation mark, in other words, each "character." "Face" referred to the fact that these character designs used to be cut into the *face* of small metal plates. Originally, printing was the process of assembling the individual letters, inking them, and then transferring their message to paper by *pressing* the paper and inked typefaces together on a large machine, called a printing *press*.

Technically the term "font" refers to a *single size and style* of a particular typeface, for example, 12-point Helvetica bold. In practice, however, the terms "font," "typeface," and even "face" are used nowadays to mean the same thing. In this book, I use them interchangeably.

There are easily several thousand different typefaces. However, I focus on the ones that come with most PostScript laser printers and compatibles (such as Hewlett-Packard printers operating in PostScript mode). These printers generally advertise that they come with 35 or 39 typefaces—but when you look on your Font menu in Word for Windows you only see ten or so. Students frequently ask where the other two dozen are.

What you see listed on your menu are typeface *families*. A typeface family includes all the letters, numbers, styles, and so on associated with a particular typeface. For instance, the Helvetica family includes Helvetica bold and Helvetica italic as well as plain old Helvetica. Most of the families include four different *styles* of that face—regular, bold, italic, and bold italic. The two fonts Zapf Chancery (a fancy script typeface) and Zapf Dingbats (little pictures, ornaments, and symbols) come only in the regular style.

As you read along, you'll notice that I frequently use the expression "set in"—as in: "This headline is *set in* Times bold, 36 point." This is shorthand for: "Times is used for this headline. It's bolded, and its size is 36 points." The term "set in" is another artifact from bygone days when typesetters actually hand-set metal letters in place one by one, ordering them into words and sentences and phrases. (And you think Word for Windows can be hard!)

THE MANY CHARACTERS OF TYPE

Although each typeface is designed differently, most of them fit into one of two broad categories—they are either **serif** or **sans serif**. Serif faces have tiny end-strokes at the tops and bottoms of letters; sans serif faces don't. The following example shows the difference.

T T

The letter on the left is a serif face (Times) and the letter on the right is a sans— literally *without*—serif face (Helvetica-Narrow).

In most cases, serif typefaces tend to make lengths of *text* easier to read because the serifs help the eye move along from letter to letter and from word to word. The text you are now reading, Times, has a serif face. Sans serif faces, on the other hand, generally stand out more clearly from the page. This makes sans serif faces like Helvetica-Narrow easier to read in *short bursts,* and at both very small and large sizes. (By the way, very large-sized type is often called **display** type.) The example compares two blocks of text—one set in Helvetica-Narrow and the other in Times. Which would you rather read?

This text is set in 10-point Helvetica-Narrow (a sans serif face). It shows how a lot of sans serif text can be harder to read than a lot of serif text. This text is set in 10-point Helvetica-Narrow (a sans serif face). It shows how a lot of sans serif text can be harder to read than a lot of serif text. This text is set in 10-point Helvetica-Narrow (a sans serif face). It shows how a lot of sans serif text can be harder to read than a lot of serif text. This text is set in 10-point Helvetica-Narrow (a sans serif face). It shows how a lot of sans serif text can be harder to read than a lot of serif text.

Which one would you rather read?

This text is set in 10-point Times (a serif face). It shows how a lot of serif text can be easier to read than a lot of sans serif text. This text is set in 10-point Times (a serif face). It shows how a lot of serif text can be easier to read than a lot of sans serif text. This text is set in 10-point Times (a serif face). It shows how a lot of serif text can be easier to read than a lot of sans serif text. This text is set in 10-point Times (a serif face). It shows how a lot of serif text can be easier to read than a lot of sans serif text.

Sometimes, a font is designed especially for a particular function. For instance, the New Century Schoolbook typeface (described by some as a "big-on-the-body" face, and by others as "fat-bodied") was in fact designed for schoolbooks. Its precursor, Century Schoolbook, was used for the old Dick and Jane primers. Looking at New Century Schoolbook, you see that it does make for easy reading—it's big and round, and each letter is very distinct. Compare the following paragraphs. One is set in New Century Schoolbook, and the other is set in Times. (The passage is borrowed from Eric Gill, *An Essay on Typography*.)

". . . although the Roman alphabet has remained essentially unchanged through the centuries, customs & habits of work have changed a great deal. In the time of the Romans, say A.D. 100, when a man said the word 'letters' it is probable that he immediately thought of the kind of letters he was accustomed to seeing on public inscriptions. Altho' all sorts of other kinds of lettering existed . . . the most common kind of formal lettering was inscription in stone."

". . . although the Roman alphabet has remained essentially unchanged through the centuries, customs & habits of work have changed a great deal. In the time of the Romans, say A.D. 100, when a man said the word 'letters' it is probable that he immediately thought of the kind of letters he was accustomed to seeing on public inscriptions. Altho' all sorts of other kinds of lettering existed . . . the most common kind of formal lettering was inscription in stone."

The passage on the left is set in 12-point New Century Schoolbook; the same passage is shown on the right in 12-point Times. Note that although New Century Schoolbook certainly makes it easy to distinguish each letter, it also takes up more space. It's not a great font to use when you're trying to squeeze a lot into a little. Also, notice how much *darker* it is than Times.

When designers talk about choosing the right typeface for a headline or for outquotes, they generally refer to the "character" of type, its "personality," and how typefaces—like human faces—have "expressions." But what exactly does this mean? The following two "demon" examples show how the character of the typeface you choose influences your message, for better

THERE'S A
DEMON
WHO LIVES
ON THE
DEAD

THERE'S A
DEMON
WHO LIVES
ON THE
DEAD

When this headline is set in Helvetica bold, it says "horror" much more loudly than when set in Times italic which has a refined, literary quality. However, because Times has that literary quality, it would be a perfect typeface if this were the title of a classic gothic novel.

or for worse. In this case, the Times italic typeface undermines the ghoulish, tabloid-esque point.

Although you should also consider the *character* of a typeface when you're selecting one for your main text, pay special attention when selecting typefaces for headlines because they're so much bigger. Since people are more likely to read your headline than anything else, it should definitely be your main typo*graphic* element.

A lot of typefaces are like your basic black dress or pair of khaki pants—you can use them for almost any occasion. However, there are times when a particular typeface can help you make a particular point, so why not use it? Naturally, you want to steer clear of typefaces that make an *opposite* point. Let's look at a few other cases where the character or design of the typeface becomes part of the message itself.

Of course, most typefaces can be used in any number of different contexts and work fine in all of them. However, you should be aware that some are better messengers for certain messages than for others.

MODERN (Avant Garde)	MODERN (New Century Schoolbook)
MOD **(Bookman bold)**	MOD (Bookman)
IMPERATIVE **(MACHINE)**	**IMPERATIVE** **(Times bold)**
Pretty poetic *(Zapf Chancery)*	**Pretty poetic** **(Helvetica-Narrow bold)**
Professional (Palatino)	*Professional* *(Palatino italic)*
Typewritten (Courier)	*Typewritten* *(Avant Garde italic)*
Just the facts **(Helvetica bold)**	*Just the facts* *(Times italic)*

In the left-hand column, the typeface reinforces the idea that is in the word. The typefaces in the right-hand column do not. At best they are neutral. At worst—as with "typewritten" and "just the facts"—they actually undercut the message.

FACE-OFF

There are thousands of fonts, but who could possibly remember them all? Most designers develop a "stable" of a dozen or so typefaces that are versatile and suit their particular style. They turn to these faces again and again in their work, and they supplement this stable with "specialty" typefaces as the need arises.

If you're working with a PostScript laser printer or compatible, you can think of its built-in fonts as your "stable." This limited number of typefaces doesn't have to make your work boring or predictable. For instance, all but one of the page designs shown in Chapter 2 use standard PostScript-printer typefaces, and a majority of them use only Times and Helvetica. Still, they all look different.

I have been desktop publishing since there *was* desktop publishing, and I have purchased a grand total of *three* typeface packages to supplement the standard PostScript stable. These were Goudy, Helvetica Black and Light (the same package), and Machine (which also includes American Typewriter). In the first two cases, the companies I purchased them for used those faces as their *main* faces, and the one that used Goudy featured it in its logo as well. I purchased the Machine typeface for work I was doing with a company that sells a product called "Power Tools." I couldn't imagine *not* using Machine for the product name, as shown here.

POWER TOOLS

Machine is the only "specialty" typeface I've ever purchased. Clearly it is the perfect messenger for the Power Tools message.

Whenever people think they need *more* typefaces to make their work more interesting, I refer them to one of my favorite quotations. It appeared in the book *TypeWise,* written by the designer Kit Hinrichs. "I've always found that true creative freedom was derived from working with numerous constraints—time, money, size, color, whatever. Restrictions force you to review the options available. A limited number of typefaces allows you the opportunity to explore the variety within

This is Helvetica-Narrow set at 18 points, in bold.

This is Helvetica-Narrow set at 18 points, in italic.

THIS IS HELVETICA-NARROW SET AT 14 POINTS, IN ALL CAPS.

This is Helvetica-Narrow set at 14 points, in bold italic. I recently discovered that this works great for subheads.

This is Helvetica-Narrow set at 24 points.

This is Helvetica-Narrow set at 10 points.

A typeface is really a whole family of different faces—each with its own color, weight, shape, and size.

the character of each face, to ask yourself how it works at different sizes, mixed with the other faces, in all caps, etc."

✦ Getting to Know the Faces in Your Stable

Experienced designers are always advising beginners to get to know the typefaces they work with "intimately." This is the recommended remedy to most design woes, including the "I wanna have good graphics" woe. In other words, if you want to pack some graphic punch in your pages, get to know how a typeface looks in all its different styles and sizes. Once you know the many faces of a face, you'll think of creative ways to use them. Not only will your work become more graphically interesting, but you'll become a better communicator as well.

Besides having their own personalities, typefaces have certain distinctly designed letters and numbers which you can use to recognize them. These "key" letters include capital T, M, and R; lowercase g; numbers; and some punctuation marks. The Ts for the standard PostScript-printer fonts are shown following (all are sized at 72 points).

Some people I know can glance through a magazine and tell you the typefaces it uses. I can't do that by a long shot, but I can recognize a few faces—Helvetica, for example, which is

Avant Garde   Bookman   Courier   Helvetica

Helvetica-Narrow   New Century Schoolbook   Palatino   Times

See how the serifs help make the letters distinct? How much bigger New Century Schoolbook looks than the others? How Bookman is somewhat wider than the others?

probably the easiest. I can also recognize Avant Garde when it's set in all caps, or when it uses a capital Q or R, both of which are quite distinctive. I usually recognize Times, and I know that Palatino italic has a great ampersand (&), which I use whenever I need one with a little class. (As you look through the following typefaces, you'll see that all the other ampersands are pretty much alike.) Whenever I need oversized numbers or punctuation marks, I use Bookman bold. As you work with different faces, you'll discover little idiosyncrasies like these that make you prefer one over another in certain circumstances.

THE FOURTH QUADRANT
&
1 2 3 4 5 6 7 8 9 # $!

The top example shows Avant Garde's distinctive Q and R—which could come in handy if you ever work with a client or product whose name includes these letters, and whose style fits. The middle example shows an ampersand in Palatino italic. The last example shows numbers and a few punctuation marks in Bookman bold. All three examples are set in 20-point type.

Color It Bookman. Designers talk about "color" and "tone" as specific and concrete aspects of a typeface's character. **Color,** in this context, has to do with the blackness of the font on the page. In the following example, Bookman bold is the most "colorful."

Notice how the color of the heads for each of the blurbs contrasts with the main text. This is an effective way to make the heads stand out. Except where indicated, all text is set at 10 points. (Again, the passage is borrowed from Eric Gill, *An Essay on Typography.*)

Text in Palatino w/ Helvetica Bold Head

". . . the most common kind of formal lettering was the inscription in stone. The consequence was that when he made letters . . . it was the stone inscription that he took as his model. He did not say: Such & such a tool or material naturally makes or lends itself to the making of such and such forms. On the contrary, he said: Letters are such and such forms; therefore, whatever tools & materials we have to use, we must make these forms as well as the forms & materials will allow."

Text in Times Bold Italic (10 pts) with Helvetica-Narrow Bold Head (11 pts)

". . . the most common kind of formal lettering was the inscription in stone. The consequence was that when he made letters . . . it was the stone inscription that he took as his model. He did not say: Such & such a tool or material naturally makes or lends itself to the making of such and such forms. On the contrary, he said: Letters are such and such forms; therefore, whatever tools & materials we have to use, we must make these forms as well as the forms & materials will allow."

AVANT GARDE TEXT, TIMES BOLD HEAD

". . . the most common kind of formal lettering was the inscription in stone. The consequence was that when he made letters . . . it was the stone inscription that he took as his model. He did not say: Such & such a tool or material naturally makes or lends itself to the making of such and such forms. On the contrary, he said: Letters are such and such forms; therefore, whatever tools & materials we have to use, we must make these forms as well as the forms & materials will allow."

Text in Bookman Bold (10 pts) w/ Helvetica-Narrow Italic Head Set at 12 pts

". . . the most common kind of formal lettering was the inscription in stone. The consequence was that when he made letters . . . it was the stone inscription that he took as his model. He did not say: Such & such a tool or material naturally makes or lends itself to the making of such and such forms. On the contrary, he said: Letters are such and such forms; therefore, whatever tools & materials we have to use, we must make these forms as well as the forms & materials will allow."

Notice that there's no space between the heads and the text. The only thing that separates them is their contrasting colors, typefaces, styles, and sizes—and that's enough.

Tone It Up, Tone It Down.   The **tone** of a typeface is how it "sounds" to the eye. The demon example shown earlier illustrates how the loud, brash quality of Helvetica bold makes it a good choice for announcing disturbing events. It's one of the headline faces most common in tabloid newspapers. By contrast, Times, which is also used widely in newspaper headlines, suggests a more deliberate, less alarmist tone.

The particular style a face is set in also affects its tone. For instance, in the following example, the announcement looks light and lyric when set in Helvetica-Narrow. But it looks *dissonant* when set in bold caps. It looks like an entirely different typeface. This is what designers mean when they say there are many faces to a face.

The POETRY SOCIETY sponsors a night of... whimsy poesy limericks rhymes jingles jangles *&* vaulting meters	*The POETRY SOCIETY sponsors a night of...* **WHIMSY** **POESY** **LIMERICKS** **RHYMES** **JINGLES** **JANGLES** *&* **VAULTING METERS**

Setting Helvetica-Narrow in bold caps puts quite a different face on things.

Meet the Faces. The following typefaces are standard on most PostScript laser printers and compatibles. When you look through them, notice how individual letters, numbers, and punctuation marks differ both from one face to the next, and from regular to italic to bold within the *same* face. Which ones look most suitable to the kinds of work you do? Which ones do you like best? Do any individual characters stand out as being something you could use?

Serif Faces: Note that all the typefaces shown here are set at 16 points.

Bookman
A B C D E F G H I J K L M N O P Q R S T U V W X Y Z
a b c d e f g h i j k l m n o p q r s t u v w x y z
1 2 3 4 5 6 7 8 9 0 ! @ # $ % ^ & * ( ) " " ?

Bookman bold
A B C D E F G H I J K L M N O P Q R S T U V W X Y Z
a b c d e f g h i j k l m n o p q r s t u v w x y z
1 2 3 4 5 6 7 8 9 0 ! @ # $ % ^ & * ( ) " " ?

Bookman italic
A B C D E F G H I J K L M N O P Q R S T U V W X Y Z
a b c d e f g h i j k l m n o p q r s t u v w x y z
*1 2 3 4 5 6 7 8 9 0 ! @ # $ % ^ & * ( ) " " ?*

Bookman bold italic
A B C D E F G H I J K L M N O P Q R S T U V W X Y Z
a b c d e f g h i j k l m n o p q r s t u v w x y z
1 2 3 4 5 6 7 8 9 0 ! @ # $ % ^ & * ( ) " " ?

Courier
A B C D E F G H I J K L M N O P Q R S T U V W X Y Z
a b c d e f g h i j k l m n o p q r s t u v w x y z
1 2 3 4 5 6 7 8 9 0 ! @ # $ % ^ & * ( ) " " ?

Courier bold
A B C D E F G H I J K L M N O P Q R S T U V W X Y Z
a b c d e f g h i j k l m n o p q r s t u v w x y z
1 2 3 4 5 6 7 8 9 0 ! @ # $ % ^ & * ( ) " " ?

Courier italic
A B C D E F G H I J K L M N O P Q R S T U V W X Y Z
a b c d e f g h i j k l m n o p q r s t u v w x y z
*1 2 3 4 5 6 7 8 9 0 ! @ # $ % ^ & * ( ) " " ?*

Courier bold italic
A B C D E F G H I J K L M N O P Q R S T U V W X Y Z
a b c d e f g h i j k l m n o p q r s t u v w x y z
1 2 3 4 5 6 7 8 9 0 ! @ # $ % ^ & * ( ) " " ?

New Century Schoolbook
A B C D E F G H I J K L M N O P Q R S T U V W X Y Z
a b c d e f g h i j k l m n o p q r s t u v w x y z
1 2 3 4 5 6 7 8 9 0 ! @ # $ % ^ & * ( ) " " ?

New Century Schoolbook bold
A B C D E F G H I J K L M N O P Q R S T U V W X Y Z
a b c d e f g h i j k l m n o p q r s t u v w x y z
1 2 3 4 5 6 7 8 9 0 ! @ # $ % ^ & * ( ) " " ?

New Century Schoolbook italic
A B C D E F G H I J K L M N O P Q R S T U V W X Y Z
a b c d e f g h i j k l m n o p q r s t u v w x y z
*1 2 3 4 5 6 7 8 9 0 ! @ # $ % ^ & * ( ) " " ?*

New Century Schoolbook bold italic
A B C D E F G H I J K L M N O P Q R S T U V W X Y Z
a b c d e f g h i j k l m n o p q r s t u v w x y z
1 2 3 4 5 6 7 8 9 0 ! @ # $ % ^ & * ( ) " " ?

Palatino
A B C D E F G H I J K L M N O P Q R S T U V W X Y Z
a b c d e f g h i j k l m n o p q r s t u v w x y z
1 2 3 4 5 6 7 8 9 0 ! @ # $ % ^ & * ( ) " " ?

Palatino bold
A B C D E F G H I J K L M N O P Q R S T U V W X Y Z
a b c d e f g h i j k l m n o p q r s t u v w x y z
1 2 3 4 5 6 7 8 9 0 ! @ # $ % ^ & * ( ) " " ?

Palatino italic
A B C D E F G H I J K L M N O P Q R S T U V W X Y Z
a b c d e f g h i j k l m n o p q r s t u v w x y z
*1 2 3 4 5 6 7 8 9 0 ! @ # $ % ^ & * ( ) " " ?*

Palatino bold italic
A B C D E F G H I J K L M N O P Q R S T U V W X Y Z
a b c d e f g h i j k l m n o p q r s t u v w x y z
*1 2 3 4 5 6 7 8 9 0 ! @ # $ % ^ & * ( ) " " ?*

Times *(Note that Times is called "Tms Rmn" in Word for Windows unless you are using Adobe Type Manager.)*
A B C D E F G H I J K L M N O P Q R S T U V W X Y Z
a b c d e f g h i j k l m n o p q r s t u v w x y z
1 2 3 4 5 6 7 8 9 0 ! @ # $ % ^ & * ( ) " " ?

Times bold
A B C D E F G H I J K L M N O P Q R S T U V W X Y Z
a b c d e f g h i j k l m n o p q r s t u v w x y z
1 2 3 4 5 6 7 8 9 0 ! @ # $ % ^ & * ( ) " " ?

Times italic
A B C D E F G H I J K L M N O P Q R S T U V W X Y Z
a b c d e f g h i j k l m n o p q r s t u v w x y z
*1 2 3 4 5 6 7 8 9 0 ! @ # $ % ^ & * ( ) " " ?*

Times bold italic
A B C D E F G H I J K L M N O P Q R S T U V W X Y Z
a b c d e f g h i j k l m n o p q r s t u v w x y z
*1 2 3 4 5 6 7 8 9 0 ! @ # $ % ^ & * ( ) " " ?*

Sans Serif Faces: Note that all the typefaces shown here are set at 16 points.

Avant Garde
A B C D E F G H I J K L M N O P Q R S T U V W X Y Z
a b c d e f g h i j k l m n o p q r s t u v w x y z
1 2 3 4 5 6 7 8 9 0 ! @ # $ % ^ & * ( ) " " ?

Avant Garde bold
**A B C D E F G H I J K L M N O P Q R S T U V W X Y Z
a b c d e f g h i j k l m n o p q r s t u v w x y z
1 2 3 4 5 6 7 8 9 0 ! @ # $ % ^ & * ( ) " " ?**

Avant Garde italic
*A B C D E F G H I J K L M N O P Q R S T U V W X Y Z
a b c d e f g h i j k l m n o p q r s t u v w x y z
1 2 3 4 5 6 7 8 9 0 ! @ # $ % ^ & * ( ) " " ?*

Avant Garde bold italic
***A B C D E F G H I J K L M N O P Q R S T U V W X Y Z
a b c d e f g h i j k l m n o p q r s t u v w x y z
1 2 3 4 5 6 7 8 9 0 ! @ # $ % ^ & * ( ) " " ?***

Helvetica   *(Note that Helvetica is called "Helv" in Word for Windows unless you are using Adobe Type Manager.)*
A B C D E F G H I J K L M N O P Q R S T U V W X Y Z
a b c d e f g h i j k l m n o p q r s t u v w x y z
1 2 3 4 5 6 7 8 9 0 ! @ # $ % ^ & * ( ) " " ?

Helvetica bold
**A B C D E F G H I J K L M N O P Q R S T U V W X Y Z
a b c d e f g h i j k l m n o p q r s t u v w x y z
1 2 3 4 5 6 7 8 9 0 ! @ # $ % ^ & * ( ) " " ?**

Helvetica italic
A B C D E F G H I J K L M N O P Q R S T U V W X Y Z
a b c d e f g h i j k l m n o p q r s t u v w x y z
*1 2 3 4 5 6 7 8 9 0 ! @ # $ % ^ & * ( ) " " ?*

Helvetica bold italic
A B C D E F G H I J K L M N O P Q R S T U V W X Y Z
a b c d e f g h i j k l m n o p q r s t u v w x y z
1 2 3 4 5 6 7 8 9 0 ! @ # $ % ^ & * ( ) " " ?

Helvetica-Narrow
A B C D E F G H I J K L M N O P Q R S T U V W X Y Z
a b c d e f g h i j k l m n o p q r s t u v w x y z
1 2 3 4 5 6 7 8 9 0 ! @ # $ % ^ & * ( ) " " ?

Helvetica-Narrow bold
A B C D E F G H I J K L M N O P Q R S T U V W X Y Z
a b c d e f g h i j k l m n o p q r s t u v w x y z
1 2 3 4 5 6 7 8 9 0 ! @ # $ % ^ & * ( ) " " ?

Helvetica-Narrow italic
A B C D E F G H I J K L M N O P Q R S T U V W X Y Z
a b c d e f g h i j k l m n o p q r s t u v w x y z
*1 2 3 4 5 6 7 8 9 0 ! @ # $ % ^ & * ( ) " " ?*

Helvetica-Narrow bold italic
A B C D E F G H I J K L M N O P Q R S T U V W X Y Z
a b c d e f g h i j k l m n o p q r s t u v w x y z
1 2 3 4 5 6 7 8 9 0 ! @ # $ % ^ & * ( ) " " ?

Some Specialty Typefaces: Script, dingbat, and symbol fonts are used for particular purposes. The script typeface, Zapf Chancery, is used for fancy things such as invitations. Dingbats is a practical-graphics typeface that can dress up anything from a form to an artistically rendered statement of purpose. The Symbol font comes with Windows and is used mainly for mathematically oriented publications, typesetters' punctuation marks, and a few picture symbols. See Chapter 6 for information on how to use the Dingbats and Symbol fonts.

Zapf Chancery

ABCDEFGHIJKLMNOPQRSTUVWXYZ
abcdefghijklmnopqrstuvwxyz
1234567890!@#$%^&*()""?

Zapf Dingbats

Symbol

ΑΒΧΔΕΦΓΗΙϑΚΛΜΝΟΠΘΡΣΤΥςΩΞΨΖ
αβχδεφγηιφκλμνοπθρστυϖωξψζ
1234567890!≅#∃%⊥&*()•…?

TYPE-AS-GRAPHICS TOOLS

Before desktop publishing, you would have typed in your text, a designer would have "spec'd" it (in other words, *specified* the font, size, style, and so on that the typesetter was to put it in), and then the typesetter would have set the text according to the designer's specs. But with desktop publishing, you can typeset your text as you type it in.

Of course, it's not really typography simply to set your text in 12-point Times. Typography requires some refinement. This section explains the typographic tools—leading (line spacing), kerning (letter spacing), type sizing, styling, aligning, and so on—that turn type into graphics. For instructions on how to use these tools in Word for Windows, see Chapter 5.

Type Specs

Type **specs,** or specifications, describe how type is set—what face is used, the style, size, leading, and alignment. For instance, the type specs for this text are: 10-point Helvetica on 12 points of leading, flush left (which would end up looking like this in typographer's shorthand: Helvetica 10/12 flush left).

When you spec type, all you're doing is deciding how you want your headlines, your subheads, the main text, and so on. Every time you decide to type a letter in 12-point Times or 10-point Helvetica, you've spec'd type.

✦ Type Sizes

Type sizes are measured in points. There are 72 points to an inch, which makes a 72-point letter 1 inch tall. Most text for reports, brochures, and so on is set in 10 or 12 points. Anything smaller than 6 points is practically impossible to read. Word for Windows lets you size type anywhere from 4 to 127 points. The word "points" is often abbreviated to "pt."

4 pts

6 pts

12 pts

18 pts

48 pts

72 pts

127 pts

◆ Leading, or Line Spacing

Leading (also called line spacing) is the white space that separates each line of type from the one above it. In the old days, printers would actually insert a *strip of lead* between two lines in order to increase the line spacing.

Leading, like the size of type, is generally measured in points. It falls into one of three broad categories. Type is said to be set "open" if there's a lot of extra space between the lines. It's said to be set "solid" when the leading is the *same size* as the type, and "minus" (sometimes called "tight") when the leading is *smaller* than the type.

You're probably familiar with double-spaced text—well, that's just text with open leading. **Paragraph spacing** is similar to leading, but it refers specifically to the amount of space between two paragraphs.

TOYS FOR TOTS TOYS FOR TOTS TOYS FOR TOTS

The headline on the left is set solid (the type size equals the amount of leading); the middle headline is set minus (the size of the leading is less than that of the type); and the headline on the right is set open (the amount of leading is greater than the size of the type).

✦ **Type Style**

A font's style includes its weight (**bold** or regular), width (e x p a n d e d , condensed, or normal), slant (*italic*), whether it's in ALL CAPS or SMALL CAPS, and whether it's <u>underlined</u>. The following example illustrates how a different type style can make a different point.

WHY ME?

Why *me?*

The example on the left says something like "Why are you always picking on me, buster?" The one on the right says something along the lines of "Why me and not him?" They're the same words, but a different type style—and a different message.

✦ **Kerning, or Letter Spacing**

Kerning, or letter spacing, refers to the amount of space between letters—e x p a n d e d , condensed, or normal. This capability is useful when you want to even out lines of type in a headline, shorten text to fit on a single page (you could condense it), and improve the appearance of type set in large sizes.

WHAT'S UP?

WHAT'S UP?

The top example is unkerned. See how the H and A, and the U and P run into each other? You can expand the letter spacing between them and make the whole headline look better, as in the bottom example.

✦ Alignment

There are four ways to align text in relation to the margin. It can be centered between the margins; flush (or straight) against the left margin and ragged along the right margin; flush against the right margin and ragged along the left; or justified, which means flush against both the right and left margins. Most text you see in newspapers, magazines, brochures, reports, and so on, is either flush left or justified. Centered text tends to be reserved for headlines, outquotes, advertising copy, and poetry. Flush right text—the rarest of the four alignments—is used most often in outquotes and stylish heads.

Note: *By the way, the poem used to illustrate these alignment options is by the humorist James Thurber; it first appeared in* The New Yorker *in the 1930s. I found it in Thurber's book about the magazine,* The Years with Ross.

Bachelor Burton

Allen Lewis Brooksy Burton
Went to buy himself a curtain,
Called on Greenberg, Moe, and Mintz,
Bought a hundred yards of chintz
Stamped with owls and all star-spangled
Tried to hang it, fell, and strangled.

by James Thurber

Centered

Bachelor Burton

Allen Lewis Brooksy Burton Went to buy himself a curtain, Called on Greenberg, Moe, and Mintz, Bought a hundred yards of chintz Stamped with owls and all star-spangled Tried to hang it, fell, and strangled.

by James Thurber

Justified

Bachelor Burton

Allen Lewis Brooksy Burton
Went to buy himself a curtain,
Called on Greenberg, Moe, and Mintz,
Bought a hundred yards of chintz
Stamped with owls and all star-spangled
Tried to hang it, fell, and strangled.

by James Thurber

Flush Left (or Ragged Right)

Bachelor Burton

Allen Lewis Brooksy Burton
Went to buy himself a curtain,
Called on Greenberg, Moe, and Mintz,
Bought a hundred yards of chintz
Stamped with owls and all star-spangled
Tried to hang it, fell, and strangled.

by James Thurber

Flush Right (or Ragged Left)

✦ Drop Caps

Drop caps are often used to start something—an article in a magazine, the main text in a fund-raising piece, a new section, and so forth. They "drop down" into a paragraph, which "wraps around" them, as in this example. This drop cap is set in Times bold at 66 points; it's dropped into the paragraph using Word's FORMAT, FRAME command. See Chapters 10 and 13 for more information.

✦ Stick-Up Caps

Stick-up caps are like drop caps, except that they stick up and out of the paragraph they're in. This one is set in Times bold at 66 points. There are two tricks used to create professional-looking stick-up caps and drop caps in Word—negative leading and subscripting. Stick-up caps are somewhat easier to create in Word than are drop caps. See Chapters 10 and 13 for more information.

✦ Large Initial Caps

The term "large initial caps" can refer to both drop caps and stick-up caps, as well as to ones that are neither, as in the following example. You can create large initial caps in Word for Windows by using either a hanging indent or a table.

M embership at the MUSEUM…

CHAPTER 4

From Start to Print Shop

This chapter explains the whole desktop publishing process, from typing what you want to say into the computer, to desktop publishing it, to getting it out of your computer, to sending it to the offset printer. It's written for people who haven't done this sort of thing before—at least not very often or very recently.

The writing, editing, and formatting you do on your computer is the "desktop" part of desktop publishing. The first section of this chapter, *You've Got to Have a Plan*, covers how to organize that part of the job. The second section, *The* Publishing *in Desktop Publishing* explains how to get desktop-published material out of your computer and on its way to the printer.

In some ways, the "publishing" part of desktop publishing is a lot like photocopying. For instance, when you photocopy something, you put the original down on the glass and set the machine to print the copies. When you send something to an offset printer, you give the printer the original—in this case, called "camera-ready copy," or a "mechanical"—and indicate how many copies you want. (Remember that print shops actually print from photographic plates, which they make by taking a picture of your camera-ready copy.)

Sometimes, you doctor up the original you use for photo-copying—you use correction fluid to hide mistakes, or you do a little cut and paste to add some text or a picture that wasn't there in the first place. Preparing camera-ready copy is much the same. Sometimes you can't do everything that needs to be done on your computer, so you have to doctor it up by hand before sending it off to the print shop. This chapter explains the special cases when this might happen and what to do when it does.

A lot of times—maybe even most times—you don't need a full-service print shop to handle your document or publication. All you need is a quick-copy shop, or even a photocopier. In that case, you may just want to skim the section *The* Publishing *in Desktop Publishing*.

YOU'VE GOT TO HAVE A PLAN

Someone once said that the way to plan a publication is to get its "name, rank, and serial number." In other words, pin down just what and why you're doing it in the first place. To do that, I always start by working through answers to the following questions. Notice that the questions are not about design per se. Rather, they concern the nature of the publication, its purpose, and the materials you want to fit into it. Once you have answers to these questions, you can then focus on questions of design—formatting your publication to put its best foot forward so that the most important information catches the reader's attention.

- Remember Rule of Thumb #1 and ask yourself: "Who's going to read this? What do I want to say to them?" The answers will help you decide whether you want to produce a brochure or a booklet, and will point to the ideas or information you want the design to call attention to.

- What look or impression do you want? Professional, lively, traditional, bold, modern, fun, elegant, '50s art deco, oriental, academic, funky, official . . . ?

- What is the single most important thing you have to say (or to show)? What would you say if you had only one sentence to say it in?

- What is the second most important thing? The third? Are there key elements you have to emphasize (such as a picture of the chairman on page 3)?

- If you don't have pictures to illustrate the things you have to say, should you? If so, can you create them or obtain them easily, or do you have to move mountains? If you have to move mountains, invoke Dos and Don'ts #3: *Keep It Simple*.

- If you don't have relevant pictures, think about other ways of getting some graphic appeal into the publication, for instance, dressing up a headline or using outquotes.

- What text and/or pictures would you like to include *if* you have room?

- How much can you spend? I like the designer Kit Hinrichs' approach to this question. "Budget is not a deterrent to creativity," he wrote in his book *TypeWise*. "But it does affect how you implement that creativity."

    For instance, knowing your budget helps determine whether you should even think about using color inks, and how many. It will also help determine the *dimensions* of your publication (it's less expensive if it fits on standard paper that the printer doesn't have to trim), the kind of paper you want, the kind of binding, and so on. You should talk to printers *in the planning stages* to determine what works best for your budget.

    Note: *Paper usually accounts for nearly 50% of the cost of a print job, so here's a pocketbook saving tip: Most printers have a* **house sheet**—*a certain type of paper that they buy in bulk and always keep on hand. Ask your print shop whether they have one; if they do and you like it, you can save yourself a bundle.*

- How will you distribute the publication? If by mail, you'll probably want to control its weight to the ounce, and produce it on a light-weight paper.

- How big will your publication be? Again, if you're planning to mail it, it's helpful to check on the standard-sized envelopes available for letter-sized pieces, booklets, catalogs, and so on.

✦ Design: Putting Your Plan into Practice

Once you've pinned down the nature and purpose of your publication, you're ready to focus on design—spec'ing the type for headlines, subheads, and body copy, for example; fitting the text into columns; placing illustrations, graphs, and outquotes on the page; and adding rules, borders, headers, and footers. For inspiration and instruction, see Chapters 1, 2, and 3.

Remember that the design, too, needs to take into account the answers to the preceding questions. For instance, the answer to "Who's going to read this?" has some design implications.

A client of mine, for example, is editor-in-chief of a well-established magazine and knows his audience quite well. *Because* he knows who they are, he pressed his staff to make a significant design change.

His audience, he knew, is getting older. More and more of them wear glasses, as he now does. The magazine has many serious stories on public policy, and he knows how to entice his readers into these stories with great headlines and leads. But he felt readers needed to be able to see these leads—so he could hook them into the story—without bothering to put their glasses on. So he had the pages redesigned to accommodate larger-than-usual type on the opening spread. This is a perfect example of format following function.

THE *PUBLISHING* IN DESKTOP PUBLISHING

Desktop publishing is what you do when you use your computer to create camera-ready copy to send to the print shop. It essentially replaces traditional typesetting and paste-up. If you haven't already, you should probably read *So, What Is Desktop Publishing Anyway?* in Chapter 1.

This section explains the key elements of the "publishing" half of desktop publishing:

- How to use photos and scanned images.

- How printers fold sheets of paper to produce publications in various sizes.

- How to find and work with service bureaus in order to produce the highest quality camera-ready copy.

- How to get your camera-ready copy to the printer.

CHECKLIST: Getting It All Together

Here's a basic checklist of things to keep in mind when you're preparing a publication. The list is not chronological because the process isn't a particularly chronological one, especially given the tight deadlines under which desktop publishers usually operate.

✓ Write, edit, and proofread text. (When you're working with complex designs, it usually helps to *finalize* the text before you start formatting it on the computer.)

✓ Decide on a size for the publication, for example, a letter-sized flip sheet, double-sided.

✓ Make a rough layout to figure out how the different elements of the publication fit together. My rough layouts usually go through two stages. I sketch the first one (you don't need to draw well to do this, by the way; my sketches are pretty sorry looking). I do the second one on the computer to make sure I can actually do what I think I can.

✓ Spec the type for text: main text, headlines, subheads, captions, and so forth.

✓ Select the tables, graphs, clip art, and so on that you want to use. *Create* them, if necessary.

✓ Format the publication on the computer. Add rules, borders, headers, footers, and so forth.

✓ Select the paper it will be printed on.

✓ Select the ink color(s) (if you want to use colored inks).

✓ Get bids from offset printers (or copy shops). You need to tell them the dimensions of the publication (called the "finished page size"); the number of pages; the number of ink colors (remember that black ink only is called a one-color job); the kind of paper, including the paper to be used for the cover if the publication has one; how the publication is to be folded, scored, or bound; how many photos, if any; the quantity you'll be ordering; and the delivery date. (If you're not sure what kind of paper you want, you can visit printers to see what they have that you like, and have them bid on that.)

✓ Prepare camera-ready copy for delivery to the printer.

✓ Deliver the mechanicals to the printer. It's often a good idea (especially when using a print shop you've never worked with before) to deliver your mechanicals in person. That way you can explain the materials you have and what you want done with them, and the printer can ask you about anything that's not clear. The more complex the print job, the more I urge you to deliver your mechanicals yourself.

✓ Approve proofs (sample pages of the publication) to ensure that what you see is what you want a thousand copies of.

**✦ Photo
Opportunities**

It's easy to deal with black-and-white photos. Here's what you have to do:

1. You have to pick out a good one.

2. You have to make a picture window for each photo (a picture window is just an empty box that you create in Word for Windows to hold the place for the picture that will go there).

3. You have to "key" each photo to its respective picture window—mark an A in the picture window and on the back of the A photo, B in the window and on the back of the B photo, and so on. (Always use a felt-tip pen or china marker when writing on the backs of photos.)

Photo

In some ways, it's even easier to deal with photos that are **scanned** into a computer file, rather than with the photos themselves. Scanning turns a photo into a complex, computerized pattern of dots. You can change how these scans look with what's called a gray-scale editor such as PC Paintbrush IV Plus (ZSoft Corporation) or Gray F/X (Xerox Imaging Systems). Or you can bring it right into Word for Windows using the IN-SERT, PICTURE command (see Chapter 11 for instructions). You can then **crop** it (that is, clip off the portions you don't want); size it to fit the available space (also called scaling); and place it on the page, along with the headline, main text, outquotes, and so on. You don't have to "key" a scanned picture to the page because it's already *in* the page.

There's an interesting similarity between scans and printed photographs. When photos are printed, they are converted into a dot pattern called a **halftone**. Although the image looks like a regular photograph from a reading distance, when you look closer, you'll notice that it's really made up of a complex series of tiny dots. The same is true of a scan, except that the dot pattern for the scan is stored in a file on your computer.

Whenever you print an image from a series of dots—whether it's a scanned image or a photo—you have to specify the quality at which you want that image printed. This is known as the **line screen**. You can specify line screens from 65 to 150 lines per inch (lpi), with the higher numbers producing better quality. A newspaper photo is usually printed at about 85 lines per inch; magazines usually use 133 or even 150 lpi.

Whenever you decide to use a line screen greater than 90 lpi (for instance, for a brochure), you should create it on film (referred to as a negative), rather than on paper. If you create a line screen greater than 90 lpi on paper, it tends to look dark and muddy when printed. (See *Settling Down with a Good Service Bureau* on the next page for more information on the choice of film versus paper.)

Scan

Two elements decide the quality of a printed photo: the quality of the original and the line screen at which it's printed. The quality of a scanned photo depends on these two elements, plus two more: the shades of gray used by the scanner (256 shades of gray is a whole lot better than the other possibilities—64, 16, or black-and-white, which is called **monochrome**) and the resolution or density at which the scan is produced (most scanners produce resolutions between 75 and 300 dots per inch, with denser definitely being better; a few can manage 400 dpi).

Although a picture produced directly from a black-and-white photo is generally of better quality than one produced from a scan, the question is "How much better?" For instance, compare the Scottish phone booths labeled "Photo" and "Scan." The photo was printed from an actual black and white photograph at a line screen of 133 lpi. Notice that it's somewhat brighter, with more contrasts than its counterpart.

The scan was printed from a scanned image of that same photo. It was scanned at a resolution of 300 dpi, and then produced using the same line screen as the photo (133 lpi). Notice that it was doctored up a bit by my service bureau. They erased the mottled sign hanging on the top of the phone booth, and they also lightened it up a little.

Scanned photos work well for many publications, under a lot of different circumstances. For instance, I would feel comfortable using a "phone booth–quality" scan instead of the photo in most newsletters. Scans can also turn mediocre photos into fairly artistic images. If you can touch up the image using a gray-scale editor, you can sometimes improve it significantly.

You can also use scans as the basis of computer art. For instance, take the headline treatment for "Rules of Thumb." That thumb-print belongs to a friend of mine. I scanned it into a TIFF file at 180 dots per inch and printed it (on paper) with a 90-lpi line screen. I then colored it gray in Micrografx Designer (just to add a lighter tone to it) and imported it into Word for Windows using the INSERT, PICTURE command. Then I fiddled with it until I came up with this headline treatment.

Settling Down with a Good Service Bureau

Service bureaus started springing up around the country at about the same time that desktop publishing did. They generally have all the expensive equipment necessary for top-of-the-line desktop-published products: very high–resolution printers (1270 or 2450 dots per inch), slide equipment, scanners, color printers, and so on.

So, instead of investing in this equipment yourself, you can just use theirs. You give them a disk with the computer file you want printed out at high resolution, and they give you back camera-ready copy. In addition to getting a quality product, you can tap their usually considerable knowledge to sort out vexing questions like, "What line screen should I use for this scanned image?"

If you're looking for a service bureau, look in the phone book under "computers—software & services" or "desktop publishing services." If you can't find one there, try your local newspaper (my local paper features a weekly computer page where several service bureaus advertise). If you still can't find one, try the classified ads at the back of computer magazines such as *PC Magazine* or *Publish*. Usually a few service bureaus that work by modem and mail are listed, so it doesn't matter where they're located. You can still get the high-quality **output** you need. ("Output" is just a generic term referring to the product you can get out of your computer, for example, a printed page or a slide.)

The service that I use most often is high-resolution printing (1270 dpi; I've never had occasion to use 2450 dpi). Because so many service bureaus use a Linotronic printer for this sort of "typeset quality," I'll explain a little about Linotronics here.

Rules OF Thumb

This thumb-print was scanned into a TIFF file and brought into Word.

Note: *The rule of thumb for working with a scanned image is that you should scan it into the computer file using roughly twice as many dots per inch as the line screen you're going to use.*

The Linotronic is a PostScript image-setting device, not a laser printer. It actually processes your page *photographically*. Because it processes images photographically, you usually have a choice between printing your page on special image-setting paper or on film. Although printing to film is more expensive, sometimes it makes sense—for instance, if your document includes scans or TIFF files that you want to print at a high-quality line screen like 133 lpi (see *Photo Opportunities* for more information on scans). Although many offset printers *can* print from film, others can't. So always check with yours to be sure.

Ideally you'll be able to find a service bureau that has its Linotronic (or other high-resolution printer) hooked up to a PC running Word for Windows. Then all you have to do is save your document and get it to them. However, finding a service bureau that's set up with Word for Windows can sometimes be trickier than you'd think. If you can't find one, you can simply send the service bureau a PostScript file or an Encapsulated PostScript file (EPS). *This is not a big deal; you don't even need a PostScript printer. Let Those Presses Roll!* walks you step by step through how to do it—and you'll be relieved to hear there aren't very many steps.

Some service bureaus also have souped-up laser printers that print at 400 to 1000 dots per inch. Depending on the sort of publication you're doing, this can be a great option. For instance, while I'm comfortable producing camera-ready copy for most reports and informational booklets at 300 dpi, I usually go with 1270 for marketing or fund-raising pieces. However, if you're not in a blue-chip corporation, 600 or 1000 dpi might serve just as well.

Some service bureaus have poster printers, which allow you to create huge documents (like 3 feet by 3 feet) *in color*. Again, if the service bureau doesn't have Word for Windows, you should be able to send them a PostScript or EPS file. Just call to be sure.

✦ Getting It to the Printer

It's very easy to create camera-ready copy for a report. You print the report on your laser printer and send it to the copy shop. That's it.

Each page of your report serves as its own mechanical. In some cases, you might want the copy shop to print the report double sided (make sure you set it up for double-sided printing in Word for Windows). In some cases, you might want them to print it on special paper. After it's photocopied, you might have it spiral-bound or put in a three-ring binder.

But say you want to create camera-ready copy for a letter-fold brochure, like the Little Bank brochure shown in Chapter 2. Whenever a publication (usually a brochure, booklet, or newsletter) is to be *folded* into final form, you have to handle it differently; you have to deal with the sometimes-confusing question of how to sequence the pages. Whether the publication is to be printed by an offset printer, the copy shop down the street, or by you on your own photocopy machine makes no difference. You still have to arrange your publication in Word for Windows so that the pages to be printed on the *same side* of a single sheet of paper are next to each other.

Folding Paper Into Publications.　When I first started desktop publishing, one of the hardest things for me was to translate a page on the computer screen into camera-ready copy for the printer, and then into the publication I got back from the printer. I always ordered my pages as I did when I was writing—first page 1, then page 2, and so on.

So I delivered my first desktop-published brochure (a letter-fold brochure, incidentally) to a traditional paste-up artist, who was making arrangements with the printer. Looking over the pages I was so proud of, he commented acerbically that he thought I was delivering camera-ready copy. I protested that it was. It had a 1270-dpi resolution, and all the text and graphics were perfectly positioned on the page. That's when I learned that when you prepare camera-ready copy for brochures or newsletters—any publication where the printed sheets will be folded—you need to lay out the pages in the order in which the printer (or photocopier) has to print them. In other words, not in the usual manner of page 1, page 2, and so on. (This order is known as **printer spreads**; the order in which you read a publication is known as **reader spreads.**)

For instance, look again at the sample letter-fold brochure for Little Bank on the next page. It was printed on both sides of a single, letter-sized sheet, and then folded into six 3.6 × 8.5-inch panels. (Sample A illustrates how to fold a letter-fold brochure.)

Two sheets of camera-ready copy were necessary to produce this brochure (shown in sample B). One sheet was used for the *outside* of the brochure (including the front cover, the back cover, and the fold-out panel), and another sheet was used for the *inside* (the inner left panel, the center panel, and the right panel).

Note that the outside panels of the brochure are arranged somewhat counter intuitively. The cover panel is on the right-hand side of the paper, and the back panel is in the middle. To this day, whenever I create one of these brochures, I actually fold up a piece of paper, label each panel, and then lay it out flat again so I can plan where each page goes. (If you're not sure how to lay out your pages in printer spreads, just ask your printer!)

So how do you actually create these two sheets of camera-ready copy in Word for Windows? First, you set your document to landscape mode. Then you have a choice to make. You can format a section of your document for three columns, or you

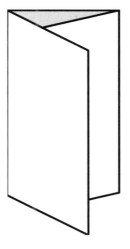

Sample A: How to fold a letter-fold brochure.

Sample B: These are the two sheets of camera-ready copy necessary to produce the Little Bank letter-fold brochure.

The LITTLE
SUPER SAVINGS
ACCOUNT

**Five great ways of
ensuring that *everybody*
can get richer.**

Not just the rich.

1. A minimum balance of $1,000.

2. Free checking.

3. Bounce protection.

4. Free Visa Card (if you qualify).

5. Preferred interest rates linked to how long you've been a customer... *not* to how much money you have in the bank.

LITTLE BANK
**We're the little bank
on your corner...**

... wherever you are.

We all need to save for the future. But who can afford to?

At LITTLE BANK, who can afford *not* to?

LITTLE BANK is an insured bank

Fold-out panel   Back cover   Front cover

How do I open a Little Super Savings Account?

Ipsum dolor sit amet, consectetuer adipiscing elit, sed diam nonummy nibh euismod tincidunt ut laoreet dolore magna aliquam erat volutpat. Ut wisi enim ad minim veniam.

Quis nostrud exerci tation ullamcorper suscipit lobortis nisl ut aliquip ex ea commodo feugiat consequat.

Lorem ipsum dolor sit amet, consectetuer adipiscing elit, sed diam nonummy nibh euismod tincidunt ut laoreet dolore magna aliquam erat volutpat dolore magna aliquam erat volutpat dolore magna aliquam erat.

How is the Little Super Savings Account better than similar accounts at other banks?

Lorem ipsum dolor sit amet, consectetuer adipiscing elit, sed diam nonummy nibh euismod tincidunt ut laoreet dolore magna aliquam erat volutpat.

Ut wisi enim ad minim veniam, quis nostrud exerci tation ullamcorper suscipit lobortis nisl ut aliquip ex ea commodo feugiat consequat.

Dolor sit amet, consectetuer adipiscing elit, sed diam nonummy nibh euismod tincidunt ut laoreet dolore magna aliquam erat volutpat volutpat.

Wisi enim ad minim veniam, quis nostrud exerci tation ullamcorper suscipit lobortis nisl ut aliquip ex ea commodo feugiat consequat. Wisi enim ad minim veniam, quis nostrud.

Quis nostrud exerci tation ullamcorper suscipit lobortis nisl ut aliquip ex ea commodo feugiat consequat aliquip ex ea commodo feugiat consequat.

What kind of benefits do long-time customers get?

Dolor sit amet, consectetuer adipiscing elit, sed diam nonummy nibh euismod tincidunt ut laoreet dolore magna aliquam erat volutpat. Ut wisi enim ad minim veniam.

Quis nostrud exerci tation ullamcorper suscipit lobortis nisl ut aliquip ex ea commodo feugiat consequat. Lorem ipsum dolor sit amet, consectetuer adipiscing elit, sed diam nonummy nibh.

- lobortis nisl ut aliquip ex ea commodo feugiat consequat
- exerci tation ullamcorper suscipit lobortis nisl ut aliquip ex ea commodo feugiat
- suscipit lobortis nisl ut aliquip ex ea commodo feugiat consequat
- enim ad minim veniam, quis nostrud exerci tation ullamcorper suscipit lobortis nisl ut aliquip ex ea commodo feugiat
- nostrud exerci tation ullamcorper suscipit lobortis nisl
- tation ullamcorper suscipit lobortis nisl ut aliquip ex ea commodo
- ut wisi enim ad minim veniam, quis nostrud exerci tation
- ullamcorper suscipit lobortis nisl ut aliquip ex ea commodo suscipit lobortis nisl ut aliquip ex ea commodo

Lorem ipsum dolor sit amet, consectetuer adipiscing elit, sed diam nonummy nibh euismod tincidunt ut laoreet dolore magna aliquam erat volutpat.

Ut wisi enim ad minim veniam, quis nostrud exerci tation ullamcorper suscipit lobortis nisl ut aliquip ex ea commodo feugiat consequat. Wisi enim ad minim veniam, quis nostrud exerci tation ullamcorper suscipit lobortis nisl ut aliquip ex ea commodo feugiat consequat.

What other advantages does LITTLE BANK give its customers?

Consectetuer adipiscing elit, sed diam nonummy nibh euismod tincidunt ut laoreet dolore magna aliquam erat volutpat. Ad minim veniam, quis nostrud exerci tation ullamcorper suscipit lobortis nisl ut aliquip ex ea commodo feugiat consequat.

Lorem ipsum dolor sit amet, consectetuer adipiscing elit, sed diam nonummy nibh euismod tincidunt ut laoreet dolore magna aliquam erat volutpat.

Ut wisi enim ad minim veniam, quis nostrud exerci tation ullamcorper suscipit lobortis nisl ut aliquip ex ea commodo feugiat consequat.

How do I get more information?

Ut wisi enim ad minim veniam, quis nostrud exerci tation ullamcorper suscipit lobortis nisl ut aliquip ex ea commodo feugiat consequat.

Enim ad minim veniam, quis nostrud exerci tation ullamcorper Enim ad minim veniam, quis nostrud exerci tation ullamcorper.

Inner left panel   Center   Right

can create a three-column table. The first choice is the easiest way to handle the *inside* panels for the Little Bank brochure because the text flows from column to column. The second is easiest for the outside panels because the text and graphics stand entirely on their own in each panel. See Chapters 12 and 17 for more information on this.

You have to prepare camera-ready copy in a similar way when you're producing a single-fold publication such as a brochure or newsletter (sample C). When you use letter-sized paper for a single-fold brochure, each page will be 5.5 inches wide by 8.5 inches tall. But you could just as easily use legal-sized paper, which would make each page 7×8.5 inches; or even 11×17-inch paper, which would give you the standard-sized four-page newsletter.

Sample D shows how most four-page publications, including single-fold brochures and newsletters, should be laid out to produce camera-ready copy. Note that the page labeled 1 is the front cover, and the page labeled 4 is the back cover.

Now, what if you want to produce an eight-page newsletter, brochure, or booklet? Sample E shows the pages you would have to pair up to produce the camera-ready copy.

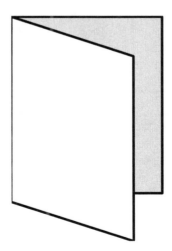

Sample C: How to fold a single-fold publication such as a booklet, brochure, or newsletter.

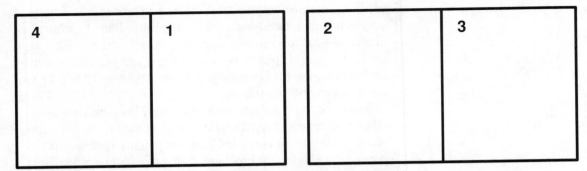

Sample D: How to lay out a four-page, single-fold publication to produce camera-ready copy.

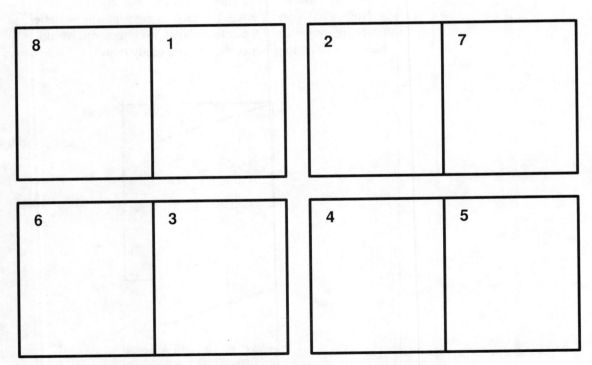

Sample E: How to lay out an eight-page, single-fold publication to produce camera-ready copy.

Getting Your Hands Dirty. You can do a lot of desktop publishing with Word for Windows, but it does have two limitations. One is the way it handles **crop marks**, the small markings that indicate the edges of the page for the printer. The other is how it handles nonstandard page sizes (standard page sizes are letter-sized and legal-sized). These two limitations bring us to the last topic in this chapter—making camera-ready copy the old-fashioned way.

First, the problems. Let's start with the standard, four-page newsletter. Each page of the newsletter is 8.5 × 11 inches. However, because newsletters are generally *folded* into their final form (see the previous section if you have questions on this), the printer prints the entire newsletter on a single 11 × 17-inch sheet. You have to produce two pages of camera-ready copy for the printer—one includes the front and back covers side by side, and the second includes the two inner pages side by side (see sample D in the previous section).

Although you *can* create an 11 × 17-inch page in Word for Windows, it would be *one* page. There is no way of joining two letter-sized pages and printing them out as the single sheet you need for camera-ready copy. Although you *could* divide the 8.5 × 17-inch page into two sections using Word's tables or columns functions, it would make all but the simplest newsletter design too complicated to handle.

The only way around this problem is to paste up the newsletter on mounting boards the old-fashioned way. This sounds like a nuisance, but it's really quite easy. The section *Camera-ready Copy the Old-fashioned Way* explains how to do it.

You'll notice that one of the things the sidebar explains is how to place crop marks on a page. Camera-ready copy has to clearly indicate the edges of the printed page for the printer. This is easy enough to do when, for instance, you're using letter-sized paper out of your laser printer as the mechanical for a letter-fold brochure. The edge of your mechanical is the edge of the printed page. End of story.

However, if you're using camera-ready copy produced by a high-quality printer like a Linotronic (see the sidebar on service bureaus), you *don't get* letter-sized paper. Instead, your pages are produced on a roll of special image-setting paper that's cut around the edges of your text, but not into perfect letter-sized pages. To indicate exactly where the edge of the printed page is to be, you have to paste the high-quality output on a board and draw the crop marks yourself. Again, the section on camera-ready copy explains how.

Note: *Some print shops may require you to paste Linotrinic output on boards so that it's easier for them to work with.*

Camera-ready Copy the Old-fashioned Way

Here's what you need to create camera-ready copy by hand:

- A grid or mechanical board with **non-repro** blue lines, that is, lines that don't show up in photocopies or photographs. These are available in a variety of sizes from all graphic arts stores.
- Glue. I always use an "adhesive stick" because it's so easy to apply. It doesn't stick so firmly that *I'm* stuck if I don't lay it down right the first time. Although this would not be appropriate for a traditional mechanical, it's fine for this kind of desktop-published mechanical.
- A ruler.
- A non-repro blue pencil. This enables you to draw lines that won't show up when the document's printed.
- A Magic Marker or pen.

Here's how you do it.

1. Rub the adhesive stick around the edges of your page.
2. Stick the page onto the grid-lined board so that the first and last lines of type on the page line up precisely with the blue grid lines. (If you're pasting down two pages side by side—preparing a mechanical for a newsletter, for example—*make sure* you measure the space between the two pages accurately. Also, draw a dotted line on the board itself to indicate the center fold between the two pages.)
3. After you have your page lined up evenly and glued down tightly, measure your margins onto the board with your non-repro blue pencil. For instance, let's say you want 1-inch margins around your entire page—top margin, bottom margin, left, and right. Start with the top of your text, measure 1 inch from your text, and draw a line across the top margin. Then measure 1

inch from the right side of your text, and draw a line down *that* margin. Continue doing this until you have drawn non-repro blue lines for all four margins.

4. Overlap the lines at the corner, as illustrated left.

5. Use a marker or pen (something the printer can see clearly) to trace a portion of the lines *outside* the margins. Finished crop marks are shown right.

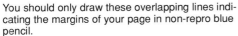

You should only draw these overlapping lines indicating the margins of your page in non-repro blue pencil.

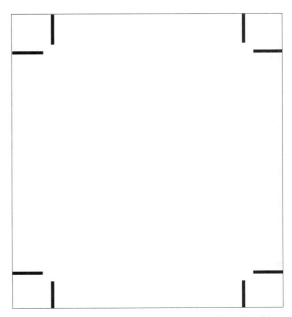

Your finished crop marks should look something like this.

Looking Great with Word for Windows

An acquaintance once told me, "I only read the instructions when I'm beat." If you're feeling "beat" as you read this, you should feel better when you're done. It's not hard to create great-looking publications with Word. For the most part, it's just a matter of getting comfortable with the table commands, and a few essentials under the Format menu—the Paragraph dialog box, the Frame dialog box, the Borders dialog box, and so on.

This part of the book teaches you step by step how to use these features to make everything you do look as though a designer did it. Chapter 5, *Tools of the Trade*, explains how to use Word's basic typographic and desktop publishing features, including fonts, type styles, and line spacing. Chapter 6, *Those Special Typesetting Characters*, shows how to exploit the special characters, dingbats, and symbols that give your work a truly typeset flair.

If you want to know how to format complex publications quickly and consistently, turn to Chapter 7, *Looking Stylish*. Chapter 8, *Designing with Tables*, explains how you can use tables to create great-looking designs, from ads to informational presentations. Then, when you have the basics down, Chapter 9, *Let Those*

Presses Roll!, gives you pointers on printing so that things turn out the way you want them.

At some point, you'll probably want to use clip art, create graphs, and design your own rules and borders. Chapter 10, *Graphs and Graphic Touches,* shows how you can use Microsoft Draw and Microsoft Graph (both included with Word) to add real graphic appeal without a lot of hassles or expense. Chapter 11, *Graphically Speaking,* gives clear examples of how you can use graphs and artwork created in other programs—such as CorelDraw! or Lotus 1-2-3—in Word. Chapter 12, *Good Design is in the Details,* and Chapter 13, *Designing a Page,* focus on turning these capabilities into professional-looking pages.

The last two chapters in this section—*Templates Save Time* and *Tips for Handling Long Documents*—cover more advanced topics that you can turn to as the need arises. ✦

CHAPTER 5

Tools
of
the
Trade

To anyone working on an important report or a brochure, word processing means a lot more than churning out pages of correctly spelled text. It means arranging this text invitingly on a page so that it's both eye-catching and easy to read. In other words, it means doing some typography. You might want to glance through Chapter 3 (if you haven't done so already) before continuing with this chapter.

Despite the invention of desktop publishing, the basic tools of typography have not changed much since Gutenberg's day. You still work with typefaces (or "fonts"); type sizes, which are measured in points; and the spacing between letters, lines, and paragraphs. In Word, these tools are found primarily on the Ribbon, and in the Character and Paragraph dialog boxes. Although you may have worked with some of these tools before, this chapter focuses on how to use them to produce professional-looking designs with type.

The Ribbon is essentially an abbreviated version of the Character and Paragraph dialog boxes. The Ruler is a formatting tool, as well as a measuring rod. It works in conjunction with both the Ribbon and the Toolbar, as well as on its own. Although I introduce the Ruler and the Toolbar in this chapter, they have useful features that keep coming up in other chapters.

This chapter makes its way from the simplest of Word's typographic tools to the most advanced. First you'll learn how to work with the Ribbon and the Ruler, then with the Character and Paragraph dialog boxes. These four closely related features of Word make up all the tools of the typographic trade.

This chapter covers everything you need to know to start your typographic work immediately. I go through the following topics:

- How to set up Word for Windows so the tools you need are handy.

- How to use the Ribbon, including the Font menu, the Point size menu, type styles, paragraph styles, and so forth.

- How to use the Ruler, including how to set tabs.

- How to use the Character dialog box.

- How to kern (adjust the space between letters).

- How to turn sub- and superscripting into powerful design tools.

- How to use colors if you have a color printer, or if you're creating slides.

- How to use the Paragraph dialog box.

- How to fine-tune the amount of space between lines of text and between paragraphs.

READY . . . SET . . .

Like all computer books, this one has a particular way of noting commands and indicating which keys you should press. The next section, *Things You Must Know Before You Read Further,* tells you what they are.

This book also assumes you have certain standard settings turned on, so that we're both looking at the same things and have the same features handy. Whenever I use settings different from the ones described here, I'll let you know. In addition, this section explains some of the other settings available, and how you might use them in your work. You can find information about the settings I don't explain by referring to your Word for Windows manual.

✦ Things You Must Know Before You Read Further

- VIEW, TOOLBAR refers to the Toolbar option on the View menu; FORMAT, CHARACTER refers to the Character option on the Format menu; and so on.

- Special keys are flanked by angle brackets (< >), for example, the <TAB> key, the <F3> key, the <ALT> key, and so on.

- <ALT> + V, P means: "Press the <ALT> key and the V key simultaneously, then press P." By the way, if you actually use this command, you'll end up turning the Page Layout view on or off, depending on which it was to begin with.

  Note: *Word uses two types of keyboard commands. The first type uses the letters underlined in the names of menus and options. For example, F is underlined in the File menu, so to open that menu, press <ALT> + F. Because S is underlined in the Save option, press S in order to save your work. The second type of keyboard command is called a "hot key." If you open the File menu, you'll notice that the Save option has <SHIFT> + <F12> written after it. This is the "hot key." It's quicker than the other type of keyboard command because it bypasses the menu entirely. Whenever you want to save, just press <SHIFT> + <F12>.*

- There are often several—and sometimes many—ways to do anything in Word. For instance, you can use your mouse to select commands from menus, or you can use the keyboard. Sometimes, all you need to do is click on a button (or icon) on the Ribbon or Toolbar. To be consistent but not too long-winded, I say things such as: "Select Normal from the View menu (<ALT> + V, N)." This makes it easier to use the keyboard commands *if you want to*. If it's just a matter of clicking on an icon, I usually say so, without giving the keyboard equivalent.

- An item on a menu is checkmarked (✔) when it's on. Select it again to turn it off.

Setting Up the View Menu

1. Turn the Normal view on. To do this, select Normal from the View menu (<ALT> + V, N). When Normal is on, a bullet (•) appears instead of the usual checkmark. This indicates that it

```
┌─────────────────────────┐
│ View                    │
├─────────────────────────┤
│ • Normal                │
│   Outline               │
│   Page Layout           │
├─────────────────────────┤
│   Draft                 │
├─────────────────────────┤
│ √ Toolbar               │
│ √ Ribbon                │
│ √ Ruler                 │
├─────────────────────────┤
│   Header/Footer...      │
│   Footnotes             │
│   Annotations           │
│   Field Codes           │
├─────────────────────────┤
│   Zoom...               │
└─────────────────────────┘
```

This is how your View menu should look after you finish setting it up.

has an additional option—in this case Draft mode (explained below).

Word lets you see your work in several different ways. When you open the View menu you'll notice three views listed at the top—Normal, Outline, and Page Layout. "Normal" is the view you'll normally use. It shows your text in WYSIWYG mode (What-You-See-Is-What-You-Get, and pronounced "wizzy-wig"). However, it doesn't show columns or specially positioned graphics as they'll appear on the printed page. Instead, newspaper-style columns appear as one long, thin column; and graphics are shown one after the other in the order in which you inserted them—*not* in the place you positioned them on the page.

The Page Layout view, by contrast, shows WYSIWYG text, columns, *and* positioned graphics. Be warned, though— WYSIWYG graphics can be slow. I usually work with long documents that have lots of graphics in Normal view right up to the very last minute.

Outline view is a tool that helps to reorganize as well as outline documents. It lets you move whole sections around by dragging and clicking.

Draft mode is non-WYSIWYG. It can be much faster to type and edit long documents using either the Normal or Outline view in Draft mode, because the screen doesn't have to re-draw the different typefaces you use, the different sizes, or the styles. Draft mode displays everything in the same font, with the various type styles (such as bold or italic) underlined. Also, Draft mode doesn't show any graphics you may have used, only empty boxes that serve as picture placeholders.

To use Draft mode, open the View menu and select Draft (which is on when it's checkmarked). To turn Draft view off, just select it again.

Note: *Draft mode can be great if your eyes tend to get tired (like mine) looking at the computer screen all day. It's easy to read the largish, thick font that's displayed.*

2. Turn the Toolbar, Ribbon, and Ruler on. To do this, select each of these options from the View menu, one after the other. Remember, an option is on when it's checkmarked. If you select an item that's checkmarked, you turn it off.

This is an example of text set in 12 point Helvetica, with the word **BOLD** in bold caps. It's shown in Normal view.

This is an example of text set in 12 point Helvetica, with the word BOLD in bold caps. It's shown in Normal view, with Draft mode "on."

The top example illustrates how text in Normal view looks on your screen. The bottom example illustrates how it looks in Draft mode. Although Normal view lets you see WYSIWYG text, it can be slow. If you find it too slow, use Draft mode. Draft mode isn't pretty, but it's the fastest mode for typing and editing long documents.

Setting Up the Tools, Options Dialog Box

Dialog boxes are another way you can tell Word which features you want to use. A menu item brings up a dialog box when it has three dots after its name; for example, selecting "Options . . ." on the Tools menu opens the Options dialog box.

1. Open the Options dialog box by selecting Options from the Tools menu (<ALT> + O, O). Select the View category by clicking on the View icon at the left of the dialog box. Make sure each of the options pictured in the following dialog box are on (in other words, are "X-ed"). If options that should be selected aren't, click on them, or press <ALT> + the letter underlined in the option's name. For instance, you can turn on the Horizontal scroll bar by pressing <ALT> + H.

Options		
Category:	Modify view settings	
View	┌Window─────────────────────┐	OK
General	☒ Horizontal Scroll Bar	Cancel
Print	☒ Vertical Scroll Bar	
Save	☒ Status Bar Style Area Width: 0"	

Window
- ☒ Horizontal Scroll Bar
- ☒ Vertical Scroll Bar
- ☒ Status Bar   Style Area Width: 0"

Show Text with
- ☒ Table Gridlines
- ☒ Text Boundaries
- ☐ Picture Placeholders
- ☐ Field Codes
- ☒ Line Breaks and Fonts as Printed

Nonprinting Characters
- ☐ Tabs
- ☐ Spaces
- ☐ Paragraph Marks
- ☐ Optional Hyphens
- ☐ Hidden Text
- ☐ All

To see more options, click on the category list at left.

> **Note:** *The options listed in the dialog box as Nonprinting Characters should all be off. This allows you to see them or hide them simply by clicking on the Show/Hide ¶ button on the Ribbon. For more information see* The Show/Hide ¶ Button and How It Works *later in this chapter.*

2. While still in the Options dialog box, select the General category by clicking on that icon. Although you can see from the following dialog box how I have my system set, only two

Useful Things to Know

- Whenever you're in a dialog box or a menu you don't want to be in, hit the \<ESC> key (called the Escape key) to get out. In those instances where there's a Cancel button available, this is the same as clicking on it.

- If you make a mistake, you can undo it in one of three ways. You can select Undo from the Edit menu; use the hot key \<CTRL> + z; or click on the Undo icon on the Toolbar (see *Anatomy of the Toolbar* later in this chapter). Remember, you can only undo the last thing you did, so if you make a mistake, undo it immediately.

- To repeat the last thing you did, select Repeat from the Edit menu, or use the \<F4> hot key. For instance, if you want to bold a number of words that aren't next to each other, highlight the first one and bold it. Then highlight the second one, and this time hit \<F4> to bold it. Then highlight the third one, hit \<F4> again, and so on.

- To highlight your entire document, choose Select All from the Edit menu, or use the hot key— \<CTRL> + 5 on the numeric keypad (the numeric keypad is usually located on the right side of your keyboard; make sure \<NUM LOCK> is on).

- To go to a particular page quickly, select Go To from the Edit menu, type the page number, then press \<ENTER>. Or, simply press \<F5>, type the page number, then \<ENTER>.

  Note: *When you use the \<F5> hot key, the Go To prompt appears on the Status Bar in the lower left corner of your screen.*

- Here's how to *copy* and paste: Highlight the text or graphic you want to copy, then choose Copy from the Edit menu (the hot key is \<CTRL> + c), or click on the Copy icon on the Toolbar. Place your cursor where you want the copied item to go, then choose Paste from the Edit Menu (the hot key is \<CTRL> + v), or click on the Paste icon on the Toolbar.

- Here's how to *cut* and paste: Highlight the text or graphic you want to cut, then choose Cut from the Edit menu (the hot key is \<CTRL> + x), or click on the Cut icon on the Toolbar. Place your cursor where you want the cut item to go, then choose Paste from the Edit Menu (the hot key is \<CTRL> + v), or click on the Paste icon on the Toolbar.

options need to be in sync: Drag-and-drop Text Editing and Measurement Units. Drag-and-drop Text Editing allows you to move text without cutting and pasting. I explain how this works in *Useful Things to Know,* following.

Set the Measurement Units to inches by clicking on the downward pointing arrow to the right of the box, and selecting Inches from the menu. This sets the Ruler to inches.

Note: *You can paste cut and copied items as many times as you want. However, you can only paste the last thing you cut or copied.*

- To get to the top of your document, press <CTRL> + <HOME>.

- To get to the bottom of your document, press <CTRL> + <END>.

- To insert a page break, press <CTRL> + <ENTER>.

Mouse Shortcuts

- You can *drag-and-drop text and graphics*—in other words, move it without bothering to cut and paste (I love this feature). First, highlight whatever you want to move, then point at it with your mouse. When the mouse pointer becomes a left-pointing arrow, hold down the left mouse button and drag the arrow to the place you want the item to go. Don't let up on the mouse button until the arrow and the dotted vertical line symbolizing the item are positioned exactly where you want the item to move. To copy text and graphics using the drag and drop feature, hold down the <CTRL> key as you drag.

  Note: *To use this feature, the Drag-and-drop Text Editing option must be on in the General category of the Options dialog box on the Tools menu.*

- You can highlight a word by double-clicking on it.

- If you move your mouse pointer way over to the left of the screen (known as the selection area), it turns into a right-pointing arrow. You can highlight an entire line of text by clicking once on that arrow. You can highlight the entire paragraph by double-clicking. To highlight several lines of text or even several paragraphs, click once, then drag the arrow down the left side of the screen.

- In Word, you generally use only the left mouse button. However, you can use your *right* mouse button to select text *vertically.* For instance, if you have to select a vertical line of numbers, hold down your right mouse button, and drag down the page until they're all selected. You can drag to the right or left, too, until you get just the right area highlighted. (You really have to try this to see what I mean.)

When you're done, click on OK (or press <ENTER>) to get back to your document.

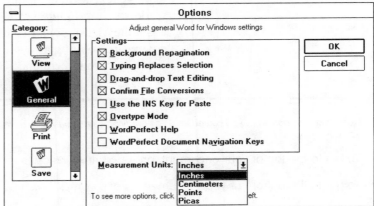

ANATOMY OF THE TOOLBAR

The Toolbar includes a variety of commonly used commands that cover everything from opening new documents to starting the drawing and graph programs that come with Word. I introduce the Toolbar here because it's one of the first things you see on your screen. However, I explain how to use many of these features in later chapters. For instance, I explain how to use the Numbered and Bulleted List buttons in Chapter 7; the Table icon in Chapter 8; and the Draw and Graph program icons in Chapter 10.

Diagram of the Toolbar

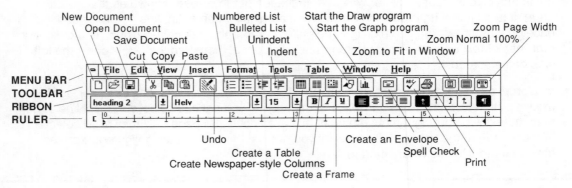

All the features on the Toolbar work basically the same way.

1. Click on the Toolbar icon representing the feature you want to use.

2. If a dialog box opens, select the options you want, and click on OK or press <ENTER> when you're done. (If a dialog box doesn't open, Word just goes ahead and does the thing requested.)

ANATOMY OF THE RIBBON AND THE RULER

Word's Ribbon (named after the old typewriter ribbon) makes it easy to format text. Together with the Ruler, it provides a shortcut for doing some of the things you can do in the Character and Paragraph dialog boxes. The things you have to do in these dialog boxes themselves are covered later in *Designing Characters* and *Designing Paragraphs,* later in this chapter.

The Ribbon includes some features which are known as *character* formatting—typeface, point size, and type style (bold, italic, and so forth)—and other features known as *paragraph* formatting—alignment, tabs, and paragraph styles. There is one important difference between character and paragraph formatting: Character formatting applies to the individual characters you highlight, while paragraph formatting applies to nothing less than an entire paragraph, whichever one your cursor happens to be in.

Diagram of the Ribbon and the Ruler

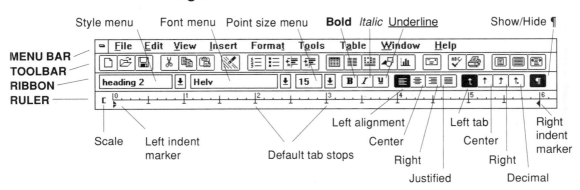

119

And how do you tell whether a particular formatting tool affects characters or paragraphs? All the character formatting options are found in the Character dialog box; paragraph formatting tools are in the Paragraph dialog box. Although the differences between these two types of formatting can seem confusing at first, you'll feel more comfortable once you try them out for yourself. And remember, if in doubt, just highlight *everything* you want to change. You won't go wrong.

✦ Character Formatting

The Ribbon has five character formatting tools—the Font menu; the Point Size menu; and the bold, italic, and underline type style icons. When you apply this formatting to your text—in other words, when you select a typeface, decide on a point size, or choose a type style—you first have to highlight the text to which you want that format to apply. The formatting only affects whatever is highlighted, whether it's a single letter, a whole paragraph, or even an entire document.

I describe each of the Ribbon's character formatting tools in the following sections.

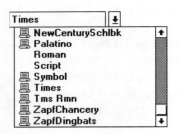

In Word, printer fonts are listed on the Font menu next to printer symbols. The next version of Windows, version 3.1, will include what's known as True Type. True Type fonts essentially include both a printer and screen font together, and provide WYSIWYG quality no matter what size you use. If you are using Windows 3.1, True Type fonts are listed on the Font meu with double Ts next to them. As of this writing, the True Type Arial font is the same as Helvetica, and Times New Roman is the same as Times.

The Font Menu and How It Works.   The Font menu lists the typefaces available on your system. When you're first learning Word, however, it isn't always clear just what "available" means. This is because there are two different types of fonts—**screen** fonts and **printer** fonts. When you have screen fonts (which show how a particular typeface looks on the screen) *and* matching printer fonts (which your printer uses), what you see on the screen is very close to what you get from the printer.

In Word, you can always tell whether a particular font is a printer font because, if it is, it will be listed in the Font menu with a little printer next to it. Fonts that don't have printers next to them are strictly screen fonts (there's no matching printer font), which means they might not look as good as you'd like on the printed page.

In some cases—for instance, if you have a PostScript printer or compatible—you might not have screen fonts to match your built-in printer fonts. In this case, the different typefaces you use print out just fine, but you can't see them on the screen—no matter which one you choose, they all look pretty much the same. You can get screen fonts to match your printer fonts by getting a good **font manager**. If you have a PostScript printer or compatible, the best font manager currently available is Adobe Type Manager (ATM). ATM gives you high-quality "Type 1 PostScript Outline fonts" that let you see on your screen what your printer will print. ATM also lets you print these fonts on all Windows-compatible printers—from dot matrix to Hewlett-Packard laser jets—at quite high-quality (you'll get the best quality from a PostScript printer). Using ATM, you can also install and use additional screen and printer fonts easily (see *What to Do When WYSIWYG Isn't What You Get* in Chapter 6).

Both Word for Windows and Windows itself include several screen fonts, some of which—Courier, Helv, Tms Rmn, and Symbol (Σψμβολ), for example—print out quite well on most printers. Others are most useful if you're printing on a plotter.

When you install your printer, Windows automatically installs the printer fonts that come with that printer (see the Windows manual for information on printer installation). These fonts, together with whatever screen fonts you've installed, appear on your Font menu. For instance, if you have a PostScript printer or compatible, you probably have these fonts listed on your menu (this might vary somewhat depending on your brand of printer): Avant Garde, Bookman, Courier, Helv, Helvetica-Narrow, New Century Schoolbook, Palatino, Symbol (Σψμβολ), Tms Rmn, *Zapf Chancery*, and Zapf Dingbats (❋❀□❊ ❖❄■❊❂❀▼▲). Remember, however, that even when your printer fonts are correctly installed, what you see on screen *isn't* what you get, until you have the matching screen fonts as well.

Note: *"Times" and "Tms Rmn" are different names for the same typeface; the same with "Helvetica" and "Helv." Windows calls these typefaces Tms Rmn and Helv; Adobe Type Manager calls them Times and Helvetica. But they're the same thing. When I indicate you should use Times or Helvetica, it means either Times or Tms Rmn, or Helvetica or Helv, depending on whether you're using Adobe Type Manager.*

To format text with a particular font:

1. Highlight the text you want to format. You can format a single letter, a paragraph, or the whole document—you've just got to highlight it first.

You MUST highlight whatever you want to change, or it WON'T change.

2. Select the typeface you want from the Font menu. You can do this using either the mouse or the keyboard. If you're using a mouse, first click on the down-pointing arrow to the right of the Font menu. Then click on the typeface you want.

Or, if you prefer to use your keyboard, press <CTRL> + F (yes—the "F" is for "Font menu"). Then use the <UP> and <DOWN> arrow keys to highlight a typeface. Press <ENTER> to actually select it.

The Point Size Menu and How It Works. The Point Size menu lets you size any typeface from 4 through 127 points. It works just like the Font menu.

To make text a particular point size:

1. Highlight the text you want to size. You can highlight anything from a single letter to the whole document.

2. Select the point size you want from the Point Size menu. You can do this using either the mouse or the keyboard. If you're using a mouse, first click on the down-pointing arrow to the right of the Point Size menu. Then click on the size you want.

If you prefer to use your keyboard, press <CTRL> + P ("P" for "Point Size"). Then type the point size you want to use, and press <ENTER> when you're done.

Type Styles and How They Work. Word has two kinds of styles—type styles and paragraph styles. Type styles (bold, italic, and so on) have two general purposes. The first is to give a typeface a certain "bearing," or flair, appropriate to a particular occasion. The second is simply to make that typeface recognizably different, so it will stand out as a heading, for example.

The Ribbon includes three type style icons—one for bold, italic, and underline. Paragraph styles, which provide an easy way to format complex documents quickly and consistently, are also listed on the Ribbon—in the Styles menu on the left-hand side. Paragraph styles are explained briefly in the next section, and more fully in Chapter 7.

Another way to enlarge text is to highlight it and then press <CTRL> + <F2>. Every time you hit this "grow font" command, the text gets 1 size larger. You can also use the "shrink font" command (<CTRL> + <SHIFT> + <F2>) to reduce text size. These commands are especially handy when you want text to be as large as possible in a limited space.

The following list shows the type styles available in Word and their keyboard shortcuts. Only the first three of these are shown on the Ribbon, but they're all listed in the Character dialog box (see *Designing Characters* later in this chapter).

Naturally, you can mix these styles to suit the occasion. For example, you can style text as ***BOLD***, ***ITALIC***, and *SMALL CAPS* all at once. However, you can use only one style of underlining at a time, and you can't use SMALL CAPS and ALL CAPS simultaneously. "Hidden" text means that you can't see it on the screen; nor will it print unless you turn on a special print option (see your Word for Windows manual for more information).

Type Style	Keyboard Shortcut
Bold	<CTRL> + B
Italic	<CTRL> + I
<u>Underline</u>	<CTRL> + U
~~Strikethrough~~	<CTRL> + Z
Hidden	<CTRL> + H
SMALL CAPS	<CTRL> + K
ALL CAPS	<CTRL> + A
<u>Words Only Underline</u>	<CTRL> + W
<u>Double Underline</u>	<CTRL> + D

Note: *Many of these keyboard shortcuts are easy to remember because they use the <CTRL> key + the first letter of the type style, such as "B" for "bold." The <CTRL> key is always used for formatting commands. The <ALT> key is used to access the commands found on menus and in dialog boxes.*

Bold Solutions to Pressing Problems

Bold Solutions to Pressing Problems

Lorem ipsum dolor sit amet, consectetuer adipiscing elit, sed diam nonummy nibh euismod tincidunt ut laoreet dolore magna aliquam erat volutpat. Ut wisi enim ad minim veniam, quis nostrud exerci tation ullamcorper suscipit lobortis nisl ut aliquip ex ea commodo feugiat consequat.

The example on the left shows how a type style (in this case, bold) can give a typeface a certain flair. The example on the right shows how a type style (in this case, italic) can help distinguish a heading from the text that follows. Note that the example on the left is most likely the heading for a booklet, brochure, cover page of a report, or magazine article.

To format text with a particular type style:

1. Highlight the text you want to style.

2. Select the type style either by clicking on the button pictured on the Ribbon, or by using its keyboard shortcut.

   Note: *You can also format text before you type it in. Just select the style, point size, and typeface you want to use, and then start typing. The formatting you selected will stay in effect until you change it.*

Type styles are known as "toggles," which means that the same command that turns a style on, turns it off as well. If you want to *un*format text formatted with a particular type style, you essentially do the same thing you did to format that text in the first place.

1. Highlight the text you want to *un*format.

2. Select the type style you want to get rid of either by clicking on the button pictured on the Ribbon, or by using its keyboard shortcut.

✦ Paragraph Formatting

The Ribbon has four paragraph formatting tools—the paragraph Style menu, Alignment icons, Tabs, and the Show/Hide ¶ icon. When you apply paragraph formatting to your text—in other words, when you select a style, an alignment, or set tabs—all you have to do is put your cursor anywhere in the paragraph you want to format. Paragraph formatting always affects the entire paragraph. Of course, if you want to format several adjoining paragraphs at once, it makes sense to highlight them all.

I describe each of the Ribbon's paragraph formatting tools in the following sections.

The Show/Hide ¶ Button and How It Works. Clicking on the Show/Hide ¶ button shows the invisible (or nonprinting) characters that represent spaces between words, the carriage returns at the end of paragraphs, the tabs made by the <TAB> key, and so on. It's *very* useful to see these marks when you're doing complex formatting. For instance, they tell you whether that odd space you see between words is due to a few extra taps on the space bar or a misplaced <TAB>.

The Show/Hide ¶ button is another toggle—it turns the invisibles on when they're off and off when they're on.

To display invisible characters on your screen:

- Click on the Show/Hide ¶ button, or use the keyboard shortcut, which is <CTRL> + <*> (in other words, <CTRL> + <SHIFT> + 8).

To make the invisible characters invisible again:

- Click on the ¶ icon again, or press <CTRL> + <*>.

The following table shows what some of these invisible characters look like on your screen. Note that they look somewhat different depending on the font and style that you're using. This is because invisible characters get formatted just like regular text.

Invisible Character	Description
¶	A carriage return (sometimes called a paragraph marker or an end-of-paragraph marker) that's formatted as 12-point Times.
¶	A carriage return formatted as 12-point Times, bold.
¶	A carriage return formatted as 24-point Times.
↵	A new line break (which starts a new line but *not* a new paragraph) formatted as 12-point Times.
¤	An end-of-cell marker formatted as 12-point Times. End-of-cell markers replace paragraph markers in tables.
·	A blank space formatted as 12-point Times.
·	A blank space formatted as 24-point Times.
→	A tab formatted as 12-point Times.

125

PUTTING IT ALL TOGETHER: From Typing to Typography

Just because you *can* select different fonts, point sizes, type styles, and so on for each letter you type, doesn't mean you'll want to very often. This example, however, puts into practice everything covered so far. Note that I have you type the text first, then format it. This is a general rule I follow (and encourage my students to follow). My experience is that it takes longer to format text *as* you type it in than to format it *after* it's typed, unless you're using styles; see Chapter 7.)

Note: *In this example I use most of the fonts that come standard with PostScript printers and compatibles. If you have a different sort of printer—or don't like the typefaces I use—substitute the fonts you like.*

aLL mixEd Up

You can give each character its own font, point size, and type style.

1. Type in the phrase "all mixed up." It doesn't matter which font or point size you use. Make all the letters lowercase.

2. Highlight the "a." Select Bookman from the Font menu, and 49 from the Point Size menu. Note that you can select as many different formats as you want, and the highlighted text remains highlighted.

3. Highlight the two "l"s. Capitalize them by pressing <CTRL> + A. (Remember: The "A" stands for ALL CAPS). Select Helvetica (Helv) from the Font menu and 30 from the Point Size menu. Make both "l"s bold by clicking on the Bold icon on the Ribbon, or by pressing <CTRL> + B.

4. Highlight the word "mixed," and select 46 from the Point Size menu.

5. Highlight the "m." Select Times (Tms Rmn) from the Font Menu and the italic type style from the Ribbon (<CTRL> + I).

6. Highlight the "i." Select New Century Schoolbook from the Font menu and the bold type style from the Ribbon.

7. Highlight the "x." Select Times from the Font menu and 24 from the Point Size menu. Apply the small caps type style by pressing <CTRL> + K.

8. Highlight the "e." Select Palatino from the Font menu and 38 from the Point Size menu. Select the underline type style from the Ribbon (<CTRL> + U). Apply the small caps type style by pressing <CTRL> + K.

9. Highlight the "d." Select Helvetica from the Font menu.

10. Highlight the "u." Capitalize it by pressing <CTRL> + A. Select Palatino from the Font menu and 48 from the Point Size menu. Select the italic type style from the Ribbon (<CTRL> + I).

11. Highlight the "p." Select Bookman from the Font menu and 38 from the Point Size menu. Select the type styles bold (<CTRL> + B) and italic (<CTRL> + I) from the Ribbon.

The Style Menu and How It Works. Styles (sometimes called "paragraph" styles, and not to be confused with *type styles*) enable you to apply complex formatting quickly and consistently to text that isn't next to each other, or even in the same document. Styles can include all sorts of things—from fonts and point sizes to page breaks and borders (see Chapter 7 for complete information).

Working with the Style menu differs from working with the Font and Point Size menus in one key respect—you don't have to highlight the paragraph you're formatting.

1. Put the cursor anywhere in the paragraph.

2. Select the style you want from the Style menu. You can do this using either the mouse or the keyboard. If you're using a mouse, first click on the down-pointing arrow to the right of the Style menu. Then click on the style you want.

   If you prefer to use the keyboard, press <CTRL> + s. Then type the name of the style you want to use, and press <ENTER> when you're done.

   Note: *If you want to format several adjoining paragraphs with the same style, highlight them.*

Alignment and How It Works. Alignment describes how text stands in relation to the margin of the page. Word includes the four most common forms of alignment: left (also known as *flush left* or *ragged right*); center; right (also known as *flush right* or *ragged left*); and justified (which is *flush*, or *even*, against both the left and right margins). The following list shows the available alignments and their keyboard shortcuts. See Chapter 3 if you have questions about alignment.

Alignment	Keyboard Command
Left	<CTRL> + L
Center	<CTRL> + E
Right	<CTRL> + R

This is an example of justified text. See how it's even against both the right and left margins (except in the last line)?   <CTRL> + J

So, what is a paragraph any-way? A paragraph is anything that ends with a carriage re-turn. In Word, a paragraph can consist of several related sen-tences, a single number, or even a graphic. If you put a car-riage return after it (sometimes called an end-of-paragraph marker), it's a paragraph. If you're having trouble figuring out what's what on your screen, use the Show/Hide ¶ button to turn the invisibles on. That way you can *see* where the carriage returns are.¶

To align your text:

1. Put your cursor somewhere in the paragraph you want to align (if you want to align several adjoining paragraphs at the same time, highlight them).

2. Click on the alignment icon you want to use, or use its key-board shortcut.

Tabs and How to Use Them. Tabs (sometimes called "tab stops") are usually used in one of two ways: to indent the first line of a paragraph, and to align text in columns on the page. In Word, the only reason you need to use tabs is to align text in columns. You can *automatically* indent the first line of every paragraph using styles (see *Using Indents* in Chapter 7).

Note that you should never use the space bar to line up text in Word; always use tabs. Things that appear lined up with spaces *on your screen* will rarely look as good when printed. This is because most typefaces that you'll use in Word—with the exception of Courier—are **proportionally spaced**, meaning that each letter has a different width. An "m," for example, takes up a great deal more space than an "i." Since each letter takes up a different amount of space, it's next to impossible to know just how many spaces you'll need to line things up evenly. Courier—unlike Times, Helvetica, Palatino, and so forth—is a **fixed** or **monospaced font**, in which every letter and every space has the same width.

Word has four types of tabs: left, center, right, and decimal. Here are examples of how you might use each one. You can find additional information on tabs in Chapter 7.

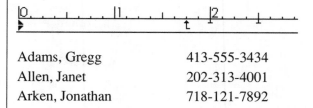

Adams, Gregg   413-555-3434
Allen, Janet   202-313-4001
Arken, Jonathan   718-121-7892

This example shows the phone numbers lining up along a left tab set at 1.75 inches. Note that each line of this example is its own paragraph (in other words, the typist hit <ENTER> at the end of each line).

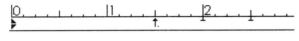

Network TV Stock Prices As of 6/28/91 Capital Markets Group

This example shows a report heading with a center tab set at 3⅝ inches and a right tab set at 6⅛ inches. Note that the text aligned along the center tab ("As of 6/28/91") is not centered on the page. It's centered around the tab itself.

Year	Return on standard index
1973	(14.8)%
1974	(26.4)
1975	37.2
1976	23.6
1977	(7.4)

This example shows the benefits of using a dec (or decimal) tab. It lines up a series of numbers along the decimal point.

You use both the Ribbon and the Ruler to set tabs. First you use the Ribbon to select the type of tab you want—left, center, right, or decimal. Then you place this tab on the Ruler.

You can set as many different tabs (and types of tabs) on the Ruler as you want. Just be aware that if you try to work with more than a few tabs on a line, you can easily lose track of which is which. To create more than two or three different columns of material, I strongly recommend that you use Word's table function, instead of tabs (see Chapter 8).

Note: *If you don't want to bother setting your own tabs, you can always use Word's default tabs, which are set every half inch (for more information, see* Using the Tabs Dialog Box *in Chapter 7).*

To set tabs on the Ruler:

1. Make sure your cursor is in the paragraph for which you want to set tabs (if you want to set tabs for several adjoining paragraphs at the same time, highlight them).

2. Click on the *type* of tab you want to set—the center tab, for example. You know that you've selected a tab type when it's highlighted on the Ribbon.

3. Click under the marker on the Ruler where you want the tab set. For instance, if you want to set the center tab at 3 inches, click just under the 3-inch marker on the Ruler. The tab stop icon appears where you click.

4. To move your text to the tab stop you just set, place the cursor to the left of that text and press the <TAB> key.

To move a tab you've already set to another measurement:

- Click once on the tab stop icon set on the Ruler, *hold down the mouse button*, and *drag* the icon to where you want it. Don't let up on the mouse button until the tab stop icon is where you want it.

To get rid of tab stops you no longer want:

- Grab hold of the tab stop icon you want to get rid of by clicking on it and holding down the mouse button. Then *drag* the icon off the Ruler. It disappears.

What to Do When Your Tabs Don't Line Up

It's easy to forget that you can (sometimes by accident) set entirely different tabs for *each* paragraph. When this happens, things stop lining up as they should. The solution is to clear all tabs from the section that's askew and reset them. To do this:

1. Highlight the adjoining paragraphs where you have set tabs. Make sure you highlight *every* paragraph you want to line up.

2. Select Tabs from the Format menu. This opens the Tabs dialog box (explained in Chapter 7).

3. Click on the Clear All button in the lower right corner of the dialog box, then click on OK or press <ENTER> to get back to your document.

4. Highlight the entire section you want to line up with tabs, then reset the tab stop(s) on the Ruler.

The Scale Icon and How to Use It. If you click once on the Scale icon, you see the margins of the page. If you drag these flat brackets, you can actually change the margins. You can also set the margins using the FORMAT, PAGE SETUP and FILE, PRINT PREVIEW commands (see Chapter 12 for more information). Word lets you set different margins for each page of your document.

If you click on the Scale icon while the flat-bracketed document margins are showing, you return to the normal view of the Ruler, where you see the Left and Right Indent markers. The following example illustrates what these two views look like.

The top example shows the margins of your page; the bottom example shows the Ruler as you normally see it—showing the Left and Right Indent markers. Note that the Scale icon itself looks different depending on whether the Ruler is displaying margins or indent markers. You can't set tabs when the Ruler is set to show document margins.

DESIGNING CHARACTERS

Now that you're familiar with the basic typographic tools on the Ribbon and the Ruler, you can turn mere formatting into great-looking typography using the Character and Paragraph dialog boxes on the Format menu. This section covers tools available in the Character dialog box, but not on the Ribbon: kerning, or character spacing; sub- and superscripts; and how to use color. The next section *Designing Paragraphs* covers some of the tools in the Paragraph dialog box that didn't make it onto the Ribbon.

A lot of the discussion in this section focuses on rather small point sizes—1 point, 3 points, and so on. Although points *are* very small (it takes 72 to make an inch), they add up surprisingly fast. You'll see that 1 or 2 points can make a big difference.

You can open the Character dialog box in several ways:

- Select Character from the Format menu with your mouse.

- Use the keyboard shortcut <ALT> + T, C.

- Double-click on the Ribbon.

Diagram of the Character Dialog Box

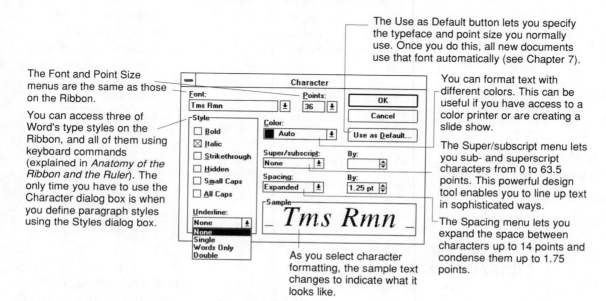

The Font and Point Size menus are the same as those on the Ribbon.

You can access three of Word's type styles on the Ribbon, and all of them using keyboard commands (explained in *Anatomy of the Ribbon and the Ruler*). The only time you have to use the Character dialog box is when you define paragraph styles using the Styles dialog box.

The Use as Default button lets you specify the typeface and point size you normally use. Once you do this, all new documents use that font automatically (see Chapter 7).

You can format text with different colors. This can be useful if you have access to a color printer or are creating a slide show.

The Super/subscript menu lets you sub- and superscript characters from 0 to 63.5 points. This powerful design tool enables you to line up text in sophisticated ways.

The Spacing menu lets you expand the space between characters up to 14 points and condense them up to 1.75 points.

As you select character formatting, the sample text changes to indicate what it looks like.

✦ Kerning, or Character Spacing

Kerning, or *character spacing* as Word calls it, allows you to adjust the space between letters. Kerning has two purposes: to make text fit into a given amount of space, and to make large headlines or other important text look better. You can adjust the character spacing through the Character dialog box.

Word recognizes three types of character spacing: **normal** (no kerning), **condensed**, and **expanded**. You can specify the exact amount of expanded character spacing from 0 through 14 points in .25-point increments, for example, .25 pts, 3.5 pts, and 6.75 pts. You can specify the amount of condensed character spacing from 0 through 1.75 pts (also in .25-point increments).

Kerning in Word adds space to (or deletes space from) the *right* side of the letter(s) kerned. In the following examples, the word "for" is set in 36-point Helvetica.

for   Normal

for   Condensed to 1.75 points

f o r   Expanded to 4 points

To condense or expand the character spacing of a word, paragraph, and so on:

1. Highlight the text you want to kern.

2. Open the Character dialog box (<ALT> + T, C).

3. Do one of the following, depending on whether you want to expand or condense the character spacing:

   a. To condense the character spacing, click on the down-pointing arrow to the right of the pull-down Spacing menu (<ALT> + G). Select Condensed. Use the arrows on the By box to choose the number of points by which you want to condense the spacing between characters.

   You can also <TAB> to this box and type in the number of points if you don't want to use the mouse. Just type the number (such as 1) without bothering to type "pt"—Word knows it's in points.

   b. To expand the character spacing, click on the down-pointing arrow to the right of the pull-down Spacing menu (<ALT> + G). Select Expanded. Use the arrows on the By box to choose the number of points by which you want to expand the spacing between characters. Again, you can <TAB> to this box and type in the number of points if you don't want to use the mouse.

4. Click on OK or press <ENTER> when you're done.

To reset condensed or expanded character spacing to normal:

1. Highlight the text you want to reset to normal character spacing.

2. Open the Character dialog box (<ALT> + T, C).

3. Click on the down-pointing arrow to the right of the pull-down spacing menu (<ALT> + G), and select Normal.

4. Click on OK or press <ENTER> when you're done.

In addition to adjusting the space between letters in a whole word (or a whole document), you can adjust the space between individual letters. Designers often kern individual letters in headlines because at larger point sizes some letters have a tendency to bump into each other, and others tend to get too far apart. In the following examples, "Woolly" is set in 48-point Avant Garde.

Normal character spacing

Space condensed 1.75 points

Space expanded 2 points

Kerning: Making Text "Shorter."   One reason to *condense* text is to shorten it so that it fits the available space; for instance, to make sure that the last two lines of a one-page letter don't spill over to a second page. The smaller the type size, however, the less you should condense it—it starts looking cramped pretty fast. You should be aware that there are several condensed typefaces specially designed to pack a great deal of text into a relatively small space. One—Helvetica Narrow—comes with most PostScript printers and compatibles.

If you feel strange vibrations when you drive, beware: There may be a wheel bearing letting loose, a drive shaft universal joint breaking, a transmission giving out, or a drive line part on the verge of failure. If the situation has developed suddenly, slow down, put on your flashers, and proceed with caution to a service station.

From How to Make Your Car Last Almost Forever *by Jack Gillis*

If you feel strange vibrations when you drive, beware: There may be a wheel bearing letting loose, a drive shaft universal joint breaking, a transmission giving out, or a drive line part on the verge of failure. If the situation has developed suddenly, slow down, put on your flashers, and proceed with caution to a service station.

From How to Make Your Car Last Almost Forever *by Jack Gillis*

If you feel strange vibrations when you drive, beware: There may be a wheel bearing letting loose, a drive shaft universal joint breaking, a transmission giving out, or a drive line part on the verge of failure. If the situation has developed suddenly, slow down, put on your flashers, and proceed with caution to a service station.

From How to Make Your Car Last Almost Forever *by Jack Gillis*

The upper-left example is set in 12-point Palatino with normal character spacing. The upper-right example is also set in 12-point Palatino, but it's condensed by .75 points, which makes it a full line shorter. The lower-left example shows 10-point Palatino condensed by .75 points. It looks a little overcondensed to my eye.

Kerning: Professional-looking Designs with Type.

The other reason to kern text is to make it look as though it were set professionally. You can add a graphic touch to a head-line by expanding text so that one line of type is more nearly the same length as another line (illustrated in the first of the following examples). You can also use character spacing to improve the appearance of type set in large sizes (illustrated in the second example). Like so many design elements, there's no magic formula for finding the right character spacing. There's only the time-honored technique of trial and error.

GABE'S CATALOGUE OF
NUTS & BOLTS

GABE'S CATALOGUE OF
NUTS & BOLTS

This example shows how expanded character spacing can add a little typographic panache by "evening up" lines of type (the overline "Gabe's Catalogue of" is expanded by 3 points). See how the extra white space in the bottom headline makes it appear somewhat "lighter" than the top one? These headlines are set in Helvetica. The "overlines" are 24 points; the main heads are 50.

GOTTA HAVE IT

GOTTA HAVE IT

This example shows how a little kerning can make a headline look professional. See how some of the letters in the first headline run into each other (or *practically* run into each other)? Remember: When you kern individual letters, Word adds or removes space to the right of the letter you've highlighted. In this example, I expanded the "G" by 2 points and the "O" by 1.5 points in "GOTTA." I expanded the "H" by 5 points, *condensed* the "A" by 1.75, and expanded the "V" by 3 in "HAVE." Despite the different character spacing I had to insert between letters, the final effect is to make the letter spacing *look* more even. These headlines are set in 50-point Bookman bold.

✦ How to Turn Sub- and Superscripting into a Powerful Design Tool

When you superscript text, you make it a little higher than it would be normally; subscripted text, by contrast, is a little lower than normal. In Word, sub- and superscripts don't have to do with mathematical equations. Instead, they are powerful tools for adjusting how words and letters line up next to each other.

9-pt subscript 3-pt subscript Normal (or baseline) text 3-pt superscript 9-pt superscript

The baseline text is positioned normally; the subscripted text is below the baseline and the superscripted text is above it. Using the Character dialog box you can select any sub- or superscript between 0 and 63.5 points.

I've found two main ways to use sub- and superscripts. One is to help line up oversized numbers, symbols, and dingbats (decorative symbols) with the regular-sized text that follows (see *Putting It All Together: Using Oversized Numbers* later in this chapter). The other is to dress up the "th"s and "st"s at the end of dates, numbered street addresses, and the like—for instance May 21st and 333 West 29th Street.

To format text as a sub- or superscript:

1. Highlight the text you want to format.

2. Open the Character dialog box (<ALT> + T, C).

3. Do one of the following, depending on whether you want to sub- or superscript text:
    a. To superscript text, click on the down-pointing arrow to the right of the pull-down Super/subscript menu (<ALT> + T). Select Superscript. Use the arrows on the By box to choose the number of points by which you want to raise the text from the baseline.
    You can also <TAB> to this box and type in the number of points you want to superscript the text.
    b. To subscript the text, click on the down-pointing arrow to the right of the pull-down Super/subscript menu (<ALT> + T). Select Subscript. Use the arrows on the By box to choose the number of points by which you want to lower

the text from the baseline. Again, you can <TAB> to this box and type in the number of points if you don't want to use the mouse.

4. Click on OK or press <ENTER> when you're done.

Note: *If you want to sub- or superscript text by exactly 3 points, you can use a hot key. After highlighting the text you want to sub- or superscript, press <CTRL> + <=> to subscript it, and <CTRL> + <+> (in other words, <CTRL> + <SHIFT> + <=>) to superscript it.*

TEST RUN: Handling "th"s and "st"s

May 21st, 1991   May 21st, 1991

Here's how to turn the example on the left into the one on the right. If you want to use text you're actually working on, just type your text in place of mine.

1. Type the text "May 21st, 1991."

2. Highlight all the text you typed, and format it with the correct typeface and point size. For instance, to use 12-point Helvetica (which is what I used in this example) select Helvetica from the Font menu, and 12 points from the Point Size menu.

3. Highlight only the text you want to superscript; in this case, "st."

4. Open the Character dialog box (<ALT> + T, C).

5. Select Superscript from the pull-down Super/subscript menu.

6. Specify 2 points in the By box.

7. Click on OK or press <ENTER> to return to your document.

8. The superscripted text should still be highlighted. If it isn't, however, highlight it again. I generally make superscripted "th"s and "st"s somewhat smaller than the main text, so select 10 from the Point Size menu.

9. Last thing—to underline the superscript click on the Underline icon on the Ribbon, or press <CTRL> + U. (Remember: you have to highlight text before you can underline it).

✦ Using Color

Color:

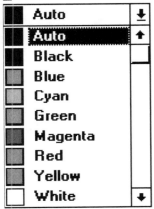

This is Word's Color menu, which appears in the Character dialog box. Even if you personally don't have a color printer, you can use color in your documents and presentations, and have them printed out by a service bureau.

The first thing to remember about color is that even if you have a color monitor and can see your brightly colored design on screen, you still need a color printer to get that color down on paper. If you don't have a color printer, you can probably find a service bureau that does. (Service bureaus generally have all the expensive equipment necessary for top-of-the-line desktop publishing; see Chapter 4.)

If you don't have a color monitor, you can still select colors. A VGA gray-scale monitor, for example, shows the "colors" as different shades of gray. If you have a monochrome (black-and-white) monitor, the colors appear as black. However, when printed on a color printer or made into slides, they *will* print in color.

Keep two things in mind:

- Many publications do *not* need color inks. If you want to use some color, the most inexpensive way of doing so is to print your brochure or booklet on colored paper (see *You Don't Need Colors to Add Color* in Chapter 2). Use preprinted paper if you want to use a color logo or some other color design (see *Flip Sheets* in Chapter 2). However, you'll almost always want to use color when you create slide presentations (see Chapter 20, *Create Your Own Slide Show*).

- When you do use color inks *and* you have your publication printed at a print shop, you don't have to give the printer a color mechanical. You can just deliver a regular black-and-white mechanical. However, make sure you indicate clearly the exact words, rules, boxes, and so on that you want printed in color, and which color you want each of them to be (see Chapter 4).

To use color:

1. Highlight the text you want to print in a particular color. Word automatically prints all text in black (referred to as "Auto" in the Character dialog box) unless you format it otherwise.

2. Open the Character dialog box.

3. Select the color you want from the Color menu (<ALT> + C).

4. Click on OK or press <ENTER> when you're done.

A final word about colors. One of the colors available is white. This is only practical if you're printing on dark-colored paper. In fact, even yellow works better if you're printing on dark-colored paper. Remember that it's always easier to read black letters on a light page than light letters on a dark page. However, you can make light letters on a dark background somewhat easier to read by making them bigger than usual.

DESIGNING PARAGRAPHS

Now that we know about formatting characters, we're ready to move ahead with formatting paragraphs. However, because the Paragraph dialog box includes so many features, I won't try to cover them all here. Instead, I'll deal with some of them in later chapters. This section focuses on how to use the Paragraph dialog box to produce sophisticated line and paragraph spacing.

Diagram of the Paragraph Dialog Box

The Alignment menu provides the same options as the icons on the Ribbon.

You can put extra space before and/or after paragraphs. This is especially useful when using paragraph styles (see Chapter 7).

Word's Indentation options enable you to adjust paragraph margins, first line indents, and hanging indents easily (see Chapters 6 and 7).

Word's Pagination options help you control how your document breaks into pages.

Word's Line Numbers option is especially useful for legal documents (see the manual that came with Word for Windows for more information).

You can set tabs using the Ribbon and the Ruler (see *Anatomy of the Ribbon and the Ruler*), or the Tabs dialog box (see Chapter 7).

The Line Spacing menu enables you to use leading—the space between lines—as a design tool. The menu also includes the old stand-bys—single, 1.5, and double—for those times when you don't want to bother with leading.

As you select paragraph formatting, the sample page changes to indicate what it looks like.

Paragraph
Alignment: Justified
Indentation
From Left: 0"
From Right: 0"
First Line: 0"
Pagination
☐ Page Break Before
☐ Keep With Next
☐ Keep Lines Together
Line Numbers
☐ Suppress
Spacing
Before: 0 li
After: 0.5 li
Line Spacing: At:
Double
Sample
OK
Cancel
Tabs...

This paragraph is set for single line spacing. A typographer would refer to a paragraph with single line spacing as being "set solid." The more space between lines, the more "open" the leading is said to be. A paragraph with very little space between lines is said to be set "minus," or "on negative leading."

This paragraph is set for 1.5 line spacing. A typographer would refer to a paragraph with single line spacing as being "set solid." The more space between lines, the more "open" the leading is said to be. A paragraph with very little space between lines is said . . .

This paragraph is set for double line spacing. A typographer would refer to a paragraph with single line spacing as being "set solid." The more space between lines, the more "open" the leading is said . . .

These three examples show how line spacing works. Note how the first lines of these paragraphs start progressively lower as you move from left to right. The reason is that Word places the leading *above* each line. This becomes very important when you're trying to get a headline to look just right.

✦ Leading, or Line Spacing

Leading, or line spacing, is the white space that separates each line of type from the one above it. Word has three hot keys that let you set line spacing to single, 1.5, and double. Using the Paragraph dialog box, you have a much wider range of options—anything from 0 to 132 lines (1584 points).

To select basic line spacing—single, 1.5, or double—you can use the Paragraph dialog box.

1. Put your cursor somewhere in the paragraph you want to line space (if you want to line space several adjoining paragraphs at the same time, highlight them).

2. Open the Paragraph dialog box.

3. Click on the down-pointing arrow to the right of the pull-down Line Spacing menu (<ALT> + I), and select the spacing you want—single, 1.5, or double.

To select basic line spacing *without* using the Paragraph dialog box, use the hot keys listed below.

Line Spacing	Hot Keys
Single	<CTRL> + 1
1.5	<CTRL> + 5
Double	<CTRL> + 2

Generally, there are four things you need to keep in mind when deciding how much leading to use:

1. If you don't want to think about leading, you have two choices. Either use one of Word's basic line spacing options (single, 1.5, or double), or use Word's default line spacing, called "Auto," which is essentially the same as single spacing.

2. The larger the type, the more leading you need. For instance, single-spaced text set in 12-point Times requires at least 12 points of leading; single-spaced text set in 24-point Times requires at least 24 points of leading. In typographic terms, "single spaced" means "set solid"—the point size of the type is at least equal to the amount of leading.

   Word provides three *types* of line spacing: "Auto," "At Least," and "Exactly." Auto line spacing (the default) adjusts to fit the largest type size or graphic in a line—you can't specify a particular point size. "At Least" allows you

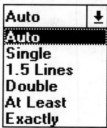

When you set your line spacing to "Exactly," the point size you specify is exactly what you get—no matter what.

to set a minimum line spacing which Word can increase as needed to accommodate text and graphics. If you set line spacing to "Exactly," however, Word can't adjust it. If you have text or graphics on a particular line that are too large for the line spacing set, they just get cut off.

3. Depending on the type of document and the look you're trying to achieve, you might want more or less leading. For instance, a fund-raising brochure might get more leading than a report, in order to give it a lighter feel.

4. In some cases, leading is a function of the space available. If you have a lot of text but not a lot of space, you might have to be stingy with the leading; if you have lots of space, you can be more generous. In fact, open leading is a nice way of lengthening text to fill a space. (Next time you're reading a newspaper, note the way different stories—even different paragraphs within stories—have somewhat different leading. This is one of the techniques layout people use to make stories fit exactly.)

Emma Inch looked no different from any other middle-aged, thin woman you might glance at in the subway or deal with across the counter of some small store in a country town, and then forget forever. Her hair was drab and abundant, her face made no impression on you, her voice I don't remember— it was just a voice.

Emma Inch looked no different from any other middle-aged, thin woman you might glance at in the subway or deal with across the counter of some small store in a country town, and then forget forever. Her hair was drab and abundant, her face made no impression on you, her voice I don't remember—it was just a voice.

Emma Inch looked no looked no different from any other middle-aged, thin woman...

All three examples are set in Palatino. The one on the left is set at 10 points on At Least 10 points of leading (in other words, single spaced or "solid"); the middle example is set at 11 points on 16 points of leading ("open"); the one on the right is set at 20 points on At Least 20 points of leading (single spaced). Again, the text is from from James Thurber's short story *The Departure of Emma Inch.*

To set text "tight" (or "negative") you essentially need to use a smaller point size for the leading than you did for the text. However, in Word, you must also set the line spacing to Exactly. While negative leading is often useful for headlines (especially headlines set in all caps or small caps), it doesn't work well for most text because the bottom of letters like "y" and "g" run into the tops of letters like "t" and "d" (see the leftmost of the following examples). A good rule of thumb is that you shouldn't set text that includes both upper and lower cases on negative leading unless you're using very large point sizes.

In the following examples, the leftmost and middle examples are both set in 13-point Palatino on Exactly 12 points of leading. In the one to the left, notice how the "g" in "middle-aged" nearly collides with the "i" in "might." Although the middle example avoids this pitfall by using all caps, it's also harder to read. The right-hand example is set in 20-point Palatino on Exactly 19 points of line spacing.

Emma Inch looked no
different from any
other middle-aged, thin
woman you might
glance at in the subway
or deal with across the
counter of some small
store . . .

EMMA INCH
LOOKED NO
DIFFERENT FROM
ANY OTHER
MIDDLE-AGED, THIN
WOMAN YOU MIGHT
GLANCE AT IN THE
SUBWAY OR DEAL . . .

EMMA INCH
LOOKED NO
DIFFERENT

These are all examples of negative leading. The first example shows the danger of using negative leading with upper-lower case text; the middle example shows how, all else being equal, negative leading works better with capital letters; and the last example shows that capitals and negative leading tend to be more effective in headlines than as body text.

To adjust your line spacing:

1. Put the cursor anywhere in the paragraph you want to set the line spacing for (if you want to set the same line spacing for several adjoining paragraphs, highlight them).

2. Open the Paragraph dialog box (<ALT> + T, P).

3. Click on the down-pointing arrow to the right of the Line Spacing menu, and select the type of spacing you want—Single, At Least, Exactly, and so on. If you prefer to use the keyboard commands press <ALT> + I.

4. Position your cursor in the At box and type the leading you want—for instance, "14pt" for 14 points. The keyboard command is <ALT> + A. At this writing, unfortunately, Word only lists line spacing in the At box in .5-line increments, so the arrows are not generally precise enough. To use them, however, simply click on the up-pointing arrow to increase the line spacing, and on the down-pointing arrow to decrease it.

    Note: *If you don't type "pt" when using points, Word will assume you mean "lines," which are a lot bigger than points. Also, if you select Single, 1.5, Double, or Auto, Word doesn't let you specify a measurement.*

5. Click OK or press <ENTER> when you're done.

✦ Paragraph Spacing

Word lets you put space above and/or below paragraphs. Although this has much the same effect as adding a carriage return between paragraphs, it has two important advantages:

*   You can include this extra space as part of your paragraph style definitions, so it's inserted automatically whenever you use that style (see Chapter 7).

*   You can use a very small amount of space (much smaller than a carriage return) to create a distinctly professional look.

It's almost impossible to tell whether someone has added space above or below the paragraphs of running text in a report; after all, the space shows up *between* paragraphs. However, when the paragraph you're dealing with is a headline, it's quite easy to imagine that it would look better with a fair amount of extra space above it and relatively little below. Here are the guidelines I follow when trying to decide whether to put extra space *before* or *after* a paragraph:

- Add space *after* paragraphs in the main text (the advantage is that you can easily format various levels of headings spaced different distances *before* the text).

- Add a substantial amount of space *before* headings to separate them from the previous section; add a smaller amount of space *after* headings to distinguish them from the text that follows.

- Add space both *before* and *after* tables and pictures. (You usually add the same amount, unless you're using captions. When you use captions, add only a small amount after the picture and a larger amount after the caption.)

There's only one way to decide exactly *how much* space you should add around a paragraph—by fiddling with it until you get it right. However, certain cases generally require relatively more or less space. For instance, you generally need only a small amount of space (4 to 6 points) between paragraphs in normal text. The following example uses 11-point Palatino on Auto line spacing, and .5 lines (6 points) of space between paragraphs.

Note: *If you don't set paragraph spacing, Word defaults to no paragraph spacing.*

Emma Inch looked no different from any other middle-aged, thin woman you might glance at in the subway or deal with across the counter of some small store in a country town, and then forget forever.

Her hair was drab and abundant, her face made no impression on you, her voice I don't remember—it was just a voice.

From James Thurber's short story, The Departure of Emma Inch. *The paragraph break has been added.*

This example shows .5 lines (6 points) of space *after* paragraphs. It's generally easier to add space below paragraphs in the main text because it allows you better control over the space between the text and different levels of headings.

On the other hand, you might put a significant amount of space (24 points, or even 36) above main headings in a report, and a significantly smaller amount above subheads. Remember that a heading should always be *closer to the text below it* than to the section above it. In the following example, there are 24 points (2 lines) of space above the main heading "Internal Factors" and 12 points (1 line) below it. Similarly, there are 12 points of space above the subhead "Academic challenges" and 4 points below it. The main text is set in 11-point Palatino, on Auto line spacing.

In 1979, the College initiated a plan for a Liberal Arts Education. While it received substantial national media coverage, the College has not capitalized on that visibility in terms of increased enrollment.

Internal Factors

During the course of this study, the marketing team interviewed a broad spectrum of the College family —students, faculty, staff, administration—to gain a better understanding of their view of the College's Plan and its impact on the College's goals and strategies. This section discusses the main problems perceived by this community.

Academic challenges

Those interviewed repeatedly named a single problem as being, in their view, the most pressing faced by the College . . .

This example shows varying amounts of space placed both before and after different levels of headings, depending on whether they're main heads or subheads.

To add space before or after paragraphs:

1. Put your cursor anywhere in the paragraph for which you want to set the paragraph spacing (if you want to set the same paragraph spacing for several adjoining paragraphs, highlight them).

2. Open the Paragraph dialog box.

3. To add space *before* a paragraph, position your cursor in the Before box (<ALT> + B). Depending on the amount of paragraph spacing you want, you can either type it in or use the arrows, which list spacing in .5-line increments. If you type in a measurement, you can specify either points (as in "4pt") or lines (simply type "1").

   To add space *after* a paragraph, position your cursor in the After box (<ALT> + E). Again, you can either type the measurement or use the arrows.

   Note: *If you don't type "pt" when using points, Word assumes you mean "lines"—there are 12 points to a line.*

4. Click on OK or press <ENTER> when you're done.

PUTTING IT ALL TOGETHER: Designing Characters and Paragraphs

This section walks you through two examples that illustrate different uses of typography. They draw on many of the formatting techniques you've learned in this chapter. If you happen to be on deadline and want to format your own work in a similar way, you can use these general instructions to help get your document out the door.

Using Oversized Numbers

This example (taken from the Little Bank brochure in Chapter 2) shows how to *vertically center* oversized numbers with the text that follows them. It uses several of the tools covered in this chapter—the Font and Point Size menus, type styles, tabs, and subscripting.

1. A minimum balance of $1,000.   **1.** A minimum balance of $1,000.

2. Free checking.   **2.** Free checking.

3. Bounce protection.   **3.** Bounce protection.

4. Free Visa Card (if you qualify).   **4.** Free Visa Card (if you qualify).

5. Preferred interest rates.   **5.** Preferred interest rates.

The above examples are the same, except for one thing. In the left-hand example, I subscripted the oversized numbers so they're vertically centered with the line of text that follows them. This gives the list a little more flair. (Incidentally, it also increases the space between the lines.)

1. Type in the text, including the numbers that begin each line. Put a tab (with the <TAB> key) between the number and the words that follow.

2. Highlight all the text, click on the left tab icon, and then click under the 3/8-inch marker on the Ruler to set the tab stop there. See how all the text immediately lines up at the new tab setting?

    Note: *There's no magic about 3/8 of an inch—if you like half an inch better, go for it. Just make sure you have enough space to enlarge the numbers.*

3. Highlight all the numbers—*only* the numbers and their associated periods. (Do this exactly the way you would highlight any text, *but use your right mouse button*. This lets you highlight text *vertically*.) I set my numbers in 26-point Times bold (again, there's no magic about the size—you might fiddle with different sizes to see what you like best).

   Note: *Each time you use your right mouse button to select text and then choose a formatting option, your text un-highlights,* so you have to re-highlight it. *This is a nuisance, but it's how Word works.*

4. Highlight all the *text* (again, use the right mouse button). Format it as 15-point Palatino.

5. Highlight all the *numbers* (periods included); open the Character dialog box; select Subscript, and enter 4 in the By box.

Why use Times bold for the numbers? If you compare Times numbers (shown in the top example in 20-point bold), with the Palatino numbers (bottom, also 20-point bold), you'll see that the Times numbers are a little rounder and less "serif-ed," especially the 2, 3, 4, and 5—which I like.

1 2 3 4 5 6 7 8 9

1 2 3 4 5 6 7 8 9

Kerning and Leading

When you do typography, all you're really doing is using the tools you learned in this chapter. You select a typeface, a type style; you do a little kerning and some careful line spacing. Before you know it, you have dressed up a phrase into a graphic image.

The headlines on the next page are both set in 48-point Avant Garde caps, centered; and the left one is set with Auto line spacing. Each line of these heads is its own paragraph. In other words, each line ends with a carriage return (just press the <ENTER> key). To turn the left one into the right one:

1. Highlight "makes"; open the Character dialog box; and condense the character spacing to 1.75 points.

   Note: *Word's default setting for Condensed is 1.75 points, so you don't have to change it.*

2. Highlight "rules" and expand the character spacing to 4 points.

3. Highlight "the" and use the Point Size menu to reduce it to 20 points. Then expand its character spacing to 9 points.

4. Highlight the question mark and set it in 72-point Bookman bold.

WHO MAKES THE RULES?

WHO MAKES THE RULES ?

The left-hand headline is set in 48-point Avant Garde, centered, with leading or line spacing set to auto. The right-hand headline has been dressed up with a little typography. It could easily serve as the main graphic element for a page.

5. The left-hand example and the first line of the right-hand example are both set with Auto line spacing. (Remember that Word puts line spacing *above* the paragraph.) Insert your cursor anywhere in "makes"; open the Paragraph dialog box; open the Line Spacing menu and set it to Exactly. Then type "48pt" in the At box.

6. Insert your cursor anywhere in "the" and set the line spacing to Exactly 24 points.

7. Insert your cursor anywhere in "rules" and set the line spacing to Exactly 54 points.

8. Insert your cursor next to the question mark and set the leading to Exactly 64 points.

You've just done some typography.

CHAPTER 6

Those Special Typesetting Characters

Special typesetting characters are the symbols that make a document look as though it was typeset by a professional, not just typed on a typewriter. They include foreign letters (such as the "é" in "résumé"); special symbols (©, ®); symbols and practical graphics, known as dingbats (☞, ✂); currency signs (¢, £, ¥); common fractions (¼, ½, ¾); and typesetters' punctuation marks (such as em dashes "—").

These special typesetting characters are so simple to use—and they upgrade the look of your work so effectively—that it's hard to understand why people don't use them more. The only time I don't use them is when I actually want the product to *look* typed (a direct-mail letter, for example). Otherwise, I use them for reports, flyers, brochures, proposals—whatever I send out of the office.

This chapter covers everything you need to know to start using special typesetting characters immediately. I go through each topic in the following order:

- How to turn everyday letters and numbers into symbols and dingbats.

- How to use Word's Symbol palette.

- How to use the special extended character set that comes with Windows.

- How to use typesetters' punctuation marks.

- How to set up glossaries and create macros that make special characters even easier to use.

- What to do when WYSIWYG *isn't* what you get.

- How to make the most of the Zapf Dingbats and Symbol fonts that come with most PostScript printers and compatibles.

DIFFERENT STROKES FOR DIFFERENT FACES

The keys on your keyboard can produce many more symbols than the ones actually printed on them. The common keyboard characters—the letters, numbers, and punctuation marks you use every day—are called the **ASCII character set**. However, you can access another whole realm of characters, called the **ANSI character set**, with some simple codes.

A Word About ASCII

ASCII is an acronym for the American Standard Code for Information Interchange. "Standard Code" means that virtually all word processing, database, and spreadsheet programs can understand ASCII, which is called "text only" in some applications, including Word for Windows.

One reason that it's hard to use documents typed into one program with another program is that every computer program formats information in its own way. However, ASCII is the actual *un*formatted letters and numbers you type in, so practically every program understands it. This means you can use the *text* from your Word documents (but not graphics or fancy formatting) with other programs if you first save it as a text-only file. To do this:

1. Choose Save As from the File menu.

2. Choose Text Only from the menu at the bottom of your screen called Save File as Type (note that Word Document is the default).

3. Name the file.

4. Click on OK or press <ENTER> when you're done.

   Note: *Word automatically saves text-only documents with a "txt" extension.*

Many people feel intimidated by such terms as ASCII (pronounced "as-kee") and ANSI (pronounced "an-see") character sets, but the only difficult thing is the technical-sounding names. A character set is nothing more than the letters and numbers you type into the computer. However, depending on the fonts you have available, it's possible to end up with "❀✿✳" when you type "abc."

You can tap into different character sets and expand the range of symbols available to you in three basic ways:

1. You can use fonts that actually come with their own character set, like the Symbol font and the Zapf Dingbats font.

2. You can take advantage of the symbols "hidden" in the extended character set that comes with Word. This works with all the regular typefaces—Times, Helvetica, Palatino, and so on.

3. You can use the symbols "hidden" in the extended character sets that come with the Symbol and Zapf Dingbats fonts.

✦ Using Symbol and Dingbats Fonts

As you know, different typefaces make letters, numbers, and punctuation marks look different. For instance, when you type "*#!?" and select the Avant Garde typeface, you get this: *#!?. When you select Bookman bold, you get this: **#!?**.

Some fonts (such as the Symbol and Zapf Dingbats fonts) do more than merely change the appearance of letters and numbers; they actually produce different characters altogether. The following example illustrates how this works. In each case, I typed in "Every good fox deserves fudge," but I formatted the middle one using the Symbol font and the bottom one using Zapf Dingbats.

The Symbol font comes with Windows and works with most printers. If you don't see it on your Font menu, refer to your Windows manual for instructions on installing it. In addition, Word itself comes with several of its own symbol-like fonts, such as MS LineDraw and MT Extra. The Zapf Dingbats font comes with most PostScript printers and compatibles. If you have a PostScript printer or compatible and don't see it listed

Every good fox deserves fudge.

Εϖερψ γοοδ φοξ δεσερϖεσ φυδγε.

❖❖❊◻❙ ❊◻◻❊ ❖◻❙ ❊❊▲❊◻❖❊▲ ❖◆❊❊❊❊✎

I typed in the same phrase "Every good fox deserves fudge" for all three examples. But I formatted the top example in 10-point Times; the middle one in 10-
point Symbol; and the bottom in 10-point Zapf Dingbats. The Symbol and Zapf
Dingbats fonts produce their own character sets.

on your Font menu, you may not have installed your printer correctly (refer to your Windows manual), or you may not have selected it correctly in Word itself.

To make sure your printer is selected correctly in Word:

1. Choose Printer Setup from the File menu (<ALT> + F, R).

2. Select the printer you're using.

3. Click on the Setup button (<ALT> + S).

4. In the Setup dialog box, check that the printer settings are
   correct.

5. Click on OK or press <ENTER>. Then click on OK or press
   <ENTER> again to get back to your document.

Note: *See Chapter 9 for more information about printing.*

Printer Fonts versus Screen Fonts

Because computer systems require a **screen font** to show you what a typeface looks like on
your screen and a **printer font** to print it, you can end up with a few problems. For instance,
if you have a PostScript printer or compatible, you may be able to *print* Zapf Dingbats but not
see them on your screen. This is because the Zapf Dingbats printer font comes with your
printer, but the screen font does not. To get it, you need a font manager that has a Zapf Dingbats screen font, such as Adobe Type Manager. However, the Symbol font comes with Windows, so you can actually see the symbols on your screen as well as print them out (see *The
Font Menu and How It Works* in Chapter 5).

If you don't have a PostScript printer, you can still purchase and use the Zapf Dingbats font—it comes with Adobe Type Manager. You can also purchase different dingbat fonts from other vendors, such as Bitstream. In this case, your dingbats may be different from the ones shown in this book, but the principle is still the same. (See *What to Do When WYSIWYG Isn't What You Get* later in this chapter.)

Here's HOW

Formatting text in a symbol or dingbat font is the same as formatting it in any other typeface:

1. Type the letter, number, or punctuation mark corresponding to the symbol or dingbat you want.

2. Highlight it.

3. Select the font from the Font menu that produces the desired symbol or dingbat.

   > **Note:** *You can also format text in symbols and dingbats before you type it in. Just select the font, point size, and so on, and start typing. When you want to go back to the typeface you normally use, just select it from the Font menu.*

The hard part of working with special characters is finding the one you want. There are almost 200 different dingbats in the Zapf Dingbats typeface. There are almost as many symbols in the Symbol font. Plus, there are over 100 symbols "hidden" in what's known as the "extended" character set for regular fonts such as Times (you have to type a short code to access these; see *The Extended Character Set* later in this chapter). Sorting through this thicket can be daunting. Memorizing is one approach. For instance, I like to use the Zapf Dingbat ❏ for check lists on forms. Because I use it frequently, I have it memorized. (Just type a lowercase "o" and format it in Zapf Dingbats.) But you clearly can't memorize hundreds of these special characters, so Word has a handy tool for finding them—the Symbol palette.

Using the Symbol Palette. The Symbol palette enables you to use special characters without remembering which key you have to press to find them. The palette lets you simply click on a symbol in order to insert it into your document.

Turning Letters and Numbers into Symbols and Dingbats

Regular	Symbol	Dingbats	Regular	Symbol	Dingbats	Regular	Symbol	Dingbats	Regular	Symbol	Dingbats
~	~	✽	a	α	❀	A	Α	✡	{	{	❛
!	!	✁	b	β	❂	B	Β	✢	}	}	❜
@	≅	✂	c	χ	✳	C	Χ	✣	|	|	❟
#	#	✄	d	δ	❆	D	Δ	✤	:	:	✚
$	∃	✄	e	ε	❄	E	Ε	✥	"	∀	✁
%	%	☎	f	φ	❅	F	Φ	◆	<	<	✜
^	⊥	✿	g	γ	✶	G	Γ	◇	>	>	✝
&	&	©	h	η	✴	H	Η	★	?	?	✞
*	*	☞	i	ι	✻	I	Ι	☆	[	[	✻
(	(	✈	j	φ	✺	J	ϑ	✪	]	]	✼
)	)	✉	k	κ	✹	K	Κ	☆	\	∴	❄
_	_	❀	l	λ	●	L	Λ	✭	;	;	✛
+	+	☜	m	μ	○	M	Μ	★	'	϶	☮
`	‾	❁	n	ν	■	N	Ν	✩	,	,	✌
1	1	☛	o	ο	❏	O	Ο	✫	.	.	✍
2	2	☚	p	π	❐	P	Π	✰	/	/	✎
3	3	✓	q	θ	❑	Q	Θ	✱			
4	4	✔	r	ρ	❒	R	Ρ	✲			
5	5	✕	s	σ	▲	S	Σ	✳			
6	6	✖	t	τ	▼	T	Τ	✴			
7	7	✗	u	υ	◆	U	Υ	✵			
8	8	✘	v	ϖ	❖	V	ς	✶			
9	9	✢	w	ω	◗	W	Ω	✷			
0	0	✐	x	ξ	|	X	Ξ	✸			
-	−	✑	y	ψ	❙	Y	Ψ	✹			
=	=	†	z	ζ	∎	Z	Ζ	✺			

To use these symbols and dingbats, type the letter, number, or punctuation mark corresponding to the symbol you want to use. Then highlight it, and format it with the Symbol or Zapf Dingbats font.

Extending Your Fonts

Code	Regular	Symbol	Dingbats	Code	Regular	Symbol	Dingbats	Code	Regular	Symbol	Dingbats	Code	Regular	Symbol	Dingbats
0145	'			0186	º	≡	❺	0218	Ú	∨	↗	0250	ú	|	→
0146	'			0187	»	≈	❻	0219	Û	⇔	→	0251	û	⌋	↔
0147	"			0188	¼	…	❼	0220	Ü	⇐	→	0252	ü	⟩	➤
0148	"			0189	½	|	❽	0221	Ý	⇑	→	0253	ý	⟩	➡
0149	•			0190	¾	—	❾	0222	Þ	⇒	→	0254	þ	⌋	⇒
0150	–			0191	¿	↵	❿	0223	ß	⇓	→	0255	ÿ		
0151	—			0192	À	ℵ	①	0224	à	◊	→				
0161	¡	ϒ	✠	0193	Á	ℑ	②	0225	á	⟨	→				
0162	¢	′	✂	0194	Â	ℜ	③	0226	â	®	➢				
0163	£	≤	✄	0195	Ã	℘	④	0227	ã	©	➢				
0164	¤	⁄	♥	0196	Ä	⊗	⑤	0228	ä	™	➤				
0165	¥	∞	♣	0197	Å	⊕	⑥	0229	å	∑	➤				
0166	¦	ƒ	✿	0198	Æ	∅	⑦	0230	æ	⌠	➤				
0167	§	♣	✺	0199	Ç	∩	⑧	0231	ç	|	●				
0168	¨	♦	♣	0200	È	∪	⑨	0232	è	⌡	→				
0169	©	♥	♦	0201	É	⊃	⑩	0233	é	⌈	⇨				
0170	ª	♠	♥	0202	Ê	⊇	❶	0234	ê	|	⇨				
0171	«	↔	♠	0203	Ë	⊄	❷	0235	ë	⌊	⇦				
0172	¬	←	①	0204	Ì	⊂	❸	0236	ì	⌈	⇦				
0173	-	↑	②	0205	Í	⊆	❹	0237	í	{	⇨				
0174	®	→	③	0206	Î	∈	❺	0238	î	|	⇨				
0175	¯	↓	④	0207	Ï	∉	❻	0239	ï	|	⇨				
0176	°	°	⑤	0208	Ð	∠	❼	0240	ð						
0177	±	±	⑥	0209	Ñ	∇	❽	0241	ñ	⟩	⇨				
0178	²	″	⑦	0210	Ò	®	❾	0242	ò	∫	⟳				
0179	³	≥	⑧	0211	Ó	©	❿	0243	ó	⌈	➣				
0180	´	×	⑨	0212	Ô	™	→	0244	ô	|	↘				
0181	µ	∝	⑩	0213	Õ	∏	→	0245	õ	⌋	➣				
0182	¶	∂	❶	0214	Ö	√	↔	0246	ö	⟩	✈				
0183	·	•	❷	0215	×	·	↕	0247	÷	|	↘				
0184	¸	÷	❸	0216	Ø	¬	↘	0248	ø	⌡	➣				
0185	¹	≠	❹	0217	Ù	∧	→	0249	ù	⌉	✈				

The symbols and dingbats listed here are available in the extended character set. To use these characters, make sure the <NUM LOCK> key is on. Hold down the <ALT> key and type the four-digit code on the numeric keypad. The symbols listed in the column marked Regular appear when you're using an everyday typeface such as Times or Helvetica. To use a character from the Symbol or Zapf Dingbats font, simply type its code and format the resulting character in the appropriate font.

To use the Symbol Palette:

1. Put your cursor where you want the symbol to be.

2. Select Symbol from the Insert menu. This opens the palette.

3. Select the font you want to use from the Symbols From menu (<ALT> + F). All regular typefaces—Helvetica, Palatino, Times, and so forth—are lumped together under Normal Text. The other symbol and dingbat fonts are listed individually.

4. When you select a font, Word shows you the symbols, pictures, ornaments, and so forth that it includes.

5. If you have trouble identifying a particular symbol, simply point at it with your mouse and hold down the left mouse button to enlarge it. If you drag the mouse over the face of the palette, Word magnifies each symbol in turn. If you prefer the keyboard to the mouse, use the <ARROW> keys. Move the cursor onto the palette itself with the <TAB> key.

6. To insert a symbol into your document, double-click on it or select it (using either the mouse or <ARROW> keys) and press <ENTER>.

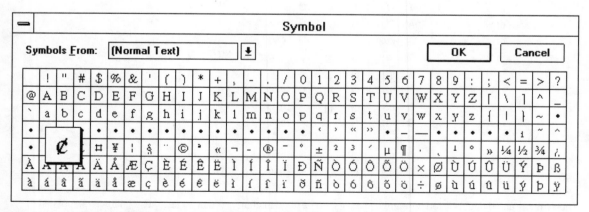

When you select Normal Text from the menu on the Symbol palette, you'll notice that the top three rows contain the letters, numbers, and punctuation marks you use every day. The bottom four rows, by contrast, contain the "hidden" symbols in the extended character set. If you don't use the Symbol palette, you have to type a four-digit code to access these characters.

Although the palette is a useful tool, it has a few drawbacks if you use symbols frequently. First, it's slow. If you know the symbol you want, it's noticeably quicker to simply type the underlying character or code than to select it from the palette. Second, you need the screen font for the typeface you want to use (such as Zapf Dingbats) in order to see the symbols in the palette. If you don't have the screen font, the special characters look like a regular typeface.

To get around these drawbacks, I've included two tables, *Turning Letters and Numbers into Symbols and Dingbats* and *Extending Your Fonts*. They provide a listing of all the symbols available using regular fonts, the Symbol font, and Zapf Dingbats.

The Extended Character Set. Word's extended character set contains 102 symbols. It includes typesetters' punctuation marks, foreign currency symbols, foreign letters, the copyright symbol, common fractions, and so on. These characters (sometimes called ANSI characters) are an extremely easy way of upgrading the look of your work.

You get each character by typing its particular 4-digit code, called an **ANSI code**. When you use a regular font such as Times, you can see the symbols on your computer screen so you always know whether you got the right one. Although you don't need either the Symbol or Zapf Dingbats font to use the extended character set, both fonts have their own particular characters for each of the codes.

To use the extended character set:

1. Turn the <NUM LOCK> key on (a light usually indicates when it's on).

2. Put your cursor where you want the special character to go, and hold down the <ALT> key.

3. While holding down the <ALT> key, use the numeric keypad to type the four numbers that represent the ANSI code you want (the code always starts with zero). For instance, typing "0169" gives you the copyright symbol (©).

Note: *You must use your numeric keypad to type the code for the extended character set. The numeric keypad is usually on the right side of your key-*

PUTTING IT ALL TOGETHER: Creating a Checklist for Forms

This example explains how to create a checklist such as the one shown below. It uses several of the tools covered so far, including tabs, point sizes, and line spacing. If you are trying to do something similar in your own work, you can use the directions below and simply substitute your text for mine.

Note: *You have to have Zapf Dingbats to create the check boxes. If you have another dingbat font that includes similar boxes, refer to the manual that came with the font to find the letter that corresponds to the box. You can also use the Symbol palette to insert the check boxes into your document.*

LANGUAGES:

❏ English   ❏ Creole

❏ French   ❏ Yiddish

❏ Italian   ❏ Braille

❏ Spanish   ❏ Signing

❏ Other _____

1. Make sure the Show/Hide ¶ option is on so that you can see the invisible characters on your screen. If it isn't, click on the ¶ icon on the Ribbon.

2. Format the text in 10-point Times by selecting Tms Rmn (or Times if you have Adobe Type Manager) from the Font menu, and 10 from the Point Size menu.

3. Type the text. Since the check box is simply a lowercase "o" formatted in the Zapf Dingbats font, type "o"s for now. Put a space or two between the "o"s and the text that follows. Put a carriage return at the end of every line, and a <TAB> between each language on the same line. Don't bother with the underline at the bottom for now, and don't worry if things don't line up—they will soon. The following picture shows essentially what your text should look like after you've typed the text, invisibles (or nonprinting characters) and all.

```
Languages:¶
o·English    →    o·Creole¶
o·French     →    o·Yiddish¶
o·Italian→o·Braille¶
o·Spanish    →    o·Signing¶
o·Other¶
```

4. After you've typed the text, set a tab. Highlight the four lines that start with English and end with Signing. Select the Left tab icon on the Ribbon by clicking on it. Set a tab at 1 and 1/8th inches by clicking under that marker on the Ruler. The second column of text should now line up. If you want, you can drag the tab icon on the Ruler to position the second column more to your liking. However, be sure you highlight *all* the text affected by the tab before moving it. Otherwise you risk adjusting the tabs for some lines, but not for others.

Note: *Depending on the typeface and point size you're using, your text might have lined up evenly when you first typed it.*

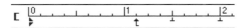

5. Use your right mouse button to highlight the first column of "o"s. Select Zapf Dingbats from the Font menu. Repeat this procedure for the second column of "o"s. If you have the Zapf Dingbats screen font, you should now see the check boxes on your screen. If you only have the printer font, not the screen font, the "o"s should now look bold.

6. If you didn't capitalize "languages" as you type it, highlight it now. Then capitalize it using <CTRL> + A, and bold it (click on the Bold button on the Ribbon or use <CTRL> + B).

7. While there are a few ways of creating the underline at the bottom of the list, one way is to use **non-breaking spaces**. Non-breaking spaces have a fixed space that allow you to create lines of a certain length easily. (Word doesn't let you underline regular spaces if they're not between text.) Give yourself an extra space after "Other," then type a bunch of non-breaking spaces by pressing <CTRL> + <SHIFT> + <SPACE BAR> simultaneously. A non-breaking space appears as a ° on your screen.

8. Highlight the string of non-breaking spaces and underline them (click on the Underline button on the Ribbon or use <CTRL> + U).

9. Adjust the list's line spacing by opening the Paragraph dialog box (<ALT> + T, P). Select At Least from the Line Spacing menu (<ALT> + I). Type "14pt" in the At box (<ALT> + A), and then click on OK or press <ENTER> to see how it looks.

board. However, if you have a laptop, the keypad is probably embedded in the regular keyboard. Look in the manual that came with your computer to find out how to get to it.

4. After you type the 4-digit ANSI code, let up on the <ALT> key.

5. If you're using a code for a regular font such as Times, the symbol you want should now appear on the screen. However, if you want to use a character that comes with the Symbol or Zapf Dingbats font, you have to take an extra step: Highlight the extended character now on your screen, and format it with the font you want.

TEST RUN: Using Checkmarks

There are two ways to get a √ in your document (note this symbol is actually a radical symbol):

Use the Symbol palette:

1. Put your cursor where you want the special character to go.

2. Select Symbol from the Insert menu. The palette opens.

3. Select the Symbol font from the pull-down menu. (If you haven't already used the palette and selected a different font, Word should automatically open to the Symbol font.)

4. Double-click on the √ character to insert it into your document. If you prefer using the keyboard, <TAB> to get onto the palette itself; use the <ARROW> keys to select the √ symbol; then press <ENTER>.

Use the ANSI code:

1. Put your cursor where you want the special character to go.

2. Turn the <NUM LOCK> key on.

3. Hold down the <ALT> key and type "0214." Until you format it with the Symbol font, it looks like this: Ö.

4. Highlight the Ö and select Symbol from the font menu. Now it should look like a √ (unless you're in Draft mode).

✦ Using Typesetters' Punctuation Marks

Typesetters' punctuation marks have a professionally set quality that distinguishes them immediately from their typewriter-like counterparts. These include curved open and close quotation marks (instead of straight ones) and em dashes (instead of double dashes). They're illustrated in the following table. As you look over the illustrations, note that different typefaces draw these punctuation marks somewhat differently.

You can access these typesetters' punctuation marks in two basic ways:

1. You can type the codes listed in the "codes" column (see *The Extended Character Set* earlier in this chapter for instructions).

Typesetter versus Typewriter

	Typewriter	Typesetter (Times)	Typesetter (Palatino)	Code <ALT> + code	Example
Open and close single quote	' '	' '	' '	0145 0146	"So he finally said 'Yes,' but I know he doesn't mean it."
Apostrophe	'	'	'	0146	don't
Open and close double quote	" "	" "	" "	0147 0148	My grandfather says, "Never worry about your heart until it stops beating."
Bullet	-	•	●	0149	used in lists
En dash	-	–	–	0150	1989–1991
Em dash	--	—	—	0151	The closing ceremony—a dazzling Hollywood spectacle—lasted longer than the main program.
Ellipsis	...	… (Symbol font only)		0188	Many sports (squash, bicycling, swimming…) are good for you.

Note: *The bullets shown here don't look like bullets on your screen. They look more like misshapen "o"s. But they print fine.*

2. You can use the Symbol palette and select the font for Normal Text (see *Using the Symbol Palette* earlier in this chapter for instructions).

   Note: *As of this writing, the palette doesn't display all typesetters' punctuation marks unless you're using a font manager.*

Typesetters' punctuation marks are a simple way to upgrade the look of your work. However, it can be cumbersome to type a four-digit code or open the Symbol palette every time you want to open or close a quote. Fortunately, there is a fairly easy way to get around this: by storing these punctuation marks in either the glossary or a macro. In this case, there a few advantages to using macros over the glossary, and macros are almost as easy to do (see *Creating Your Own Glossaries and Macros*).

Although the glossary and macros work fine for several typesetters' punctuation marks, they're not the best solution for curved open and close quotes. The best solution is a document called NEWMACRO.DOC in your main Word directory (usually called Winword). By installing the SmartQuotes macro that comes in this document, you can use curved quotation marks by typing the ordinary quotation marks and the apostrophe. To use this feature:

1. Open the NEWMACRO.DOC as you would any Word document.

2. Select SmartQuotes from the list of macros, and then click on Install.

3. Choose to install this macro on the Normal template (the default) and on a particular menu, such as the Tools menu. Click on OK, and Word installs the macro.

4. To return to your document, "cancel" the dialog box that lists the macros, and then select Close from the File menu (<ALT> + F, C). If Word prompts you to save NEWMACRO.DOC, *don't*.

5. You'll find two new options on the menu you chose in step #3: Enable SmartQuotes and Disable SmartQuotes. Select Enable SmartQuotes to start using them. Choose Disable SmartQuotes to use the straight quotes—for instance, if you want your document to look typed.

6. Select Save All from the File menu <ALT> + F, E). If Word prompts you to save the document you're currently working on, answer Yes or No as you wish. When Word prompts you to save the global glossary and command changes, answer Yes. Word saves the newly installed SmartQuotes entry and adds this capability to your Normal template.

Creating Your Own Glossaries and Macros

Glossaries

The glossary is an extremely useful feature of Word. It lets you store text that you use frequently so you don't have to retype it. Instead you just press a few keys and it's inserted into your document. No matter what document or template you're working on, you can always use your glossary.

You can create a glossary entry for just about anything you don't want to type over and over again: company names; signature lines (yes, you can include a scanned image such as the boss's signature in a glossary); return addresses; stationery headings (including a logo); and typesetters' punctuation marks, which I'll cover here.

To make a glossary entry for a typesetters' em dash.

1. Make sure the <NUM LOCK> key is on.

2. Hold down the <ALT> key and type "0151." Let up on the <ALT> key and you should see an em dash.

3. Highlight just that em dash. Don't highlight spaces or anything around it.

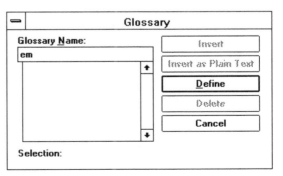

Grayed commands are not currently available.

4. Select Glossary from the Edit menu (<ALT> + E, O).

5. Type a name for your glossary entry (I always try to keep these names short and easy to remember; I call my em dashes "em").

6. Click on the Define button (<ALT> + D). Your em dash is now in your glossary.

   Note: *You can follow these general directions to create a glossary entry for every typesetters' punctuation mark and symbol you expect to use frequently.*

To use the em dash once it is in your glossary:

1. Place your cursor where the em dash goes, and type the name you gave it (in my case, "em"—but don't put a space after it).

2. Press the <F3> key (known as the "expand glossary" key).

To save your glossary entries:

1. Select Save All from the File menu (<ALT> + F, E).

2. Word prompts you to save the document you're currently working on. Answer Yes or No as you wish.

3. Word then prompts you to save the "global glossary and command changes." If you want to save your glossary entries, click on Yes or press Y.

   Note: *If you forget to save any glossary or macros changes that you've made, Word prompts you to save them when you exit. If you've made changes you don't wish to save—if you accidentally deleted a glossary entry, for example—answer No.*

If you format the text you put in the glossary with a particular typeface, size, and so on, whenever you use that glossary entry, it will have that same typeface, size, and other formatting. This is great for things like stationery headings, but what about typesetters' punctuation marks, return addresses, and the like, which should appear in whatever typeface and size you're currently using?

The answer is that you don't format such entries. If you don't specifically format your text with a particular typeface, size, and so on, that glossary entry takes on the *style* of whatever paragraph you use it in (see Chapter 7 for more on styles). This can create a problem if you're not using styles because even if you *think* you're not using styles, Word acts as though you are. You can solve this problem in one of two ways.

1. You can highlight the text and reformat it however you like.

2. You can redefine the Normal style so that it uses the typeface you're currently working with. This preferred method of handling the problem is fully explained in Chapter 7.

Other things you should know about glossaries include:

- You can delete glossaries. Just open the Glossary dialog box (<ALT> + E, O); scroll through the list of glossaries; highlight the one you want to delete by clicking on it; then click on the Delete button (<ALT> + L).

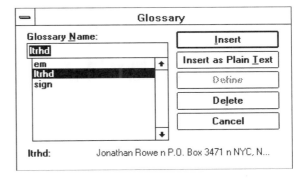

- You can *redefine,* or change, a glossary entry if you make a mistake. Just follow the instructions for defining a glossary entry, type in the name of the glossary you want to change, and click on Define. Word for Windows flashes a message asking whether you want to redefine the existing glossary. Click on Yes (or press Y) if you do.

- If you forget the names you've assigned varies glossary entries, open the Glossary dialog box. When you select an item's name, its text appears at the bottom of the dialog box. (Unfortunately, this feature doesn't show special characters such as em dashes.) You can also print these entries as a reference.

- You can insert a glossary entry whose name you've forgotten. Make sure your cursor is positioned where you want to insert the entry, and open the Glossary dialog box. Scroll through the entries, click on the one you want, and then click on the Insert button (<ALT> + I). If you want to insert an entry that you formatted in a particular way *without* the formatting, click on the Insert as Plain Text button (<ALT> + T).

Macros

When automating typesetters' punctuation marks, it can be somewhat easier to use macros than to use glossaries. There are two basic reasons for this. First, when you use macros, there's no need to worry about which typeface you're currently using, or about styles. Whatever typeface you're using is the one the macro will use. Second, typesetters frequently don't use spaces around em and en dashes. However, this can be a nuisance when using glossaries since there has to be a space before you type the glossary's name, else you'll get a message that the glossary doesn't exist.

Be careful when you record a macro. Everything you do during the recording session becomes part of the macro, and when you use it, the macro repeats every action. Also, when you're recording a macro, you can only use your mouse to open menus and select items from the Ribbon, dialog boxes, and so forth. You have to use your ARROW keys to move around the text area of your document.

To create a macro that stores an em dash:

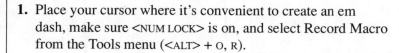

1. Place your cursor where it's convenient to create an em dash, make sure <NUM LOCK> is on, and select Record Macro from the Tools menu (<ALT> + O, R).

2. Type a name for the macro in the Record Macro Name box (I called mine EmDash). You can't use spaces or dashes in a macro's name.

3. Select a Shortcut key so you can use the macro without opening a menu (I selected <CTRL> + <SHIFT> + M). To do

this, simply select a key from the pull-down menu (or type one in, for example M). Word indicates whether that shortcut is currently Unassigned, or whether it's being used by another command. If it's being used by another command, just select a different key.

4. If you want, type a brief description of the macro.

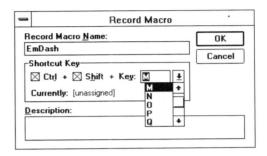

5. Click on OK or press <ENTER> when you're ready to start recording the macro. Once you're in your document, be careful. Whatever you do becomes part of the macro.

6. Create the em dash by holding down the <ALT> key and typing "0151" on the numeric keypad. Make sure <NUM LOCK> is on. Let up on the <ALT> key when you're done.

7. Select Stop Recorder from the Tools menu. You can do this with your mouse; or by pressing <ALT> + O, then R.

   Note: *You can follow these general directions to create a macro for every typesetters' punctuation mark and symbol that you expect to use frequently.*

To use a macro:

1. Place your cursor where you want the results of the macro to go.

2. Press the Shortcut keys to which you assigned the macro. For instance, if you want to use the em dash you recorded, press its Shortcut keys, such as <CTRL> + <SHIFT> + M.

You save macros just as you save glossary entries:

1. Select Save All from the File menu (<ALT> + F, E).

2. Word prompts you to save the document you're currently working on. Answer Yes or No as you wish.

What to Do When WYSIWYG *Isn't* What You Get

What you see on the screen isn't always what you get. In many cases, this can be fixed by a font manager such as Adobe Type Manager (ATM) or Bitstream's FaceLift. In other cases, you have to live with it. In any case, I highly recommend using a font manager because I find it's much easier to create high-quality documents and presentations the closer what I see on screen is to what I get when I print. The next version of Windows (version 3.1) is expected to include what's known as True Type, which should improve Word's WYSIWYG capabilities when you're using True Type fonts. You'll still need a font manager to provide WYSIWYG for your other fonts.

If you don't have a font manager, fonts look fine on your screen at relatively small sizes, but they look worse and worse as they get bigger (though they still print out fine if you have a laser printer). As a client of mine said when she saw her first 60-point Times on screen, "The rough edges are very apparent when it's as big as this."

The image on the left shows a 60-point Times "R" with the WYSIWYG capabilities of Windows 3.0. The one on the right shows that same "R" with Adobe Type Manager.

Both ATM and FaceLift give you much truer WYSIWYG than does Windows 3.0 alone. They draw screen fonts "on the fly"—in other words, when you use them—to any size up to 127 points, in any style, without jagged edges. However, ATM and FaceLift are substantially different in other ways, and those are worth mentioning here.

Adobe Type Manager

ATM provides high-quality "Type 1 PostScript outline fonts" for both your screen and printer. This means three things:

1. What you see is almost always what you get.

3. Word then prompts you to save the "global glossary and command changes." If you want to save your macros, click on Yes or press Y.

   Note: *If you forget to save glossary or macro changes that you've made, Word prompts you to do so when you exit. If you've made changes you don't wish to save—if you accidentally deleted a macro, for example—answer No.*

2. ATM works with all Windows printers, from dot-matrix printers to Hewlett-Packard LaserJets to high-resolution Linotronics used in service bureaus.

3. ATM gives you access to the largest number and highest quality computerized typefaces available.

Although Adobe Type Manager doesn't affect the print quality of PostScript printers, it does make it much easier to use additional "down-loadable" PostScript fonts (that is, fonts that don't come with the printer, but which you have to purchase and install separately). ATM also greatly improves the capabilities of dot-matrix printers. It not only enables them to use the same fonts as a PostScript printer, but it actually makes them print those fonts better than before. Type Manager also gives HP LaserJets the ability to use typefaces you used to need a PostScript printer to use.

Bitstream's FaceLift

FaceLift is another alternative to the dreaded "jaggies." Although many reviews of this product rate it as "second-best" to Adobe Type Manager, it excels in one area—it works with DOS applications as well as Windows. At the time of this writing, you can use the same Bitstream fonts with both FaceLift for Windows and FaceLift for WordPerfect 5.1.

Two other points are worth mentioning here. One is that Bitstream makes most sense for non-PostScript printers. If you have a PostScript printer, you should probably have Adobe Type Manager (Adobe Systems, Inc., actually invented PostScript). Second, although Bitstream's fonts are widely regarded as very good, Adobe's fonts are better still.

Dealing with Problems You Can't Fix

Although ATM and FaceLift can fix almost all of your WYSIWYG-that-isn't problems, occasionally you'll still bump into one they can't. An example is when a word spills over onto another line when it prints, even though on the screen it looks fine. One remedy for this is to use FILE, PRINT PREVIEW before printing. Although occasionally even this is wrong, in my experience it's wrong less often than either Normal or Page Layout view.

To correct a mistake made while recording a macro (in other words, to re-record a macro):

1. Select Record Macro from the Tools menu. Give the macro the same name you gave it previously. You can select either the same or different Shortcut keys.

2. Click on OK or press <ENTER> when you're ready to start recording the macro.

3. Word flashes a message asking whether you want to replace the existing macro. Click on Yes (or press Y) if you do.

You can use the Macro dialog box (<ALT> + O, M) to do the following:

- Select macros and Run them (you don't need to use the Shortcut keys).

- Delete them.

- Rename them.

- Edit them (this is a more advanced function).

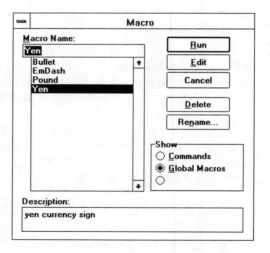

You can use the Options dialog box to reassign Shortcut keys, and to add macros to menus and to the Toolbar (see your Word for Windows manual for more information).

GREAT-LOOKING STUFF WITH DINGBATS AND SYMBOLS

There are literally hundreds of great ways to use the Symbol and Zapf Dingbats fonts. I'll show just a few here to get you started. These fonts are the easiest way I know to get "pictures" onto an otherwise pictureless page. I'm always using them in calendars, forms, reports, and as borders between sections.

✦ Dingbat Designs

Four groups of my favorite dingbat designs are presented in this section. You can use the first group, *Dingbat Ornaments,* to grace an important statement such as a fund-raising brochure, or to decorate a dull list in paragraph form. You can use the second group, *Dingbat Pictures,* when no other artwork is handy. The third group of designs, *Dingbat Bullets,* provides some alternatives to round bullets in bulleted lists. You can use the fourth group, *Dingbat Dividers,* to separate items on the same line, and as borders to separate sections. If you find a symbol or dingbat you'd like to use, look it up in the tables presented earlier in this chapter to see how to get it, or use the Symbol palette.

Dingbats and symbols can be formatted just like every other font, except that they don't accept type styles. If you boldface or italicize them, they won't *look* bolded or italicized. However, you can make them any size, you can expand or condense the character spacing between them, and sub- and superscript them. In fact, if you change a dingbat's size more than a few points, you'll *need* to sub- or superscript it in order to keep it in line with the surrounding text. Consider the following example.

Office of Graduate Admissions ☞

Office of Graduate Admissions ☞

Office of Graduate Admissions ☞

The top example is in 12 points. The middle example shows the text in 14-point bold, and the dingbat in 28 points. See how much higher it is than the rest of the line? The bottom example shows the dingbat subscripted by 5 points.

Dingbat Ornaments. The first example is adapted from a fund-raising brochure I helped produce for The Graduate School of Political Management. It shows one way to use dingbats to grace an important statement. The second example is part of a flyer design, taken from Chapter 2. It also uses dingbats as ornamental dividers—but this time to separate items for sale, instead of statements of purpose and mission.

The Trustees have established The Graduate School of Political Management to contribute to the advancement of professional politics. ❧ But the word "professional" itself suggests something more than the acquisition of technical skills. It implies a system of values which governs the conduct of the practitioner, and contributes to the public interest. ❧ Those who have been associated with The Graduate School of Political Management's development regard politics as a high calling. ❧ In the words of the English philosopher Bernard Crick, we hope to contribute "to the task of restoring confidence in the virtues of politics as a great and civilizing human activity." ❧

This example shows how to use dingbats to grace an important statement.

VASES ■ JEWELRY ■ MUGS ■ HAND-WOVEN RUGS ■ SILVERWARE ■ CUPS ■ PLATES ■ BOWLS ■ MUGS ■ JEWELRY ■ FURNITURE ■ PAINTINGS ■ PORTRAITS ■ SCULPTURE ■ ETCHINGS ■ CANDLE-STICKS ■ RINGS ■ PLATTERS ■ HAND-KNIT SWEATERS ■ LAMPS ■ CLOCKS ■ FRAMES ■ POTTERY ■ VASES ■ JEWELRY ■ MUGS ■

This example shows how to use dingbats to divide a long list of elements presented in paragraph form. The text is in 10-point Times caps. The square bullets are in 8-point Zapf Dingbats, subscripted by 1.5 points. (Remember that you have to use the Character dialog box to set subscripts and superscripts.)

Dingbat Pictures. The first example shows a good use of dingbats as pictures. Although the message is serious, the tone is light and the simple design is eye-catching. The second example illustrates a number of other uses of dingbats.

If you agree with the opinions expressed in this ad, express your own opinion by clipping ✂ this coupon, filling it ✎ out, and sending it ✉ straightaway to your state legislator. Or phone him ☎ and let him know that enough is enough.

This example shows how you can use dingbats as pictographs—pictures that represent ideas. In this case the pictures don't replace the words, but are used to reinforce what the reader can do to help solve the problem. In some cases, you can actually substitute pictures for words, which is what a true pictograph does (see the next example).

✔ IT OUT

Put Outgoing ✉ Here for Pickup

Sewing ✂ *Club*

✎ NOTES

Restrooms ☞

continued on the next page ➡

❏ Yes ❏ No

Happy ❤ *Valentine's Day* ❤❤

✘TRA! ✘TRA!

These examples show how easy it is to use dingbats to dress up headings, notes, or signs. If you'd like to try the Valentine's Day example, these are the specs. The first heart is 20 points, subscripted by the default of 3 points. The second and third hearts are both 10 points; the second is superscripted by 3 points; the third is subscripted by the same.

Dingbat Bullets.   Although you might feel more comfortable sticking with the tried and true "round bullet" for your lists, here are some dingbat alternatives just in case. Note that some dingbats are better suited to particular sizes than others. For instance, I usually reduce the black square (■) to 8 points (as shown in the following example). I think the circled numbers tend to look better in the larger type sizes that make them easier to read (they're shown here at 14 points). I also like the checkmarks a little oversized (12 points). Everything else in these examples is set at 10 points.

✔ save ALL receipts over $25

■ fill out form TE-1 for cash expenses (attached)

❸ fill out form TE-2 for credit card expenses (attached)

④ save ALL receipts over $25

◆ fill out form TE-1 for cash expenses (attached)

Here are five dingbat alternatives to the round bullet. The Zapf Dingbats font actually has four different sets of circled numbers—two sets of white numbers in black circles (one using serif numbers, the other sans serif) and two sets of black numbers in white circles (again, both serif and sans serif).

Dingbat Dividers.   Here are two ways to separate different items on the same line. The first example is from stationery; the second is from a flyer heading shown in Chapter 2.

Jonathan Rowe ▪ P.O. Box 3471 ▪ NYC, New York 10011 ▪ 212-777-4369

This stationery heading could just as easily use round bullets instead of these dingbats for dividers. The dingbats are set at 8 points and superscripted by 1.5 points.

OVER 75 REGIONAL ARTISTS & CRAFTSMEN

POTTERY ▪ PAINTINGS ▪ WOODWORK ▪ SCULPTURE

This heading is taken from a flyer shown in Chapter 2. The text is in 17-point Times and the dingbats are 10 points, superscripted by 2 points.

The following examples show some of the dingbat combinations you can use to create borders to separate sections in a booklet, brochure, newsletter, and so on.

All the dingbats shown here are 12 points, except for the second example, which is 7 points.

✦ Symbol Designs Although the Symbol font is somewhat specialized toward mathematics, it does have a few items that are more generally useful. It also has a few symbols you can't get anywhere else, including a round bullet that actually looks like a round bullet on your screen, a real ellipsis (…) with dots somewhat farther apart than if you just type in three periods, sans serif Registration and Copyright marks, and the Trademark symbol (both serif and sans serif). Since the Symbol font actually comes with Windows, you have it whether or not you have a PostScript printer or Adobe Type Manager.

Here are the Symbol fonts I've found most useful. Note that some of them are very similar to Zapf Dingbats (making them an excellent choice if you don't have Zapf Dingbats).

Code	Symbol	Code	Symbol
0167	♣	0211	©
0168	♦	0212	™
0169	♥	0214	√
0170	♠	0219	⇔
0171	↔	0220	⇐
0172	←	0221	⇑
0173	↑	0222	⇒
0174	→	0223	⇓
0175	↓	0224	◊
0183	•	0226	®
0188	…	0227	©
0190	—	0228	™
0210	®		

The following examples both use characters that come with the Symbol font. I've found the Symbol font particularly good for the simple flowcharts that are easy to do with Word's table functions (the arrows used here are also available as Zapf Dingbats). The second example is a simple border.

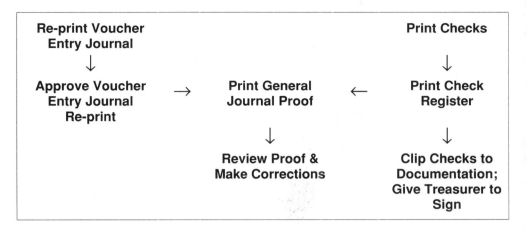

This is a portion of a flowchart describing a company's Accounts Payable process. The arrows are formatted in 14-point Symbol. Another example of this flow chart—created using Microsoft Draw—is shown in Chapter 20.

The white diamonds in this example are subscripted by 1.5 points.

CHAPTER 7

Looking Stylish

A paragraph **style** is nothing more than formatting you can reuse. It can be as simple as a preferred typeface and point size, or it can include all the formatting options you can think of. Once you format the styles for your main text, headings, captions, and so on, much of your design is done, too. The great thing about styles is that they make formatting and design easy. Once you develop a **style sheet**—in other words, set up the styles you want to use—for a report, brochure, slide show, whatever, you can reuse those styles as often as you like, even for different types of documents. You can also change a style sheet with just a few keystrokes and still maintain a consistent look.

I create styles for almost everything I do. Every time I work on a flip sheet or a manual, I set up the styles I'm going to use first. (This usually takes a grand total of about five or six minutes, even on those days when everything goes wrong.)

Many of the documents I produce frequently—reports, proposals, even invoices and letterhead—have a similar look. I have a special footer that gives my last name and the page number. My heads are often formatted the same, as is my main text. I use a standard cover page and follow a standard outline (I ardently believe in Dos and Don'ts #1: "Reuse your good ideas").

To speed the process of putting these documents together, I use special templates that include the styles I use and some standard text (Chapter 14 shows how to create your own templates and clarifies the differences among styles, templates, glossaries, and macros). While setting up a template can take ten or fifteen minutes, I can't possibly estimate how many hours it can save.

This topic of styles (with or without templates) may sound complex, but it really only *sounds* that way. The fact is, styles are the easiest way to improve the look of your publications and presentations. With them, you end up doing basic design and typography *while you're typing*. When you finish typing and applying styles, you've basically finished "typesetting" your document as well.

This chapter covers everything you need to know to start using styles right now. I go through each topic in the following order:

- The case for using styles.

- How to create styles using the Style dialog box.

- How to redefine Normal.

- How to create styles by example.

- How to access all Word's standard styles.

- How to use borders.

- How to use Word's pagination options.

- How to use indents.

- How to use the Numbered and Bulleted List icons on the Toolbar.

- How to use the Tabs dialog box.

- How to use advanced styling options—Based On, Next Style, and Merge.

USING STYLES TO MAKE YOUR LIFE EASIER AND YOUR DOCUMENTS BETTER LOOKING

Dos and Don'ts #11 is "Be consistent," but you can have too much of a good thing. A client of mine recently switched their magazine from a traditional to a desktop publishing system. Like many first-time desktop publishers, they were using all the typefaces they had in order to create "interest," and it wasn't a pretty sight. So, when I came on board, I campaigned for consistency. We eventually selected typefaces and type styles for the text, headlines, subheads, and so on and settled on a few different standard layouts, plus some special ones for regular features.

And did I get consistency. Once the basic design was set, it was set in stone. I then started a new song and dance: "Be consistent, not monotonous."

Sometimes, for example, no matter what your headline style is, a word needs special emphasis, like this headline from *New York Newsday*. "Seems" *needs* to be italicized, even if the standard headline style doesn't call for italics.

Well, Albany *Seems* Close To a Budget

Sometimes a headline requires other common-sense adjustments to the predetermined style. A short headline, for example, might need to be set in a larger type size than usual; an especially long headline might need smaller type; and so on. It's important to be consistent but to still use common sense. Styles help you do this.

When you define styles, you are simply specifying how you want different elements of your document to look—your headings, main text, captions, outquotes, and so on.

Consistency plays an even larger role in business publications because they tend to have fewer special cases. Still, you may not want every proposal, report, and presentation to look exactly like the last one. Styles let you change your mind quickly—and change it back again if you don't like the results. By using styles, you also expand the range of options available to you, for instance, generating a table of contents and an index automatically, and using Word's outlining feature.

✦ Styles in a Nutshell

Later sections cover all the subtleties of styles, but the basics are fairly straightforward.

A style is simply a name assigned to certain formatting (it is sometimes called a "paragraph style" because it affects whole paragraphs instead of individual words and letters). A style can specify typeface, point size, line spacing, alignment, and so on. When you apply a style to a paragraph, that whole paragraph immediately takes on the formatting specified in the style.

Word comes with several standard styles built-in; these appear on the Style menu on the Ribbon (see *Using* All *Word's Standard Styles* later in this chapter). The standard styles include Normal (for main text), and headings 1 through 3. Word automatically formats everything as Normal text unless you format it otherwise. To use a style other than Normal, just put the cursor anywhere in the paragraph you want to format, and then select a style from the Style menu (see the section *The Style Menu and How It Works* in Chapter 5 if you have questions about this).

These are the standard styles that appear on the style menu when you open a new document.

Although Word's standard styles are extremely useful, many people don't like how they look and want to redefine them right away. With this in mind, I explain how to redefine standard styles before I explain how to create them from scratch.

Word provides two methods for defining and redefining styles: 1) the Style dialog box method, and 2) the "by-example" method. Throughout this book, I generally use the dialog box method when giving instructions on styles. However, I explain the second method in *Styles by Example* later in this chapter. Although you should use the method you feel more comfortable with, be aware that there are options—such as Next Style— that are available only through the Style dialog box.

The Style dialog box (on the Format menu) is described in the following diagram.

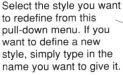

Word considers all text to be Normal text unless you format it otherwise by selecting a different style.

Diagram of the Style Dialog Box

Select the style you want to redefine from this pull-down menu. If you want to define a new style, simply type in the name you want to give it.

You can use Shortcut keys for styles, just as you can for macros. Simply select the keys you want to use. Word alerts you to whether that shortcut is currently Unassigned, or whether it's used by another command.

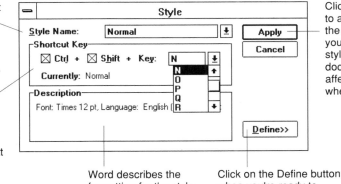

Click on the Apply button to apply the style listed in the Style Name box to your text. The Normal style affects the entire document; other styles affect only the paragraph where your cursor is.

Word describes the formatting for the style currently listed in the Style Name box.

Click on the Define button when you're ready to define or redefine a style.

To redefine existing styles using the Style dialog box:

1. Select Style from the Format menu (<ALT> + T, S). The Style dialog box opens (shown in the diagram above).

2. To redefine Normal, select it from the Style Name menu (it's already selected if your cursor is in a paragraph with Normal formatting). To redefine another style, for instance heading

187

1, select it now. See how the description of each style's formatting appears as you select it from the menu?

3. If you want, you can assign Shortcut keys to your styles. This enables you to apply styles to your text using keyboard commands, as well as by selecting them from the Style menu on the Ribbon. To assign a Shortcut key, simply select a key from the pull-down menu (or type one in—for example, N). Word indicates whether that shortcut is currently Unassigned, or whether it's being used by another command. If it's being used by another command, just select a different key.

   Note: *If you assign a Shortcut key to a style, you can apply that style simply by placing your cursor in the paragraph you want to style, and pressing the Shortcut key—for example, <CTRL> + <SHIFT> + N.*

4. Click on the Define button (<ALT> + D) when you're ready to redefine the style. When you do this, the dialog box expands to include additional options.

These buttons open the Character dialog box, Paragraph dialog box, Tabs dialog box, and so on. Each of these dialog boxes works the same whether or not you're defining styles.

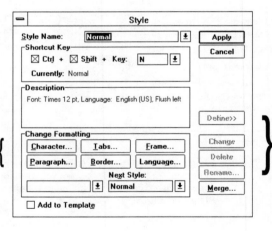

These commands become available depending on the selections you make. For instance, once you change a style, the Change button becomes available. If you select a non-standard style from the Style Name menu, you can Delete it or Rename it (you can't delete or rename Word's standard styles).

5. If you want to redefine any of the Character options—typeface, point size, type style, and so on—click on the Character button (<ALT> + C). If you want to change paragraph formatting options—line spacing, alignment, and so on—click on the Paragraph button (<ALT> + P). If you want to use borders in your style—as part of a heading, for example—click on the Border button (<ALT> + B).

The Tabs button (<ALT> + T) enables you to set tabs as part of your style; the Language button (<ALT> + G) enables you to select a language other than English (the spelling checker and other proofing tools automatically use the appropriate dictionary); and the Frame button (<ALT> + F) enables you to position the styled text or graphics in a specific location on the page (see Chapter 13). This last technique is great for creating a style for outquotes, by the way.

6. After you've made your changes to the selected style, you have an important choice to make. You can click either on the Change button (<ALT> + A), or the Apply button (just press <ENTER>). Here's the difference between the two options:

   a. When you click on the Apply button, Word saves the style, returns to your document, and applies the style to the paragraph where your cursor is (or to adjoining paragraphs that you highlighted).

   b. When you click on the Change button, Word saves the style but does *not* return to your document. This way, you can define or redefine several styles at one sitting, so to speak. When you've defined all the styles you want to define, click on Close to return to your document. If you want to automatically apply the *last* style you defined to the paragraph where your cursor is (or to any paragraphs you highlighted), however, click on Apply.

   Whether you choose Apply or Change, Word pops up a dialog box asking whether you want to "change the properties of the standard style." Answer Yes if you do (click on the Yes button, press Y, or press <ENTER>).

Note: *Whenever you redefine styles that you've already used in your document, Word automatically updates your text to use the new formatting. However, if you've redefined styles you haven't yet used in your text—heading 1 or heading 2, for example—you now have to apply those styles to the appropriate paragraphs.*

To define a style from scratch using the Style dialog box:

1. Select Style from the Format menu.

2. Type a name for this new style in the Style Name box.

3. If you want, you can assign a Shortcut key.

Redefine Old Styles or Create New Ones?

You should *redefine* all the standard styles. For example, redefine Normal for the main text, and redefine heading 1, heading 2, and so on for your headings. If you create new styles for your headings (such as Chapter Head, Chapter Subhead, and so on), you can't *automatically* generate a table of contents. Instead, you have to go through your document and mark the headings you want included in the contents with table entry fields (see Chapter 15).

If Word doesn't have a standard style to handle the type of formatting you need—an outquote, for example, or a caption—then create a new one.

4. Click on Define when you're ready to define the style (<ALT> + D).

5. Select the other formatting options using the appropriate dialog boxes. For example, select Paragraph to define paragraph formatting, Character to define character formatting, and so on.

6. When you've finished defining the style, click on Apply to save the style, apply it to the paragraph where your cursor is (or to highlighted text), and return to your document. However, if you don't want to apply the style immediately—or if you want to define or redefine other styles as well—click on Add to save the style (the Change button turns into an Add button when you define a new style). When you're ready to return to your document, click on Close.

Note: *If you want to make any changes to the new style, you can now redefine it just as you would a standard style.*

TEST RUN: Redefining Normal

The following example leads you through the process of redefining Normal. However, the process works the same no matter what style you redefine. Word comes out of the box with its

Normal style defined as 10-point Times, Auto line spacing, and flush left. It looks like the left-hand example below. However, you can easily format the Normal style so that each paragraph starts with an indent, or so that space automatically separates the paragraphs, as shown in the right-hand example.

Note: *You can redefine the Normal style using the by-example method, too.*

How wrong Emily Dickinson was! Hope is not the "thing with feathers." The thing with feathers has turned out to be my nephew. I must take him to a specialist in Zurich.
Had coffee with Melnick today. He talked to me about his idea of having all government officials dress like hens.
From Woody Allen's *Without Feathers*

How wrong Emily Dickinson was! Hope is not the "thing with feathers." The thing with feathers has turned out to be my nephew. I must take him to a specialist in Zurich.

Had coffee with Melnick today. He talked to me about his idea of having all government officials dress like hens.

From Woody Allen's *Without Feathers*

The example on the left is Word's default Normal style. The example on the right redefines Normal so that it has 13 points of leading (instead of Auto leading) and automatically puts .5 lines (6 points) of space After paragraphs.

To turn the left-hand example into the one on the right:

1. Type in some text (for instance, the text shown in the example). Although you don't need to type text before you define a style, it does let you see how the formatting looks.

2. Put your cursor anywhere in that paragraph, and select Style from the Format menu. If Normal isn't selected in the Style Name menu, select it. If you want, assign it a Shortcut key.

3. When you're ready to redefine Normal, click on Define (<ALT> + D). Then click on Paragraph (<ALT> + P) to change the style's line and paragraph spacing. Add .5 lines (6 points) of space after each paragraph by using the arrows or typing "6pt" in the After box (<ALT> + E).

4. Change the line spacing by selecting At Least from the Line Spacing menu, and typing "13pt" into the At box. Then click on OK or press <ENTER> to return to the Styles dialog box.

5. Click on Apply or press <ENTER> to return to your document. Word pops up a dialog box asking whether you want to "change the properties of the standard style." Answer Yes to redefine (click on the Yes button, press Y, or press <ENTER>).

When you return to your document, your Normal text will be formatted with the new Normal style. From now on, all the text you type will look like the text in the right-hand example, rather than the one on the left. However, styles are document-specific, which means that when you start a new document you'll have to redefine Normal again (or use Word's Merge styles command). If you want to redefine styles for use in new documents, you need to redefine the *Normal template* (see Chapter 14 for step-by-step instructions) or turn on the Add to Template option (<ALT> + E) in the Style dialog box.

Just Give Me a Different Face

Although it's easy to redefine Normal, it might be that all you want to change is the typeface and/or the point size. If this is the case, there's an even easier way. Simply select Character from the Format menu (<ALT> + T, C). Select the typeface and point size you want to use, and then click on the Use as Default button (<ALT> + D). Word pops up a dialog box asking whether you want to change the font for the Normal style to the typeface and point size you indicated. Answer Yes if you do (click on the Yes button, press Y, or press <ENTER>). When you use this feature, you're actually changing the typeface and/or point size for the Normal template—in other words, Word now uses these type specs for all your documents.

TEST RUN: Creating a Style from Scratch

Here's how to define a style for captions from scratch. The example uses essentially the same text as the previous example.

How wrong Emily Dickinson was! Hope is not the "thing with feathers." The thing with feathers has turned out to be my nephew (shown in the picture above left). I must take him to a specialist in Zurich.

This formatting above works well as a style for captions: auto-spaced 8-point Helvetica bold, with .5 lines (6 points) of space Before it to separate the caption from the graphic, and 16 points (slightly less than 1.5 lines of space After) to separate it from the next graphic, the main text, or whatever.

1. Type in some text (for instance, the text shown in the example).

2. Put your cursor anywhere in that paragraph, and select Style from the Format menu.

3. Type "caption" or the name you want to give the new style in the Style Name box. If you want, assign it a Shortcut key.

4. When you're ready to define the caption, click on Define (<ALT> + D). Then click on Character (<ALT> + C) to change the style's character formatting. Select Helvetica (or Helv) from the Font menu; 8 from the Point Size menu; and click on the bold button (<ALT> + B). Click on OK or press <ENTER> when you're done.

5. Click on Paragraph (<ALT> + P) to change the style's line and paragraph spacing. Use the arrows to select .5 lines in the Before box (or type ".5" or "6pt"), and type "16pt" in the After box. Click on OK or press <ENTER> when you're done.

6. Click on Apply or press <ENTER> to return to your document and apply the new style to the paragraph where your cursor is.

✦ Styles by Example

When you define or redefine styles by example, you bypass the Style dialog box. All you have to do is type some text, format it the way you want the style to look, and then tell Word that *that's* what you want the style to look like.

To redefine an existing style by example:

1. Put your cursor anywhere in the paragraph you want to use as the example. Then select the style you want to redefine from the Style menu on the Ribbon. For instance, if you want to redefine Normal, make sure Normal is selected. If you want to redefine heading 1, select that now.

2. Format the text the way you want the style to look. Select the formatting—typeface, point size, line spacing, and so on—using the Ribbon, and the Character and Paragraph dialog boxes on the Format menu.

3. When you finish formatting the paragraph just as you want the style to look, reselect the style from the Style menu on the Ribbon.

4. Word pops up a dialog box asking whether you want to redefine the style based on the selection. Answer Yes if you do (click on the Yes button, press Y, or press <ENTER>).

To create a style from scratch using the by-example method:

1. Type the text you want to use as the basis for a new style—for instance, the text for a caption you want to create, or the text for an outquote.

2. Format the text the way you want the style to look.

3. When you finish formatting the text, type the name you want to give that style in the Style menu on the Ribbon. There are two ways to do this:
   a. You can highlight the current name in the Style menu with your mouse, type over it, and then press <ENTER>.
   b. You can press <CTRL> + s. The cursor jumps into the Style menu. Type the new style's name, then <ENTER>.

Note: *If you want to make any changes to the new style, you can now redefine it just as you would a standard style.*

✦ Using *All* Word's Standard Styles

Word has 34 standard styles, although you generally see only four (Normal and headings 1 through 3). The additional styles include a header and footer; nine levels of headings (named headings 1–9); eight table of contents levels; and seven index levels. All of Word's standard styles are listed on the pull-down Style menu in the diagram labeled *Standard Styles*.

Note: *This is the only place you'll ever get to see all Word's standard styles at a single glance because Word only lets you see ten items at a time on its pull-down menus.*

You can add standard styles to your Style menu in a few ways:

Normal
annotation referenc ↑
annotation text
footer
footnote reference
footnote text
header
heading 1
heading 2
heading 3
heading 4
heading 5
heading 6
heading 7
heading 8
heading 9
index 1
index 2
index 3
index 4
index 5
index 6
index 7
index heading
line number
Normal
Normal Indent
toc 1
toc 2
toc 3
toc 4
toc 5
toc 6
toc 7
toc 8 ↓

Here's a menu showing all Word's standard styles. Note that many of them—header and footer, for example—appear automatically on the Style menu when you use the feature.

- You can use a feature attached to a style. For instance, when you use a header or footer, that style *automatically* appears on your Style menu. This is also the case with styles for tables of contents and indexes, annotations, footnotes, and line numbering.

- You can use the Style dialog box. Put your cursor in the paragraph you want to format using one of the standard styles not listed on the Style menu. Select Style from the Format menu and press <CTRL> + Y. This command lists all Word's standard styles on the Style Name menu. Open the menu and scroll through the list until you find the style you want—heading 4, for example—and select it. If you like, you can redefine the style at this point, or simply click on Apply or press <ENTER> to return to your document (this will also apply the style to the paragraph where your cursor is). If you check the Style menu on the Ribbon, the standard style you applied is now listed.

Note: *Generally, you'll only need to add a few standard styles to the Style menu, for example, headings 4 and 5. Most of the other standard styles are attached to specific features, so that when you use that feature, its style appears automatically on the Style menu.*

- You can type the name of one of these standard styles into the Style menu on the Ribbon. This is similar to defining a new style by example. Put your cursor in the paragraph you want to format using a standard style that isn't listed on your Style menu. Then press <CTRL> + S to highlight the Style

Type Specs for Word's Standard Styles

Style	Spec
Normal	10 pt Tms Rmn, flush left
Normal Indent	Normal + indent of .5 inches
Annotation Reference	Normal + 9 pt
Annotation Text	same as Normal
Footer	Normal + Center tab at 3 inches & a right tab at 6 inches
Footnote Reference	Normal + 8 pt, superscript 3 pt
Footnote Text	same as Normal
Header	Normal + Center tab at 3 inches & a right tab at 6 inches
Heading 1	Normal + 12 pt Helv bold, underline; 12 pt of space Before; Next style = Normal
Heading 2	Normal + NOT underlined; 10 pt of space Before; Next style = Normal
Heading 3	Normal + 12 pt Tms Rmn bold; NOT underlined; Indent of .25 inches; 8 pt of space Before; Next style = Normal Indent
Heading 4	Normal + 12 pt Tms Rmn; underlined; Indent of .25 inches; 6 pt of space Before; Next style = Normal Indent
Heading 5	Normal + 10 pt Tms Rmn bold; NOT underlined; Indent of .5 inches; 4 pt of space Before; Next style = Normal Indent
Heading 6	Normal + 10 pt Tms Rmn; underlined; Indent of .5 inches; 0 pt of space Before; Next style = Normal Indent
Headings 7–9 **(These three are the same.)**	Normal + 10 pt Tms Rmn italic; NOT underlined; Indent of .5 inches; 0 pt of space Before; Next style = Normal Indent
Index heading	Normal + Next style = Index 1
Indexes 1–7	Normal + an indent you need an equation to figure out: .25 inches x (level number −1)... e.g., **Index 5** is indented by (.25 x (5−1)) = 1 inch
Line number	Normal
TOC level 1	Normal + Right indent of .5 inches; Left tab at 5.75 inches and right tab at 6 inches
TOC levels 2–8	Normal + another indent you need an equation to figure out: .5 inches x (level number −1)... e.g., **Index 5** is indented by (.5 x (5−1)) = 2 inches

menu. Type the name of the style you want to use, for example, heading 4. (If you don't like to use keyboard commands, you can also highlight the Style menu with your mouse and then type the style name.)

The table on the preceding page shows the type specs (or formatting) for each of Word's standard styles. Notice that all of the styles say "Normal +," which means that they're *based* on Normal—that is, they have some formatting in common with Normal.

DESIGNING IN STYLE

Word's styles are a powerful design tool. Not only can you easily standardize your headings, captions, and so on with a specific typeface and point size, but you can create styles that include sophisticated formatting as well. When used in conjunction with templates (see Chapter 14), styles can turn even the complex job of designing a newsletter into a fairly routine matter. In this section, I cover many of the features that transform styles from a mere formatting feature into a professional design tool.

Students frequently ask: When is it worth creating a style? I've already mentioned that I create styles for almost everything I do. Even if I expect to use a particular style only two or three times in a document, I'll go ahead and create that style. The reason? It's likely that you or a co-worker or your boss will wake up one morning and decide that the headings (or some other element) don't look as good as they could. The type should be bolder or bigger or there should be more space between the lines.

When this happens—and it usually does—you will be glad you used styles. You can change them all at once simply by redefining the style, and that will be the end of it. If you want my advice, unless you're typing a laundry list, use styles.

This section covers four of the main features you can use to turn styles into professional design tools—borders, pagination, indents, and tabs. These features work the same whether or not you use them with styles. But combined with styles, these features enable you to create sophisticated designs as you type.

✦ Border Basics

Word has a great selection of borders. You can use them to create horizontal rules, boxes, grids, vertical rules, shadow boxes, and shaded boxes. Although I introduce borders here, the subject is too big to cover fully in this section. So I explain how to use borders with tables in Chapter 8, and with imported graphics in Chapter 11. The chart *Boxes and Rules* shows just some of the borders you can create in Word.

No matter what you want to border—a headline, a table, or a graph imported from Excel—you have to use the Border command on the Format menu to do it. This dialog box is shown in the following diagram.

Diagram of the Border Dialog Box

Click here to set a rule to the right of paragraphs.

Click here to set a rule above paragraphs.

Click here to set a rule to the left of paragraphs.

Click here to set a rule between paragraphs.

Click here to set a rule below paragraphs.

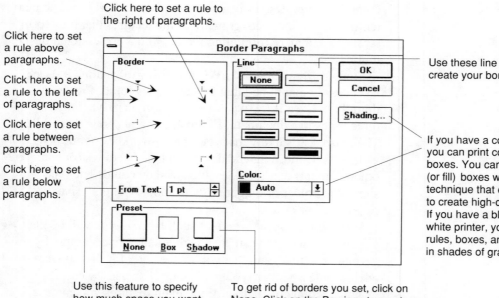

Use these line styles to create your borders.

If you have a color printer, you can print color rules and boxes. You can also *shade* (or fill) boxes with colors—a technique that enables you to create high-quality slides. If you have a black-and-white printer, you can print rules, boxes, and filled boxes in shades of gray.

Use this feature to specify how much space you want between the borders and the text.

To get rid of borders you set, click on None. Click on the Box icon to create a regular box, and the Shadow icon to create a shadow box.

To create boxes and rules:

1. Put your cursor anywhere in the paragraph where you want to use a border. If you want to *box* several paragraphs, highlight them all.

   Note: *When you are using this feature in connection with styles, you don't have to select the text until you apply the style.*

2. Select Border from the Format menu (<ALT> + T, B). The Border dialog box opens.

3. Select one of the Preset borders—Box (<ALT> + B) or Shadow (<ALT> + H)—or click on the sample page to indicate where you want the border to go. When you click on the sample page, all the **selection markers** (the tiny arrows marking the corners of your text) disappear, except for the ones which indicate where the rule will go. If you click in the wrong place, simply click somewhere else to position the rule where you want it. In the following sample, the rule will be placed *above* selected text.

4. Select the type of line you want the box or rule to use by clicking on it. The rule appears in position on the sample.

   Note: *To get rid of all the borders you've set and start over, click on None in the lower-left corner (<ALT> + N).*

5. If you want to position more than one rule around the text—for instance, one rule above and another below—click on the sample page to indicate where you want the next border to go, and then select the type of line you want it to use. You can position five different rules around text, as shown in the following example.

6. Click on OK or press <ENTER> when you're done.

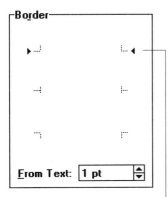

These selection markers indicate that the rule will be placed above the selected text.

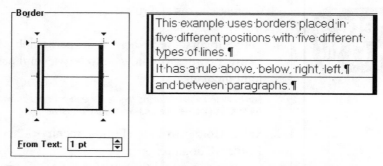

The sample border on the left created the "design" shown on the right.

Boxes and Rules

Horizontal Rules

Vertical Rules

Boxes

Grids

Shadow Boxes

Shaded Boxes

◆ Pagination

Word has three pagination options: Page Break Before, Keep With Next, and Keep Lines Together. You can use two of these options whether or not you use styles: Keep With Next (which keeps two paragraphs together on the same page) and Keep Lines Together (which keeps a single paragraph intact on a page). However, you should only use the third option, Page Break Before, when you want to define a style so that it *always* starts a new page. When you're typing—*not* defining styles— and want to start a new page, press <CTRL> + <ENTER> (this puts a page break just *above* the cursor).

You access these three pagination commands in the Pagination section of the Paragraph dialog box.

Pagination Options in the Paragraph Dialog Box

Use Page Break Before to define a style so that it always starts on a new page. This can be useful for chapter headings.

Use Keep With Next to keep paragraphs together on the same page. This is useful if you want to put a box around a group of paragraphs. If a page break falls within them, they move to the next page, box and all.

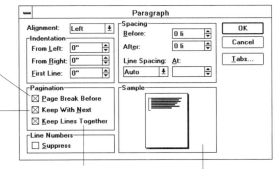

Use Keep Lines Together to prevent a single paragraph from breaking and spilling over onto the next page. This is useful if you want to box a paragraph. If a page break falls within such a paragraph, the entire paragraph moves to the next page.

Note how the sample page changes to reflect the options you have chosen.

To include a page break as part of a style:

1. As you are defining the style, click on Paragraph (<ALT> + P).

2. Click on Page Break Before (<ALT> + P).

3. Finish defining the style as usual.

Murder the Orphans But Save the Widows

Short lines at the end of a paragraph—a single word, for example—and the last line of a paragraph printed by itself at the top of a page or column are both called "widows." An "orphan" is the *first* line of a paragraph printed at the bottom of a page or column. Although both are considered to be bad form in publishing, orphans are considered to be worse because they interrupt the reader's eye movement at the beginning of a new thought. Most publishers get rid of orphans; many leave widows.

Word is set to automatically prevent both widows and orphans when printing. Although you may generally find this is a good idea, you may also find that it prevents you from fitting your text precisely on a page. This option can also make it next to impossible to make columns even along the bottom (see Chapter 13 for more information on columns).

To turn Widow/Orphan Control off:

1. Select Options from the Tools menu (<ALT> + O, O).

2. Select the Print category by clicking on the Print icon.

3. Click on Widow/Orphan Control to turn it off.

    Note: *You can turn this option off only for the document you're currently working on.*

4. Click on OK or press <ENTER> when you're done.

After you turn Widow/Orphan Control off, you will have to eliminate orphans (if they occur) by hand. To do this, you can edit the text; adjust the line spacing to allow another line to move up onto the page; or force the orphan onto the following page with a page break (<CTRL> + <ENTER>).

Note: *You should only use the Page Break Before option as part of a style definition. The only way to get rid of this type of page break is to open the Paragraph dialog box and turn it off.*

To prevent a page break from occurring within a group of paragraphs:

1. Highlight all the paragraphs you want to keep in the group, except the last one. (If you select the last one, the paragraph below it—in other words, the *next* paragraph—will become part of the group.)

   Note: *When you are using this feature in connection with styles, you don't have to select the text until you apply the style.*

2. Select Paragraph from the Format menu.

3. Click on Keep With Next (<ALT> + N).

4. Click on OK or press <ENTER> when you're done.

To prevent a page break from occurring within a single paragraph:

1. Put your cursor anywhere in the paragraph you want to keep intact on a page.

2. Select Paragraph from the Format menu.

3. Click on Keep Lines Together (<ALT> + K).

4. Click on OK or press <ENTER> when you're done.

To get rid of the Keep With Next and Keep Lines Together options:

1. Select the appropriate text.

2. Open the Paragraph dialog box and turn the Keep With Next option or the Keep Lines Together option off.

3. Click on OK or press <ENTER> when you're done.

PUTTING IT ALL TOGETHER: Styles, Glossaries, and Tabs

Say you have to do a weekly sales report, and you want to format it like the first of the following two examples. Every week you want to use this same exact heading; the only thing you want to change is the date. If this is what you want to do, you can't use styles to do it.

Styles have two important limitations. First, a style can handle only one set of formatting commands, not two. It can't handle 10-point text *and* 14-point text in the same paragraph (remember that styles apply to an *entire* paragraph). Second, a style can only store formatting, not text. Therefore, you can format the second of these two examples using styles (though you'll still have to type the heading in every week), but not the first.

Sales Summary   Folk Music and Jazz Department   Week ending 9/9/91

You can't format this heading as a style because Word can only use one set of formatting commands; it can't handle both 14- and 10-point text. Also, if you want to store the words as well as the formatting, you need to make this into a glossary entry. Be sure to include the carriage return as part of the entry—that's how the glossary remembers paragraph formatting.

Sales Summary

You can format this heading as a style. However, Word's styles only remember the formatting, not the words used.

You can easily store and reuse the heading in the first example—text, formatting, and all—by creating a glossary entry (see *Creating Your Own Glossary Entries and Macros* in Chapter 6 for more information).

To create the heading and store it as a glossary entry:

1. Type the text for the heading, putting a tab (that is, press the <TAB> *key once) between "Sales Summary" and the department name, and another tab between the department name and the date. (Remember: never use spaces to line up text.)*

   Note: *You don't have to adjust the tab settings on the Ruler now. As long as you use the <TAB> key when you're typing text, you can set the tab stops later.*

2. Format "Sales Summary" as 14-point Palatino bold. Format the department name and the date as 10-point Palatino bold.

3. Place the tab stops on the Ruler. Put a center tab at 3 inches and a right tab at 6 inches. (If you have trouble getting the right tab precisely to 6 inches, place it at some other measurement first and then *drag* it to the 6-inch marker). When you set the tabs, the text immediately lines up.

4. Make sure the cursor is somewhere in the heading, and then select Border from the Format menu (<ALT> + T, B). Click on the bottom of the sample page to indicate that you want the border to go *below* the paragraph. Then click on the second-to-thinnest line available. Click on OK or press <ENTER> when you're done.

5. Once you're back in your document, highlight the entire heading. Make sure you highlight the carriage return as well since this is what carries the paragraph formatting, including the border.

6. Use the EDIT, GLOSSARY command (<ALT> + E, O) to open the Glossary dialog box. Type the name you want to assign the heading, such as "sales." Then click on Define (<ALT> + D).

Now your heading is available at all times, no matter what document you're in. Just type the name you gave the glossary entry, such as "sales," and press <F3>.

Style	A standard format—including typeface, point size, line spacing, type style, and so on—that you can save and use for different design elements, for example, main text, headings, or outquotes.
Glossary entry	Text (both formatted and unformatted) that you can store for easy retrieval.
Macro	A series of commands (both keystrokes and mouse clicks) that you save for future use. You can assign a macro (or series of commands) to a Shortcut key, to a menu, or to the Toolbar.
Template	A "model" document that can contain customized menus, text and graphics (a logo, for example), special macros, special styles, a special glossary, and even a customized toolbar.

TEST RUN: Creating Styles Using Both Borders and Page Breaks

This example shows how to use Word's borders and Page Break Before command to create a style for a heading that always starts on a new page. Even if you use this heading only for new sections, you should call it heading 1, instead of, say, "Section Head." By redefining heading 1, you'll be able to automatically generate a table of contents. If you're following these instructions to create a heading style that you actually intend to use, you can tailor them to your own preferences.

Retirement Planning News

1. Type the heading "Retirement Planning News" or any other text you want to use.

2. Put your cursor anywhere in the heading, and select Style from the Format menu.

3. Select heading 1 from the Style Name menu. If you want to assign the heading to a Shortcut key, select a key from the pull-down menu—for example, 1.

4. When you're ready to define the style, click on Define (<ALT> + D).

5. Click on Character (<ALT> + C) and select the following: 18-point Palatino bold. Turn the single underline off (remember that Word's standard style for heading 1 includes an underline). Click on OK or press <ENTER> when you're done.

6. Click on Paragraph (<ALT> + P) and select the following: Centered alignment, Page Break Before, 1 line (12 points) of space Before, and 2 lines (24 points) of space After. Click on OK or press <ENTER> when you're done.

    Note: *If you have redefined your Normal style, you may also have to reset the line spacing to Auto and the indents to zero.*

7. Click on Border (<ALT> + B). Click on the top of the sample page to indicate that you want the border to go *above* the paragraph. Then click on the thickest line style available. It appears at the top of the sample page.

8. Set the From Text option to 3 points (you can do this either by typing "3" or by using the arrows; you don't have to type "pt" because Word's default measurement for this option is points). Click on OK or press <ENTER> when you're done.

9. Click on Apply to save the style and apply it to the paragraph where your cursor is. Word pops up a dialog box asking whether you want to redefine the standard style. Answer Yes if you do (click on the Yes button, press Y, or press <ENTER>).

Now, whenever you choose heading 1 from the Style menu, your text will be formatted in 18-point Palatino bold centered, with a thick border above. It will also be at the top of a new page.

✦ Using Indents

Word enables you to use four different types of indents: right and left paragraph indents, first line indents, and hanging indents. You can use the Ruler and the Paragraph dialog box to create all of these indents; you can use the Toolbar to create two of them (left paragraph indents and hanging indents). Each of these tools gives you a different degree of precision and flexibility, with the Toolbar being the least precise but the simplest to use and the Paragraph dialog box being the most precise but somewhat harder to use.

You don't have to use indents in connection with styles. But doing so gives you an important design tool. It spares you the trouble, for example, of creating an indent each time you want one. Just set the indent once when you define the style, and then simply apply (or select) that style to use that formatting again. This section explains how to create and use Word's four types of indents.

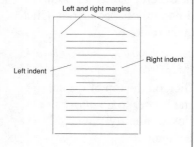

Left and right margins

Right indent

Left indent

Right and Left Paragraph Indents. The margins of your document indicate how far text and graphics print from the edge of the page. You can use **left and right paragraph indents** to emphasize particular paragraphs of text and graphics by setting them off from the margin, as shown in the example at left.

To create a left paragraph indent using the Toolbar:

1. Put your cursor anywhere in the paragraph you want to indent (if you want to indent several adjoining paragraphs at the same time, highlight them).

2. Click on the Indent icon on the Toolbar ⊞ . The left edge of the paragraph *indents* (in other words, moves to the right) by a half inch.

3. If you want to indent the paragraph further, click on the Indent icon again.

   Note: *The size of the indent equals the size of the default tab stops specified in the Tabs dialog box (see* Using the Tabs Dialog Box *later in this chapter).*

To *un*indent an indented paragraph using the Toolbar:

1. Put your cursor anywhere in the paragraph you want to unindent (if you want to unindent several adjoining paragraphs at the same time, highlight them).

2. Click on the Unindent icon on the Toolbar ⊞ . The left edge of the paragraph moves to the left by a half inch.

3. If you want to unindent the paragraph further, click on the Unindent icon again.

> **Note:** *The Unindent icon is also handy when you're typing indented text and want to return to the usual margin. When you get to the end of the indented text, press <ENTER> to start a new paragraph. Since Word copies the formatting from the previous paragraph when you start a new one, your new paragraph is also indented. Simply click on the Unindent icon to get back to the normal margin, and continue typing.*

Notice that as you indent and unindent your paragraphs, the Left Indent marker on the Ruler moves to the right. If you put your cursor in an indented paragraph and open the Paragraph dialog box, you'll see that the From Left measurement has also changed. Instead of zero, it now measures .5 inches.

As mentioned previously, you can use both the Ruler and the Paragraph dialog box themselves to set an indent. The advantage of using the Ruler is that you can set indents to any measurement within a sixteenth of an inch. The Paragraph dialog box lets you be even more precise—you can type *whatever* measurement you want, in inches or in points. You can also set

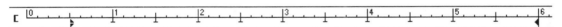

Lorem·ipsum·dolor·sit·amet,·consectetuer·adipiscing·elit,·sed·diam· nonummy·nibh·euismod·tincindunt.·Lorem·ipsum·dolor·sit·amet,· consectetuer·adipiscing·elit,·sed·diam·nonummy·nibh·euismod·tincindunt.¶

When you indent a paragraph, its Left Indent marker moves from zero (the margin) to the right, in this case to .5 inches.

Indentation		
From Left:	0.5"	⬍
From Right:	0"	⬍
First Line:	0"	⬍

When you indent a paragraph, the Paragraph dialog box—as well as the Ruler—reflects the change. In this case, the From Left measurement indicates that the selected paragraph has a .5-inch indent.

4

4

LOOKING STYLISH

right paragraph indents, as well as left indents, using both these tools.

To set a left indent using the Ruler:

1. Put your cursor anywhere in the paragraph whose left margin you want to adjust.

2. Grab the Left Indent marker by the *bottom*. If you grab it by the top, only the top half will move (which, by the way, is how you create a first-line indent).

3. Drag the marker to where you want it.

To set a right indent using the Ruler:

1. Put your cursor anywhere in the paragraph whose right margin you want to adjust.

2. Grab the Right Indent marker ◀ .

3. Drag the marker to where you want it.

To set a left indent using the Paragraph dialog box:

1. Put your cursor anywhere in the paragraph whose left margin you want to adjust.

   Note: When you are using this feature in connection with styles, you don't have to select the text until you apply the style.

2. Select Paragraph from the Format menu (<ALT> + T, P).

3. Word automatically positions your cursor in the From Left box. You can either type a measurement for the left indent (such as ".73"—no need to type "inches"), or you can use the arrows to select a measurement.

4. Click on OK or press <ENTER> when you're done.

To set a right indent using the Paragraph dialog box:

1. Put your cursor anywhere in the paragraph whose right margin you want to adjust.

2. Select Paragraph from the Format menu (<ALT> + T, P).

3. Position your cursor in the From Right box (<ALT> + R). You either can type a measurement for the right indent (such as ".73"), or you can use the arrows to select a measurement.

4. Click on OK or press <ENTER> when you're done.

Using Right and Left Paragraph Indents in a Style
When you define a style using the Style dialog box, just click on the Paragraph button (<ALT> + P) to set a left and/or right indent (the button opens the Paragraph dialog box). When you define a style by example, however, you can use either the Ruler or the Indent icon on the Toolbar to create the indent used as the example. (Remember that the Indent icon can only create a left indent.)

The method you use depends mainly on your own style. If you feel more comfortable dragging icons on the Ruler (which lets you see how things line up immediately) than typing measurements in a dialog box, here's one idea you might consider. Define the bulk of your style—everything except the indents—using the Style dialog box. Then *re*define the style using the by-example method, adding the indents to the definition.

First Line Indents. First line indents are often used to start new paragraphs. Although you have to press the <TAB> key on a typewriter (and even in many word processing programs) if you want a first line indent, you don't in Word. You just set the first line indent, and Word *automatically* indents the first line of a paragraph. If you like the look of first line indents, consider redefining Normal to include them. You can use both the Ruler and the Paragraph dialog box to create first line indents.

To set a first line indent using the Ruler:

1. Put your cursor anywhere in the paragraph for which you want to set a first line indent.

2. Grab the *top half* of the left indent marker.

3. Drag it to where you want it. (First line indents are often set at .2 or .25 inches.)

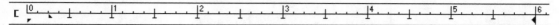

Lorem ipsum dolor sit amet, consectetuer adipiscing elit, sed diam nonummy nibh euismod tincindunt. Lorem ipsum dolor sit amet, consectetuer adipiscing elit, sed diam nonummy nibh euismod tincindunt. ¶

The first line indent in this example is set to .25 inches. When setting this indent on the Ruler, remember to grab just the *top half* of the Left Indent marker.

To set a first line indent using the Paragraph dialog box:

1. Put your cursor anywhere in the paragraph for which you want to set a first line indent.

    Note: *When you are using this feature in connection with styles, you don't have to select the text until you apply the style.*

2. Select Paragraph from the Format menu (<ALT> + T, P).

3. Position your cursor in the First Line box (<ALT> + F).

4. You can either type a measurement for the first line indent (such as ".2") or you can use the arrows to select a measurement.

5. Click on OK or press <ENTER> when you're done.

✦ Great-Looking Lists

Whenever you create a list, consider dressing it up with hanging indents. As a rule, hanging indents make lists more interesting to look at and easier to read. You can create them using the Toolbar, the Ruler, and the Paragraph dialog box.

The Toolbar gives you instant access to two types of lists—numbered lists and bulleted lists. Both are formatted as hanging indents. When you use the Numbered List icon to create a list, Word automatically numbers the items as you type. (Unfortunately, if you decide to delete items or move them around, you have to renumber them by hand.) The Bulleted List function is identical to the Numbered List function, except that it begins each item with a bullet. You can select the symbol you want for bullets and the numbering system you prefer in the Bullets and Numbering dialog box.

You can change the look of your lists easily by using the Bullets and Numbering dialog box on the Tools menu. This dialog box allows you to change the number format used by the Numbered Lists icon on the Toolbar and the bullets used by the Bulleted List icon. (It also allows you to change the number format used by Word's outlining feature; refer to the manual that came with Word for Windows for more information on this.)

To create a numbered or bulleted list using the Toolbar:

Here's HOW

1. Put your cursor where you want the list to go.

2. Click on the Numbered List icon ▤ or the Bulleted List icon ▤ on the Toolbar. Word automatically inserts a "1" or a bullet, formats the item as a hanging indent, and repositions the cursor at the indent, where you should start typing.

3. After you type the first item, press <ENTER> to start a new paragraph for the second item. Click again on the Numbered or Bulleted List icon. Word automatically inserts a "2" or a bullet, formats the item, and repositions your cursor. Keep doing this until you're done.

   Note: *When you're creating a numbered list, you might find it quicker to simply type subsequent numbers yourself and press the <TAB> key to reposition the cursor at the indent. The Numbered List icon is most important as a tool to create a hanging indent. Since Word copies the formatting from the previous paragraph when you press <ENTER>, subsequent paragraphs all have the hanging-indent format. The Bulleted List icon remains useful throughout the list because it saves you the trouble of typing a code or using macros or glossary entries to create the bullet.*

4. When you finish typing the list, you will probably want to get rid of the hanging indent format and reset your left paragraph margin to zero. To do this, simply press <CTRL> + G, or reselect Normal from the style menu.

   Note: *If you reselect Normal from the style menu, Word pops up a dialog box asking whether you want to redefine Normal based on the selection. Answer No.*

To change the bullets used by the Bulleted List icon on the Toolbar:

1. Select Bullets and Numbering from the Tools menu (<ALT> + O, B).

2. When the dialog box opens, click on the bullet you want to use.

3. If you want, you can change the size of a bullet. Simply click on the one you want to change, and then type a new size in the Point Size box (<ALT> + P). You can also use the arrows to select a size.

4. If you don't like any of the bullets listed in the box, you can get new ones. Click on the one you want to replace, and then click on the New Bullet button (<ALT> + N). The Symbol palette opens (see *Using the Symbol Palette* in Chapter 6). Select the symbol you want included in the list of bullets. When you return to the dialog box, it's there. You can now select it and size it just as you would any other bullet.

Diagram: Designing with Bullets

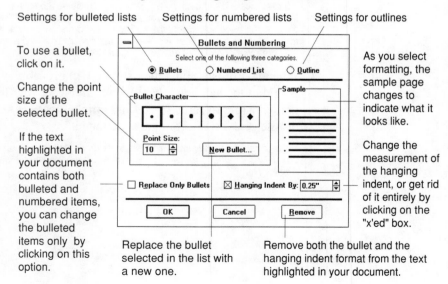

Settings for bulleted lists   Settings for numbered lists   Settings for outlines

To use a bullet, click on it.

Change the point size of the selected bullet.

If the text highlighted in your document contains both bulleted and numbered items, you can change the bulleted items only by clicking on this option.

As you select formatting, the sample page changes to indicate what it looks like.

Change the measurement of the hanging indent, or get rid of it entirely by clicking on the "x'ed" box.

Replace the bullet selected in the list with a new one.

Remove both the bullet and the hanging indent format from the text highlighted in your document.

Bullets and Numbering
Select one of the following three categories.
○ Bullets   ○ Numbered List   ○ Outline
Bullet Character
Point Size: 10
New Bullet...
Sample
□ Replace Only Bullets   ⊠ Hanging Indent By: 0.25"
OK   Cancel   Remove

5. If you want to change the size of the hanging indent created by the Bulleted List icon, type the measurement you want in the Hanging Indent By box (<ALT> + H), or use the arrows.

6. Click on OK or press <ENTER> when you're done.

> **Note:** *You can also change the bullets in a list you've already typed. Simply highlight the list, and open the Bullets and Numbering dialog box (<ALT> + O, B). Select the bullet you want, and click on OK or press <ENTER> when you're done. You can use this same procedure to turn a numbered list into a bulleted list.*

Diagram: Designing with Numbers

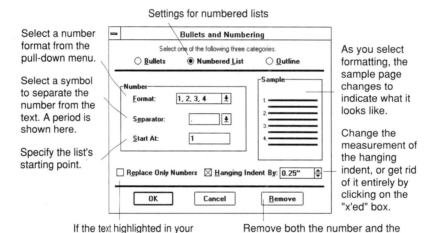

Settings for numbered lists

Select a number format from the pull-down menu.

Select a symbol to separate the number from the text. A period is shown here.

Specify the list's starting point.

As you select formatting, the sample page changes to indicate what it looks like.

Change the measurement of the hanging indent, or get rid of it entirely by clicking on the "x'ed" box.

If the text highlighted in your document contains both bulleted and numbered items, you can change the numbered items only by clicking on this option.

Remove both the number and the hanging indent format from the text highlighted in your document.

To change the number format used by the Numbered List icon on the Toolbar:

1. Select Bullets and Numbering from the Tools menu (<ALT> + O, B).

2. When the dialog box opens, click on the Numbered List option (<ALT> + L).

3. Select a number format from the Format menu (<ALT> + F), for example, "i, ii, iii."

4. Select the symbols you want to separate the numbers from the text from the Separator menu (<ALT> + E), for example, "( )."

5. If you want the list to start at a number other than 1, type the starting point in the Start At box (<ALT> + S).

6. If you want to change the size of the hanging indent created by the Numbered List icon, type the measurement you want in the Hanging Indent By box (<ALT> + H), or use the arrows.

7. Click on OK or press <ENTER> when you're done.

> **Note:** *You can also change the format for numbers in a list you've already typed. Simply highlight the list, and open the Bullets and Numbering dialog box (<ALT> + O, B). Select the format you want, the separator, and so on, and click on OK or press <ENTER> when you're done. You can use this same procedure to turn a bulleted list into a numbered list.*

Hanging Indents. Technically, hanging indents are the opposite of first line indents. In a first line indent, the first line of text is indented, and the rest of the text lines up along the left margin. In a hanging indent, the first line of text starts at the margin (where you place a number or bullet), and the rest lines up at the indent. If you place your cursor in a paragraph formatted as a hanging indent, you'll notice that the Left Indent markers on the Ruler are also in a position opposite to that of a first line indent.

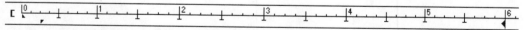

• → Lorem ipsum dolor sit amet, consectetuer adipiscing elit, sed diam nonummy nibh euismod tincindunt. Lorem ipsum dolor sit amet, consectetuer adipiscing elit, sed diam nonummy nibh euismod tincindunt.¶

The hanging indent in this example is set to .25 inches. When setting this indent on the Ruler, hold down the <SHIFT> key, and grab only the *bottom half* of the Left Indent marker. After the number or bullet identifying the item, press the <TAB> key to position the cursor at the indent, where you should start typing.

There are two handy keyboard commands for use with hanging indents: <CTRL> + N creates a hanging indent at the first default tab stop, and <CTRL> + G gets rid of it.

Indentation

From Left:	0.25"	⬍
From Right:	0"	⬍
First Line:	-0.25"	⬍

This is how a .25-inch hanging indent looks in the Paragraph dialog box. Notice that the measurement for the first line of the indent is negative—in other words, it's to the left of the indent itself.

To set a hanging indent using the Ruler:

1. Put your cursor anywhere in the paragraph for which you want to create a hanging indent.

2. Hold down the <SHIFT> key, and then grab the bottom half of the Left Indent marker. (You must always hold down the <SHIFT> key to move the bottom half of the marker separately from the top half.) Drag the bottom half of the marker to where you want the indent to begin (for example, .25 inches). Don't let up on the <SHIFT> key until you have the bottom half of the marker correctly positioned.

3. When you finish typing the list and are ready to get rid of the hanging indent format and reset your left paragraph margin to zero, press <CTRL> + G or reselect Normal from the Style menu.

   Note: If you reselect Normal from the Style menu, Word pops up a dialog box asking whether you want to redefine Normal based on the selection. Answer No.

To set a hanging indent using the Paragraph dialog box:

1. Put your cursor anywhere in the paragraph for which you want to set a hanging indent.

   Note: When you are using this feature in connection with styles, you don't have to select the text until you apply the style.

2. Select Paragraph from the Format menu (<ALT> + T, P).

3. In the From Left box, you can either type a measurement for the hanging indent (such as .25), or you can use the arrows to select a measurement.

4. Position your cursor in the First Line box (<ALT> + F), and type (or select) the same number as that in the From Left box, but *precede it with a negative number.* This indicates that the first line of the hanging indent starts to the left of the rest of the indent, which it does.

5. Click on OK or press <ENTER> when you're done.

✦ Using the Tabs Dialog Box

There are five reasons to use the Tabs dialog box instead of setting tabs on the Ruler.

1. If you want to use tabs as part of styles (especially when defining styles with the Style dialog box).

2. If you want to set tab stops with extreme precision, say, at 2.83 inches.

3. If you want to use a particular tab measurement which you can then apply consistently in different circumstances (for instance, to the two columns at either end of a table).

4. If you want to get rid of *all* the tabs in a particular paragraph and start over with a clean slate. This is an important feature because it's possible to unwittingly place tabs on the Ruler (outside the margins) that you can't find, but you need to eliminate because they are wreaking havoc with other settings.

5. If you want to use **tab leaders**, which is what Word does when it generates a table of contents. (Tab leaders are

Diagram of the Tabs Dialog Box

Set default tab stops by typing a measurement or using the arrows.

Type the measurement at which you want to place a tab on the Ruler.

The scroll box lists the tabs in the text highlighted in your document.

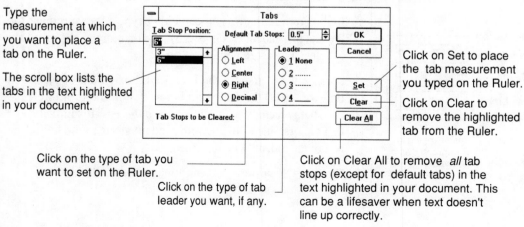

Click on Set to place the tab measurement you typed on the Ruler.

Click on Clear to remove the highlighted tab from the Ruler.

Click on the type of tab you want to set on the Ruler.

Click on the type of tab leader you want, if any.

Click on Clear All to remove *all* tab stops (except for default tabs) in the text highlighted in your document. This can be a lifesaver when text doesn't line up correctly.

dotted, dashed, or solid lines that "lead to" the tab stop. They're common in directories and in other kinds of publications where readers have to follow along from one side of a page to the other in order to find the information they want.)

To use the Tabs dialog box:

1. Put the cursor in the paragraph for which you want to set tabs.

   Note: *When you are using this feature in connection with styles, you don't have to select the text until you apply the style.*

2. Select Tabs from the Format menu (<ALT> + T, T).

3. If you want to get rid of some tabs that have already been set, click on the Clear All button. You can also clear tabs individually by selecting the one you want to delete and then clicking on Clear.

4. Select the *type* of tab you want to set—right, center, and so on.

5. Select a leader if you want one; the default is None.

6. Type the measurement at which you want this tab set. Click on Set to place it on the Ruler. If you want to set another tab stop on the Ruler, you can do so now.

7. Click on OK or press <ENTER> when you're done.

   Note: *You can also change the type of a tab stop already on the Ruler, or add a leader. To do this, simply select the text containing the tab, and open the Tabs dialog box. Select the tab you want to change from the scroll box, and then select the type of tab you want it to be and/or the leader you want it to use.*

✦ More Styling Options

Now that you know the basics of most of the formatting that can be included in styles, all that's left is three features: Based On, Next Style, and Merge. (I cover how to use styles with the Frame command in Chapter 13; see the manual that came with Word for Windows for information on using styles with the Language command.)

Merge. The Merge command lets you use the styles you set up in another document (or in a template) in the document you're currently working on. For instance, if you created styles for a report or pamphlet, and decide you'd like to use these same styles in the document you're now working on, you can.

To merge styles from another document or a template with the document you're currently working on:

1. Select Style from the Format menu (<ALT> + T, Y).

2. Click on Define (<ALT> + D).

3. Click on Merge (<ALT> + M). This opens the Merge dialog box, which works like the dialog box you use to open documents, except that it automatically lists *templates* instead of documents. If you want to use the styles on a particular template, select it from the list. If necessary, change the directory to locate the template you want.

4. If you want to merge styles from a *document* rather than a template, change the File Name to read "*.doc" (this way, the scroll box lists all files with the "doc" ending that Word assigns documents, rather than the "dot" ending it assigns templates). If you want, you can select the Word Document file type from the menu at the bottom of the dialog box. Select the document whose styles you want to use from the list. If necessary, change the directory to locate the correct document.

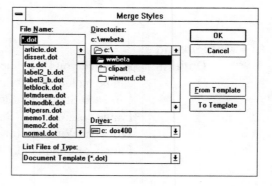

5. Click on OK or press <ENTER> when you're done. Word pops up a dialog box that asks whether you want to replace the styles of the same name in your current document with those in the document you've selected. Answer Yes if you do (click on Yes, press Y, or press <ENTER>).

6. Click on Close to get back to your document.

Based On. The Based On command enables you to create several related styles with similar formatting characteristics. This way, if someone decides that the headings should be in Helvetica-Narrow rather than Helvetica, you can change them all simply by changing the style they're based on.

Remember that Word's standard styles are all based on Normal. This means that if you change the line spacing for Normal to, let's say double, other standard styles will then be double-spaced—the footer, for instance, and the headings. One way to get around this problem is to get rid of the link between certain standard styles and Normal.

To get rid of the link between a standard style and Normal:

1. Select Style from the Format menu.

2. Select the standard style you no longer want to have based on Normal.

3. Click on Define (<ALT> + D).

4. Highlight Normal in the Based On menu and delete it (just hit the <DELETE> key).

   Note: *At this writing, you have to press the <TAB> key or click on another formatting option to make the Change button available.*

5. Click on Change (<ALT> + A), then click on Close.

   Note: *You can use this technique to break the link between* any *style that's based on another that you want to change.*

To base one style on another:

1. Select Style from the Format menu.

2. Select or create the style you want to use as the **base** style. For instance, if you want to define a series of related headings, use heading 1 as the base style—in other words, the style on which the other headings will be based.

3. Click on Define (<ALT> + D) and redefine heading 1 as you want it. As part of this redefinition, you'll probably want to break the link between it and Normal (see the previous section if you have any questions).

4. When you're done, click on Change (<ALT> + A).

5. Select the next style you want to create or redefine, for instance, heading 2.

6. Select the style you want to base it on—such as heading 1—from the Based On menu. Then make whatever changes you want to the style. Styles that are based on one another can look quite different, despite having certain formatting—such as typeface—in common. For example, heading 1 might have a border above it, while the other heading styles—all based on heading 1—don't have borders. In this case, you would have to delete the border from each of the other heading styles. Click on Change when you're done.

7. Click on Close to get back to your document.

Next Style.   You can set up your styles so that they automatically apply the next style that should come in your document. This enables you to truly typeset your document as you type. For example, you probably want Normal text to follow your headings. You can define these headings in such a way that when you press <ENTER> at the end of a heading, Word automatically formats the next paragraph as Normal. Similarly, you might have a style for graphs that you always want followed by a caption style. The Next Style feature enables you to do this.

To use the Next Style feature:

1. Select Style from the Format menu.

2. Select the style you want to define.

3. Click on Define (<ALT> + D), and define the style. If you want, base it on another style.

4. Select the style you want to use as the Next Style from the Next Style menu (<ALT> + X).

5. Click on Change, and then on Close.

PUTTING IT ALL TOGETHER: Designing in Style

The following example shows how to use the Style dialog box to take full advantage of Word's styling options to simplify the creation, not only of styles themselves, but of an entire page design. The example used is from an office procedures manual, but the layout works just as well for reports and even booklets. Once you define the styles in this example, you need only type the text and apply the styles to produce the design shown here. You can use the Bulleted List icon on the Toolbar (explained earlier in this chapter) to create the hanging indents.

OFFICE PROCEDURES

Tipsum dolor sit amet, consectetuer adipiscing elit, sed diam nonummy nibh euismod tincidunt ut laoreet dolore magna aliquam erat volutpat. Ut wisi enim ad minim veniam, quis nostrud exerci tation ullamcorper suscipit lobortis nisl ut aliquip ex ea commodo feugiat consequat:

- lorem ipsum dolor sit amet lorem ipsum dolor sit amet lorem ipsum dolor sit amet

- ipsum dolor sit amet nonummy nibh euismod

- magna aliquam erat volutpat

- quis nostrud exerci tation ullamcorper suscipit

- lorem ipsum dolor sit amet lorem ipsum dolor sit amet lorem ipsum dolor sit amet

- dolor sit amet lorem ipsum dolor sit amet lorem ipsum dolor sit amet quis nostrud exerci tation ullamcorper suscipit

Internal Control Procedures

Tipsum dolor sit amet, consectetuer adipiscing elit, sed diam nonummy nibh euismod tincidunt ut laoreet dolore magna aliquam erat volutpat. Ut wisi enim ad minim veniam, quis nostrud exerci tation ullamcorper suscipit lobortis nisl ut aliquip ex ea commodo feugiat consequat.

Consectetuer adipiscing elit, sed diam nonummy nibh euismod tincidunt ut laoreet dolore magna aliquam erat volutpat. Ut wisi enim. Lorem ipsum dolor sit amet, consectetuer adipiscing elit, sed diam nonummy nibh euismod tincidunt ut laoreet dolore magna aliquam erat volutpat. Ut wisi enim ad minim veniam, quis nostrud exerci tation ullamcorper suscipit lobortis nisl ut aliquip ex ea commodo feugiat consequat.

Approvals

Dolor sit amet, consectetuer adipiscing elit, sed diam nonummy nibh euismod tincidunt ut laoreet dolore magna aliquam erat volutpat. Ut wisi enim ad minim veniam, quis nostrud exerci tation ullamcorper suscipit lobortis nisl ut aliquip ex ea commodo feugiat consequat. Dlore magna aliquam erat volutpat. Ut wisi enim ad minim veniam, quis nostrud exerci tation ullamcorper suscipit lobortis nisl ut aliquip ex ea commodo feugiat.

Tipsum dolor sit amet, consectetuer adipiscing elit, sed diam nonummy nibh euismod tincidunt ut laoreet dolore magna aliquam erat volutpat. Ut wisi enim ad minim veniam, quis nostrud exerci. Lorem ipsum dolor sit amet, consectetuer adipiscing elit, sed diam. Tipsum dolor sit amet, consectetuer adipiscing elit.

3

Here are the specs for the four styles used in this document.

Normal 11-point Helvetica on At Least 16 points of line spacing; .5-line (6 points) of space After each paragraph; indented .25 inches From Left

heading 1	14-point Times bold, caps on Auto line spacing; 12 points of space Before, and 3 points of space After; rule above; 0 indent From Left
heading 2	heading 1 + NO rule; upper/lowercase
heading 3	heading 2 + italic; upper/lowercase; indented .25 inches From Left; 9 points of space Before

This example shows how you can define each of the four styles in this report using the Style dialog box. One of the advantages the Style dialog box has over the by-example method is that the dialog box lets you define styles *before you type in a word of text*. That's how to handle this example.

1. Select Style from the Format menu (<ALT> + T, Y).

2. If it's not already selected, choose Normal from the Style Name menu. If you want, assign Normal to a Shortcut key, such as N.

3. Click on Define (<ALT> + D) to redefine Normal.

4. Click on Character (<ALT> + C). Select Helvetica (Helv) from the Font menu and 11 from the Point Size menu. Click on OK or press <ENTER> when you're done.

5. Click on Paragraph (<ALT> + P). Type ".25" in the From Left box (remember that this moves the left paragraph margin a quarter of an inch to the *right*). Select .5 line (or type "6pt") in the After box. Set the line spacing to At Least, and type "16pt" in the At box. Click on OK or press <ENTER> when you're done.

6. Although you've finished formatting Normal, you still have four more styles to do. Click on Change (<ALT> + A). Word pops up a dialog box asking whether you want to change the standard style. Answer Yes.

7. Select heading 1 from the Style Name menu. If you want, assign it to a Shortcut key, such as 1. If you look at the Based On menu at the bottom of the dialog box, you'll see that heading 1 is based on Normal. You should unlink it from Normal so that any changes you later make to the main text won't affect your headings. To do this, highlight Normal in the Based On box (<ALT> + O), and delete it.

8. Click on Character, then select Times (Tms Rmn) from the Font menu, and 14 from the Point Size menu. Select bold and all caps; *un*select the single underline. (Remember that the underline is part of Word's standard style for heading 1.) Click on OK or press <ENTER> when you're done.

9. Click on Paragraph. Type "3pt" in the After box. Notice that "1 li" (which equals 12 points) already appears in the Before box; again, this is part of Word's standard style. You know that

you have successfully unlinked heading 1 from the Normal style if there's a zero on the From Left box instead of .25, which is now the left paragraph indent for the Normal style. Make sure Line Spacing is set to Auto. Click on OK or press <ENTER> when you're done.

10. Click on Border (<ALT> + B). Click on the top of the sample page to indicate that you want the border to go above the paragraph. Then click on the second-to-thinnest line available. Set the From Text option to 2 points (you can do this either by typing "2" or by using the arrows). Click on OK or press <ENTER> when you're done.

11. Make sure the Next Style (<ALT> + x) is Normal. Click on Change to redefine heading 1.

12. Select heading 2. If you want, assign it to a Shortcut key, such as 2. Notice that it's currently based on Normal. To make it possible to change all your headings simply by redefining heading 1, base heading 2 on heading 1. To do this, select heading 1 from the Based On menu. Then format heading 2 as 14-point Times bold, upper/lowercase (in other words, *not* all caps) with 1 line (12 points) of space Before, and 3 points After. Make sure the heading is at the left margin of the page—in other words, that it does *not* have a quarter of an inch left paragraph indent—and that the line spacing is set to Auto. Delete the Border above it by opening the Border dialog box and clicking on None in the lower left corner. Again, make sure the Next Style is Normal. After you define heading 2, move on to heading 3.

13. Set heading 3 so that it's based on heading 1. Note that part of Word's standard styling is to follow heading 3 with text formatted in the Normal Indent style. You don't want this! So select Normal from the Next Style menu. Then format heading 3 as 13-point Times bold, italic, and upper/lowercase. Note that you *want* heading 3 to be indented .25 inches From Left, so make that change in the Paragraph dialog box. Put "9pt" Before the heading and "3pt" After. Delete the Border above heading 3 by opening the Border dialog box and clicking on None in the lower left corner.

14. Click on Change, and then click on Close to return to your document.

15. Now you can see how styles really do allow you to typeset your documents as you type. Select heading 1 from the Style menu before you type the text for that heading (if you assigned the heading a Shortcut key, you can simply press it). As you type, Word automatically formats it with the style you defined as heading 1. When you press <ENTER>, Word automatically starts formatting text as Normal. When you come to a second-level head, select the style for heading 2. Again, Word formats the heading as you type, and when you press <ENTER>, it returns to the Normal style.

16. One last thing: I generally use footers to number pages because they allow you to add design touches and useful information, as well as page numbers. However, if all you need is a page number—as in this example—here's another way. Select Page Numbers from the Insert menu (<ALT> + I, U). Then select the options Bottom of Page and Center.

CHAPTER 8

Designing with Tables

When most people think of tables (*if* they think of tables), they picture tedious columns of numbers. When I think of tables, however, I think of how easily you can use them to create all sorts of publications and presentations. Tables in Word are really a design tool that lets you lay out text and graphics in interesting ways. When you use tables to design a publication, only you will ever know it's a table. Readers will see an appealing design—nothing more or less. Chapter 2 contains several examples of what I mean: the Little Bank letter-fold brochure, the Membership at the Museum brochure cover, and the Busy People catalog.

This chapter focuses on how to use tables to create appealing designs—with and without columns of numbers. This chapter is organized around two examples: an advertisement (adapted from Chapter 2) and an informational report or presentation. Each design uses some essential features of tables.

This chapter covers these topics in the following order:

- How to create a table.

- How to change column widths.

- How to use the formatting features on the Table menu.

- How to use borders and shading with tables.

- How to add using Word.

BASIC TABLES

Most features of Word work the same with or without tables. You format text exactly the same way; you adjust line and paragraph spacing using the commands you used in the other chapters; and you handle styles the same way. However, tables introduce a number of new and easy-to-use design tools as well—from the ability to create no-nonsense columns to complex forms. You can put almost anything in a table: text, rules, WordArt (see Chapter 10 for information on this), and graphics of all sorts. The only thing you can't put in a table is another table.

✦ Getting Started

Word refers to the act of creating a table as "inserting" the table into a document. You can insert tables in one of two ways: by mouse or by menu. Before you create a table, however, make sure that the Gridlines option on the Table menu is on so you can see the "invisible" border that outlines the table.

Note: *You can add "visible" borders to tables as well (see* Designing Borders *later in this chapter).*

To insert a table using your mouse:

1. Put your cursor where you want the table to go (give yourself a few extra carriage returns around this point so you have some extra room to work).

2. Click on the Table icon on the Toolbar ▦.

3. Word displays a small grid. Simply drag the mouse over the grid to indicate the number of columns and rows you want in the table. Practically speaking, selecting the correct number of columns is much more important than selecting the correct number of rows, because it's so easy to add additional rows. I generally start my tables with only one or two rows.

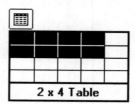

2 x 4 Table

To create a table using menu commands:

1. Put your cursor where you want the table to go (remember to give yourself a few extra carriage returns around this point so you have some extra room to work).

2. Select Insert from the Table menu (<ALT> + A, I) to open the Insert Table dialog box.

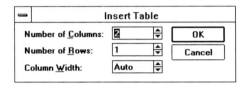

3. Word defaults to two columns, so if you're creating a two-column table, just click on OK. If you want some other number of columns, type that number here or use the arrows. Don't bother to specify the number of (horizontal) rows—you can create them as you go along. Unless you have a specific column width in mind, leave that setting at Auto. You can adjust them later if you want.

Note: *The Auto setting says, in effect, "Make every column as wide as possible so that they all fit on the page."*

4. Click on OK or press <ENTER> when you're done.

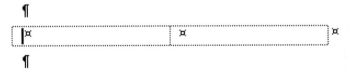

This is the "invisible" border that outlines tables. You can only see it when the Gridlines option on the Table menu is turned on. You have to turn the Show/Hide¶ feature on the Ribbon on before you can see the other invisible characters.

✦ Eleven Things You Must Know about Tables

1. Each "box" in a table is called a "cell." In the preceding illustration, the cursor is in the left-hand cell.

2. Every cell of a table is a separate paragraph. Instead of ending with carriage returns, they end with end-of-cell markers ¤ (which look a little like space invaders).

3. Use the <TAB> key to move forward one cell.

4. Use the <SHIFT> + <TAB> keys to move back one cell.

5. When you're in the last cell of a table, just press <TAB> to start a new row.

6. To highlight an entire column, point at that column with the mouse and click once with the *right* mouse button. Click on the right mouse button *and* drag to select more than one column at a time. You can select the entire table this way.

7. Here's another way to highlight a column: Put your cursor in the column and choose Select Column from the Table menu (<ALT> + A, C).

8. To highlight a row: Put your cursor in the row, and choose Select Row from the Table menu (<ALT> + A, R).

9. To select the entire table, put your cursor anywhere in the table and choose Select Table from the Table menu (<ALT> + A, A).

10. Word gives you three different "views" of tables. You can work with the Left and Right Indent markers, the Table (or column) markers, and the Margin markers for the page. Each of these tools gives you different formatting capabilities and enables you to make certain changes. You change views by clicking on the Scale icon on the Ruler. Here's what each view can do for you:

    • Word's Indent markers work the same in tables as in regular text. You use the Left and Right Indent markers to change the width of the text and nothing else. *Changing the width of the text does not affect the width of the column itself*—just the text within the column (see *Using Indents* in Chapter 7). You have to be in the Indent "view" to set tabs.

Left and Right Indent markers

- You use Table markers (**T**s) to adjust column widths. Note that the first Table marker doesn't look like a "T," but like the Left Indent marker. However, it acts like a Table marker.

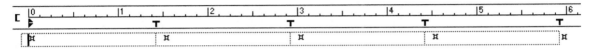

Table (or column) markers

- As always, you use the Margin markers to adjust the page margins.

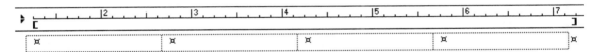

Margin markers

11. To **split a table** (in other words, to put a carriage return between two rows so that you can insert material), put your cursor in the row *below* the place you want the carriage return to go. Then select Split Table from the Table menu (<ALT> + A, S).

Note: *This technique comes in handy when the first thing in your document is a table, and you decide to put text above it.*

◆ Changing Column Widths

After you create a table, you will almost always want to change the width of the columns to fit the sort of design you're creating. Word enables you to do this in several different ways; following are two.

To change column widths using Table markers:

1. Put your cursor anywhere in the table.

   Note: *You can also use this technique to change the width of a single cell. To do this, simply highlight the cell you want to change and continue following these directions.*

2. While the column is highlighted, click on the Scale icon once or twice until you see the "T"s that stand for Table markers.

3. Drag the "T" to the *right* of the highlighted column to narrow or widen that particular column. If you drag the "T" to the *left* of the highlighted column, you'll narrow or widen the column next door. You can adjust the column width for any of the columns in the table—not just the highlighted one. Try this to see what I mean. As you widen or narrow particular columns, notice that the entire table gets wider or narrower. There are two ways to prevent this from happening:

   • Hold down the <SHIFT> key as you drag the "T"s. In this case, only two cells change width—the cells to the right and to the left of the "T" you're dragging. The width of the table itself doesn't change.

   • Hold down the <CTRL> key as you drag the "T"s. In this case, you narrow or widen the column to the *left* of the "T" you're dragging, and all the columns to the *right* of that "T" become the same width. Again, the width of the table itself doesn't change.

   Note: *This is a great technique to use when you want to make all your columns the same width and fit them inside the margins. To do this, drag the last Table marker so that it's equal with the right margin (if you're in Page Layout view and have Text Boundaries on in the Options dialog box, dotted lines mark the page margins). Hold down the <CTRL> key and drag the first Table marker (which looks like the Left Indent marker) slightly. This forces the columns to "equalize." Keep holding down the <CTRL> key and drag the first marker back to its starting point to return the table to its original width.*

To change column widths by dragging a column's edges:

1. Position your mouse pointer along the right edge of the column you want to change. When you're exactly on the edge, your cursor turns into a double line with arrows pointing from either side.

2. Click on the left mouse button and drag to resize the column. You can prevent changing the overall width of the table by holding down either the <SHIFT> or <CTRL> key as described in the previous section.

Note: You can use this same technique to change the width of a single cell. Simply highlight the cell you want to change and drag that cell's right edge.

Which Is Better—Dragging "T"s or Dragging Column Edges?

As you know, there are generally lots of different ways to do something in Word, and your choice depends mostly on which you remember. Personally, however, I find that the bigger my table is and the more stuff I have in it, the easier it is to use "T"s to change column widths. The reason is that the more "selectables" you have near one another, the harder it can be to select the particular thing you want, especially when the thing you want is as thin as a column edge.

✦ Working with the Table Menu

If you want to add or delete columns, add rows to the middle of your table, delete rows, merge cells, or change the structure of your table in almost any other way, use the Table menu.

Table
Insert Columns
Delete Columns
Merge Cells
Convert Table to Text...
Select Row
Select Column
Select Table   Alt+NumPad 5
Row Height...
Column Width...
Split Table
√ Gridlines

Adding and Deleting Rows and Columns. When you're in the last cell of a table and want to add an extra row to the bottom, just press <TAB> and it's yours. But what if you want to add a row to the middle of the table? Or a column? Or delete an extra row? It's easy.

PUTTING IT ALL TOGETHER: Transforming a Table into an Advertisement

This advertisement is adapted from Chapter 2. It's a leaner version of the original, which has holly branches adorning the corners and is proof that tables don't have to look like ledger sheets. Unless you're a number cruncher, you should think of tables as a design tool that enables you to lay out text and graphics in columns.

TOYS
FOR
TOTS

This Christmas, give a gift to *all* the children of our city.

Donate toys to the **Chelsea WEE CARE Center.**

Gifts are tax-deductible. Chelsea Wee Care Center is a non-profit organization.

111 Mockingbird Lane • Our Town, CA 11111
111-222-2121

Come to our open house! December 18, 10 am - 6 pm. Lorem ipsum dolor sit amet, consectetuer adipiscing elit, sed diam nonummy nibh euismod tincidunt ut laoreet dolore magna aliquam erat volutpat. Ut wisi enim ad. *Supervised games for kids. Refreshments will be served.*

To add rows to your table:

1. Put your cursor in the row *below* the one you want to add (Word adds rows *above* the cursor position).

2. Select Insert Cells from the Table menu (<ALT> + A, I).

Here's how to turn a table into an ad.

1. Position your cursor where you want to put the table, and then create one; it should be one row high and two columns wide. You can either use the Table button on the Toolbar, or select Insert from the Table menu (<ALT> + A, I).

2. Drag the column edges so that the first column is 2.75 inches wide, and the second one is 1.25 inches wide—the combined width is 4 inches. Your table is done.

   Note: *If you prefer, use the "T"s on the Ruler.*

3. Now you only have to type and format the text, just as you would if you weren't using tables. You can use carriage returns, new line breaks (<SHIFT> + <ENTER>), and so on. Of course, if you use the <TAB> key, you'll end up in the next cell, so you have to use <CTRL> + <TAB> (see *Tables and Tabs,* later in this chapter). As you type, the cells "grow" to accommodate the text.

Here are the specs for this ad if you want to try it yourself: All the text in the first column is centered, and "toys" is in 58-point Bookman on Exactly 47.5 points of line spacing, with 5 points of space Before. The word "for" is in 36-point Bookman on Exactly 33 points of line spacing; and "tots" is in 58-point Bookman on Exactly 56 points of line spacing, with 3 points of space After.

The rest of the text is in Times. The two paragraphs starting with "This Christmas..." are set in 14-point Times, single-spaced; there are 2 points of space After the first paragraph and 4 points After the second. The last two paragraphs in the first column are in 9-point text on 9 points of leading; 2 points of space separates them.

A bullet separates two sections of the address in the last line. You can create a bullet by holding down the <ALT> key and typing "0149" on the numeric keypad (be sure the <NUM LOCK> key is on). Although the misshapen "o" that appears on your screen doesn't look much like a bullet, it prints just fine. If you prefer to use the Symbol palette, open it and select the bullet that's part of the Symbol font.

The second column is set entirely in 11-point Times on 14 points of lead, flush left.

Note: *When you're working in a table, Insert Table changes to Insert Cells.*

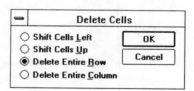

3. Select the option Insert Entire Row by clicking on it with the mouse, or by pressing R.

To add columns to your table:

1. Put the cursor in the column to the *right* of the one you want to add (Word adds columns to the *left* of your cursor position).

2. Select Insert Cells from the Table menu (<ALT> + A, I).

3. Select the option Insert Entire Column (C).

To delete rows from your table:

1. Put the cursor in the row you want to delete.

2. Select Delete Cells from the Table menu (<ALT> + A, D).

3. Select the option Delete Entire Row by clicking on it with the mouse, or by pressing R.

To delete columns from your table:

1. Put the cursor in the column you want to delete.

2. Select Delete Cells from the Table menu (<ALT> + A, D).

3. Select the option Delete Entire Column (C).

Here's another way to add or delete columns or rows. Highlight the column or row that you either want to delete, or that is to the right of or below the one you want to add. Then select Insert Columns, Delete Columns, Insert Rows, or Delete Rows from the Table Menu.

Shifting Cells.   If you don't want to add an entire row or column, just shift specific cells down a row or over to the right, you can. However, you need to understand exactly how things shift, or you could be in for a few nasty surprises. When you shift cells down or right, you're adding cells above or to the left of the selected cell(s). When you shift cells up or left, you're deleting cells above or to the right of the selected cell(s).

To shift cells down or right:

1. Put your cursor in the cell you want to shift. If you want to shift several adjoining cells, highlight them.

2. Select Insert Cells from the Table menu (<ALT> + A, I).

3. Select the option you want—down or right.

Original table

This·row·lines¤	¤	¤
¤	up·with·this·one¤	¤
¤	¤	¤
¤	¤	¤
last·cell¤	last·cell¤	¤

This cell has been shifted down. To move it back to its original position, shift it up.

¤	¤	¤
¤	¤	¤
This·row·lines¤	up·with·this·one¤	¤
¤	¤	¤
¤	¤	¤
¤	last·cell¤	¤
last·cell¤	¤	¤

¤	¤	¤
¤	This·row·lines¤	¤
¤	up·with·this·one¤	¤
¤	¤	¤
¤	¤	¤
last·cell¤	last·cell¤	¤

This cell has been shifted right. To move it back to its original position, shift it left.

To shift cells up or left:

1. Put your cursor in the cell you want to shift. If you want to shift several adjoining cells, highlight them.

2. Select Delete Cells from the Table menu (<ALT> + A, D).

3. Select the option you want—up or left.

Merging Cells.   Unfortunately Word only lets you merge two or more cells in the *same* row; it won't let you merge a cell with the one above or below it.

To merge cells:

1. Highlight the cells you want to merge.

2. Select Merge Cells from the Table menu (<ALT> + A, M).

   Note: *When you merge two cells, Word actually turns one cell into a carriage return; when you merge three cells, it turns two into carriage returns, and so forth. So when you get back to your table you'll have a few unwanted carriage returns to delete.*

Centering Tables on the Page.   The ability to *align* the rows of a table—so that they are centered on the page, for example—enables you to create very professional-looking presentations. You'll probably want to center your tables for many reports, most handouts and overheads, and for *all* slides.

Note: *You use the Row Height dialog box to align rows in a table. You can also use this dialog box to specify a row's height. This feature works very much like line spacing in the Paragraph dialog box.*

To align the rows of a table:

1. Select the entire table. You can either click on your right mouse button and drag, or you can choose Select Table from the Table menu (<ALT> + A, A).

   Note: *You can center or right align individual rows of the table as well as the whole table. Just put your cursor anywhere in the specific row and continue with these instructions.*

2. Select Row Height from the Table menu (<ALT> + A, H).

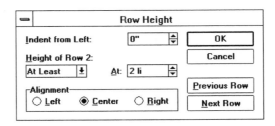

3. Click on Center (<ALT> + C), Left (<ALT> + L), or Right (<ALT> + R).

Specifying Column Widths Right Down to the Inch

Usually it's enough to adjust the widths of columns by dragging either their edges or the "T"s on the Ruler. However, when you need an exact width, use the Column Width dialog box.

Note: *You can also use this dialog box to specify the width between columns (in other words, how far to indent whatever's in a cell from the column's edge).*

To specify column width:

1. Highlight whichever column you want to format first.

2. Select Column Width from the Table menu (<ALT> + A, W).

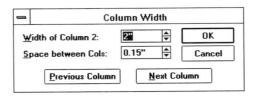

3. Type a width for that column, for example, 1 or .25 (Word assumes you mean inches). If you prefer, use the arrows to select a width.

4. Click on the Next button (<ALT> + N) and specify a column width.

> **Note:** *Sometimes you can see the highlight jump to the next column behind the dialog box. You can* always *see which column you're in by noting the Width of Column option; it indicates the column number.*

5. If you want to return to the previous column, click on the Previous button (<ALT> + P). When you're done, click on OK or press <ENTER>.

✦ **Tables and Tabs**

You set tabs in tables pretty much the way you set them anywhere else. Remember that you can only set tabs between Left and Right Indent markers—not between "T"s. (See Chapter 5 for information on how to use the Ribbon and the Ruler to set tabs; see Chapter 7 for information on how to use the Tabs dialog box.)

To set tabs in tables:

1. Select the column over which you want to set a tab.

2. Select the tab stop you want from the Ribbon (left, center, and so on).

3. Click under the Ruler measurement at which you want to place that tab. It's easy, and it'll be easier still if you follow these tips:

- When possible, set the same tabs for an entire column. To do this, *you must highlight the entire column.* Although you can set different tabs for each individual cell, it's easy to get confused about what's where.

- When you set a decimal (or dec) tab for a column, the text in that column aligns automatically; you don't need to <TAB> to it.

- When you use another sort of tab (left, center, or right), you must *manually* put a <TAB> in each cell. To do this, insert the cursor to the left of the text, and then press the <CTRL> + <TAB> keys. (Remember that if you press just the <TAB> key, you'll jump to the next cell.)

TURNING TABLES INTO DESIGNS

This section focuses on the various tools available to turn tables into finished designs. Although the Table menu is clearly a key tool, you also can use virtually all of Word's other design tools in tables—kerning, line spacing, styles, special typesetting characters, borders, and so on.

◆ Designing Borders

It's hard to overstate the power of borders as a design tool for informational presentations. You place borders in a table just as you place them in text (see *Border Basics* in Chapter 7).

To add borders:

1. Highlight the column(s), row(s), or specific cells to which you want to add rules or borders.

2. Select Border from the Format menu (<ALT> + T, B).

3. Select one of the Preset borders—Box (<ALT> + B) or Grid (<ALT> + G)—or click on the sample page to indicate where you want the border to go.

4. Select the type of line you want the box or rule to use by clicking on it. The border appears in position on the sample.

5. Click on OK or press <ENTER> when you're done.

   Note: *If you want to get rid of a border, highlight the cells and select Border from the Format menu. Then select None in the lower-left corner (<ALT> + N).*

You can also **shade** (or color) specific cells in your table, as well as paragraphs. If you have a color printer, you can use color backgrounds for your text. If you have a black-and-white printer, colors appear as dot patterns or shades of gray. You can also use a variety of patterned backgrounds, including screens from 5 to 90 percent. A diagram of the Shading dialog box follows.

1. Highlight the column(s), rule(s), or specific cells that you want to shade.

2. Select Border from the Format menu (<ALT> + T, B).

Diagram of the Shading Dialog Box

To get rid of shading, click on None.

You can create custom patterns by selecting different colors from the Foreground and Background menus. If you want to create a pattern for use on a black-and-white printer, you should try setting Foreground to white and Background to black (which is the reverse of their defaults).

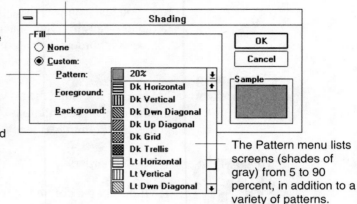

The Pattern menu lists screens (shades of gray) from 5 to 90 percent, in addition to a variety of patterns.

3. If you want to use borders as well as shading, indicate where you want the borders to go. Then select a line style.

4. Click on Shading (<ALT> + s). This opens the Shading dialog box.

5. Select the shading or pattern you want to use from the Pattern menu. If you want to custom-make your own pattern, set the foreground and background colors you want to use, and then select a pattern.

6. Click on OK or press <ENTER> when you're done.

    Note: *To get rid of shading, select None from the Shading dialog box.*

Effective Shading

Here are a few rules of thumb for effective shading.

- It's easier to read dark letters on a light-colored background than light letters on a dark-colored background.

- However, if you're using light-colored text, make the background as dark as possible. The greater the contrast between the text and the background, the clearer the message.

- Make the text printed on shaded backgrounds somewhat larger than usual so that it stands out. Generally, you should not shade small text (small, in this case, being anything less than 9 points or so).

- Depending on the size of your text, it might be significantly easier to read sans serif faces (such as Helvetica) than serif faces. If you're working with anything less than 12-point type, you should at least experiment with a sans serif (or perhaps a bold) face.

- The quality of shading varies depending on the resolution of your printer. This is especially true if you're using shades of gray or screens. The screens used in this section, for example, were created on a computer and printed at 1270 dots per inch (with a 133-lpi line screen) on a Linotronic. If you want to create truly professional-looking screens, you have to use a high-resolution printer. However, depending on the sort of publication or presentation you're working on, the 300-dpi resolution of the everyday laser printer might be fine. You should, however, experiment a little to see what suits your purposes best. I generally use shading of either 10 or 20 percent with a black (or Auto) foreground and a white (or Auto) background.

PUTTING IT ALL TOGETHER: From Tables to Presentations

Besides being a powerful page layout tool, tables enable you to make great tables! There are two main means of visually boiling down numerical information and presenting it appealingly—the chart (or graph) and the table. I cover tables here and touch on charts in Chapters 10 and 20. We've all seen tables that *don't* summarize information and present it attractively—in government documents, for example. They just lay it all out there, pages of tabular data. You can easily do that, too, with the table features discussed. Just make a 14-column table (or whatever), stick headings at the top and along the left side, and type in the numbers.

If you *do* want to present information attractively—no matter how much—good formatting is indispensable. Rules, borders, varied typefaces, and so on help make data easier to understand. At the same time, these formatting tools can turn a string of numbers into an eye-catching visual aid that conveys your message as effectively as a good headline. The tables labeled A and B are really the same table with different messages. When you're finished with the following example, you'll have created Table A.

Note: *If you want to create Table B after you finish A, just highlight it (I would highlight a few extra carriage returns at the top and bottom as well) and copy it (<CTRL> + C). Put your cursor somewhere farther down the page and paste it (<CTRL> + V). If you prefer, use Word's drag and drop feature. Then* remove *the border and shading for the last column, and add a border and shading for the bottom row.*

2nd & 3rd Quarter Sales, By Product ($000)

		PRODUCT		
	A	B	C	Total
July	69	41	58	**168**
August	76	43	61	**180**
September	78	45	65	**188**
October	82	46	66	**194**
November	81	47	67	**195**
December	79	47	72	**198**

A. The message of this table can be summarized as: "Sales have risen steadily since July."

2nd & 3rd Quarter Sales, By Product ($000)

		PRODUCT		
	A	B	C	Total
July	69	41	58	168
August	76	43	61	180
September	78	45	65	188
October	82	46	66	194
November	81	47	67	195
December	**79**	**47**	**72**	198

B. This table is exactly the same as Table A, but the boxed row emphasizes a different point. Its message could be summarized as follows: "Sales of Product C have grown rapidly since July, to the point that they almost equal sales of A."

1. Before you create a table, add a few extra carriage returns both above and below the place where the table will start, to provide a little room to maneuver. Create a table using either the Table button on the Toolbar or the Table menu. Table A is 7 columns by 9 rows. You have two choices: You can simply specify the number of columns and create the rows as you go along, or you can also specify for the number of rows and be done with it.

2. If you count the columns in Table A, you probably won't count 7. That's because there is a thin column at the very left and right of the table, and there's also a thin extra row at the bottom. These extra columns and rows can give your table an attractive margin inside the border. Although it usually makes sense to adjust the column widths *after* you finish typing the text (otherwise, how will you know how wide they should be?), in this case it might be helpful to narrow both the first and seventh columns now.

   To do this, highlight the first column, click on the Scale icon until you see the "T"s, and drag the "T" *to the right* of the first column to narrow it. Repeat this procedure with the seventh column. These columns are both less than a quarter of an inch wide in the finished example.

   Note: *If you prefer, you can narrow these columns by dragging their edges, or by using the Column Width dialog box.*

3. Before you start typing, you should start with the column headings (A, B, C and so forth) *in the second row of the second column*. Although the main heading ("2nd & 3rd Quarter Sales" through "Product") is in the first row of the table, you have to merge the first row of cells into one cell. *Whenever you merge cells, make it your last step*. This will save you from a lot of extra work.

   Type the column headings into row 2 (just press the <TAB> key to get from cell to cell), and the rest of the text and numbers into rows 3 through 8. Remember that row 9 should be left blank. (Don't worry if everything looks awful as you're typing; it will look great by the time you finish step 4.)

4. Once the text is typed, format it. All the text so far should be 13 points with Auto line spacing and .5 lines (6 points) of space After, so highlight the entire table and format it with these specs. Then you're ready to format the column headings, labels (July, August, and so on), and numbers with their respective typefaces and alignments.

   The column headings are Helvetica bold, centered. The easiest way to format them is to highlight that whole row and format all the headings at once. The numbers are Bookman, centered (click in the first cell you want to format, and then drag down and across until the whole section is highlighted). The labels are in Helvetica, flush left.

   Note: *13-point Bookman and 13-point Helvetica are quite different sizes. Because of this, you may find that the labels don't line up with the data. To correct this, superscript the labels (I superscripted mine by 2.5 points).*

5. With the text formatted, it makes sense to adjust the column widths. Although you can certainly do this by dragging the "T"s or the column edges, I'll go through the instructions for using the

Column Width dialog box. Set the first and seventh columns to .2 inches, and the other columns to 1 inch.

Highlight the first column, and open the Column Width dialog box (<ALT> + A, W). Type ".2", then click on the Next Column button (<ALT> + N). Type "1" for the width of column 2, and click on Next Column again. Keep this up until you've finished all seven columns. (Be sure to make the seventh column .2 inches wide—not 1 inch!)

If you make a mistake, use the Previous Column button (<ALT> + P) to go backward. Click on OK or press <ENTER> when you're done.

It Even Adds!

I used Word for Windows to add up the numbers in Tables A and B. This is a great little feature.

1. Highlight the cells you want to add—they can be in columns or rows.

2. Select Calculate from the Tools menu (<ALT> + O, C). Word does the rest.

But, where does Word put the answer? It's in two places. If you check the left corner of the status bar at the bottom of the screen (*before* you click on your mouse or type anything), you'll see it.

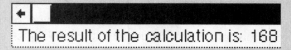

The result of the calculation is: 168

Check the left corner of the status bar to see the answer.

Word also copies the answer onto the clipboard. To get it into your document, simply put the cursor where you want the answer to go, and then paste (<CTRL> + V). You can format it as you would anything else.

Note: *Word also can calculate all sorts of formulas. To learn more about these computational skills, refer to the Word for Windows manual.*

6. When you get back to your table, you may find that the "r" in September has spilled over onto another line. If this is the case, here's how to fix it. If this *isn't* the case, glance at this fix anyway. Someday you'll need it.

   - Put your cursor in September's cell. If you don't see the Left and Right Indent markers on the Ruler, click on the Scale icon until you do.

   - When you're in the Indent view, drag the Right Indent icon to the right in order to increase the amount of space available for text inside the column. This does not change the width of the column itself; it simply gives "September" a little more room. This technique enables text to stick out beyond the bounds of the column.

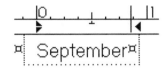

Adjusting the Left and Right Indent markers does not affect the column width itself; only the width of the text inside the column.

7. Now you're ready to merge the top row of cells into one cell. Highlight the top row, and select Merge Cells from the Table menu. Notice all the extra carriage returns you have to delete from that cell.

8. After you get rid of the extra carriage returns caused by merging cells, type the table's main heading, including "product," which is on the second line of the heading. Just insert a carriage return between "($000)" and "product."

9. The specs for the heading "2nd" through "by product" are: 17-point Helvetica bold, centered, with .5 line (6 points) of space Before and 1 line (12 points) of space After. Format "($000)" as 13-point Helvetica bold.

   Format "product" in the second line of the heading as 14-point Helvetica bold, centered, with .5 line of space After.

10. Put your cursor in "product." Select Border from the Format menu, and place the thinnest available border above the selected text. In your table, the rule above "product" probably extends most of the way across the cell. To narrow this rule:

    - Put your cursor in the word "product." If you don't see Indent markers on the Ruler, click on the Scale icon until you do.

- When you see the Indent markers, drag the Left and Right Indent icons to narrow the width of that paragraph, and therefore that of the rule.

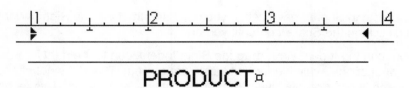

PRODUCT¤

These are the Indent markers used for the heading "product" in Table A.

11. These steps outline and shade the "total" column. Highlight the relevant cells, and open the Border dialog box. Click on the preset Box (<ALT> + B), and select the second-to-thinnest line. Click on Shading (<ALT> + S), and select 10% from the Pattern menu. Click on OK or press <ENTER> when you're done.

12. After you screen the "total" column, you might want to make the text bold, as I did. I also thought that the first number in that column was too close to the border. To correct this, I put .5 line of space Before the first row of numbers.

13. These steps outline the entire table and center it. Highlight the table, and box it with the thinnest available line. When you're done, select Row Height from the Table menu (<ALT> + A, H). Select Center (<ALT> + C) from the Alignment section. Click on OK or press <ENTER> when you're done.

CHAPTER 9

Let Those Presses Roll!

No matter how great your Word for Windows documents look on the computer screen, they're not done until they look just as good on paper. Some days all you have to do to make this happen is to click on the print icon in the Toolbox. Other days the printed version won't line up for some reason, and you have to fuss with it until it does. Then there are those days when you don't want to print at all; you want to send your work to a service bureau and have them turn it into camera-ready copy (from 300 to 2450 dots per inch), a color printout, or slides. On these days, you have to take one more step: You need to create a PostScript or Encapsulated PostScript (EPS) file for the service bureau to work with.

Of course, if your service bureau uses Word for Windows, you don't need to create a PostScript file. However, at this writing, very few do. In fact, you may run into some that are skeptical that you can produce professional-quality publications and presentations from Word—*but you can*. The first time I tried, my service bureau couldn't get over it. They kept saying, "You did *this* in a word processing program?" If your service bureau balks, assure them that it can be done. It's just that people are only now starting to use these techniques.

You might decide to create a PostScript file for another reason: You might want to edit that file to create special effects such as outlined or screened (grayed) text as explained in Chapter 21.

No matter what your reason for wanting to create a PostScript file, this chapter covers the basic information you need to deal with Word, your printer, and PostScript—whether or not you actually have a PostScript printer. (That's right! You don't need a PostScript printer to use PostScript.)

This chapter covers these topics in the following order:

- Printing basics.

- Setting up your printer.

- Color printing.

- What is PostScript?

- How to create a PostScript file.

- How to create an Encapsulated PostScript file.

ALL-PURPOSE PRINTING

Whether you're printing an ordinary Word for Windows document or creating a PostScript or EPS file, the easiest way is to click on the Toolbar's Print icon. However, there are a number of cases when it isn't practical to use the icon—for example, when you want to print only a few pages of your document, or when you first want to set the printer to create PostScript files. In these cases, you have to use the Print dialog box, which is shown in the diagram of the Print dialog box on the next page.

To use the Print dialog box:

1. Select Print from the File menu (<ALT> + F, P).

2. Select the print options you want to use, such as the number of copies, the page range, and so on.

3. Click on OK or press <ENTER> when you're ready.

Diagram of the Print Dialog Box

This opens the Print Setup dialog box. Clicking on this button is the same as choosing Print Setup from the File menu.

Word allows you to print style sheets, glossary entries, and a number of other useful items, as well as documents. Use this pull-down menu to select what you want to print.

Clicking on this button is the same as choosing Options from the Tools menu and then selecting the Print category.

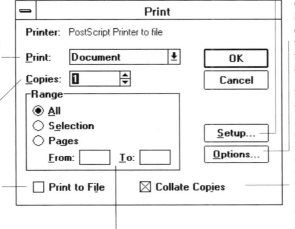

Select the number of copies you want to print.

When you're printing two or more copies of a document, use this option if you want Word to print one full copy before printing subsequent copies. If you don't use this option, Word will print every copy of the first page, every copy of the second page, and so on. This option's only drawback is that your document prints more slowly.

Turn this option on if you want to create a PostScript file. (You must have a PostScript *driver* set up in your system to create a PostScript file.)

If you have highlighted a portion of your document, the middle option reads "Selection." Use this option if you want to print only whatever is highlighted. If, however, *nothing* is highlighted, this option reads "Current Page." If you use it, only the page where your cursor is will print. Use the From... To options to print particular pages.

✦ Setting Up Your Printer

The actual act of printing a document is the easiest part of the printing process. Setting things up to print can be somewhat harder because you have to make several choices. If you have more than one printer set up in Windows, you first have to select the one you want to work with. Of course, if you have only one printer on your system, this isn't much of a choice. If you don't have a PostScript printer but want a service bureau to print PostScript files for you, you'll have at least two printers listed on your system—your regular printer and the PostScript printer driver. You'll have to select the printer you want *before* printing, and before you do that, you'll have to install the printer using Windows' Control Panel. See your Windows manual for instructions.

To select the printer you want to work with in Word:

1. Select Print Setup from the File menu.

or

If you already have the Print dialog box open, click on the Setup button (<ALT> + s).

2. Select the printer you're going to use from Word's Print Setup list box. If you want to use that printer's standard settings (or the settings you last specified), all you have to do is click on OK or press <ENTER>. However, if you want to specify or confirm the print capabilities you plan to use, you need to go into the Setup dialog box for the printer you've chosen.

   Note: *Since each printer has somewhat different print capabilities, their Setup dialog boxes can look quite different.*

3. Click on Setup (<ALT> + s) to change or confirm the printer's settings.

   Note: *You have to specify Orientation, Paper Size, and Paper Source in Word's Page Setup dialog boxes (these are under the Format menu). If you enter specifications in the Print Setup dialog box, Word ignores them.*

4. When you've set up the printer the way you want, click on OK or press <ENTER>.

   Note: *These settings stay in effect until you change them.*

✦ Color Printing

You print to a color printer just as you print to any other printer. However, if you *have* a color printer and want to print in color, you have to do three things:

1. Make sure you use colors in your document.

2. Select the color printer from the pull-down list of printer models. If your printer model isn't listed—or if you're creating a color PostScript file to print at a service bureau—select a widely used model such as the QMS ColorScript 100.

   Note: *If you're using Windows 3.1, you have to install a separate printer driver if you want to use the capabilities of a color PostScript printer. You then have to select that printer driver in Word as described previously.*

3. Make sure the Use Color option is on. As of this writing, Windows 3.0 and 3.1 put this option in different dialog boxes.

In 3.0 it's on the main PostScript printer setup dialog box; in 3.1 you have to click on the More button (<ALT> + M) to find it.

If you don't have a color printer but plan to use a service bureau to produce a color printout or slides, you still have to do these same three things, plus, you have to turn on the Print to File option in the Print dialog box (select Print from the File menu). For more information on creating PostScript files, see *Printing Your Work As PostScript Files* later in this chapter.

You *must* select a color PostScript printer (such as the QMS ColorScript 100) to create a PostScript file that prints in color. Black-and-white printers ignore colors. See Chapter 20 for information on creating color slides and overheads.

WORKING WITH POSTSCRIPT

Before you can work with PostScript, you need to install a PostScript printer **driver** in your system, using Windows' Control Panel. The beauty of Windows is that you use the exact same procedure to install all printers, whether it's an HP LaserJet, an IBM QuietWriter, a PostScript black-and-white printer, or a PostScript color printer. (See your Windows manual on how to do this, and make sure you have your Windows disks handy before you start. If your office uses a network, the system administrator can help with this.) You only have to install printer drivers once; then it's done forever.

You don't need a PostScript printer to use PostScript, and you don't need a color PostScript printer to use color. You simply need to install the PostScript printer driver that comes with Windows, and then select the type of printer suitable for the work you're doing. For instance, if you're creating a PostScript file with black and white and shades of gray, use the Apple LaserWriter IINTX driver. If you're creating a color PostScript file, use the QMS ColorScript 100. If you want to use oversized pages such as 11 × 17 inches, use the Linotronic 500. The brand of the printer doesn't matter since you're creating a file and not actually sending information to the printer; rather, you need to tap the *capabilities* that the particular driver includes when you're creating your PostScript or EPS file.

After you've installed your PostScript printer driver using Windows' Control Panel, you're ready to create PostScript files.

✦ **Printing Your Work As PostScript Files**

Once you've set up your PostScript printer driver(s) using Windows' Control Panel, it's simple to turn your work into PostScript files.

1. Open the document you want to turn into a PostScript file. Select Print from the File menu (<ALT> + F, P).

What Is PostScript?

PostScript is a sophisticated "language" that's specially designed to handle graphics and page layouts. In fact, the introduction of PostScript and its use with the Apple LaserWriter and Linotronic printers is largely what enabled people to create complete pages of camera-ready copy off a PC—in other words, to desktop publish—in the first place. This language works with a variety of different programs, including Word for Windows, to tell PostScript printers or **slide recorders** (which make slides) what a printed page should look like. For this reason, PostScript is often called a "page description" language. It allows you to position letters, numbers, pictures, and other design elements precisely on a page.

PostScript treats everything, including text, as a graphic. This means that you can make letters and numbers any size, shape, and shade you want, just as you can change the size of a clip art illustration. The ability to use PostScript is one of the things that boosts Word from a mere word processor to a desktop publishing system.

Word itself doesn't use all the capabilities that PostScript makes available. However, when you create a PostScript file, you can make certain changes to it easily that will enhance your publications and presentations. Chapter 21 shows how to edit your PostScript files to get two of these features: outlined and screened (or grayed) text.

Because of PostScript's power, service bureaus almost always use PostScript printers and slide recorders. So, even if they don't use Word (and at this writing, most do not) they *can* use the PostScript files you create to produce camera-ready copy and slides.

PostScript Files versus Encapsulated PostScript Files

Encapsulated PostScript (EPS) files are just like regular PostScript files, with these two exceptions:

1. They contain an extra two lines of PostScript language code that enable you to import them as *graphics* into several word processing programs (including Word), into page layout programs, and into slide presentation packages.

2. When the Print dialog box appears, turn on the Print to File option (<ALT> + L).

3. Click on Setup (<ALT> + S) to select the PostScript printer model you want to use, and to set any options, such as Use Color.

2. You create them differently than regular PostScript files (see *Encapsulating PostScript* later in this chapter).

Since many service bureaus can use both PostScript and EPS files, which one you use depends on two things: the preference of the service bureau, and whether you're preparing a printed document or slide presentation. If you're creating slides, you might choose to use Encapsulated PostScript files if the service bureau can place them into a slide presentation program and work with them more easily (ask them about this). However, if you do choose this method, be sure to create a *separate* EPS file for *each* slide.

It's also possible to **download** (or send) an EPS file directly to a printer, just the way you handle a PostScript file. You can change your EPS files exactly as you do a regular PostScript file, so it's just as easy to add special effects. Unfortunately EPS files tend to be somewhat more unreliable than PostScript files, so unless you have a reason to use them, don't bother.

In PostScript, letters, numbers, shapes, and pictures are all treated as graphics. PostScript lets you change the size, shape, and color of any graphic you can create on the computer.

When you print to a PostScript file, Word creates a text-only computer file (or document) containing the PostScript commands that explain to printers and slide recorders how the pages should look. (A text-only file is unformatted and can be used by almost any program.) You can open and change this file in Word, just as you would any other document.

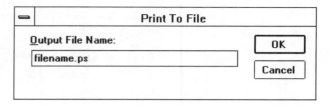

When you print a PostScript file, Word creates a text-only file on a hard disk (or floppy disk). Word then prompts you to name the PostScript file you're creating. If you want to save it on a special drive or in a special directory, just type that information before the name, for instance, B:\BROCHURE\FILENAME.PS.

4. Return to the Print dialog box and print the document by clicking on OK or pressing <ENTER>. When it "prints," it creates a PostScript file instead.

5. Word prompts you to name the file. (I always make sure I add a .PS extension so that my PostScript files are easy to identify.)

Note: *Once you set up your system to create PostScript files, you can create additional files just by clicking on the Print icon on the Toolbar. When you want to stop creating PostScript files and start printing normally again, turn off the Print to File option, and reselect your usual printer model and settings.*

✦ Encapsulating PostScript

Although you create EPS files differently than regular PostScript files, they work pretty much the same, with one exception. You can only *download* regular PostScript files (in other words, send them) to a PostScript printer or slide recorder; you can't use them in other programs. You can actually place EPS files into other programs *as graphics*.

EPS files can be handy if you want to use a table or page layout that you did in Word for Windows as a graphic in another program, or if your service bureau wants to use the EPS files to create slides. However, whenever you create an EPS file for use in another program, be sure to create a *separate* EPS file for *each* page of your document. Although this can be time consuming, it's better than having all your pages print on top of one another, which is what happens if you don't take this precaution.

Note: *To print a single page per file, use the From... To... option in the Print dialog box.*

What If My Service Bureau Has Trouble Printing My PostScript File?

Many service bureaus are still more familiar with Macintosh than IBM-compatible computers. If you use an IBM-compatible system, the service bureau may have trouble printing your PostScript files. This is because your file contains a special character in two places (one at the very start of the file and the other at the very end) that the Macintosh doesn't know how to handle.

However, you can fix this problem quickly. After you've created a PostScript file, open it and delete the two problem characters. Then save the document as Text Only.

1. In Word, open the PostScript file you created. When Word prompts you to convert the file from "Text Only," just click on OK or press <ENTER>.

2. Delete the short black bar (ı) from the beginning of the text (it's the first thing you see).

3. Press <CTRL> + <END> to get to the very end of the file, and then delete the short black bar there.

4. Select Save As from the File menu (<ALT> + F, A). Make sure that "Text Only" appears in the Save File as Type menu at the bottom of the screen. If it doesn't, select it now.

5. You can keep the file's present name, so just click on OK or press <ENTER>.

Your service bureau can now print this file from a Macintosh computer.

To create EPS files:

1. Open the document you want to turn into an EPS file. Select Print from the File menu (<ALT> + F, P).

2. When the Print dialog box opens, click on Setup (<ALT> + s) to select the PostScript printer model you want to use, such as a black-and-white or a color printer. (If you want to create a color EPS file, make sure you set up your printer as QMS ColorScript 100 or another color printer.)

3. Choose to print to an Encapsulated PostScript File rather than the printer (<ALT> + c). Although you can name the file here, I generally don't. Instead, I wait for Word to prompt me to name the file when I actually print. I recommend that you do this, too, if there's even a possibility you're going to create more than one EPS file at a time; otherwise, you have to keep returning to this dialog box and renaming the files. Word just prints the new EPS file over the old one without warning. Also, I always give my EPS files an .EPS extension to make them easier to find and identify.

Note: *If youre using Windows 3.1, you may have to use the More button rather than the Options button to specify that you want to print to an EPS file.*

4. Return to the Print dialog box and print the document by clicking on OK or pressing <ENTER>. Then print, just as always. If you didn't give the EPS file a name, Word prompts you to do so now. (This works exactly as it does when you're creating a PostScript file.)

Note: *You have to retrace your steps through the Setup process to reset the system to print to your printer.*

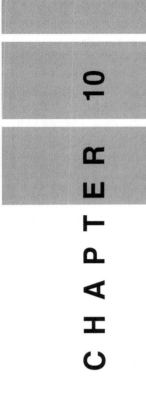

CHAPTER 10

Graphs and Graphic Touches

Word comes with three graphics programs—Microsoft Draw, Graph, and WordArt. You don't need to know how to draw to use these programs. If you can drag your mouse across the screen, you can create custom rules, sophisticated headline treatments, and graphs for presentations.

Since I don't have space to explain everything there is to know about Draw, Graph, and WordArt, I'll focus on those techniques that enable you to add graphic appeal quickly and easily to your publications and presentations. Microsoft Graph has so many uses, however (it's essentially the same charting program found in Excel) that I cover aspects of it in Chapter 20 as well. If you have any trouble using these programs, or if you want to know more, refer to the Word for Windows manual or the Help system that comes with each program.

This chapter covers these topics in the following order:

- Microsoft Draw basics, including how to use clip art.

- How to create graphic headline treatments with Draw.

- How to create custom graphs with Draw.

- Microsoft WordArt basics.

- Microsoft Graph basics.

- How to create professional charts with Graph.

DRAW BASICS

Once you've embedded a Draw graphic in Word, you can move that graphic wherever you like in the document, just as you move text. You can also copy it to other Word documents, and you can change the copied graphic as easily as the original.

Microsoft Draw comes with Word and enables you to create all sorts of graphic designs, rules, and dingbats. It also enables you to use clip art images, and to modify these images to suit your needs. In a lot of ways, "drawing" is just a matter of clicking and dragging the mouse.

Draw enables you to **embed** graphics—in other words, include them—in Word documents. (This capability is called "OLE," which stands for Object Linking and Embedding.) When you create a Draw graphic, it's essentially saved within your Word for Windows document. To edit it, you simply have to double-click on the image. This way, your Word document always includes the most recent drawing or graph.

Working with Embedded Graphics

In many ways, Draw, Graph, and to a lesser extent WordArt, work very much like Word. You choose commands from the menus in the same way—by mouse or by keyboard. You select dialog box options by clicking on them. You Copy, Cut, and Paste the same way; the commands are under the Edit menu, and the keyboard shortcuts are the same. Even Undo is the same (<CTRL> + z).

For all these similarities, however, there are important differences between how you handle Word documents and how you handle drawings, graphs, and WordArt. You'll see what I mean if you look under the File menus in both Microsoft Draw and Graph. The commands New, Open, Save, Print, and so on aren't listed. It's not that they're listed on another menu, either; they aren't listed at all. The reason is that you don't save these documents the same way you save Word documents—as individual files. Instead, you embed drawings and graphs in a Word document by using the Update command on the File menu. It doesn't exist as an individual file *per se*; rather, it exists inside the Word document. Whenever you want to edit the embedded graphic, simply double-click on it in Word (or select the graphic, and then choose the "Object," as it's called, from Word's Edit menu). The Draw, Graph, or WordArt window opens so you can change the graphic however you like.

Once you've embedded a graphic in Word, you can move that graphic wherever you like in the document, just as you move text. You can also copy it to other Word documents, and you can change the copied graphic as easily as the original.

Unfortunately, Word documents that include embedded graphics can be quite large. This is because the graphics you embed—whether they're graphs, drawings, or WordArt—are technically **fields** that include all the information necessary to create and edit them using the source program, for instance, Microsoft Draw. (A field is a special set of codes that tells Word where to find

There are two ways to get into Draw:

1. In Word, position your cursor where you want to place the Draw graphic, and then click on the Draw program icon on the Toolbar ⬚ .

or

Select Object from the Insert menu (<ALT> + I, O) and Microsoft Drawing from the scroll box of Object Types. Then click on OK or press <ENTER>.

Note: *After you place the Draw graphic in Word, you can move it wherever you like.*

certain information, and what to do with it when it's found.) You can reduce the size of your documents by *un*embedding embedded graphics—in other words, isolating them from their source program by unlinking their field. If you unembed a graphic created in WordArt, or a chart created in Graph, you can *not* re-embed it. However, you can always re-embed a graphic created in Draw.

Note: *To see the fields in your document, choose Field Codes from the View menu (<ALT> + V, C). If you do this, you'll see that your embedded graphics are all fields. Follow the same procedure to stop viewing fields. For more information on fields, see the entry in the Visual Glossary at the end of this book.*

To unembed an embedded graphic:

1. Select the graphic.

2. Press the UNLINK FIELD command, <CTRL> + <SHIFT> + <F9>. If you choose to view fields now, you'll see that the field codes have disappeared. What used to be an embedded graphic is now a plain old graphic. (See Chapter 11 for more information on handling plain old graphics in Word.)

In addition to being able to re-embed a graphic created in Draw, you can *embed* most any graphic imported or pasted into Word simply by changing it in Draw. This turns it into an embedded Draw graphic. To do this:

1. Select the graphic you want to change.

2. Double-click on it to open Draw. (Or select it, and choose Picture from the Edit menu.)

3. After editing the graphic, choose Update from the File menu, and then Exit and Return to get back into Word.

Note: *Depending on the graphic, you may find that you can't edit it quite the way you want (see Using Clip Art in Draw later in this chapter).*

2. Word opens Draw in a small window. To enlarge that window to take up your whole screen, click on the Maximize button in the upper-right corner (you can use this same technique to make any window full-size).

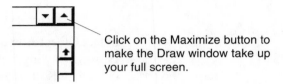

Click on the Maximize button to make the Draw window take up your full screen.

You can use Draw to create original graphics and modify clip art graphics. This section explains how to do so.

✦ The Toolbox

Here are descriptions of the tools available in Draw. Step-by-step instructions for using these tools follow.

Arrow: Select, size, and move graphics.

Zoom In/Zoom Out: See your graphic close up, or at a reduced size.

Line: Draw straight lines vertically, horizontally, or at an angle.

Ellipse/Circle: Draw circles and ellipses.

Rounded Rectangle/Square: Draw both rectangles and squares with rounded corners.

Rectangle/Square: Draw rectangles and squares.

Arc: Draw curved lines.

Freeform: Draw free-hand.

Text: Add a line of text to your graphic.

Select a color or shade of gray for
lines or text. The default color,
black, is currently selected.

Line [color palette] **Other...**
Fill [color palette] **Other...**

Select a color or shade of gray to
fill shapes. The default color,
white, is currently selected.

Drawing Lines and Boxes

- To draw something, click on the tool you want to use. For example, if you want to draw a line, click on the Line tool. The mouse pointer turns into a crosshair + when you move it into the drawing area. Hold down the left mouse button and drag to create a line or shape. Don't let up on the mouse button until you finish drawing. Once you finish drawing an object, you have to use the Arrow tool to resize or reshape it.

  Note: *To draw a straight line or a perfect circle, press the <SHIFT> key before you click on the mouse button, and hold it down until you're done.*

- You can fill any circle, ellipse, rectangle, square, or free-form shape with a pattern (select Pattern from the Draw menu), and/or a color or shade of gray from the Fill palette.

- You can change the color of any line—whether it's a straight line, a circle, square, arc, or free-form line—using the Line palette. You can change the width or pattern of a line (for instance, turn a thin line into a thick one, and a solid line into a dashed one) by using the Line Style commands on the Draw Menu.

  Note: *The Line Style commands don't work with text.*

- You can use guides to help line things up evenly and at precise measurements by choosing Show Guides from the Draw menu (<ALT> + D, W). Once you see the guides on your screen, drag them to where you want them. Notice that as you drag a guide to a new position, a small number appears. This number is the inch measurement at which you're placing the guide.

- You can have objects "Snap to Grid," which means that they automatically line up along an invisible grid when you move

263

or size them. This command is always on unless you turn it off (it's under the Draw menu). Although it can be useful, it can also complicate the task of adjusting two things in precise relation to one another.

"Drawing" Text

- To use text in your graphic, choose the font, point size, alignment, and type style from the Text menu. Then click on the Text tool.

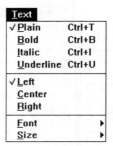

- The mouse pointer turns into a cursor when you move it into the drawing area. Type the text you want. (You can only type a *single line* at a time.) When you're done, press <ENTER> or click anywhere off the text to get out of text mode.

- To edit text, select it with the Arrow, and then choose Edit Text from the Edit menu (<ALT> + E, D).

- To change the font, point size, or type style of text, select it with the Arrow tool, and then select the specs you want from the Text menu.

- To change the color of text, select it with the Arrow tool, then click on the color or shade of gray you want in the Line palette.

Using the Arrow Tool

- To resize anything you've drawn—or to change its shape—select it with the Arrow tool. You'll know it's selected when small handles appear around the object's edges. Click on the handles and drag them to change the object the way you want.

Note: *You can resize text only by choosing a new point size from the Text menu.*

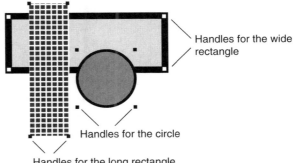

Handles for the wide rectangle

Handles for the circle

Handles for the long rectangle

- You can move both text and objects. Simply select what you want to move with the Arrow tool, and drag it from the middle (if you drag it from a handle you'll resize it). A dotted box or line serves as a placeholder for the image while you're dragging it. When you let go of the placeholder, the image itself moves into position.

- You can select several objects at once by any of three methods: 1. You can draw an invisible "selection" box around them with the Arrow tool. 2. You can click on each one while holding down the <SHIFT> key. 3. You can choose Select All from the Edit menu (<ALT> + E, A).

- You can turn several different objects into a single object by selecting them and then grouping them together. To do this, choose Group from the Draw menu (<ALT> + D, G). You can *un*group them again by selecting the group, and then choosing Ungroup from the Draw menu (<ALT> + D, U).

Draw	
Group	Ctrl+G
Ungroup	Ctrl+H
√ Framed	
√ Filled	
Pattern	▶
Line Style	▶
√ Snap to Grid	
√ Show Guides	Ctrl+W
Rotate/Flip	▶

- You can put one object (or text block) in front or in back of another one. To do this, select it, and then choose Bring to Front (<ALT> + E, F) or Send to Back (<ALT> + E, B) from the Edit menu.

- Draw lets you rotate objects or flip them—in other words, turn them over, turn them on their side, or turn them upside down. To do this, select the object you want to rotate or flip, and then choose Rotate/Flip from the Draw menu.

Note: *Draw doesn't allow you to rotate or flip text. However, WordArt does (see* WordArt Basics *later in this chapter).*

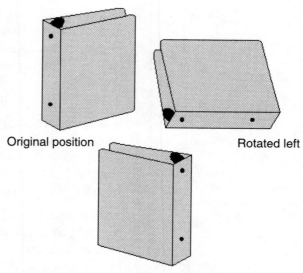

Original position   Rotated left

Flipped horizontal

Using the Zoom Tool

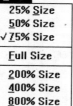

- With the Zoom In/Zoom Out tool, you can view your drawing close up to line things up more easily, or at a reduced size to make it easier to select objects that don't all fit on your screen. The Zoom In/Zoom Out tool does the same thing as the View menu.

- To zoom in, click on the Zoom In/Zoom Out tool, and then click on the object you want to see close up. The first click magnifies the object to 200%, the second click to 400%, and the third click to 800%.

- To shrink your view of the object, click on the Zoom In/ Zoom Out tool; hold down the <SHIFT> key; and then click on the object. The image shrinks one level for each click (the levels are shown on the View menu). For example, if you had magnified the object to 400%, the first click would shrink it to 200%, the second click would take it to Full Size, and a third click would reduce it to 75% of the actual size.

Deleting Mistakes. Draw is very forgiving. It's actually easier to get rid of mistakes than to make them in the first place.

- If you make a mistake, *immediately* choose Undo from the Edit menu (or use the same hot key as in Word, <CTRL> + Z).

- If it's too late to Undo the mistake, use the Arrow to select the text or object you want to delete. Press the <DELETE> key. Or, if you prefer, select Clear from the Edit menu.

Note: *It doesn't make any sense to Cut mistakes (which puts them on the clipboard) unless you want to paste them elsewhere.*

Using Colors in Draw. If you have a color monitor, the Line and Fill palettes at the bottom of your screen show colors. If you don't see these palettes, select Show Palette from the Colors menu (<ALT> + C, P).

If you have a VGA gray-scale monitor set up in Windows as a color monitor (as it should be), you will see shades of gray representing the different colors. If you print to a color printer, these shades of gray will *print* in color. If you want to do color work in Draw but have a gray-scale monitor, you should make a "color guide" for yourself so that you know what color each shade of gray represents. To do this, just draw a series of boxes and fill each one with a different shade of gray (make sure you go in order so you can identify which is which later on). Then embed the image in Word, and print it on a color printer. If you don't have a color printer, create a color PostScript or EPS file (as described in Chapter 9) that your service bureau can print out. You can use these colors to create slides or other types of presentations in Word (see Chapter 20). If you print to a black-and-white printer, each color will translate into a gray pattern.

Edit
Undo	Ctrl+Z
Cut	Ctrl+X
Copy	Ctrl+C
Paste	Ctrl+V
Clear	Del
Select All	Ctrl+A
Bring to Front	Ctrl+=
Send to Back	Ctrl+-
Edit Text	Ctrl+E

Colors
√ Show Palette	Ctrl+P
Edit Palette...	
Add Colors from Selection	
Get Palette...	
Save Palette...	

PUTTING IT ALL TOGETHER: Headline Treatments in Draw

This example shows how to use Draw to create the following headline treatments. The first headline could easily serve as the main graphic element for any number of publications—a report, newsletter, or brochure. The second headline was designed to serve as a subhead in the same publication. Notice that it retains the basic design elements—the Avant Garde typeface, the caps, and the rules—used in the main head, although it's much smaller and subtler.

Word enables you to do a great deal with rules and borders, but the easiest way to produce the design shown here—the floating rules centered vertically in a line of text—is with Draw. Unlike Paintbrush (which comes with Windows), Draw enables you to produce high-quality type that you can use in publications and presentations.

INDUSTRY ANALYSIS

——— HOMEBUILDING REPORT ———

1. In Word, position your cursor where you want to place the Draw graphic, then open Draw. To do this, either click on the Draw program icon on the Toolbar, or choose Object from the Insert menu. When your Draw window opens, click on the Maximize button to make it full size.

2. Choose Font from the Text menu (<ALT> + T, F), and then Avant Garde from the Font menu.

3. Choose Size from the Text menu (<ALT> + T, S), and then 24 points from the Size menu.

4. Click on the Text tool. Put your cursor in the drawing area, and type your headline—in this case, INDUSTRY ANALYSIS—in caps. Press <ENTER> or click anywhere off the text to get out of text mode.

   Note: *If you need to edit your text, select it, and then choose Edit Text from the Edit menu (<ALT> + E, D).*

5. Click on the Arrow tool. Select the headline and drag it to the very left of your screen. This enables you to measure the length of the head and rule together most accurately.

   Note: *If your graphic turns out to be larger or smaller than you'd like, you can resize it—and even crop (or trim) unwanted portions—in Word.*

6. Choose Show Guides from the Draw menu (<ALT> + D, W). Drag the horizontal guide so that it runs through the center of the head. Drag the vertical guide until it displays the measurement you want for the length of the headline. In this case, the headline treatment is 6 inches long

from the first letter of text to the end of the rule, so you would drag the vertical guide until it registers 6.00.

Note: *Depending on the size of your screen, this may be very near the right-hand edge. If this is the case, you might want to reduce your view of the headline to 75% to give yourself more room to work. To do this, use either the Zoom tool (remember to hold down the <SHIFT> key before you click with the mouse), or choose 75% Size from the View menu.*

7. Click on the Line tool. Choose Line Style from the Draw menu (<ALT> + D, L), and then select a 4-point line. Position the crosshair on the horizontal guide, and hold down the <SHIFT> key to draw a straight line. Click on the left mouse button and drag until you get to the vertical guide.

8. If the rule isn't quite the right length, select it with the Arrow tool and adjust it by dragging one of the handles at either end. If you have trouble selecting it, turn off the Show Guides option on the Draw menu. Make whatever other adjustments to the graphic you think are necessary, and then choose Exit and Return from the File menu (<ALT> + F, X). Answer "Yes" when Draw prompts you to update the graphic in Word.

The headline treatment now appears in your Word document. Print it to see how it looks on paper (I've noticed that rules placed to the right of text in Draw are sometimes closer to the text than they appear on screen). If you want to make further adjustments to the graphic, double-click on it (or select it, and then choose Microsoft Drawing Object from Word's Edit menu). Remember that you can move this graphic around in your document just as you can text. You can also copy this graphic into other Word documents, and then modify that copy without affecting the headline as it appears in *this* document. When you're ready to create the subhead, place your cursor where you want the subhead to appear, and open Draw.

9. Choose the Avant Garde typeface and a size of 11 points.

10. Click on the Text tool and type the headline—in this case, HOMEBUILDING REPORT—in caps.

11. When you're done, turn on the Show Guides option. The subhead is half the size of the main head, so drag the vertical guide to 3 inches. Center the text between the left edge of the drawing area and the vertical guide. Drag the horizontal guide so that it runs through the center of the head.

12. Click on the Line tool. Choose a Line Style of 2 points from the Draw menu, hold down the <SHIFT> key, and draw a short rule to the left of the head. If the rule needs to be shortened, lengthened, or repositioned, do so now. (You may have to turn the Show Guides option off to make these corrections.)

13. When the rule looks just as you want it to, copy it, and paste it to the right of the head. Line up the second rule with the first. When you're ready, choose Exit and Return from the File menu. Answer "Yes" when Draw prompts you to update the graphic in Word.

Remember that color files take up significantly more space than do black-and-white files. If you're not planning to print graphics in color, it probably makes sense to set Draw to black and white to get a sense of the shades of gray (sometimes called **dot patterns** or **screens**) that will actually print. To do this, select Get Palette from the Colors menu (<ALT> + C, G). Then select one of the two black-and-white palettes—17grays.pal or geni.pal (the latter has a larger number of patterns). Although many of these patterns are too coarse to provide a high-quality finished product, others work quite well. A little experimentation will help you decide which ones to use and which to avoid. (See Chapter 21 for information on creating high-quality text screens using PostScript.)

"Saving" Your Graphic and Returning to Word

- To "save" or embed the graphic in your Word document, choose Update from the File menu.

- To get out of Draw and return to Word, choose Exit and Return to Document from the File menu. If you haven't updated your Word document to include the most recent changes to the graphic, Draw prompts you to do so now. If you don't want to include this graphic (or your most recent changes) in Word, answer "No." Otherwise, choose "Yes."

Changing an Embedded Graphic

- To change (or edit) an embedded graphic, double-click on it. Or, if you prefer, select it, and then choose Microsoft Draw Object from the Edit menu.

File

Update	
Import Picture...	
Exit and Return to Document1	

Edit

Undo Copy	Ctrl+Z
Repeat Copy	F4
Cut	Ctrl+X
Copy	Ctrl+C
Paste	Ctrl+V
Paste Special...	
Select All	Ctrl+NumPad 5
Find...	
Replace...	
Go To...	F5
Glossary...	
Links...	
Microsoft Graph Object...	

✦ Using Clip Art in Draw

Draw enables you to use and modify graphics created with other programs (such as Paintbrush or CorelDraw!) and to use clip art. You should be aware that most graphics or drawing programs use different formats to describe the images they create. Chapter 11 explains some of the differences between these formats, so I won't rehash them here. You should know, however, that Draw uses something called .WMF files, which stands for Windows Metafile format. In addition, it translates several other different graphics formats (such as the .PCX and .BMP files created by Paintbrush). When you work with files translated into Draw from another format, you may find that you can't modify graphics as easily as you would like. For example, if you draw several different rules in Paintbrush and save them in one file, when you translate them into Draw they will be a single graphic. You won't be able to manipulate each rule individually.

The easiest way of getting a graphic created by another program into Draw is to copy and paste it. If you don't have this option, however, try to save such graphics as .WMF files before importing them into Draw. At present, this will give you the greatest flexibility to change that graphic once it's in Draw.

Word for Windows comes with several dozen clip art images (all in .WMF format). The disk that came with this kit, *Tools of the Trade*, has a number more. These images should be in the Clipart directory inside your Winword directory, or in another directory that you decided would work better (see the Introduction of this book for information on using the disk).

To use clip art:

1. Choose Import Picture from the File menu (<ALT> + F, I).

2. The Import Picture dialog box that opens is similar to the dialog box you use in Word to open files. However, it only lists graphics files that Draw can import. If necessary, change the drive or directory to locate the file you want.

3. Select the file you want to import into Draw and open it (you can double-click on it, click on OK, or press <ENTER>).

4. Once in Draw, you may need to Ungroup the graphic to

change it. To do this, select Ungroup from the Draw menu (<ALT> + D, U). If Draw doesn't give you this option, the graphic is *not* grouped. If it was grouped, you should now be able to modify the clip art just as you would any Draw graphic.

Note: *If you translated a graphic from another format, such as .PCX or .BMP, you may* not *be able to modify it in Draw as you would like. However you can change .PCX and .BMP files in Paintbrush.*

PUTTING IT ALL TOGETHER: Create a Custom Chart Using Clip Art

Although you'll generally use the Graph program to create charts for reports and presentations, sometimes a custom chart using original graphics or clip art adds a lighter touch that works better in a particular setting. In these cases, you can create a custom graph in Draw, similar to this one, shown reduced.

Everything in this chart was created in Draw except the title and border, which were set in Word.

WORDART BASICS

WordArt enables you to create special effects with text—to place it on a curve, for example, or outline it, or turn it upside down. Since these features can seem too good *not* to use, I have to begin with a warning about when you should create these effects.

1. Create the chart title in Word. It's set in 22-point Helvetica bold, centered, with 5 lines of space Before and 3 lines of space After. When you finish formatting the title, press <ENTER>. This is where you want the chart to go.

2. Open Draw. Click on the Maximize button so that it takes up your full screen.

3. Click on the Line tool, and set Line Style to 1 point.

4. Draw a vertical rule along the left edge of the screen (about 3.5 inches from top to bottom), and a horizontal rule along the bottom (about 4.5 inches from left to right). Remember that you can hold down the <SHIFT> key to draw a straight line, and you can use the Show Guides option on the Draw menu to measure the length of the rules. If you have trouble aligning the rules at the corner, magnify it using either the Zoom tool or the View menu.

5. When you have the rules drawn correctly, turn them into a single object (this ensures that you don't accidentally move one and have to start over). To do this, select them both using the Arrow tool, or choose Select All from the Edit menu (<ALT> + E, A). Then choose Group from the Draw menu (<ALT> + D, G).

6. The next thing is to import the bundle-of-money graphic. Choose Import Picture from the File menu. Open the Clipart directory (or the directory you use for clip art) and choose MONEY.WMF from the scroll box.

7. Copy the money graphic, paste it, and then drag the second bundle above the first. Paste another bundle, and then drag that one into position. Continue doing this until you've stacked all the bundles the way you want them. When you're done, select the piles of money and the rules, and group them into a single object.

   Note: *If a bundle partly covers the one above it, select it, and choose Send to Back from the Edit menu (<ALT> + E, B).*

8. Set the type specs to 14-point Helvetica bold. Type the text (each dollar amount and each year has to be created as a separate text item), and place it as indicated on the chart. You might find it helpful to reduce your view of the chart to 75%, and to turn the Show Guides option on (if it isn't already).

9. When you're done, choose Exit and Return from the File menu. To embed the chart in Word, answer "Yes" when Draw prompts you to update the graphic.

WordArt includes more than a dozen of its own typefaces. While these can work well in less formal situations, their quality is not high enough for use in most professional publications or presentations. Some of them, however, can be very effective in certain circumstances and in small doses; for example, the "novelty" typefaces reminiscent of feminine handwriting or a computer print out. A few such examples are shown in the *Here's How* section below.

Another problem with WordArt is that even though the special effects are fairly impressive in themselves, they can make your work look amateurish. However, sometimes you want a lighter piece included in an important presentation.

For instance, I was part of a small group that created some admissions and marketing materials for a meeting of university executives. While the overall presentation was highly professional, we created one handout that was meant to get a chuckle. It illustrated a confusing idea in an irreverent but accurate way. In keeping with its tone, the handout's title was set on a curve. WordArt definitely can come in handy in the right situations. When you use it, make sure it has the right tone for the publication or presentation you're creating.

In some ways, WordArt is similar to Draw. You open WordArt—as you open Draw—from within Word, and you "save" (embed) WordArt graphics in Word itself, instead of saving them as separate files. You can also cut, copy, and paste WordArt graphics, and move them just as you move text in Word. If you have any questions about handling embedded documents, see *Working with Embedded Graphics* earlier in this chapter. The WordArt dialog box is described in the diagram on the next page.

To create a graphic using WordArt:

1. In Word, position your cursor where you want to place the WordArt graphic. Select Object from the Insert menu (<ALT> + I, O) and MS WordArt from the scroll box of Object Types. Then click on OK or press <ENTER>.

   Note: *Word does not come with a Toolbar icon ready-made for WordArt. If you use the program often enough, you might want to create one (see the Word for Windows manual for more information).*

Diagram of the WordArt Dialog Box

Type the text you want to turn into art.
After each line of text, press <ENTER>.

Select a font. ————

Select a point size. If the
size you want isn't listed,
type it in. When you select
Best Fit, the program fits
the text to the Preview
frame at the right. This is
often a good starting
point; you can always
change the point size
once you see how it looks
in your document.

Select a style (in other
words, a special effect) for
your art; Button, for
example, Upside Down, or
Arch Up.

Select a color for your text.

Align your text. The default
alignment is Center.

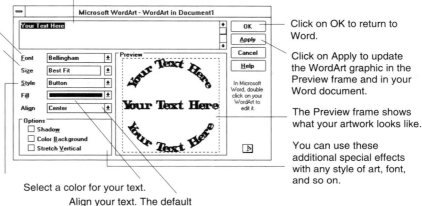

Click on OK to return to
Word.

Click on Apply to update
the WordArt graphic in the
Preview frame and in your
Word document.

The Preview frame shows
what your artwork looks like.

You can use these
additional special effects
with any style of art, font,
and so on.

2. Type the text you want to turn into art. Press <ENTER> to start a new line.

3. Select the font, size, style, color, and alignment. In WordArt, the *Style* is the special effect you use. You should experiment with the fonts and styles to decide which ones suit your work.

   Note: *To create outline text, select white from the Fill list. To create* **reverse text** *(white text on a black background) select White from the Fill list, and then turn the Color Background option on.*

4. Select the Options you want.

   Note: *When experimenting with different fonts, styles, and options, you might find that the artwork Preview doesn't update automatically. To update the Preview, click on the Apply button (<ALT> + A). The Apply button also inserts the graphic into Word.*

5. When you're ready to return to Word, click on OK.

   Note: *If you enlarge a WordArt graphic, the program pops up a dialog box when you return to Word, asking whether you want to enlarge that graphic. Click on OK or press <ENTER> if you do.*

Once you're in Word you can resize, crop, and border the graphic (see Chapter 11 for instructions). To modify the WordArt graphic, double-click on it or select it, and then choose MS

WordArt Object from the Edit menu (<ALT> + E, B). The following examples illustrate just a few of the special effects you can create with WordArt.

Computer Graphics Department

This example could serve as a headline treatment or a logo. It's set in 30-point Touchet, using the Plain style.

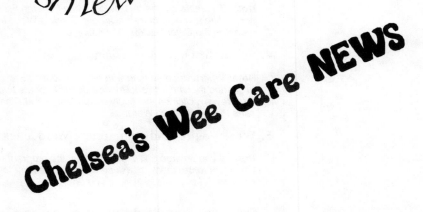

This logo is set in Marysville at Best Fit using the Button style. The Button style requires three lines of text. The first line is used at the top of the "button," the second line is used in the middle, and the third at the bottom. If you have only two lines of text, the second line will be used for both the middle and the bottom. If you don't want text across the middle, leave the second line of text blank.

This headline treatment could be a masthead for a one-page newsletter, or the headline for a column in a larger publication. It's set in 24-point Tupelo using the style called Slant Up (Less).

GRAPH BASICS

Microsoft Graph is essentially the same charting program used in Excel. In fact, one of the things it allows you to do is import graphs and their underlying data *from* Excel. Like Draw and WordArt, Graph embeds the charts you create in Word, instead of saving them as separate files. The program enables you to create a dozen different types of charts—from Bar charts to 3-D Pie charts—and to format them in dozens of different ways. This section covers the basics of using Graph and finishes with an example of how to create a Line chart. Chapter 20 includes another example of how to create a chart for use in reports and presentations.

There are two ways to get into Graph:

1. In Word, position your cursor where you want to place the chart, and then click on the Graph program icon on the Toolbar .

or

Select Object from the Insert menu (<ALT> + I, o) and Micro-soft Graph from the scroll box of Object Types. Then click on OK or press <ENTER>.

Note: *After you place the chart in Word, you can move it wherever you like.*

2. Word opens Graph in a small window. To enlarge that window, click on the Maximize button in the upper-right corner (you can use this same technique to make any window full-size).

When Graph opens, it displays two windows: a datasheet window with sample data in it, and a sample chart. When you create a chart, what you're actually doing is telling Graph to read the data in the datasheet, and then **plot** (or translate) it as a visual image. So the first thing you have to do is replace the sample data with the numbers you want to use for your chart.

Note: *To **activate** (or select) either the datasheet or the chart so you can use it, click on it. (Or, if you prefer, you can select the one you want from the Window menu.) To resize either the datasheet or the chart, select it, and then drag the edges of its window. You can drag all four sides, plus the corners. When your mouse is positioned so that it can resize the window, the pointer turns into a double-edged arrow.*

✦ Dealing with Data

You can replace the sample data with the data you want to use for your chart in one of three ways: 1. You can type new data in place of the sample data. 2. You can paste data copied from a table created in Word (or from a spreadsheet created in Excel). 3. You can choose the Import Data command from the File menu to use a file created by another program. Whichever method you decide on, you need to tell Graph whether to plot that data from rows or columns. You do this by choosing either the Series in Rows or the Series in Columns option from the DataSeries menu.

If you accept Graph's default option—Series in Rows—you have to enter data with these rules in mind:

```
DataSeries
 Plot on X Axis
 Include Row/Col...
 Exclude Row/Col...
√ Series in Rows
 Series in Columns
 Move To Overlay
 Move To Chart
```

1. Enter the data for each item in its own row. For instance, if you want to graph the sales of penny loafers versus tennis sneakers over the course of a year, you would enter all the data for penny loafers in one row, and the data for tennis sneakers in another. (In technical terms, Graph considers penny loafer data and tennis sneaker data each to be a **series**.)

2. Enter the **series names** (for instance, Penny loafers or Tennis sneakers) in the *first column* of the datasheet.

3. Enter the **labels** that describe the data (for instance, January, February, March, and so on) in the *first row* of the data sheet.

If you choose the option Series in Columns from the Data-Series menu (<ALT> + D, C), enter data according to these rules:

1. Enter the data for each item in its own column.

2. Enter the series names in the *first row* of the datasheet.

3. Enter the labels that describe the data in the *first column* of the datasheet.

Graph's DataSeries menu enables you to sift through a good deal of data and to graph only specific portions of it (use Exclude and Include Row/Column). You can also use this menu to specify the rows and columns you want plotted as particular chart elements (use Move to Overlay and Move to Chart). Although you may never have to use these "power user" features, they can help you turn very detailed information into eye-catching visuals. For information on how to use all the commands listed on the DataSeries menu, refer to the Word for Windows manual; for information on how to create a chart overlay, see Chapter 20.)

Entering Data into Datasheets.   If you know how to use Word's table functions, you know how to enter data into datasheets. There's only one real difference between typing numbers into Word and typing them into Graph. As of this writing, you can't type commas when entering data without first formatting the sheet to accept commas. For instance, if you type "3,826," Graph displays "3826." And when you create a chart, the numbers in that chart will appear comma-less.

To specify that data should include a certain number format, such as commas:

1. Highlight all the cells in which you expect to use a particular number format.

2. Choose Number from the Format menu (<ALT> + T, N).

3. Select the number format you want from the scroll box, whether it's a comma; two decimal places after the zero; or both a dollar sign and comma, *plus* parentheses around negative numbers (which is the format selected here).

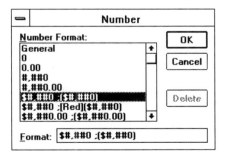

4. Click on OK or press <ENTER> when you're done.

You might take a few minutes to familiarize yourself with some of the number formats available. They actually save typing because once you format a cell to use a certain type of number—such as a comma—you don't have to type the comma; Graph adds it automatically where appropriate. Similarly, you can format numbers so they're all preceded by dollar signs—without typing the dollar signs.

Deleting Data from Datasheets. To delete data from datasheets:

1. Highlight the data you want to delete.

2. Press \<DELETE>, or choose Clear from the Edit menu. Graph pops up the Clear dialog box where you can choose to clear data, formatting (such as Number formatting), or both. Select the one you want.

3. Click on OK or press \<ENTER> when you're done.

Changing Column Width in Datasheets. Changing the width of a column in a datasheet is similar to changing it in a Word table. You can drag the column with your mouse, or use the Column Width command on the Format menu to type a measurement.

To size a column with your mouse:

1. Point at the *top* of the line dividing a cell from its right-hand neighbor.

2. When the mouse pointer turns into a double-edged arrow, drag the column to the width you want.

To size a column using the Column Width command:

1. Choose Column Width from the Format menu (<ALT> + T, W).

2. Type the measurement you want to use in points.

3. Click on OK or press <ENTER> when you're done.

✦ Graphing Charts

Once you enter the data for your chart in the datasheet, Graph immediately redraws the sample chart to reflect the new information. If you're creating a 3-D Column graph (the default), this means you're almost done. All that's left is to size the chart as you want it to appear in Word, and then choose Update from the File menu (<ALT> + F, U) to embed it there. When you're ready to return to Word, choose Exit and Return (<ALT> + F, X).

Note: *Although you can resize the graph in Word, you may not like the results. Line thicknesses may not look right, text may become distorted, and different elements of the graph may bump each other or end up too far away.* For WYSIWYG charts, size them in Graph.

Of course, Graph offers an extensive set of formatting options in addition to the ones used in the sample chart. You can use a variety of colors if you have a color printer, or a number of different patterns if you have a black-and-white printer. You can select fonts and point sizes; and you can add gridlines, arrows, and text. In short, you can customize any chart so that it delivers the information and the message you want in the way you want.

This section explains Graph's tools for creating great charts.

The Gallery Menu. Graph enables you to create a dozen different types of charts, each of which includes upwards of four or five different styles—for example, pie charts with or without percentages attached, and exploded pie charts, in which slices are disconnected for emphasis.

To select a chart type:

1. Choose a chart type—Line, Pie, or whatever—from the Gallery menu.

2. Graph opens a gallery of standard styles available for that type of chart (the pie chart gallery is shown following). Click on the one closest to what you want. You can then use the Chart and Format menus to customize it further.

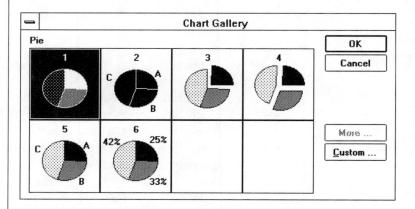

The Chart Menu.   The Chart menu lists all the things you can use to customize your chart: a title, for example, a legend, and an arrow. To use any of these items, choose it from the Chart menu. Then specify additional options in any dialog box that pops up.

Although it doesn't appear on any menu, you can always add floating (or unattached) text. To do so:

1. Click anywhere on the chart and start typing. Click anywhere off the text to get out of text mode.

2. To format the text with a particular font and point size, click on it to select it (you know it's selected when handles appear around it). Choose Font from the Format menu (<ALT> + T, F).

   Note: *Graph's Font dialog box is similar to Word's Character dialog box.*

3. To box the text, select it, and then choose Patterns from the Format menu (<ALT> + T, P). You can create a particular type of box by selecting the style, color, and weight of the borders used. Click on the Shadow option to create a shadow box.

   Note: *You can also box other text, such as the chart title.*

Chart
Titles...
Data Labels...
Add Arrow
Delete Legend
Axes...
Gridlines...

About Axes: A chart's **X-axis** is along the horizontal rule; the **Y-axis** is along the vertical rule. If you're using a 3-D chart, the **Z-axis** replaces the Y-axis.

Format
Patterns...
Font...
Text...
Scale...
Legend...
Number...
Column Width...
─────
Chart...
Overlay...
3-D View...
─────
Color Palette...

The Format Menu.   The Format menu includes options for datasheets (Number and Column Width) as well as for charts. I'll explain the three most commonly used chart formatting dialog boxes here: Patterns, Font, and Text.

You can format a **pattern** for every element on a chart—from the colors and black-and-white patterns used to distinguish different items, to the rules along the vertical and horizontal axes, to the color of the chart title. You format patterns, fonts, and text for each element individually. Depending on the type of element you're formatting, buttons will appear in the dialog box that enable you to access other formatting features (such as Font and Text) without having to go back and select these options from the Format menu.

To change the pattern used for a particular chart element:

1. Double-click on that element, or click on it once to select it and then choose Patterns from the Format menu (<ALT> + T, P). This opens a dialog box for the selected element.

2. Format the element with the available borders, colors, patterns, and so on.

3. Click on OK or press <ENTER> when you're done, or click on any available buttons to get into other formatting options.

To change the font used for a particular chart element:

1. Select that element and then choose Font from the Format menu (<ALT> + T, F).

2. Select a typeface, point size, style, and so on.

3. Click on OK or press <ENTER> when you're done, or click on any available buttons to get into other formatting options.

PUTTING IT ALL TOGETHER: Creating a Line Chart

The following Line chart shows the number of high school graduates in New York State 1989 through 1991. Here's how to create it in Graph and embed it in Word. (As always, you can follow these basic instructions to get your own chart out the door. If you're working on a project, Chapters 11 and 20 cover additional chart examples.)

NYS High School Graduates

1. In Word, position your cursor where you want to place the chart, and then open Graph. When Graph opens, click on the Maximize button to make its window full-size.

2. Activate the datasheet by clicking on it.

3. Get rid of the sample data by highlighting it and then pressing <DELETE>. When Graph pops up the clear box, delete only the data (this is the default option).

4. Make sure that the DataSeries menu is set for Series in Rows. Highlight the second row (you can simply click in the left-most box in that row) and choose Number from the Format menu. Click on "#,##0" in the scroll box to set the Number Format to accept commas.

5. This chart does not use series names (after all, there's only one series), so don't type anything in the first column. Type the labels—1987, 1988, and so on—in the first row of the datasheet. Type the number of high school graduates in the second row. Don't bother to type commas; Graph adds them automatically.

Document2 - Datasheet				
1987	1988	1989	1990	
193,780	196,112	183,042	170,262	

6. Activate the chart by clicking on it. Notice that the chart reflects the new data.

7. Choose Line from the Gallery menu. Select the fourth style of Line chart, which uses horizontal gridlines.

8. Your chart is now a Line chart. Resize it as you want it to appear in Word.

   Note: *Charts look larger on-screen than when they print. It takes some practice to get a sense of how this works.*

9. Choose Titles from the Chart menu (<ALT> + T, C), and then choose Chart from the list of available title-types. You don't have to position your cursor anywhere. As long as the title is selected (surrounded by handles), simply type the text—for example, "NYS High School Graduates." When you finish typing, choose Font from the Format menu and set it in 14-point Times bold. Click on OK or press <ENTER> to get out of the Font dialog box; then click anywhere off the title to get out of text mode.

10. Double-click on the line tracing the decline in high school students. This opens a dialog box of patterns available for Lines & Markers. Select the square from the Style menu in the Marker section. Click on OK or press <ENTER> when you're done.

11. Click on the vertical (or Y-) axis to select it. Choose Font from the Format menu and set the numbers in 10-point Times. Select the horizontal (or X-) axis and choose the same formatting.

12. To add floating text, simply start typing. In the example, I put a carriage return at the end of each line, as shown below.

This decline is not¶
expected to end¶
until 1995.

When you finish typing, choose Font from the Format menu and set it in 10-point Times bold. Then choose Patterns from the Format menu to box the text by clicking on the Shadow option in the lower-left corner. Move the boxed text (by clicking and dragging) to an appropriate place on the graph.

   Note: *To get rid of floating text, titles, and arrows, select the element, and then press the <DELETE> key.*

13. To add an arrow, select Add Arrow from the Chart menu (<ALT> + C, R). Drag the arrow so that the arrowhead is near where you want it to point. Click on the arrow's left end and drag it so that it's more-or-less parallel with the X-axis. Then size the arrow and put it wherever you want.

14. You're done. Choose update from the File menu (<ALT> + F, U) to embed the chart in Word. Choose Exit and Return (<ALT> + F, X) to return to Word.

Text formatting is available only for text elements. You can position text in a variety of ways, including sideways. To use these options:

1. Select the text element you want to position and then choose Text from the Format menu (<ALT> + T, T).

2. Select the alignment, orientation, and so on.

3. Click on OK or press <ENTER> when you're done, or click on any available buttons to get into other formatting options.

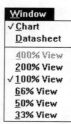

The Window Menu.   The Window menu serves two functions: 1. It allows you to select either the Chart or the Datasheet. 2. It enables you to change your view of the chart—to magnify it so that you can place text or arrows precisely, for example; or to shrink it so that you can see how everything fits together. Select the 100% View to see the graph the size at which it will be embedded in Word.

CHAPTER 11

Graphically Speaking

Graphics created with Draw, Graph, and WordArt are just one type that you can use in Word for Windows. You can also use Encapsulated PostScript graphics, TIFF files (usually scanned images of photos or artwork), .PIC files (for charts created in Lotus), and several others.

If you're not using Draw, Graph, or WordArt, the easiest way of getting graphics into your Word publications and presentations is by copying them from another Windows' program—such as Paintbrush, CorelDraw!, or Excel—and pasting them into Word. However, if you don't have that option, you can use the Picture option on the Insert menu.

The INSERT, PICTURE command also enables you to bring into Word pictures created with *programs you don't have*. This means that you can use clip art in any of the graphics formats that Word uses. There's a caveat, however. If the clip art doesn't store each graphic in a separate file, you'll have to crop out all the unwanted images. (Many clip art collections bunch graphics together in a single file. When you import one of these graphics into Word, you end up with the whole bunch.) Depending on the clip art's file format, you might be able to modify it in Draw; but if that's your plan, try to get a package that uses the .WMF (Windows Metafile) format. This way, you'll get maximum flexibility to make changes. If you are planning to use lots of clip art, you might want to investigate one of the high-level graphics programs for Windows—such as CorelDraw!—that can handle several different graphics formats.

This chapter covers these topics in the following order:

- Differences among the graphics formats that Word uses.

- How to use the INSERT, PICTURE command.

- How to put a border around graphics.

- How to scale and crop graphics.

- How to caption graphics.

- How to turn a picture into a presentation.

GETTING GRAPHIC

Every graphics or drawing program uses its own format to describe the images it creates. These different formats are called graphics formats. Word needs a graphics import **filter** to "read" and use each of these different formats; as of this writing, a dozen such filters are available. Here are the graphics formats that Word currently uses (or "supports," as the literature says):

- AutoCAD 2-D Format (*.DXF)

- AutoCAD Plotter Format (*.PLT)

- Computer Graphics Metafile (*.CGM)

- DrawPerfect (*.WPG)

- Encapsulated PostScript (*.EPS)

- HP Graphic Language (*.HGL)

- Lotus 1-2-3 Graphics (*.PIC)

- Micrografx Designer 3.0/Draw (*.DRW)

- PC Paintbrush (*.PCX)

- Tagged Image File Format (*.TIF)

- Windows Bitmaps (*.BMP)

- Windows Metafile (*.WMF)

If you used the Complete Setup option to install Word, you should have these filters on your system. To check, use the TOOLS, OPTIONS command. Select the Win.Ini category, and then select MS Graphic Import Filters from the pull-down Application menu. Word lists the available filters. If they're not there, refer to your Word for Windows manual for installation instructions.

✦ Beauty Contest

When it comes to graphics formats, beauty isn't in the eye of the beholder; it's in the format itself. While many of these formats are of comparable quality, some are clearly better than others for certain types of graphics. As long as you steer clear of the obvious problems, your graphics will turn out fine. In general, people end up using one graphics format rather than another only because they're using a program that happens to save graphic images in that particular format. For example, people don't generally run around trying to create .PIC files. Rather, if they are using Lotus 1-2-3, they use .PIC files because that's how Lotus saves charts. However, some formats are better than others for some things.

For instance, .EPS files provide some of the highest quality graphics and most advanced graphic capabilities available. Other formats have comparable print quality—such as .DRW and .WMF—but you can't do as much with them.

Paintbrush, which comes with Windows, allows you to save graphics in either of two **bitmapped** formats—.PCX or .BMP. Like all bitmap drawing programs, Paintbrush creates images using a grid system in which each square makes up a "bit" (or a "little bit") of the full picture. One advantage of bitmap drawing programs is that they're generally the easiest to use. Using them is almost like painting by numbers—you just color in the squares.

TIFF graphics (TIFF is an acronym for Tagged Image Format Files) are most often used for scanned images, whether photos or artwork. The section *Photo Opportunities* in Chapter 4 has two examples of TIFF files—the scanned image of a phone booth and the thumbprint used in Rules of Thumb. TIFF files are essentially bitmapped files (similar to .BMP and .PCX files). However, they are among the most complex files around and tend to be enormous (the phone booth was 565,288 bytes; a 3.5-inch

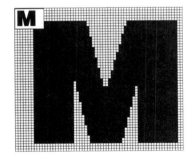

This is a close-up of a Paintbrush "M." When they're magnified, it's easy to understand why these images are called bitmaps. Each square is a "little bit" of the drawing.

double-sided disk only contains 720,000 bytes). Unwieldy as they are, TIFF files are invaluable if you want to scan (or computerize) photos or any other artwork. They are also quite easy to handle in Word for Windows.

The following examples show the difference in quality between .PCX, .BMP, and .EPS graphics. Remember that .BMP and .PCX files are virtually the same. If you stick with "square" bitmaps made from straight lines and right angles, you can't tell them from .EPS graphics.

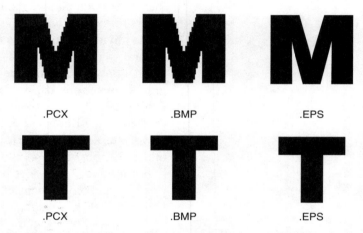

| .PCX | .BMP | .EPS |

Notice that the .PCX and .BMP images look the same. They're fine for straight lines, but angles and curves are jagged. The .EPS images, on the other hand, are perfectly formed no matter the size or shape or angle. This is essentially true for all "object-oriented" formats, such as .WMF (used by Microsoft Draw).

◆ **Inserting Graphics**

If you can't copy and paste, you can use the INSERT, PICTURE command to get graphics into your Word publications and presentations.

To insert graphics into Word:

1. Put the cursor where you want the graphic to go.

2. Select Picture from the Insert Menu (<ALT> + I, P).

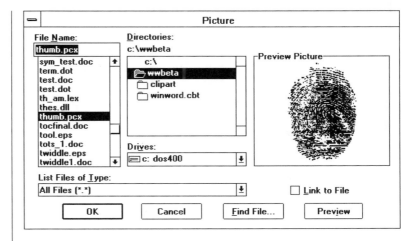

3. Choose the graphic you want to insert from the list; note that the List Files menu at the bottom of the dialog box now lists graphics formats such as .PCX. If necessary, change the drive and directory to locate the correct file.

4. If you want to preview a graphic to make sure it's the right one, highlight it and click on Preview (<ALT> + I). If you want to link your Word document to the graphic so that it can be updated automatically as the graphic changes, click on Link to File (<ALT> + L).

5. Click on OK or press <ENTER> when you're ready.

6. The graphic appears in Word. If you can't see it, make sure you're *not* in Draft view. If you still can't see it, use the TOOLS, OPTIONS command to turn the Picture Placeholders option off (it's under the View category). If that doesn't work, select Preview from the File menu (<ALT> + F, V) and try printing it. If you can print it but still don't see it, the graphic may be too large to fit in your computer's memory. You can still resize and crop it (although somewhat awkwardly).

Note: *When working with graphics and/or large documents, your system can run significantly faster if you turn the Picture Placeholders option on, or Draft view. If you have trouble inserting a particular graphic, select Draft from the View menu and try again.*

✦ Borders

You can border graphics (including those you create using Draw, Graph, and WordArt) just as you can border tables and text. However, you can't shade graphics. You don't have to be able to see the graphic itself to border it—you can put a box or rules around a placeholder just as well. (See *Border Basics* in Chapter 7 for more information.)

To border a graphic:

1. Select the graphic or its placeholder by clicking on it.

2. Select Border from the Format menu (<ALT> + T, B).

3. Select one of the Preset borders—Box (<ALT> + B) or Shadow (<ALT> + H)—or click on the sample page to indicate where you want the border(s) to go.

4. Select the type of line you want the box or rule to use.

5. Click on OK or press <ENTER> when you're done.

> **Note:** *To remove borders, click on None in the lower-left corner (<ALT> + N).*

✦ Cropping and Scaling

You can crop graphics (trim off the portions you don't want) and scale, or resize, them in two ways: you can drag the corners and edges of the image with your mouse, or you can use the Picture dialog box, which is on the Format menu. You can crop and resize graphics created with Draw, Graph, and WordArt; graphics that you copied from another program; and those that you inserted using the INSERT, PICTURE command. Word treats them all alike.

To resize graphics by dragging:

1. Select the graphic. You'll know it's selected when handles appear around its edges.

2. Click on one of those handles, and drag. You can only drag the handles on the right and left edges to the right and left; this makes the image wider or thinner. You can drag the top and bottom handles up and down; this makes it longer or shorter. As you drag, notice that the left corner of your Status Bar displays the graphic's new size as a percentage of its

original size. (If you can't see the Status Bar, use the TOOLS, OPTIONS command to turn it on.)

If you want to size your graphic proportionately so that its original shape doesn't change, simply drag from one of its four corners.

Note: If you make a mess of your graphic while trying to size it, you can always undo the damage. Select Picture from the Format menu (<ALT> + T, R), and click on the Reset button (<ALT> + S). This returns the graphic to its original size.

To crop graphics by dragging their edges:

1. Select the graphic.
2. Hold down the <SHIFT> key. Click on one of the handles, and drag. (The handles move in the same directions as described in the previous section.) If you drag the right handle to the left, you hide portions of the image. If you drag the right handle to the right, you add space to the right side of the graphic. As you drag, the Status Bar displays the crop measurements.

To crop or scale graphics using the Picture dialog box:

1. Select the graphic.
2. Select Picture from the Format menu (<ALT> + T, R). Notice that Word displays the original size of the graphic at the bottom of the dialog box. No matter what you do to this graphic, you can always return to its original size simply by clicking on the Reset button.

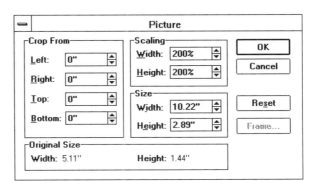

PUTTING IT ALL TOGETHER: Turning a Picture into a Presentation

This example shows how to work with clip art or other graphics that you insert into a document. However, you use the same commands to format graphics whether you're working with .EPS files, as in this case; an image copied from another program and pasted into Word; or a graphic you created with Draw, Graph, or WordArt.

You'll find the chart used in this example (KIT_CHT1.EPS) on the disk that comes with this kit. I'll just say a few words about how this chart was created in case you want to try your own. This chart is called a "combination chart" because it combines a column chart (monthly sales, measured along the left axis) with a line chart (year-to-date cumulative sales, measured along the right axis). I created it in Graph, which treats the columns as the main chart, and the line as an overlay. When I finished, I translated the file into an .EPS file for use in this example. I give instructions for creating a combination chart in Chapter 20.

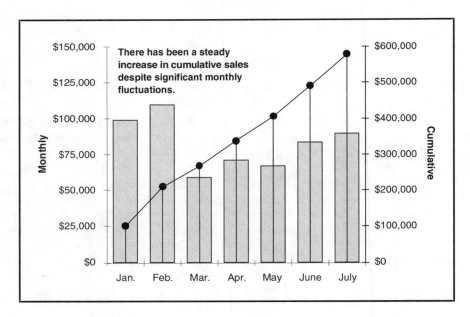

Monthly vs. Cumulative Sales, First Half 1991

This chart could easily be used in a report or handout or for an overhead transparency. If you have a laser printer, overhead transparencies are a cinch to create. All you need are transparencies suitable for laser printers, which are sold at most stationery stores. You don't have to create color charts to make effective presentations; in fact, most charts are created in black, white, and shades of gray for use in black-and-white reports. However, be careful with grays because they can turn out muddy-looking when photocopied (the lighter the gray, the better it usually looks). Stripes and other patterns can be a good alternative (see Chapter 20). As always, you can use these instructions to format a graphic you really have to get out the door.

1. When inserting graphics, it's usually a good idea to add several extra carriage returns above and below the line on which you'll insert the graphic so that you have room to move around. Then put your cursor where you want the graphic to go.

2. Select Picture from the Insert menu and then select KIT_CHT1 (it should be in your Clipart directory). Word places the graphic in your document.

3. Select the graphic, and box it using the FORMAT, BORDER command (<ALT> + T, B). I used the second thinnest line style available.

4. Once the chart is boxed, it's easy to see that there's too much white space around it. You need to crop the graphic so that the box fits as close to the chart as possible. If you're comfortable with your mouse, the easiest way to do this is to select the graphic and hold down the <SHIFT> key. Then drag the edges until the border is a respectable distance from the chart itself.

   Note: *You can see all four edges of the chart at once by zooming out to 75% of the original size. To do this, select Zoom from the View menu, and then 75% (<ALT> + V, Z, 7).*

5. You might also want to use your mouse to resize the chart; in the example it's 4.5 inches wide and 3 inches high.

   Note: *Even if you prefer to crop and resize graphics using your mouse, you might want to use the Picture dialog box to touch things up when you're nearly finished. This is an especially useful technique if you want to make several graphics the same size.*

6. All that's left is to center the chart and to give it a title. In the example, the title is set in 12-point Times bold, centered, with 3 lines of space Before (to separate it from the preceding material) and 1 line After. When you have a two-line title like this one, you should probably use the New Line command (<SHIFT> + <ENTER>) to break it where you want. Since a New Line break *doesn't* start a new paragraph with its own carriage return—it only starts a new line—you don't run into problems with line spacing.

3. To crop the graphic, type the amounts by which you want to crop the image along its left, right, top, and bottom sides. Of course, you don't have to crop the image along all four sides. If, for example, you just want to take an inch off the top, type "1" in the Top box (or use the arrows).

4. To scale the image, you can use either the Scaling options, which express the size of the graphic as a percentage of its *original* size, or the Size options, which express it in inches. No matter which option you decide to use, the other automatically changes as well. Here's an example of how this works. If you want to double the size of an image, scale it to 200% of both its original width and its original height. If you want to halve its size, scale it to 50%. Word automatically displays the new size of this graphic in the Size section. Note that the *original* size doesn't change.

Similarly, if you want to fit a 6-inch × 6-inch chart into a 3-inch × 3-inch space in your document, type 3 in both the Width and Height boxes in the Size section. Word automatically displays the corresponding percentages describing how the graphic was scaled in the Scaling section.

To change the shape of a graphic, scale the height and width to different percentages. For example, if you want it to be unusually long, scale the height to a larger percentage than its width. To make it unusually wide, scale the width to a larger percentage than its height.

5. Click on OK or press <ENTER> when you're done.

&etc... &etc... &etc...

You can change the shape of a graphic by scaling the width and height differently. The top example shows the graphic at original size. The middle one shows it at the original width, with the height scaled to 150%. The width of the bottom example is scaled to 150%, with the original height.

◆ **Captioning Graphics**

Captioning a graphic is no more difficult than typing text.

To caption a graphic:

1. Put the cursor directly to the right of the graphic you want to caption, and insert a carriage return.

2. Type the caption, and format it.

   Note: *If you're going to use several captioned graphics in your work, you might want to create a caption style and picture style to ensure consistency. If you do this, be sure to define the Next Style for the picture style as "caption" (to do this, define the caption style first).*

CHAPTER 12

Good Design Is in the Details

Good design is especially in the not-so-small details—like the basic layout of the page: whether your document is double or single sided, for example; whether it's in portrait or landscape mode; whether the margins are 1 inch all the way around or wider on the sides; whether it has a header and footer; and where the page number goes.

These "details" make up basic page design. When you start a new document, you should address these aspects of your work before anything else.

This chapter covers these topics in the following order:

- Landscape versus portrait pages (also called **orientation**).

- Page margins.

- Double-sided versus single-sided publications.

- How to use different orientations, page sizes, and margins in a single document.

- Everything you need to know about headers and footers.

- How to Preview and Zoom.

PAGE SETUP

This kit focuses on creating publications on the two page sizes that are standard for laser printers—letter and legal. However, you can use any size page up to 22 × 22 inches. *Sizing Pages (or Getting Oriented)* later in this chapter explains how to size documents so that they're smaller than usual, and *Sizing Up a Page* explains how you can break out of the laser printer letter-and-legal mold into much larger documents.

Different kinds of publications have different standard sizes. Most reports, newsletters, flyers, and so on tend to be 8.5 × 11 inches, portrait (or vertical) orientation. Complex tables of data are frequently done in landscape (or horizontal) orientation, on both letter and legal paper. Single-fold brochures are produced every day in a slew of sizes; 5.5 × 8.5 inches is a common one.

In the case of publications that you fold into final size (a single-fold brochure, for example), the finished page size can be quite different from the size of the paper on which it's printed. For instance, a single-fold brochure with a finished page size of 5.5 × 8.5 inches is printed on 11 × 8.5-inch paper (in other words, letter-sized paper in landscape orientation). A letter-fold brochure with a finished page size of 3.6 × 8.5 inches is printed on the same size sheet (see *Folding Paper Into Publications* in Chapter 4).

Depending on the type of print shop you use, the printer may use an even larger sheet to fit two or three copies of your publication on a single piece of paper. For instance, the larger print shops may well use 11 × 17-inch paper and print two letter-fold brochures at the same time. You should always sort out such matters with your printer well before you deliver the camera-ready copy, because it can make a difference as to exactly what you deliver.

You can also specify a page size that's smaller than letter-sized paper, for instance, if you were creating a 4 × 5-inch ad. In this case, you would have to *cut* the document into a finished page size.

Word enables you to set a different orientation, different page size, and individual margins for each page of your document. This is ideal for data-intensive reports that use landscape tables or diagrams. Although I have seen entire reports produced in landscape orientation, I've only seen one that wasn't awkward to read. It was short, it used largish type, and it formatted information into bulleted points instead of paragraphs, rather like a presentation (I explain how to create this format in Chapter 18).

◆ Sizing Pages (or Getting Oriented)

In Word, you use the Page Setup dialog box to control the page size and orientation of your printer as well as your document. Although you can also specify these options in the Print Setup dialog boxes, they don't affect how your documents look or print.

In Word, page size and paper size aren't necessarily the same thing, although they can be. If you select letter-sized paper from the pull-down Paper Size menu and then select Portrait mode, the Width automatically registers as 8.5 inches and the Height as 11 inches. If you select Landscape mode, the Width then changes to 11 inches and the Height to 8.5.

If you want, however, you can specify a page size that doesn't have a matching paper size. Simply type the measurements you want into the Width and Height boxes. For instance, if you want to create a 4 × 5-inch ad, simply type those measurements; Word automatically displays the paper size called "Custom Size." Although smaller-than-usual pages can certainly come in handy, they have one major drawback: you can't control where they print on the paper. They tend to come out centered, toward the bottom of the page. Because of this, you may find it easier to use a standard page size, and then create and size a frame (see Chapter 13 for more information on frames).

Note: *The paper sizes available vary according to the type of printer you have. If you have more than one printer set up for use with Word, you should select the one you want before using the Page Setup dialog box.*

To lay out your document using standard page and paper sizes:

1. Select Page Setup from the Format menu (<ALT> + T, U).

2. At the top of the dialog box (pictured following), select the Size and Orientation option (<ALT> + S).

3. Select the size you want to use from the Paper Size menu (<ALT> + Z).

4. Select the Orientation—Portrait (<ALT> + R) or Landscape (<ALT> + L). Word automatically registers the Width and the Height in the appropriate boxes, and changes the Sample to reflect your selections.

    Note: *The Sample also reflects the margins currently in effect.*

5. After you've set up the Size and Orientation, you can specify either the Margins (<ALT> + M) or the Paper Source (<ALT> + P), or you can click on OK or press <ENTER> to get back to your document.

```
┌─┬──────────────────────────────────────────────────────┐
│─│                   Page Setup                           │
├─┴──────────────────────────────────────────────────────┤
│            Select which page attributes to modify.       │
│   ○ Margins    ● Size and Orientation   ○ Paper Source   │
│  ┌────────────────────────┐  ┌─Sample──────────────┐    │
│  │ Paper Size :           │  │                      │    │
│  │ Letter (8 ½ x 11 in) ▼ │  │   ┌──────────────┐   │    │
│  │                        │  │   │ ════════════ │   │    │
│  │ Width:      8.5"    ⬍  │  │   │ ──────────── │   │    │
│  │ Height:     11"     ⬍  │  │   │ ──────────── │   │    │
│  │ ┌─Orientation────────┐ │  │   │ ──────────── │   │    │
│  │ │ ┌─┐ ● Portrait     │ │  │   │ ──────────── │   │    │
│  │ │ │A│               │ │  │   │ ──────────── │   │    │
│  │ │ └─┘ ○ Landscape    │ │  │   └──────────────┘   │    │
│  │ └────────────────────┘ │  └──────────────────────┘    │
│                              Apply To: Whole Document ▼   │
│  ┌─────────┐  ┌─────────┐  ┌──────────────────┐          │
│  │   OK    │  │ Cancel  │  │ Use as Default...│          │
│  └─────────┘  └─────────┘  └──────────────────┘          │
└──────────────────────────────────────────────────────────┘
```

You can change the margins, paper size, orientation, and paper source specified in your Normal template by clicking on the Use as Default button (<ALT> + U) in the Page Setup dialog box. When Word pops up a dialog box asking whether you want all new documents affected by this change, answer Yes.

To lay out your document using custom paper sizes:

1. Select Page Setup from the Format menu (<ALT> + T, U).

2. At the top of the dialog box, select the Size and Orientation option (<ALT> + S).

3. Type the Width you want to use (<ALT> + W); if you prefer, use the arrows. Type the Height (<ALT> + H).

4. Select the Orientation—Portrait (<ALT> + R) or Landscape (<ALT> + L).

5. After you've set up the Size and Orientation, you can go to either the Margins option (<ALT> + M) or the Paper Source options (<ALT> + P), or you can click on OK or press <ENTER> to get back to your document.

◆ Setting Margins

Outside of cutting and folding, margins are the most powerful tool you have for changing the shape of the printed page. You can narrow the text by setting wide left and right margins, and provide plenty of room for outquotes. You can give a publication a sophisticated, modern look by setting a wide top margin. You can position text artistically—for use in a brochure, for example, or a booklet—by using wide margins on all four sides.

Margins also have important practical uses, such as ensuring you have adequate room to bind the publication—for instance, when you're using a three-ring binder or spiral binding. Word's Gutter option enables you to add space specifically for this pur-

Sizing Up a Page

Word for Windows allows you to create pages in any size up to 22 × 22 inches. However, can you print it out? Unfortunately the answer may be that you *can't*. Take a moment to look at the maximum paper size available for your printer. The largest page that the Apple LaserWriter IINTX can use is legal-sized, 8.5 × 14 inches; the NEC ColorMate can only handle letter-sized sheets. The Linotronic 500, however—a high-resolution printer which is used in many service bureaus—can handle page sizes up to what is termed "tabloid extra," or 11.69 × 18 inches (tabloid is 11 × 17 inches). If you want to create documents that are too large for your own printer but can be handled by a Linotronic, here's what you do.

1. Set up your page size and margins by selecting Page Setup from the Format menu.

2. While working on the document, you can print copies *scaled to fit* (in other words, *reduced* to fit) on a sheet of paper your printer can manage. Use the Scale option in the Print Setup dialog box.

3. When you're ready to take the final document to the service bureau, use the Linotronic 500 model of printer to create a PostScript file as explained in Chapter 9. You should *always* do a one- or two-page test run at a service bureau to ensure that any new techniques you are trying actually produce the results you want. I can't overstate how important this is—service bureau fees add up pretty quickly.

Note: *If you have any questions regarding installing printer drivers, refer to your Windows manual. If you have questions about selecting printer models in Word, refer to Chapter 9 or to your Word for Windows manual.*

pose. It adds space to either the left margin (for single-sided publications) or to the inside margin (for double-sided publications). It doesn't matter whether you use the Gutter option or add extra space to the margins, as long as you leave enough room for binding.

Some printers won't print correctly unless you set a minimum page margin, because they can't print on the entire sheet of paper. Most laser printers, for example, can't print within a quarter inch of the edge of the page. If your margins don't meet this minimum, Word pops up a warning message when you go to print.

To set your margins:

1. Select Page Setup from the Format menu (<ALT> + T, U).

2. At the top of the dialog box, select Margins (<ALT> + M).

3. Type the margins you want in the appropriate box (or use the arrows).

4. After you set up the margins, you can go to either the Size and Orientation option (<ALT> + S) or the Paper Source option (<ALT> + P), or you can click on OK or press <ENTER> to get back to your document.

```
┌─────────────────────────────────────────────────────────┐
│ ▬                    Page Setup                          │
├─────────────────────────────────────────────────────────┤
│           Select which page attributes to modify.        │
│     ◉ Margins    ○ Size and Orientation   ○ Paper Source │
│                                                          │
│                              ┌─Sample──────────────┐     │
│   Top:      [1"    ] ▲▼      │                     │     │
│                              │   ═══════════        │     │
│   Bottom:   [1"    ] ▲▼      │   ──────────         │     │
│                              │   ──────────         │     │
│   Left:     [1.25" ] ▲▼      │   ──────────         │     │
│                              │   ──────────         │     │
│   Right:    [1.25" ] ▲▼      │   ──────────         │     │
│                              │   ──────────         │     │
│   Gutter:   [0"    ] ▲▼      │                     │     │
│                              └─────────────────────┘     │
│   ☐ Facing Pages      Apply To: [Whole Document    ] ▲▼  │
│                                                          │
│   ┌────────┐   ┌────────┐   ┌──────────────────┐        │
│   │   OK   │   │ Cancel │   │ Use as Default... │        │
│   └────────┘   └────────┘   └──────────────────┘        │
└─────────────────────────────────────────────────────────┘
```

Double-Sided Versus Single-Sided Publications. *Most* publications are double sided. Brochures, magazines, newspapers, and so on all use both sides of the page. Reports, however, are single sided as often as not, and flyers almost always are. You set up Word to print double-sided documents by setting the Facing Pages option on. Whether or not you turn them on depends primarily on the sort of work you do.

When you use Facing Pages (which adjust margins for double-sided pages), notice that the labels for the margins change. The left margin turns into the "inside" margin, and the right margin turns into the "outside" margin. The following diagram illustrates how this works.

When working with double-sided pages, take care to paginate your pages correctly. Right-hand pages should always be odd numbered (1, 3, 5, and so on). Left-hand pages should always be even numbered (2, 4, 6, and so on). Chapters should always start on a right-hand page. If you have to insert a blank page to *force* a chapter to open on the right, so be it.

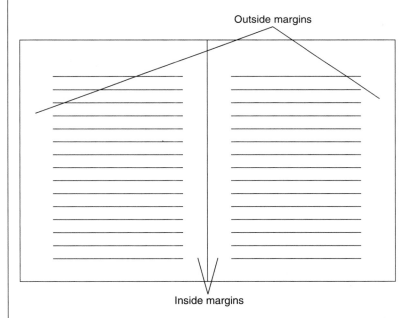

Turn the Facing Pages option on to produce double-sided publications in Word. When you do this, the labels for the margins in the dialog box change from "left" and "right" to "inside" and "outside," respectively.

To make your document double sided:

1. Open the Page Setup dialog box (<ALT> + T, U).

2. At the top of the dialog box, select Margins (<ALT> + M).

3. Click on the Facing Pages option (<ALT> + F) to turn it on. It's on when there's an "X" in the box.

4. Click on OK or press <ENTER> to get back to your document.

> **Note:** *If you change your mind and want your single-sided publication back, just turn Facing Pages off.*

✦ **Getting Reoriented**

You can include pages with different orientations and margins in a single document. You can also include different page sizes. However, if you don't use this particular option carefully, you could end up making your publications and presentations look worse instead of better.

When you use this feature, Word automatically inserts a **section** break into your document. Sections are a way of dividing your document so that each part can have its own orientation and margins, its own system of headers and footers, its own page numbering, and so on. Sections can be quite large or very small. For example, many of your documents will probably have only one section; on the other hand, you could turn every page of a document into its own section. (See *Using Section Breaks*, later in this chapter.)

Note: *On your screen, sections appear as double dotted lines, as though you have two page breaks on top of each other.*

To change the page setup options for specific pages of your document:

1. Put your cursor where you want to start the new section—in other words, where you want to start using the new orientation or margins.

2. Open the Page Setup dialog box (<ALT> + T, U).

3. At the top of the dialog box, select Margins (<ALT> + M) or Size and Orientation (<ALT> + S) depending on which options you want to change for this section.

4. Select the options, and then select This Point Forward from the Apply To menu (<ALT> + A).

> **Note:** *You can also use this menu to change the page setup for your whole document by selecting Whole Document. When your document includes more than one section, you can change the setup for each section by selecting This Section (which only appears on the menu when your document has more than one section).*

5. After you make the changes, you can go to either the Size and Orientation options (<ALT> + S) or the Paper Source options (<ALT> + P) and change them as well, or you can click on OK or press <ENTER> to get back to your document.

✦ Header and Footer Basics

Headers run along the top of every page, and footers run along the bottom. They can contain anything you want—from page numbers, to the name of the department producing the document, to a rule or logo.

Like tables, headers and footers are design and organizational tools that you can adapt to your own needs. You can use them to create headers and footers, of course. But you can also use their underlying architecture to design other aspects of a page as well. Generally, the header and footer tools enable you to do three sorts of things:

1. Repeat information and designs at the top and/or bottom of every page.

2. Set the page number with which a document starts and ends.

3. Place information very close to the edges of a page.

You can use rules, pictures, text, tables—just about anything— to dress up headers and footers, and you can create up to six different headers and footers in *each section* of a document. This may sound like a lot at first, but you'll be surprised at how quickly you use them up. A diagram of the Header/Footer dialog box follows.

Diagram of the Header/Footer Dialog Box

Select the header or footer you
want to edit from this list.

If you want to specify a
different header and/or
footer for the first page of a
document or section, turn
this option on. "First"
header and footer get
added to the list.

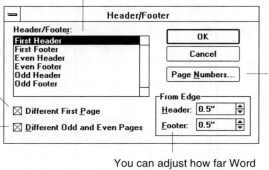

You can select
from a half dozen
page number
formats, such as
i,ii,iii or A,B,C. You
can also specify the
page number at
which the
document or
section starts.

This option is usually
used in conjunction with
the Facing Pages option,
which makes your
publication double-sided.
When it's on, you can
select Odd and Even
headers and footers.

You can adjust how far Word
places the header and footer
from the edge of the page.

To create a header or footer:

1. Select Header/Footer from the View menu (<ALT> + v, H).

   Note: *You should not be in Page Layout view when you do this. Although you can certainly create headers and footers in Page Layout view, you won't have the benefit of the icons.*

2. Select Header or Footer, then click on OK or press <ENTER>. The next thing you know you're *in* the header or footer. They look identical at first, but they're labeled clearly just to the right of the icons.

3. Be creative. You can paste graphics into headers and footers. You can type or format text. You can use dingbats, symbols, color, borders, rules, tables—whatever. Of course, you also can round up the usual suspects, for example, a page number, the date, and/or the time-of-day. Just click on the respective icon.

   What you see on your screen when formatting the header and footer depends on whether the Field Codes option is on or off (it's listed on the View menu); and whether or not you have the date and time set correctly in Windows' Control Panel. (If the wrong date or time appears, you don't; see your Windows manual to find out how to set them.)

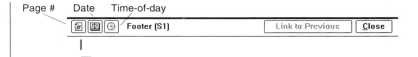

Page #   Date   Time-of-day

When the Field Codes option is on, you can see that the page number, time, and date are actually fields. This matters only when you use one of these fields, and then want to get rid of it later on. You can't just <BACKSPACE> over it; instead you have to highlight the field and press the <DELETE> key.

4. You can use all the normal formatting tools in headers and footers. When you first create one, it takes on the typeface, size, and paragraph formatting of the Normal style. It also has two tabs set—a center tab at 3 inches and a right tab at 6 inches. If you prefer other tab settings, just drag set the ones you want.

   Note: *In Word, headers and footers are styles. After you create a header or footer, it's automatically added to the Style menu on the Ribbon. You might want to redefine the header and footer styles. You might even want to unlink them from Normal so that changes you make to Normal no longer affect them.*

5. After you've finished, click on the Close button.

TEST RUN: Footer Design

Here's how to create the following footer, shown reduced:

DRAFT of 7/31/91   7   Hassett/Marketing Dept.

1. Select Header/Footer from the View menu, and then select Footer.

2. In the footer, type "DRAFT of" and then click on the Date icon. Make sure you leave a space between the "of" and the date. The actual date appears if the VIEW, FIELD CODES option is off; the date *field* appears if it's on.

3. Press the <TAB> key. The cursor jumps to the center tab, which is set at 3 inches (this is part of Word's standard footer style).

4. Click on the Page # icon. Either a page number or the page field appears, depending on whether the VIEW, FIELD CODES option is on or off.

[ruler graphic: 0 . . . |1 . . . |2 . . . |3 . . . |4 . . . |5 . . . |6]

> **Note:** *The page number that appears may not be the correct number for the page you're on. However, the page numbers are updated automatically when you print the document or "print preview" it. (The Print Preview feature is explained later in this chapter.)*

5. Press the <TAB> key again. The cursor moves to the right tab, which is set at 6 inches (again, this is part of Word's standard footer style).

PUTTING IT ALL TOGETHER: Designing with Tables and Footers

This example shows how to create this 5.5 × 1- inch single-fold brochure cover from planning to printing. It uses both tables and footers as design tools, rather than to create tables and footers per se. (If you haven't already, I recommend that you read *Brochures, Directories, and Catalogs* in Chapter 2 and *Folding Paper Into Publications* in Chapter 4.) To spare you the nuisance of making up text as you go along, I put the text for for the back cover of this brochure on the disk that came with this kit (KIT_TRST.DOC). *Don't open it yet*—I'll explain how to insert it when we get to that part of the example. If you want, you can follow these instructions to create a cover for your own single-fold brochure.

BOARD OF TRUSTEES:

Carol Salmon *lorem ipsumdolor sit amet, consectetuer adipiscing elit, sed diam nonummy nibh exerci tatton biad. Ut wisi enim ad minim veniam, quis nostrud exercis sit amet.*

Frank Walnuts *lorem ipsumdolor sit amet, consectetuer adipiscing elit, sed diam nonummy nibh quis nostrud exerci tatton biad.*

Jonathan Crowe *lorem ipsumdolor sit amet, consectetuer adipiscing elit, sed diam nonummy nibh quis nostrud exerci tatton biad. Ut wisi enim ad minim veniam, quis nostrud.*

Julia Grams *lorem ipsumdolor sit amet, consectetuer adipiscing elit, sed diam nonummy nibh quis nostrud exerci tatton biad. Ut wisi enim ad minim.*

Kevin Daniels *lorem ipsumdolor sit amet, consectetuer adipiscing elit, sed diam nonummy nibh quis nostrud exerci tatton biad. Ut wisi enim ad minim veniam, quis nostrud.*

Neil Bricant *lorem ipsumdolor sit amet, consectetuer adipiscing elit, sed diam nonummy nibh quis nostrud exerci tatton biad. Ut wisi enim ad minim veniam, quis nostrud exercis sit amet sit amet sit amet.*

P. Philips *lorem ipsumdolor sit amet, consectetuer adipiscing elit, sed diam nonummy nibh quis nostrud exerci tatton biad. Ut wisi enim ad minim venia.*

Patricia Harness *lorem ipsumdolor sit amet, consectetuer adipiscing elit, sed diam nonummy nibh quis nostrud exerci tatton biad. Ut wisi enim ad minim veniam, quis nostrud sit amet.*

Richard Michaels *lorem ipsumdolor sit amet, consectetuer adipiscing elit, sed diam nonummy nibh quis nostrud exerci tatton biad.*

Susan Branch *lorem ipsumdolor sit amet, consectetuer adipiscing elit, sed diam nonummy nibh quis nostrud exerci tatton biad. Ut wisi enim ad minim veniam ut wisi.*

SERVICE
What Membership Means
CREDITS

The Greater New York Consortium

6. Type "Hassett/Marketing Dept."

7. Highlight the text and set it in 9-point Palatino. Put a thin double border above it. Click on Close when you're done.

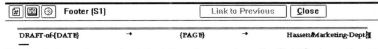

# 🔳 ⊗	Footer (S1)		Link to Previous	**Close**

DRAFT-of-{DATE}   →   {PAGE}   →   Hassett/Marketing-Dept.¶

This is what your footer should look like when you have the Field Codes option on.

Planning the Brochure Cover

If you're doing a report on letter-sized paper in portrait orientation, you don't have to think very hard about how to set it up. However, when you're creating, say, a 5.5 × 11-inch single-fold brochure, you need to have a plan. What you have to do in essence is create two columns on letter-sized paper in landscape orientation. On covers, I generally use tables to create columns—the front cover goes in the right-hand cell and the back cover goes in the left-hand cell. Keep in mind, however, that when text *flows* from column to column, it's usually easier to use Word's Column functions (which are covered in Chapter 13).

Note: *Chapter 17 goes through an example in which you create an entire letter-fold brochure in a single Word document, using tables for the cover and columns for the inside text.*

When you decide to use tables to create a cover, other issues arise—that of margins, for example. Usually, small brochures like this one have relatively slim margins. I used half an inch for both the left and right margins, and three-quarters of an inch for the top and bottom. That's easy enough, but what about the middle "margin"?

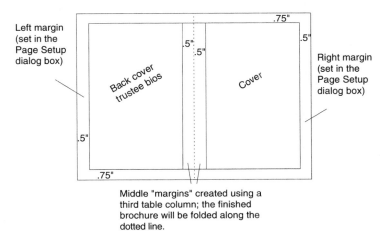

This is a tidy version of the kind of "map" I make whenever I do a fairly complex publication.

I used a third column, 1 inch wide, in the middle of the page to create a left-hand margin for the front cover and a right-hand margin for the back cover. Now that the margins are taken care of, how much room do I have left over for two columns that, in effect, serve as the front and back covers? Here's the calculation: 11 inches − (.5 inch left + .5 inch right + 1 inch middle) = 9 inches; 9 inches ÷ 2 columns = 4.5 inches. So each of the other columns is 4.5 inches wide.

By the way, I really do make these calculations before I start a brochure like this. In fact, I usually take a piece of paper, fold it in two, and mark the measurements on each side. I even scribble in the title and any other features that require special formatting. This serves as a rough map to guide me through what I have to do.

Creating the Brochure Cover

1. Start a new document by clicking on the New Document button on the Toolbar. If you prefer, select New from the File menu. Select the Normal template (the default), and then click on OK.

2. Select Page Setup from the Format menu (<ALT> + T, U). Set the Page Size to Letter, and select Landscape orientation. Set the top and bottom margins to .75 inches and the left and right margins to .5 inches.

3. Create a three-column, one-row table by using the Table icon on the Toolbar. If you prefer, select Insert from the Table menu. Make sure the Gridlines option on the Table menu is on so you can see the table on your screen.

4. Make the first column 4.5 inches wide; the second column 1 inch wide; and the third, 4.5 inches. The easiest way to do this is probably by dragging the edges of the cells. However, you can also use the Column Width dialog box, or the "T"s on the Ruler.

5. Highlight the table. In the Column Width dialog box on the Table menu (<ALT> + A, W), set the Space Between Columns option to zero. This makes the text line up with the very edge of the column, instead of being slightly indented. At this point, the three columns should take up the bulk of your landscape page. Click on the Zoom to Fit in Window button on the Toolbar to check whether this is so.

6. Let's format the front cover first. Put your cursor into the third column, and type the text for the title, just as it appears in the example. *Don't type the text at the bottom of the cover*—that's going to go into the footer in step #9. The title is *entirely* in New Century Schoolbook bold, centered. The words "SERVICE" and "CREDITS" are both 60 points, with single line spacing.

7. The phrase "What Membership Means" is set at 24 points, with 7.5 points of space After, and Exactly 21 points of line spacing.

8. When you format text in bold, 60-point caps, you'll generally need to kern it. Otherwise, some letters will run into each other, and other letters will have odd gaps between them. I kerned "SERVICE" by condensing the "R" by 1.5 points and expanding the space around the "V" by 3 points. I kerned "CREDITS" by expanding the space around the "R" by 3 points and the space around the "I" by 2 points.

   Note: *Word adjusts the space to the* right *of the letter you highlight and kern.*

9. Put the organization's name—in this case, "The Greater New York Consortium"—in the footer by selecting Header/Footer from the View menu (<ALT> + V, H). Set the footer so that it prints .25 inches from the paper's edge. Select Footer (<ALT> + F), and then click on OK or press <ENTER> to open it.

   Get rid of the two tabs included in Word's standard footer style (one at 3 inches, the other at 6) by clicking on them with your mouse and dragging them *off* the Ruler. Once the old tabs are gone, set a center tab at 7.75 inches. Then press the <TAB> key and type the text. Set it in 17-point New Century Schoolbook bold, centered.

   Note: *If you're creating a full brochure, you will probably want to turn the Different First Page option on in the Header/Footer dialog box.*

10. Insert the file containing the trustees' bios. To do this, put the cursor in the first cell. Select File from the Insert menu (<ALT> + I, L), and select KIT_TRST.DOC from the list of files (it should be in your Word program directory; see the instructions for using the disk that came with this kit in the *Introduction* if you have trouble with this).

    The text for the Board of Trustees now should fill up the cell. It should retain its formatting, but since there's no way to guarantee this, I'll give you the specs just in case. All the text is in Palatino, with .5 lines (6 points) of space After each paragraph. The title "Board of Trustees" is 14-point bold, small caps, centered, with 1.5 lines of space Before. The trustee bios are set at 10 points, justified. The names are bold and the bios themselves are italicized.

    Note: *In the example, I indented the bios slightly—9 points from both the right and left margins—so that they're* clearly *within the rule at the top of the page. To do this, highlight the text, and select Paragraph from the Format menu (<ALT> + T, P). Type "9pt" in both the From Left and From Right boxes.*

11. Highlight the "Board of Trustees" cell. Select Border from the Format menu (<ALT> + T, B), and place a single rule above it.

12. Save the document and print it. After it prints out, fold it in two. Sometimes it's hard to imagine how all the details that go into a design fit together until you have it in your hands.

✦ Using Section Breaks

Word lets you break your documents into **sections**. You can change certain basic design elements for each section of your document—for instance, orientation, page numbers, headers and footers, and the number of columns. This can be very handy if you're preparing several chapters in a single file. If you break each chapter into its own section, you can create special headers and footers for each chapter. This way, you can include chapter titles as well as page numbers. If you want, you can also *change* the page numbering process in each section. If you want the Executive Summary of your report to use small Roman numerals, for example, and the rest of the report to use Arabic numbers, just put a section break at the end of the Summary, and format the page numbers differently in each section.

If you want certain pages of your document formatted in two columns and other pages formatted in three columns—or whatever—you can do it by inserting a section break between them (see Chapter 13 for information on creating columns).

When you change a page's orientation, or its margins, Word *automatically* inserts a section break. However, if you just want to change the number of columns or the headers and footers, you have to insert a break manually.

Diagram of the Break Dialog Box

You can use this option to put a page break into your document. The result is the same as when you use <CTRL> + <ENTER>.

If you are working with columns and want to force text or graphics to start a *new* column, insert a column break. The idea is similar to a page break.

Next Page starts a new section on a new page.

Continuous starts a new section on the page you're currently working on. Practically speaking, this only makes sense when you want to design a page that includes both single- and multiple-column formats. You can't have one page with two different headers or footers, or two different orientations.

You can use section breaks to create columns, start a new series of headers and/or footers, restart page numbering, and restart footnote numbering. There are four kinds of section breaks to choose from: Next Page, Continuous, Even Page, and Odd Page.

Even Page starts the new section on the next even-numbered page. This is especially useful when you're using double-sided pages and/or different odd and even headers and footers.

Odd Page starts the new section on the next odd-numbered page.

Break

Insert:
- ○ Page Break
- ○ Column Break

Section Break
- ● Next Page
- ○ Continuous
- ○ Even Page
- ○ Odd Page

OK
Cancel

Tips on Handling Sections

Section breaks all work the same, no matter why you are using them. It may change your headers and footers, restart the page numbering, or change the number of columns snaking across the page—it makes no difference. One section break works just like every other one. Here's some basic information on how to deal with them.

- First, on your screen a section break looks a little like two page breaks stuck together.

- The only way to tell which section you're in at any given moment is to look at the Status Bar at the bottom of the screen.

Pg 2   Sec 2

- When working with headers and footers in sectioned documents, make sure the cursor is in the section whose header or footer you want to format *before* you open the Header/Footer dialog box. Word doesn't designate headers and footers according to the sections they belong to. Once you're in one, however, you can see the section number on the title bar. Always check to be sure you're in the right place. If you aren't, close the header or footer without making changes, reposition the cursor so it's *in* the section whose header or footer you want to format, and try again.

- My last tip for handling sections deals with printing. If you're going to print the entire document, it doesn't matter whether it's divided into sections or not. It matters a great deal, however, if you want to print only particular pages.

To print individual pages:

1. Select Print Preview from the File menu and "turn to" the page or pages you want to print. (Use the scroll bar or the <PAGE UP> and <PAGE DOWN> keys.)

2. When you get to a page you want to print, note both the page number and section at the right of the "button" bar. For example, the display shows P19 S1 for page 19, section 1, and P20 S2 for page 20, section 2. Note this information for every page you want to print.

3. Click on the Print button (or press P). When the Print dialog box opens, put the first page and section number you want to print in the From option (for instance, "p19s1"—no need for spaces), and the ending page and section you want to print in the To option (for instance, "p20s2").

You create a section by inserting one of Word's four different section breaks: Next Page, Continuous, Even Page, and Odd Page (see the diagram of the Break dialog box for explanations of each).

To create a section break:

1. Put your cursor wherever you want the new section to start, and select Break from the Insert menu.

2. Select the type of section break you want to use.

3. Click on OK or press <ENTER> to get back to your document.

✦ Different First Page

When you use the Different First Page option, Word creates a different header *and* a different footer for the first page of your document (or for the first page of every section in your document, if you're using more than one section).

To use a different header/footer on your first page:

1. Select Header/Footer from the View menu (<ALT> + V, H). Turn the Different First Page option on (<ALT> + P). It's on when there's an "x" in the box.

2. Immediately two more options appear in the Header/Footer list box: First Header and First Footer.

3. Select the First Header or First Footer if you want to format it in a specific way. For instance, if the first page is a cover page, you might want to place the organization's name in the footer so that it's close to the bottom of the page. If, however, you just want to leave the header and/or footer on the first page *blank*, format only the regular Header and/or Footer.

4. Click on OK or press <ENTER> when you're ready.

✦ Different Odd and Even Pages

The Different Odd and Even Pages option enables you to format odd (or left-hand) pages differently than even (or right-hand) pages. It's generally used in conjunction with the Facing Pages option.

To format right- and left-hand pages differently:

1. Select Header from the View menu. Turn the Different Odd and Even Pages option on (<ALT> + D). Immediately, four more options appear in the Header/Footer list box: Even Header, Even Footer, Odd Header, and Odd Footer.

2. Go through the list formatting the different headers and footers. If you can't remember what's in a particular one, open it and see. You can always close it without making any changes.

Note: *Remember that you can copy and paste between headers and footers; you don't have to create each one from scratch.*

✦ Page Numbers

You can use the Page Numbers feature in the Header/Footer dialog box to select one of five different number formats, including i,ii,iii, and a,b,c. You can also use this feature to start numbering pages with whatever number you wish. Simply type the starting number in the Start At option. This is invaluable for long documents spread over several chapters because you can easily start a chapter wherever the previous one left off.

Note: *If you break your document into sections, you can number the pages in each section* however you like. *For instance, each section could restart with 1.*

To use the Number feature:

1. Open the Header/Footer dialog box (<ALT> + V, H).

2. Click on the Page Numbers (<ALT> + N) to open the Page Number Format dialog box.

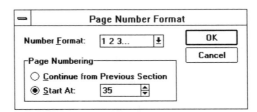

3. Select a number format from the Format menu.

Zooming and Previewing

Word has two features that enable you to work with your document at different sizes: Zoom and Print Preview.

Zoom

Zoom enables you to see your work at any magnification from 25 to 200%. You can zoom out, for instance, to 75% magnification, to fit an entire graphic on screen so that it's easier to crop or resize. You can also zoom out and see a whole page at once—this is invaluable for moving text, graphics, and frames with your mouse. (See Chapter 13 for more information on frames.) After you've moved things around in a reduced view, you can then zoom in on a particular section of your page and line things up precisely. The only drawback I've found to the Zoom tools, especially the reduced magnifications, is that they don't always provide an accurate view of your page. To see your full page accurately, you need to use Word's Print Preview feature.

To see a whole page at once in Page Layout view:

- Click on the Zoom to Fit in Window icon on the Toolbar 🔳.

To return to Normal view:

- Click on the Zoom to 100% icon on the Toolbar 🔳.

To see the entire width of your page:

- Click on the Zoom Page Width icon on the Toolbar 🔳.

You have additional Zoom options when you open the Zoom dialog box on the View menu. There you can select either the Page Width or Whole Page options (which correspond to the Page Width and Fit in Window icons on the Toolbar, respectively). You can also select one of the four standard magnifications: 50%, 75%, 100%, and 200%. And if none of these are quite what you need, you can specify another percentage.

1. Select Zoom from the View menu (<ALT> + v, z). The Zoom dialog box opens.

2. Select the magnification you want, or type it in the Custom box. You can also use the arrows.

3. Click on OK or press <ENTER> when you're done.

To *un*magnify your page, simply click on the Zoom to 100% icon on the Toolbar, or select 100% from the Zoom dialog box (<ALT> + v, z). There's an important difference between these two options. In addition to remagnifying your document to 100% size, the Zoom to 100% icon returns it to Normal view. If you want to remain in Page Layout view, you should use the Zoom dialog box.

Note: *The templates that came with this kit include four additional Zoom buttons on the Toolbar: Zoom to 100%, 75%, and 200% in Page Layout mode, and 100% in Draft mode.*

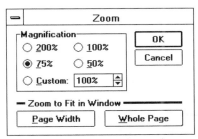

To open the Zoom dialog box, select
Zoom from the View menu.

Print Preview

Word's Print Preview feature enables you to see your "printed" page in miniature on the screen. Although it's not 100 percent accurate, it's the most reliable of Word's WYSIWYG modes. Whenever the Page Layout view and Print Preview show things lining up a bit differently, believe the latter.

The Print Preview feature shows you how things fit together at a glance. You don't have to scroll up to this corner to see how the header looks and then back down to the other corner to see the footer—it's all right there. It also provides a wonderful capability: You can simply *drag* certain page elements—your headers, footers, and margins—to where you want them to go on the page. You can also see two pages at once (click on Two Pages, or press A).

To use the Print Preview feature to reposition page elements:

1. Select Print Preview from the File menu.

2. A screen opens showing your document in the middle and a "button" bar on top.

3. Click on Margins (or press M). Dotted lines ring various page elements, including the header and footer. The margins also are shown by dotted lines, with handles attached.

4. When you point your mouse at one of the dotted elements or the handles on the margins, it turns into a crosshair. You now can move that element simply by clicking on it and dragging it with your mouse.

5. When you're satisfied with the new position, click anywhere *off* the page to make the changes take effect.

   Note: *You can't drag a header or footer past the margin into the main text. You can, however, move the margin down and* then *reposition the header exactly where you want it.*

6. You can Print (P), or Cancel (C) to return to your document.

4. Click on Start At (<ALT> + S), and type the page number with which you want the document to start (or use the arrows).

5. If you want, select a header or footer to format. Click on OK or press <ENTER> when you're done.

PUTTING IT ALL TOGETHER: Mirror Margins + Odd and Even Headers/ Footers = Double-Sided Publications

Here's how to set up your double-sided publications to take advantage of odd and even headers and footers. The instructions focus on setting up the document as a double-sided publication, changing the margins, creating headers and footers, and formatting a graphic. If you're not using these instructions to help format your own work, you can use two sample files from the *Tools of the Trade* disk that came with this kit: KIT_DUBL.DOC and KIT_CHT2.EPS.

Background

Lorem ipsum dolor sit amet, consectetuer adipiscing elit, sed diam nonummy nibh euismod tincidunt ut laoreet dolore magna aliquam erat volutpat. Ut wisi enim ad minim veniam, quis nostrud exerci tation ullamcorper suscipit lobortis nisl ut aliquip ex ea commodo feugiat consequat. Dolor sit amet, consectetuer adipiscing elit, sed diam nonummy nibh euismod tincidunt ut laoreet dolore magna aliquam. Ad minim veniam, quis nostrud exerci tation ullamcorper suscipit lobortis nisl.

Ipsum dolor sit amet, consectetuer adipiscing elit, sed diam nonummy nibh euismod tincidunt ut laoreet dolore magna aliquam erat volutpat ut wisi. Enim ad minim veniam. Ullamcorper suscipit lobortis nisl ut aliquip ex ea commodo feugiat. Sit amet consectetuer adipiscing elit, sed diam nonummy nibh. Minim veniam, quis nostrud exerci tation ullamcorper suscipit lobortis.

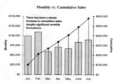

Monthly vs. Cumulative Sales

Lorem ipsum dolor sit amet, consectetuer adipiscing elit, sed diam nonummy nibh euismod tincidunt ut.

Lorem ipsum dolor sit amet, consectetuer adipiscing elit, sed diam nonummy nibh euismod tincidunt ut laoreet dolore magna aliquam erat volutpat. Ut wisi enim ad minim veniam, quis nostrud exerci tation ullamcorper suscipit lobortis nisl ut aliquip ex ea commodo feugiat consequat. Dolor sit amet, consectetuer adipiscing elit, sed diam nonummy nibh euismod tincidunt ut laoreet dolore magna aliquam. Ad minim veniam, quis nostrud exerci tation ullamcorper suscipit lobortis nisl.

Ipsum dolor sit amet, consectetuer adipiscing elit, sed diam nonummy nibh euismod tincidunt ut laoreet dolore magna aliquam erat volutpat ut wisi. Enim ad minim veniam.

Background

Ullamcorper suscipit lobortis nisl ut aliquip ex ea commodo feugiat.

Lorem ipsum dolor sit amet, consectetuer adipiscing elit, sed diam nonummy nibh euismod tincidunt ut laoreet dolore magna aliquam erat volutpat. Ut wisi enim ad minim veniam, quis nostrud exerci tation ullamcorper suscipit lobortis nisl ut aliquip ex ea commodo feugiat consequat. Dolor sit amet, consectetuer adipiscing elit, sed diam nonummy nibh euismod tincidunt ut laoreet dolore magna aliquam. Ad minim veniam, quis nostrud exerci tation ullamcorper suscipit lobortis nisl.

Ipsum dolor sit amet, consectetuer adipiscing elit, sed diam nonummy nibh euismod tincidunt ut laoreet dolore magna aliquam erat volutpat ut wisi. Enim ad minim veniam. Ullamcorper suscipit lobortis nisl ut aliquip ex ea commodo feugiat. Sit amet consectetuer adipiscing elit, sed diam nonummy nibh. Minim veniam, quis nostrud exerci tation ullamcorper suscipit lobortis.

Lorem ipsum dolor sit amet, consectetuer adipiscing elit, sed diam nonummy nibh euismod tincidunt ut laoreet dolore magna aliquam erat volutpat. Ut wisi enim ad minim veniam, quis nostrud exerci tation ullamcorper suscipit lobortis nisl ut aliquip ex ea commodo feugiat consequat. Dolor sit amet, consectetuer adipiscing elit, sed diam nonummy nibh euismod tincidunt ut laoreet dolore magna aliquam. Ad minim veniam, quis nostrud exerci tation ullamcorper suscipit lobortis nisl.

Ipsum dolor sit amet, consectetuer adipiscing elit, sed diam nonummy nibh euismod tincidunt ut laoreet dolore magna aliquam erat volutpat ut wisi. Enim ad minim veniam. Ullamcorper suscipit lobortis nisl ut aliquip ex ea commodo feugiat. Sit amet consectetuer adipiscing elit, sed diam nonummy nibh. Minim veniam, quis nostrud exerci tation ullamcorper suscipit lobortis.

Lorem ipsum dolor sit amet, consectetuer adipiscing elit, sed diam nonummy nibh euismod tincidunt ut laoreet dolore magna aliquam erat volutpat. Ut wisi enim ad minim veniam, quis nostrud exerci tation ullamcorper suscipit lobortis nisl ut aliquip ex ea commodo feugiat consequat. Dolor sit amet, consectetuer adipiscing elit, sed diam nonummy nibh euismod tincidunt ut laoreet dolore magna aliquam. Ad minim veniam, quis nostrud exerci tation ullamcorper suscipit lobortis nisl.

Ipsum dolor sit amet, consectetuer adipiscing elit, sed diam nonummy nibh euismod tincidunt ut laoreet dolore magna aliquam erat volutpat ut wisi. Enim ad minim veniam. Ullamcorper suscipit lobortis nisl ut aliquip ex ea commodo feugiat. Sit amet consectetuer adipiscing elit, sed diam nonummy nibh. Minim veniam, quis nostrud exerci tation ullamcorper suscipit lobortis.

Lorem ipsum dolor sit amet, consectetuer adipiscing elit, sed diam nonummy nibh

✦ Distance from Edge

From Edge is the last option for headers and footers. It's useful because it enables you to specify how far headers and footers should be from the edge of the page. Try different distances to see what they look like. The larger the number, the *farther* from the edge the header or footer is.

1. Open the document KIT_DUBL.DOC.

2. Because this example is a double-page spread (pages 2 and 3), you have to create a dummy first page. To do this, simply put your cursor to the left of the very first word in the document, and press <CTRL> + <ENTER> to put in a page break. Position your cursor in what's now the second page.

3. Use the Page Setup dialog box to specify the Page Size (Letter), Orientation (Portrait), Facing Pages (on), and Margins (Top = 2.3; Bottom = 1; Inside = 1.5; Outside = 1.5). The extra space in the Inside margin makes room for binding the report.

4. Format your main text. In this example, I defined Normal as 11-point Times justified, on Auto line spacing. It has a First Line indent of .2 inches and 3 points of space After.

5. Make sure your cursor is on the second page, which is an even page. Open the Header/ Footer dialog box. Turn on Different Odd and Even Pages. Set the Header 1.5 inches from the edge of the page. Leave the footer at the default value of .5 inches. Select the Even Header, and then click on OK or press <ENTER> to open it.

   Note: *If you happen to be in Page Layout view, Word only displays one header and one footer even after you turn on Different Odd and Even Pages. To get to an even header in Page Layout view, your cursor has to be positioned on an even page. To get to an odd one, it has to be positioned on an odd page. When you first start working with headers and footers, it tends to be easier to use either Normal or Draft view.*

6. On even pages, you generally want text and graphics to be positioned at the left of the page. On odd pages, you generally want them positioned at the right. In this example, the header includes the report's section title, and the footer includes the page number and the name of the department that produced the report.

   Type the section title in the even header (in this case, "Background"). Format it as 16-point Times, flush left. Since Word bases the header and footer styles on Normal, you have to get rid of the First Line indent. Add the thickest rule available in the Border dialog box; in the example, I positioned it 4 points from the text. Copy the even header—text, rule, and all—and close it when you're done.

7. Open the odd header. Paste the even header into it and make one change: align it flush right.

To use this option:

1. Open the Header/Footer dialog box.

2. Type the distance at which you want the header to start (or use the arrows); type the distance at which you want the footer to start. *These do not have to be the same number.*

3. If you want, select a header or footer to format. Click on OK or press <ENTER> when you're done.

---

8. Open the even footer. Format it as 9-point Helvetica with the second-thinnest rule available in the Border dialog box. Remember to get rid of the First Line indent. Set a page number at the left margin; separate the number from the name of the department that produced the report with an em dash (you can use either the Symbol palette or type <ALT> + 0151 on the numeric keypad); and then type the department's name. Copy the footer, and close it when you're done.

9. Open the odd footer, and paste the even footer into it. Change the alignment to flush right. Reposition the page number at the right edge of the page. Reposition the department name to the left of the number and put the em dash between them. Close the footer when you're done.

10. Three more steps to go. First, put your cursor where you want the chart to go, and use the INSERT, PICTURE command to bring it into the document (it's in KIT_CHT2.EPS). Center the chart, box it (I used the thinnest line available), and put 1 line of space above it. Scale the chart to approximately 60% of its original size. When I did this, I thought that the border around the graphic was too close to the graphic itself. If you do, too, you can fix it by "cropping" the chart using negative numbers, which adds white space around it. Although you can do this by holding down the <SHIFT> key while dragging the edges of the graphic with your mouse, you can also open the Picture dialog box and type a negative number in all the Crop From boxes. In this case, I typed "-.2" inches.

11. Add a caption to the chart (just copy and paste a sentence or two of dummy text if you're not doing this for real). Format it in the same style as the footer: 9-point Helvetica. However, put 3 points of space Before (to separate it from the graphic) and 1 line of space After (to separate it from the main text). Change the Left and Right Indents so that the caption is no wider than the graphic it describes.

12. One last thing: When you use facing pages, the text on the bottom of both pages really needs to line up evenly. Sometimes it's necessary to tweak the space around graphics and heads in order to make this happen, but you'll make a big step in the right direction if you turn off Widow/Orphan Control. You can do this in one of two ways: By using the Print Category in the Options dialog box on the Tools menu; or by using the Options dialog box from the Print dialog box itself.

Folio Treatments

Folio treatments are how designers dress up page numbers, and headers and footers generally. Often you can create a finished, professional look with the tiniest of touches. Here are examples of some easy-to-do folio treatments. Naturally there are hundreds of variations on these; this is just to get you started.

1

The number is in 10-point New Century Schoolbook, with a double line above. I adjusted the Right and Left Indents to narrow the rule to what you see here. To do this, simply put your cursor in the paragraph and drag the Left Indent marker to the right and the Right Indent marker to the left.

2

The number is in 10-point New Century Schoolbook. The 16-point Zapf Dingbat beneath it is in a separate paragraph, formatted with Exactly 11 points of line spacing. This pushes the number and the dingbat closer together. (See Chapter 6 if you have questions on dingbats and symbols, and how to use them.)

3

The number is in 8-point Helvetica bold. The three Zapf Dingbats beneath it are 6 points on Exactly 5 points of leading.

◇ 4 ◇

The number is in 12-point Palatino bold. The Zapf Dingbats on either side are set at 8 points.

5

The number is 10-point Times bold. It has the second-thinnest rule in the Border dialog box placed both above and below. I adjusted the Right and Left Indents to narrow the rules to what you see here.

6

The number is 10-point Avant Garde, with the thinnest border around it. I adjusted the Right and Left Indent markers until I got the box width I wanted.

7

This is almost identical to the previous folio treatment, except the number is bolded, the border is the second-thinnest available, and the paragraph width is quite narrow.

Page 8 of 24

With the Show/Hide¶ button on, this treatment appears in the footer as: *Page·{PAGE}·of·24¶*. The numbers and text are 10-point Times italic.

9

This folio treatment was created with Draw. The number is formatted in 12-point Bookman bold.

|10|

This folio treatment was also created with Draw.

CHAPTER 13

Designing
a Page

Up to now, we've been sifting through the pieces of what, taken together, is called "page design." This chapter puts in the two last pieces of the puzzle. It covers Word's two most sophisticated page layout features—columns and frames.

This chapter draws upon two page layouts taken from Chapter 2—a report, and a magazine-style layout. It also uses a third example guaranteed to convince you that the frame feature is as easy as it actually is. The disk that came with this kit includes the text for all three examples so you can focus on formatting instead of typing. Have the Draw files KIT_RUL1–KIT_RUL3.WMF standing by.

This chapter covers these topics in the following order:

- How to create and format frames.

- How to create drop caps.

- How to create columns.

DESIGNING FRAMES

Frames allow you to put graphics and text *anywhere* on the page. If you decide to put a framed graphic or framed paragraphs into the main text (see examples A and B), the rest of the text wraps around it. You also can put framed text and graphics (for instance, outquotes) in the margins. You can use as many frames as you want on a page.

Word provides an impressive battery of options guaranteed to get your framed text and graphics positioned exactly where you want them. There are two general methods to choose from: relative and absolute positioning. **Absolute positioning** is when you type the precise measurements at which you want to place the frame (for instance, 3.4 inches from the left). **Relative positioning** is for less exacting jobs—when it's enough that the image simply be at the top or bottom of the page or after a particular headline. This chapter covers both types, and Chapters 18 and 19 include additional examples using frames.

I rarely use Page Layout view in my work, except when I use frames and columns. Page Layout view is the only way to get WYSIWYG for positioned text and graphics while you work on them. Because it can be excruciatingly slow at times, however, you may decide to go without WYSIWYG as much as you can. But sometimes there's no way around it. When you're laying out a

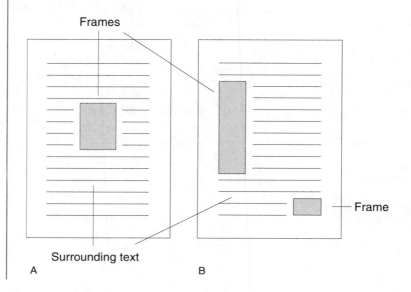

Frames

Surrounding text

Frame

A   B

page, you need to see what it looks like while you're working so you just have to grit your teeth and wait for the screen to redraw.

One other tip on working with frames. If you type in the text before you frame graphics and text, this feature is easy to use. If you don't, it can get harder.

Like most of Word's features, you can create and format frames by mouse, or by menu.

Here's HOW

To create a frame:

1. Highlight the text and/or graphics you want to put inside a frame—anything from several paragraphs to a single letter.

   Note: You can put just about anything inside a frame, including tables and other frames. However, as of this writing, working with frames inside frames has proven frustrating.

2. Click on the Frame button on the Toolbar ▦.

   or

   Select Frame from the Insert menu (<ALT> + I, F). If you're not in Page Layout view, Word pops up a dialog box prompting you to switch to Page Layout view. You have to use this view if you want to size or position frames using your mouse, or if you want to see frames correctly positioned on your screen. Answer Yes to switch.

As of this writing, when you first create a frame, Word puts a box around it. You can use the Border dialog box to get rid of this box (just click on None), or to change it to a different line style.

To a certain extent, Word treats everything inside a frame as a single object. You select a frame—and whatever's in it—by clicking on the frame. You can then drag the frame and its contents someplace else on the page. You can also resize the frame by dragging the handles.

Although you can resize a frame using the same mouse technique used to resize graphics, the results aren't quite the same. You don't change the size of the framed items themselves; rather, you change the shape of the frame, making the items inside it flow long instead of wide, for example. You change the size of the framed text itself just as you change the size of any other text, by highlighting it and selecting a new point size. Similarly, you change the size and shape of a framed graphic by selecting it and resizing it, just as you would a graphic that isn't framed.

Note: *You generally have to use the <ARROW> (or directional) keys to select text and graphics inside a frame. Remember to hold down the <SHIFT> key to high-light items using the <ARROW> keys.*

To resize a frame using your mouse:

1. Select the frame. You know it's selected when handles appear around its edges.

2. Click on one of those handles, and drag. You can only drag the handles on the right and left edges to the right and left; this makes the frame wider or thinner. You can drag the top and bottom handles up and down; this makes it longer or shorter. You drag the corner handles diagonally; this changes the frame's height and width at the same time.

To move a frame someplace else:

1. Although you don't have to zoom out in order to move a frame, it can be easier if you do. To fit the whole page on your screen, click on the Fit in Window button on the Toolbar. Select the frame.

2. Position your mouse over the frame so that the mouse pointer turns into four arrows pointing in four directions. Sometimes this can be frustrating because you have to position the mouse just right. I have the best luck when I point at the edge of the frame right next to a handle, but not on the handle. If you point *on* it, you'll get the double-edged arrows used for resizing.

3. When the mouse pointer turns into four arrows, click, and drag the frame where you want it to go. A dotted box serves as a placeholder for the frame while you're dragging it. When you let go of the placeholder, the frame itself moves into position.

Note: *You can also cut and paste a frame if you want to move it onto an-other page.*

To get rid of a frame:

1. Select it, and then choose Frame from the Format menu
(<ALT> + T, F).

2. Click on the Remove Frame button (<ALT> + R).

   Note: *As of this writing, when you remove a frame that has a box around it, Word leaves the box. To remove that, open the Border dialog box and click on None. If you want to remove the frame, the box, and its contents, select the frame and then press <DELETE>.*

✦ What the Options Are

It's pretty simple to create a frame and drag it around the page until you've got it where you want it, but it isn't always very precise. To place a frame at a specific measurement, you will probably want to use the Frame dialog box, at least to touch up the positioning after you've moved it close to where you want it. The Frame dialog box also includes several other important features. For instance, it lets you specify whether or not you want the main text to wrap around the frame; it lets you specify the distance you want to place the frame from the surrounding text and graphics; and it lets you delete a frame. This dialog box is also useful when you want to define a style that includes a frame (you can access the Frame dialog box directly from the Style dialog box). A diagram of the Frame dialog box follows.

Diagram of the Frame Dialog Box

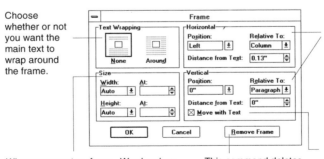

Choose whether or not you want the main text to wrap around the frame.

The options in the Horizontal and Vertical sections are especially useful for defining styles—for example, an outquote style—that always has to be positioned in a certain place on the page. When you move a frame with your mouse, you're actually specifying its horizontal and vertical position.

When you create a frame, Word makes it large enough to fit around the text and graphics inside. However, you can also set a *specific* width and height here. This is essentially the same as resizing the frame with your mouse.

This command deletes the frame but not the text and graphics inside. To delete the frame and everything that's in it, use the <DELETE> key.

When this option is on, the frame can move up or down the page depending on whether you add or delete portions of the surrounding text. When this option is off, the frame is stationary—no matter what you do to the surrounding text.

The Frame dialog box—with its Horizontal positioning and Vertical positioning and Widths and Heights—can look pretty confusing. But it all depends on *how* you look at it. When you drag a frame with your mouse, what you're really doing is setting its **horizontal** and **vertical position**, in other words, where it is on the page. You're telling Word how far you want the frame from the top of the page, or from the left side. Similarly, when you resize a frame using your mouse, you're actually specifying its width and height. After you position or resize a frame, open the Frame dialog box and check out the settings that Word itself uses to describe where your frame is and how big it is.

The following section briefly explains how to use the options in the Frame dialog box.

Size.   The Size options are the numerical equivalent of dragging the edges of a frame with your mouse. There are two options listed on the Width menu: Auto and Exactly. When you first create a frame, Word makes it large enough to fit around the text and graphics inside it, in other words, Auto. When you change the width of the frame—either by using the mouse or this dialog box—you are setting an exact measurement for the frame, for instance, Exactly 1.5 inches, or Exactly 7 inches. When you have an exact frame measurement, text flows to fit its width; if graphics are too large to fit, they get lopped off. To fix this problem you can resize either the graphic or the frame.

The Height menu lists three options: Auto, Exactly, and At Least. Auto and Exactly work the same for both width and height. At Least is a somewhat more flexible option that allows the frame to have a minimum height, but no maximum. If you keep adding text and graphics, the frame will keep getting longer so that they fit. If you are using a frame for a sidebar in a newsletter or for an outquote, you may want to set an exact height.

Horizontal and Vertical Positions.   Whenever you move a frame, you're specifying its horizontal and vertical position. Word provides many different options for doing this. Because these options literally cover the whole landscape (there probably isn't a position you can think of that Word can't manage), they can seem very confusing at first. Furthermore you don't generally need them all, except for special cases. Here I focus

Frames and Styles

Working with frames and styles at the same time is easy. If you want to create a framed style, just create a style as you normally would—using the Style dialog box or the by-example method—and include the frame as part of the style definition. (See Chapter 7 if you have any questions about creating styles.) Although it doesn't matter whether you drag the frame into position or whether you use the Frame dialog box, be sure you format the frame exactly the way you want the style to be formatted. Include these elements in the style definition: whether or not you want the text to wrap around the frame, the frame's size, the horizontal and vertical positioning, borders, shading, typeface, point size, line spacing, and so on. Then, whenever you apply this framed style to text, Word automatically formats the text and positions it on the page.

You can also apply two or more different styles to a single frame—for example, if you're creating sidebars for a publication and want each one to have a standard heading and standard text formatting. Just remember that when you define these styles, you have to define them so that the frame is *exactly* the same. Otherwise, you can end up with two different frames on top of each other, rather than two different styles in the same frame.

on the ones you're bound to use sooner or later. Once you're comfortable with these, try the others and see what they can do.

The easiest way of getting used to Word's positioning options is to move a frame with your mouse, and then open the Frame dialog box and see how Word describes its position. In fact, you may end up using your mouse to position frames more than this dialog box. However, the dialog box is invaluable for ensuring that certain design elements such as outquotes and sidebars are all the same width, start at the same height, are the same distance from the edge of the page, and so on. Although I frequently drag frames into rough position, I almost always use the Frame dialog box to finalize that it is positioned exactly where I want it. The Frame dialog box is a must when you're using framed styles.

Horizontal Positions

Whenever you position an image on the page, you have to se-lect two things: a starting point at which Word starts to measure, and a position relative to that starting point. There are three dif-ferent horizontal starting points (listed on the Relative To menu): the margin, the page, or a column (unless you're using more than one column, margin and column are the same). There are five different horizontal positions relative to each of these three starting points: left, center, right, inside, and outside. (Or, if you want to use absolute positioning, you can just type the horizon-tal measurement at which you want to place the graphic, for ex-ample, 4.2 inches Relative To Margin.) Here are some tips for deciding which of these fifteen combinations to use (see the dia-gram *Relative To Page versus Relative To Margin* following).

Position	Option
• In main text area	Relative To Margin
• Outside the margins	Relative To Page
• In a column	Relative To Column
• In main text area, left side	Left, Relative To Margin
• In main text area, right side	Right, Relative To Margin
• In main text area, center	Center, Relative To Margin
• Left margin	Left, Relative To Page
• Right margin	Right, Relative To Page
• Left side of column	Left, Relative To Column
• Right side of column	Right, Relative To Column
• Center of column	Center, Relative To Column

Vertical Positions

A frame's vertical position describes where it's placed between the top and bottom of the page. Word includes three such posi-tions: top, bottom, and center. It also includes three vertical starting points: margin, page, and paragraph. These are similar to the horizontal options—just think top and bottom instead of left and right. (If you want to use absolute positioning, simply type in the vertical measurement at which you want to place the graphic, for example, 2.3 inches Relative To Margin would

Relative To Page versus Relative To Margin

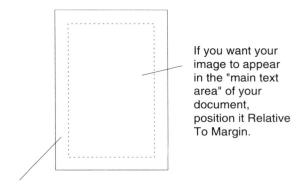

If you want your image to appear in the "main text area" of your document, position it Relative To Margin.

If you want your image to appear in the margin of your document, position it Relative To Page.

place the frame 2.3 inches from the top margin.) Again, if you want to put the image in the main text area of your document, position it Relative To Margin. If you want to put the image in the margin, position it Relative To Page.

Word's default vertical position is 0 inches Relative To Paragraph. All this means is that the frame is placed directly below the *preceding* paragraph. You can also position the frame a specific distance below that paragraph by typing a number and setting it Relative To Paragraph. If you have the Move with Text option on (Word's default), the frame will move as the preceding paragraph moves. If you have this option off, the frame is stationary.

Distance from Text

You can specify that a frame be positioned a specific Distance From Text. This enables you to leave more or less space between the frame and the text that wraps around it. Word's default value for both horizontal and vertical positions is .13 inches.

TEST RUN: Framing an Outquote

Now that you have a sense of how frames work, all you need is some practice. This example shows how to put a paragraph in a frame and then turn it into an outquote. Use the file KIT_FRAM.DOC from the *Tools of the Trade* disk. The sample page on the left shows what this file looks like when you first open it. The following instructions turn the example on the left into the page on the right.

Neil Bricant lorem ipsumdolor sit amet, consectetuer adipiscing elit, sed diam nonummy nibh quis nostrud exerci tatton biad. Ut wisi enim ad minim veniam, quis nostrud exerci sit amet sit amet sit amet.

Jonathan Crowe lorem ipsumdolor sit amet, consectetuer adipiscing elit, sed diam nonummy nibh quis nostrud exerci tatton biad. Ut wisi enim ad minim veniam, quis nostrud. Julia Grams lorem ipsumdolor sit amet, consectetuer adipiscing elit, sed diam nonummy nibh quis nostrud exerci tatton biad. Ut wisi enim ad minim. Kevin Daniels lorem ipsumdolor sit amet, consectetuer adipiscing elit, sed diam nonummy nibh quis nostrud exerci tatton biad. Ut wisi enim ad minim veniam, quis nostrud.

PLACE THE OUTQUOTE AFTER THIS PARAGRAPH.

P. Philips lorem ipsumdolor sit amet, consectetuer adipiscing elit, sed diam nonummy nibh quis nostrud exerci tatton biad. Ut wisi enim ad minim venia. Patricia Harness lorem ipsumdolor sit amet, consectetuer adipiscing elit, sed diam nonummy nibh quis nostrud exerci tatton biad. Ut wisi enim ad minim veniam, quis nostrud exercis sit amet.

Richard Michaels lorem ipsumdolor sit amet, consectetuer adipiscing elit, sed diam nonummy nibh quis nostrud exerci tatton biad. Susan Branch lorem ipsumdolor sit amet, consectetuer adipiscing elit, sed diam nonummy nibh quis nostrud exerci tatton biad. Ut wisi enim ad minim veniam ut wisi.

Carol Salmon lorem ipsumdolor sit amet, consectetuer adipiscing elit, sed diam nonummy nibh quis nostrud exerci tatton biad. Ut wisi enim ad minim veniam, quis nostrud exercis sit amet. Frank Walnuts lorem ipsumdolor sit amet, consectetuer adipiscing elit, sed diam nonummy nibh quis nostrud exerci tatton biad.

Jonathan Crowe lorem ipsumdolor sit amet, consectetuer adipiscing elit, sed diam nonummy nibh quis nostrud exerci tatton biad. Ut wisi enim ad minim veniam, quis nostrud. Julia Grams lorem ipsumdolor sit amet, consectetuer adipiscing elit, sed diam nonummy nibh quis nostrud exerci tatton biad. Ut wisi enim ad minim. Kevin Daniels lorem ipsumdolor sit amet, consectetuer adipiscing elit, sed diam nonummy nibh quis nostrud exerci tatton biad.

Neil Bricant lorem ipsumdolor sit amet, consectetuer adipiscing elit, sed diam nonummy nibh quis nostrud exerci tatton biad. Ut wisi enim ad minim veniam, quis nostrud exercis sit amet sit amet sit amet.

P. Philips lorem ipsumdolor sit amet, consectetuer adipiscing elit, sed diam nonummy nibh quis nostrud exerci tatton biad. Ut wisi enim ad minim venia. Patricia Harness lorem ipsumdolor sit amet, consectetuer adipiscing elit, sed diam nonummy nibh quis nostrud exerci tatton biad. Ut wisi enim ad minim veniam, quis nostrud exercis sit amet. Frank Walnuts lorem ipsumdolor sit amet, consectetuer adipiscing elit, sed diam nonummy nibh quis nostrud exerci tatton biad.

Richard Michaels lorem ipsumdolor sit amet, consectetuer adipiscing elit, sed diam nonummy nibh quis nostrud exerci tatton biad. Susan Branch lorem ipsumdolor sit amet, consectetuer adipiscing elit, sed diam nonummy nibh quis nostrud exerci tatton biad. Ut wisi enim ad minim veniam ut wisi.

"THIS IS AN OUTQUOTE THAT HAS BEEN FRAMED, ELONGATED, BOXED, AND DRAGGED TO THE CENTER OF THE PAGE."

Neil Bricant lorem ipsumdolor sit amet, consectetuer adipiscing elit, sed diam nonummy nibh quis nostrud exerci tatton biad. Ut wisi enim ad minim veniam, quis nostrud exerci sit amet sit amet sit amet.

Jonathan Crowe lorem ipsumdolor sit amet, consectetuer adipiscing elit, sed diam nonummy nibh quis nostrud exerci tatton biad. Ut wisi enim ad minim veniam, quis nostrud. Julia Grams lorem ipsumdolor sit amet, consectetuer adipiscing elit, sed diam nonummy nibh quis nostrud exerci tatton biad. Ut wisi enim ad minim. Kevin Daniels lorem ipsumdolor sit amet, consectetuer adipiscing elit, sed diam nonummy nibh quis nostrud exerci tatton biad. Ut wisi enim ad minim veniam, quis nostrud.

PLACE THE OUTQUOTE AFTER THIS PARAGRAPH.

P. Philips lorem ipsumdolor sit amet, consectetuer adipiscing elit, sed diam nonummy nibh quis nostrud exerci tatton biad. Ut wisi enim ad minim venia. Patricia Harness lorem consectetuer adipiscing elit, quis nostrud exercis sit amet.

Richard Michaels lorem consectetuer adipiscing elit, nostrud exerci tatton biad. Ut ipsumdolor sit amet, sed diam nonummy nibh quis wisi enim ad minim veniam ut

Carol Salmon lorem consectetuer adipiscing elit, nostrud exerci tatton biad. Ut quis nostrud exercis sit amet. ipsumdolor sit amet, sed diam nonummy nibh quis

"THIS IS AN OUTQUOTE THAT HAS BEEN FRAMED, ELONGATED, BOXED, AND DRAGGED TO THE CENTER OF THE PAGE."

ipsumdolor sit amet, sed diam nonummy nibh quis wisi enim ad minim venia. ipsumdolor sit amet, sed diam nonummy nibh quis wisi enim ad minim veniam,

ipsumdolor sit amet, sed diam nonummy nibh quis Susan Branch lorem consectetuer adipiscing elit, nostrud exerci tatton biad. Ut wisi.

ipsumdolor sit amet, sed diam nonummy nibh quis wisi enim ad minim veniam, Frank Walnuts lorem consectetuer adipiscing elit, nostrud exerci tatton biad.

Jonathan Crowe lorem ipsumdolor sit amet, consectetuer adipiscing elit, sed diam nonummy nibh quis nostrud exerci tatton biad. Ut wisi enim ad minim veniam, quis nostrud. Julia Grams lorem ipsumdolor sit amet, consectetuer adipiscing elit, sed diam nonummy nibh quis nostrud exerci tatton biad. Ut wisi enim ad minim. Kevin Daniels lorem ipsumdolor sit amet, consectetuer adipiscing elit, sed diam nonummy nibh quis nostrud exerci tatton biad. Ut wisi enim ad minim veniam, quis nostrud.

Neil Bricant lorem ipsumdolor sit amet, consectetuer adipiscing elit, sed diam nonummy nibh quis nostrud exerci tatton biad. Ut wisi enim ad minim veniam, quis nostrud exercis sit amet sit amet sit amet.

P. Philips lorem ipsumdolor sit amet, consectetuer adipiscing elit, sed diam nonummy nibh quis nostrud exerci tatton biad. Ut wisi enim ad minim venia. Patricia Harness lorem ipsumdolor sit amet, consectetuer adipiscing elit, sed diam nonummy nibh quis nostrud exerci tatton biad. Ut wisi enim ad minim veniam, quis nostrud exercis sit amet.

Richard Michaels lorem ipsumdolor sit amet, consectetuer adipiscing elit, sed diam nonummy nibh quis nostrud exerci tatton biad. Susan Branch lorem ipsumdolor sit amet, consectetuer adipiscing elit, sed diam nonummy nibh quis nostrud exerci tatton biad. Ut wisi enim ad minim veniam ut wisi.

Carol Salmon lorem ipsumdolor sit amet, consectetuer adipiscing elit, sed diam nonummy nibh quis nostrud exerci tatton biad. Ut wisi enim ad minim veniam, quis nostrud exercis sit amet. Frank Walnuts lorem ipsumdolor sit amet, consectetuer adipiscing elit, sed diam nonummy nibh quis nostrud exerci tatton biad.

Note: *In practice, you would rarely design a page quite like this one. As it's positioned, this outquote forces sentences to jump across it. Thus a sentence that starts on the outquote's left finishes on its right. In real life, you would first format the main text into columns, and then position the outquote. This is an ideal layout, however, for a flyer in which the text around the positioned image is a stylish list of some sort.*

1. This step simply ensures that your formatting matches mine. Highlight the entire document (make sure <NUM LOCK> is on, and then press <CTRL> + 5 on the numeric keypad). Format all the text with the following specs: 10-point Times on At Least 14 points of line spacing, justified, with a first line indent of .2 inches. The document margins are 1 inch top and bottom and 1.25 inches right and left.

   Note: *If you were doing this for a real, I would suggest redefining Normal with these specs.*

2. Find the outquote-to-be. It's in caps in the last paragraph.

3. Highlight the capped text and the carriage return that follows it; otherwise you'll end up with an extra carriage return.

4. Frame the text. To do this, you can either click on the Frame icon on the Toolbar, or select Frame from the Insert menu (<ALT> + I, F). If you're not in Page Layout view, Word prompts you to switch to it. Answer Yes.

5. Select the frame and drag it up toward the top of the page. Remember that the mouse pointer turns into four arrows pointing in four different directions when you can move it. Drag it and place it after the third paragraph (again, this paragraph is set in caps).

6. Resize the frame so that it's 2 inches wide, and is centered between the margins. To do this, simply drag the left edge of the frame until it's positioned at the 1.5-inch marker on the Ruler. Then drag the right edge of the frame until it's positioned at what's now the 2-inch marker on the Ruler. (Unless you have an eagle-eye, the easiest way to center a frame is to use the Center Relative To Margin options in the Horizontal section of the Frame dialog box; I come back to this later.)

7. Highlight the text inside the frame. You will probably have to use the <ARROW> keys on your keyboard to do this. Set it at 18-point Times bold, centered, on At Least 26 points of line spacing. Get rid of the .2-inch First Line indent.

8. Remember that Word automatically puts a box around frames. In this case, instead of deleting the box, change the line style to a thicker one. To do this, select the frame, open the Border dialog box, choose a line style, and then position the border 4 points from the text. If you find that the bottom of the frame is still a bit close to the text, make the frame slightly longer by dragging it.

9. If your text doesn't text wrap around the frame, select Frame from the Format menu (<ALT> + T, F), and then select Around (<ALT> + D). While you're in the Frame dialog box, notice the values Word is using for the size and position of the frame. Make sure the Width of the frame is 2 inches and its Horizontal Position is Center Relative To Margin.

✦ Drop Caps and Stick-Up Caps

Drop and stick-up caps are an easy way to get graphic appeal into a page design without using graphics (see Chapter 3). You can use frames to create them; I provide directions for both types of caps following.

To create a drop cap:

1. Type the text you want the cap to drop into.

2. Highlight the letter you want to turn into a drop cap.

3. Click on the Frame icon on the Toolbar; or, if you prefer, use the INSERT, FRAME command (<ALT> + I, F). Word frames the letter.

   Note: *If the text doesn't wrap around the letter, open the Frame dialog box and select the Around option. If Word boxes the frame, remove the box unless you want to create a boxed drop cap. If you decide to create a boxed drop cap, you'll generally want to shade the box.*

4. Highlight the letter, and format it. Generally drop caps are quite large—upwards of 48 points. The below is set in 62-point Bookman, on Exactly 60 points of line spacing. The line spacing is very important; if you have too much line spacing, the drop cap won't line up evenly with the text to the right of it. If you have too little line spacing, the top of the cap can get chopped off. If you have trouble seeing how things are lining up, work at 200% view (use the Zoom dialog box on the View menu).

5. Resize the frame to leave a respectable distance between the drop cap and the text to the right of it. Leave almost no distance between the drop cap and the text below it.

L orem ipsum dolor sit amet, consectetuer adipiscing elit, sed diam nonummy nibh euismod tincidunt ut laoreet dolore magna aliquam erat volutpat. Ut wisi enim ad minim veniam, quis nostrud exerci tation ullamcorper.

L orem ipsum dolor sit amet, consectetuer adipiscing elit, sed diam nonummy nibh euismod tincidunt ut laoreet dolore magna aliquam erat volutpat. Ut wisi enim ad minim veniam, quis nostrud exerci tation ullamcorper.

Note: *It can take a few tries before you get a drop cap you like. If you're having trouble lining everything up, it can help to change the size of the drop cap itself. The trick is to find a point size and line spacing that produces a cap whose top and bottom lines up with the top and the bottom of a line of text in the paragraph into which it drops.*

Although you create stick-up caps in a way similar to drop caps, I find them somewhat easier to do. To create a stick-up cap:

1. Type the text you want the cap to stick up from.

2. Highlight the letter you want to turn into a stick-up cap.

3. Click on the Frame icon on the Toolbar; or, if you prefer, use the INSERT, FRAME command (<ALT> + I, F). Word frames the letter.

   Note: *If the text doesn't wrap around the letter, open the Frame dialog box and select the Around option. If Word boxes the frame, remove the box unless you want to create a boxed* (and usually shaded) *stick-up cap. Although these are somewhat less common than boxed drop caps, they can add a great touch to the right piece.*

4. Highlight the letter, and format it. Like drop caps, stick-up caps tend to be quite large—upwards of 48 points. The one in the preceding example is set in 62-point Bookman. Unlike drop caps, the line spacing for the stick-up cap itself doesn't matter. However, you have to put sufficient space Before the text in the paragraph it sticks out of, to make the bottom of the first line of that text even with the bottom of the stick-up cap. In the preceding example, there's 38 points of space Before the text. Again, it might be helpful to work at 200% view.

   Note: *If you have trouble getting the stick-up cap to line up exactly with the text to the right of it, you can sub- or superscript the cap slightly. The cap in the preceding example is superscripted by 1 point.*

5. Resize the frame to leave a respectable distance between the stick-up cap and the text to the right of it. Leave almost no distance between the stick-up cap and the text below it.

his is a drop cap placed in a shaded box. The shade was created by selecting a Pattern of 10% while using Word's default values of a black (Auto) foreground and a white (Auto) background. The "T" is set in 68-point Palatino on Exactly 62 points of leading, centered.

This graphic shows a drop cap in a shaded box. Your results may differ slightly, as this one is shown reduced.

PUTTING IT ALL TOGETHER: Styles and Frames

This example creates a report that uses a frame in styles. When you're done, you should be able to place headings in the margin to the left of your text at the drop of a hat. If you're not using these instructions as the basis of your own work, use KIT_LEFT.DOC from the *Tools of the Trade* disk that came with this kit. When you're done, it should look like the example on the right. This is one of those layouts that—like a 5.5 × 8.5-inch single-fold brochure—requires a little planning. If you like this layout and want to use it as a standard report format, I definitely would set it up as a template (see Chapter 14 for information on creating templates).

This example is as much about style as it is about the frame command. It puts a lot of different design elements together, and it creates a page that is as professional-looking as any you're likely to come across.

Accounts Payable Manual, 1991/92 — Office Procedures

Office Procedures
Lorem ipsum dolor sit amet, consectetuer adipiscing elit, sed diam nonummy nibh euismod tincidunt ut laoreet dolore magna aliquam erat volutpat.Ut wisi enim ad minim veniam, quis nostrud exerci tation ullamcorper suscipit lobortis nisl ut aliquip ex ea commodo feugiat consequat.
Ipsum dolor sit amet, consectetuer adipiscing elit, sed diam nonummy nibh euismod tincidunt ut laoreet dolore magna aliquam erat volutpat. Ut wisi enim ad minim veniam, quis nostrud exerci tation ullamcorper suscipit lobortis nisl ut aliquip ex ea commodo feugiat consequat tation ullamcorper suscipit lobortis nisl ut aliquip ex ea commodo feugiat consequat.
• lorem ipsum dolor sit amet lorem ipsum
• ipsum dolor sit amet nonummy nibh euismod
• magna aliquam erat volutpat
• quis nostrud exerci tation ullamcorper suscipit
• magna aliquam erat volutpat
• diam nonummy nibh euismod tincidunt ut magna

Internal Control Procedures
Dolor sit amet, consectetuer adipiscing elit, sed diam nonummy nibh euismod tincidunt ut laoreet. Ipsum dolor sit amet, consectetuer adipiscing elit, sed diam nonummy nibh euismod tincidunt ut laoreet dolore magna aliquam erat volutpat. Ut wisi enim ad minim veniam, quis nostrud exerci tation ullamcorper suscipit lobortis nisl ut aliquip ex ea commodo feugiat consequat.
Lorem ipsum dolor sit amet, consectetuer adipiscing elit, sed diam nonummy nibh euismod tincidunt ut laoreet dolore magna aliquam erat volutpat. Ut wisi enim ad minim veniam, quis nostrud exerci tation ullamcorper suscipit lobortis nisl ut aliquip ex ea commodo feugiat consequat.

Approvals
Dolor sit amet, consectetuer adipiscing elit, sed diam nonummy nibh euismod tincidunt ut laoreet. Ipsum dolor sit amet, consectetuer adipiscing elit, sed diam nonummy nibh euismod tincidunt ut laoreet dolore magna aliquam erat volutpat. Ut wisi enim ad minim veniam, quis nostrud exerci tation nibh euismod tincidunt ut laoreet dolore magna aliquam erat volutpat. Ut wisi enim ad minim veniam, quis nostrud exerci tation.
Lorem ipsum dolor sit amet, consectetuer adipiscing elit, sed diam nonummy nibh euismod tincidunt ut laoreet. Magna aliquam erat volutpat. Ut wisi enim ad minim veniam, quis nostrud exerci tation ullamcorper suscipit lobortis nisl ut aliquip ex ea commodo feugiat. Nonummy nibh euismod tincidunt ut laoreet dolore magna aliquam erat volutpat. Ut wisi enim ad minim veniam onummy nibh euismod tincidunt.

OWR Plastic Products, Inc. — Office of Accounting   Page 3

Accounts Payable Manual, 1991/92 — Office Procedures

OFFICE PROCEDURES
Lorem ipsum dolor sit amet, consectetuer adipiscing elit, sed diam nonummy nibh euismod tincidunt ut laoreet dolore magna aliquam erat volutpat. Ut wisi enim ad minim veniam, quis nostrud exerci tation ullamcorper suscipit lobortis nisl ut aliquip ex ea commodo feugiat consequat.
Ipsum dolor sit amet, consectetuer adipiscing elit, sed diam nonummy nibh euismod tincidunt ut laoreet dolore magna aliquam erat volutpat. Ut wisi enim ad minim veniam, quis nostrud exerci tation ullamcorper suscipit lobortis nisl ut aliquip ex ea commodo feugiat consequat tation ullamcorper suscipit lobortis nisl ut aliquip ex ea commodo feugiat consequat.
• lorem ipsum dolor sit amet lorem ipsum
• ipsum dolor sit amet nonummy nibh euismod
• magna aliquam erat volutpat
• quis nostrud exerci tation ullamcorper suscipit
• magna aliquam erat volutpat
• quis nostrud exerci tation ullamcorper suscipit
• diam nonummy nibh euismod tincidunt ut magna

Internal Control Procedures
Dolor sit amet, consectetuer adipiscing elit, sed diam nonummy nibh euismod tincidunt ut laoreet. Ipsum dolor sit amet, consectetuer adipiscing elit, sed diam nonummy nibh euismod tincidunt ut laoreet dolore magna aliquam erat volutpat. Ut wisi enim ad minim veniam, quis nostrud exerci tation ullamcorper suscipit lobortis nisl ut aliquip ex ea commodo feugiat consequat.
Lorem ipsum dolor sit amet, consectetuer adipiscing elit, sed diam nonummy nibh euismod tincidunt ut laoreet dolore magna aliquam erat volutpat. Ut wisi enim ad minim veniam, quis nostrud exerci tation ullamcorper suscipit lobortis nisl ut aliquip ex ea commodo feugiat consequat.

Approvals
Dolor sit amet, consectetuer adipiscing elit, sed diam nonummy nibh euismod tincidunt ut laoreet. Ipsum dolor sit amet, consectetuer adipiscing elit, sed diam nonummy nibh euismod tincidunt ut laoreet dolore magna aliquam erat volutpat. Ut wisi enim ad minim veniam, quis nostrud exerci tation nibh euismod tincidunt ut laoreet dolore magna aliquam erat volutpat. Ut wisi enim ad minim veniam, quis nostrud exerci tation.

OWR Plastic Products, Inc. — Office of Accounting   Page 3

1. The trick to this design is the page margins (use the Page Setup dialog box). Once you have the margins down, the rest *literally* flows into place. Set the page margins as follows: 1 inch top, bottom, and right; 3.25 inches left.

2. Use the Styles dialog box to redefine four of the standard styles on your menu: Normal and headings 1–3. The specs for Normal are: 10-point Helvetica justified, with 3 points of space After; single line spacing; and a .2-inch First Line indent.

3. The specs for heading 1 are: 14-point Times bold caps, flush left, with 0 points of space After; single line spacing; and *no* First Line indent. Unlink it from Normal. To get to the Frame dialog box and include positioning as part of the style, click on the Frame button (<ALT> + F).

4. To get the headings out into the left margin of the page, you have to place them Relative To Page (see the diagram titled *Relative To Page versus Relative To Margin*). Use the following settings in the Frame dialog box: Text Wrapping is Around; the Width is 1.75 inches; the Horizontal Position is Left Relative To Page; the Vertical is 0 inches Relative To Paragraph (the default); make sure the Move with Text option is on; and Distance From Text is the default of .13 inches for the Horizontal Position. Click on OK to get back to the Styles dialog box.

5. Select the next heading to redefine. Set heading 2 as 12-point Helvetica bold, upper/lowercase (in other words, turn All Caps off). Although you can run the same gamut of paragraph and positioning options as you did for heading 1, here's an easier way: base it on heading 1. Be sure the Next Style is Normal.

6. Select heading 3 and define it as Based On heading 2 with a Next Style of Normal. (The Next Style is currently set for Word's default, which is Normal Indent.) The only other change is in the Character dialog box—select Italic. Now that everything's defined, click on Close to get back to your document.

7. Apply the style heading 1 to "Office Procedures", heading 2 to "Internal Control Procedures", and heading 3 to "Approvals." Everything should line up just as you hoped. (If it doesn't, make sure you're in Page Layout view—the most likely culprit. If that doesn't do it, check the Frame settings for heading 1 and backtrack from there.)

   Note: *You might want to insert an extra carriage return (as I did) after the text that precedes a heading.*

8. Use the Print Preview (<ALT> + F, V) command or the Fit in Window icon to see the whole page at a glance. Notice that the header and footer are positioned squarely over the main text, instead of over the entire page. You might like this look and decide to leave it.

   However, you should be aware of a problem. Take another look at the illustration that shows what this file used to look like. There was a page number in the right corner of the footer. If you look at the footer now, however, you'll see that it isn't there anymore. This is because Word's standard style for headers and footers places a right tab at 6 inches. When you changed the margins of your document, this tab setting didn't change. The page number is still out there at the 6-inch marker, but you can't see it because the main text of your document is only 4.25 inches wide. Step 10 shows how to fix this.

9. Return to your document. Make sure you're still in Page Layout view. Scroll up to the header at the very top of the page, put your cursor in it, and magnify it to 200%. You can see that the header should extend to nearly –2 inches. Open the Paragraph dialog box and type –1.9 in the From Left option. It's important to be that specific in this case because you have to make the footer the same width.

   After you finish realigning the header, redefine the header style. Just put your cursor anywhere in the header; select header from the Style menu; press <ENTER>; and say Yes to Word's Redefine? prompt.

10. Here's how to fix the footer. Open the Styles dialog box. Select footer. In the Paragraph dialog box set the From Left option to –1.9.

   Then go into the Tabs dialog box. Note that two tabs are listed—one at 3 inches and the other at 6. Click on the Clear All button to get rid of them. Then click on the Right alignment option to set a right tab. Put your cursor in the Tab Stop Position box and type 4.25, which is the width of your main text. Click on OK or press <ENTER> when you're ready. This places a right tab at the very right margin of the text and puts the page number there. Click on OK or press <ENTER> to define that style and get back to your document.

   Now when you look at the document in Print Preview mode, or print it out, it should look pretty much like the example shown earlier.

USING COLUMNS

Word lets you divide your document into sections and format each of these sections differently. When you first open your document, Word considers it to be one big section. You can add sections if you wish and format them however you like—with different headers and footers, for instance, or in two columns, or three. For the purpose of columns, a section does not need to take up an entire page; a single paragraph can be in a section all its own.

There are three ways you can create columns in Word—you can use a table, a frame, or Word's Column functions, which format text into snaking or newspaper-style columns.

When you use Word's Column functions, you almost always end up using sections as well. Although you can create newspaper-style columns without using sections, publications and presentations look unmistakably more professional when they are *not* done entirely in columns—when the title runs across the entire width of the page, or when a graphic spreads across two columns. You need to create separate sections to produce these formats.

✦ Creating Columns

The columns dialog box on the Format menu allows you to format your document (or sections of it) into newspaper-style columns. Word has a built-in formula that determines how many columns you can place on a particular page given the page size, orientation, margins, and so forth. This formula lets you place more columns on a landscape page than on a portrait page and it lets you have wider columns if you have thinner margins. Because Word calculates both the number of columns and their width, you can't adjust the width of the columns directly. However, you can adjust the margins and the amount of space between columns, and this enables you to (indirectly) widen or narrow the columns.

Word lets you create more columns on a page than you will probably ever want to create. I never use more than three columns in portrait orientation; five in letter-sized landscape orientation (only when I don't need much in the way of margins); and six when I'm using legal-sized paper in landscape mode. Columns narrower than 2 inches are generally too narrow.

If the only design element you want in your publication is newspaper-style columns, creating them requires only a few clicks of the mouse. Unfortunately publications and presentations formatted entirely in columns (title and all) can look amateurish unless done quite carefully.

To create newspaper-style columns:

1. Select Columns from the Format menu (<ALT> + T, O) and type the number of columns you want in the Number of Columns option.

2. If you want, adjust the Space Between the columns (<ALT> + S), or place a Line Between them (<ALT> + L).

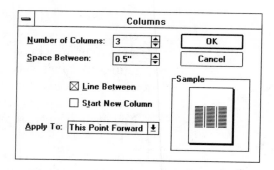

3. Click on OK or press <ENTER> to get back to your document.

To get rid of columns:

• Select Columns from the Format menu and type 1 in the Number of Columns option.

If you have text already typed in when you create newspaper-style columns—and there's enough of it to flow from column to column—it *will* flow from column to column. However, you have to be in Page Layout view to see these columns. Otherwise, you see only one skinny column of text running down the whole length of your document.

You don't have to wait until all the text is typed to format your document in columns. However, I recommend that you do so simply because there are always fewer hassles when you save complex formatting for last.

Although it's pretty easy to create columns in Word, it gets somewhat trickier when you don't want every single page and paragraph formatted with the same number of columns. When this is the case (and it usually is), you need to insert section breaks (see Chapter 12 if you have questions about handling sections in Word).

✦ Using Sections with Columns

It takes only one or two more steps to create columns *with* sections than without—and the extra steps are to create the particular section (or sections). Depending on your layout, after you create one section and format it using columns, you may have to create another section and format it to *not* use columns, or to

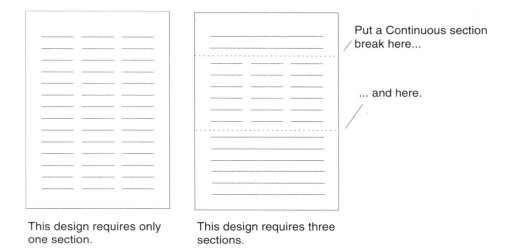

This design requires only one section.

This design requires three sections.

Put a Continuous section break here...

... and here.

The diagram on the left shows a single-section document formatted in columns. The diagram on the right shows a document formatted into three sections.

use a different number of columns. There are two ways of handling this. You can insert your own section break and then format the new section into columns, or you can use the Columns dialog box to "automatically" insert a section break. Whichever method you use, the result is the same.

To insert a section break and format the new section with a different number of columns:

1. Put your cursor *below* where you want the section break to go, and then select Break from the Insert menu (<ALT> + I, B). Remember that Word inserts page breaks and section breaks above your cursor position.

2. Choose the sort of Section Break you want—Continuous, for example, or Next Page. Click on OK or press <ENTER> when you're done. Word inserts a section break (which appears as a double-dotted line on your screen).

    Note: *Continuous section breaks create a new section on the same page. This is ideal for those times when you want to format a title to take up the entire width of the page, and the text to flow into two or more columns. You would put a continuous section break between them.*

3. Put your cursor in the section you want to format into columns. You can tell what section you're in by glancing at the left of the Status Bar where it says "Sec 1," "Sec 2," and so on.

4. Select Columns from the Format menu (<ALT> + T, O). Type the Number of Columns you want to use, and any other options you want to take advantage of. For instance, you can narrow or expand the space between each column, and/or put a line between columns. Click on OK or press <ENTER> when you're done.

To use the Columns dialog box to automatically insert a section break and format the section with a different number of columns:

1. Put your cursor *below* where you want the section break to go, and then select the Columns dialog box from the Format menu (<ALT> + T, O).

2. Select This Point Forward from the Apply To menu (<ALT> + A).

Note: *This is very similar to how you set different margins and orientation for specific pages in your document.*

3. Enter the number of columns you want to have in the new section.

4. Click on OK or press <ENTER> when you're done. Word inserts a Continuous section break and formats the new section with the number of columns you indicated.

Note: *You can only use this method to insert a continuous section break or a column break. You have to use the INSERT, BREAK command to create a section that starts on a new page, an odd page, or an even page.*

Column Breaks.   You can also force text to start a new column in one of two ways: by using the Break dialog box to insert a column break, or by using the Columns dialog box to insert one automatically. Again, the result is the same no matter which method you use.

To start a new column using the Break dialog box:

1. Place your cursor in the paragraph you want to start a new column, and then select Break from the Insert menu (<ALT> + I, B).

2. Select Column Break (<ALT> + C).

3. Click on OK or press <ENTER> when you're done. If you're in Page Layout view, you'll see that the text and/or graphics in this paragraph now show up in the next column.

To start a new column using the Columns dialog box:

1. Place your cursor in the paragraph you want to start a new column.

2. Select Columns from the Format menu (<ALT> + T, O).

3. Select the Start New Column option (<ALT> + T), and then select This Point Forward from the Apply To menu. This technique automatically inserts a column break.

4. Click on OK or press <ENTER> when you're done. The text and/or graphics following the column break now show up in the next column.

You get rid of a break—whether a page break, a section break, or a column break—by <BACKSPACING> over it, or by highlighting it and pressing <DELETE>.

PUTTING IT ALL TOGETHER: Sections, Columns, and Clip Art

This example is adapted from the *Newsletters and Other Periodicals* section of Chapter 2. It shows you how to turn the page on the left (found in KIT_COL.DOC on the *Tools of the Trade* disk that came with this kit) into the one on the right. You can find the rules for this example in the files KIT_RUL1–KIT_RUL3.WMF. If you want, you can follow these instructions to get a "columned" document you're actually working on out the door.

Although only one page is shown here, the finished product will be two pages. The second page is nothing more than a single column of text used to show you how to reset a document back to one column. There are three sections in this two-page document. The first section is the headline, the second is the three columns, and the third is the single-column page.

MOD SCOTLAND

ABERDEENSHIRE

Lorem ipsum dolor sit amet, consectetuer adipiscing elit, sed diam nonummy nibh euismod tincidunt ut laoreet dolore magna aliquam erat volutpat. Ut wisi enim ad minim veniam, quis nostrud exerci tation ullamcorper suscipit lobortis nisl ut aliquip ex ea commodo feugiat consequat.

Ipsum dolor sit amet, consectetuer adipiscing elit, sed diam nonummy nibh euismod tincidunt ut laoreet dolore magna aliquam erat volutpat. Ut wisi enim ad minim veniam, quis nostrud exerci tation ullamcorp.

ANGUS

Dolor sit amet, consectetuer adipiscing elit, sed diam nonummy nibh euismod tincidunt ut laoreet dolore magna aliquam erat volutpat. Ut wisi enim ad minim veniam, quis nostrud.

Lorem ipsum dolor sit amet, consectetuer adipiscing elit, sed diam nonummy nibh euismod tincidunt ut laoreet dolore magna aliquam erat volutpat. Ut wisi enim ad minim veniam, quis nostrud exerci tation ullamcorper suscipit lobortis nisl ut aliquip ex ea commodo feugiat consequat.

Dolor sit amet, consectetuer adipiscing elit, sed diam nonummy nibh euismod tincidunt ut laoreet dolore magna aliquam erat volutpat. Ut wisi enim ad minim veniam, quis nostrud.

Consectetuer adipiscing elit, sed diam nonummy nibh euismod tincidunt ut laoreet dolore magna aliquam erat volutpat. Ut wisi enim ad minim veniam, quis nostrud exerci tation ullamcorper suscipit lobortis nisl ut aliquip.

ARGYLL AND AYRSHIRE

Consectetuer adipiscing elit, sed diam nonummy nibh euismod tincidunt ut laoreet dolore magna aliquam erat volutpat. Ut wisi enim ad minim veniam, quis nostrud exerci tation ullamcorper suscipit lobortis nisl ut aliquip.

Lorem ipsum dolor sit amet, consectetuer adipiscing elit, sed diam nonummy nibh euismod tincidunt ut laoreet dolore magna aliquam erat volutpat. Ut wisi enim ad minim veniam, quis nostrud exerci tation ullamcorper suscipit lobortis nisl ut aliquip ex ea commodo feugiat consequat. Lorem ipsum dolor sit amet, consectetuer adipiscing elit, sed diam nonummy nibh euismod tincidunt ut laoreet dolore magna aliquam erat volutpat.

Adipiscing elit, sed diam nonummy nibh euismod tincidunt ut laoreet dolore magna aliquam erat volutpat. Ut wisi enim ad minim veniam, quis nostrud exerci tation ullamcorper suscipit lobortis nisl ut aliquip ex ea commodo feugiat consequat.

MOD SCOTLAND

Aberdeenshire

Or se tu quel Virgilio e quella fonte che spandi di parlar si largo fiume? O delli altri poeti onore e lume, vagliami 'l lungo studio e 'l grande amore che m' ha fatto cercar lo tuo volume volume volume.

Tu se' lo mio maestro e 'l mio autore; tu se' solo colui da cu' io mi tolsi lo bello stilo che m' ha fatto onore. Vedi la bestia per cu' io mi volsi: aiutami da lei, famoso saggio, ch'ella mi fa tremar le vene e i polsi.

A te convien tenere altro viaggio se vuo' campar d'esto loco sel vaggio: che questa bestia, per la qual tu gride, non lascia altrui passar per la sua.

Angus

Or se tu quel Virgilio e quella fonte che spandi di parlar si largo fiume? O delli altri poeti onore e lume, vagliami 'l lungo studio e 'l grande amore che m' ha fatto cercar lo tuo volume. O delli altri poeti onore e lume, vagliami 'l lungo studio e 'l.

A te convien tenere altro viaggio se vuo' campar d'esto loco sel vaggio: che questa bestia, per la qual tu gride, non lascia altrui passar per la sua via, ma tanto lo 'mpedisce che l'uccide; e ha natura si malvagia e ria, che mai non empie la bramosa voglia, e dopo sto ha piu fame che

pria pasto a pui fame che che pria che che pria.

Or setu quel Virgilio e quella fonte he spandi di parlar si largo fiume? O delli altri poeti onore e lume, vagliami 'l lungo studio 'l grande amore che m' ha fatto cercar lo tuo volume. Odelli altri poeti onore e lume, vagliami 'l lungo studio e 'l grande amore amore.

Argyll and Ayrshire

Or se tu quel Virgilio e quella fonte che spandi di parlar si largo fiume? O delli altri poeti onore e lume, vagliami 'l lungo studio e 'l grande amore che m' ha fatto cercar lo tuo volume e ha natura si malvagia.

O delli altri poeti onore e lume, vagliami 'l lungo studio e 'l grande amore e ha natura si malvagia e ria.

A te convien tenere altro viaggio se vuo' campar d'esto loco sel vaggio: che questa bestia, per la qual tu gride, non lascia altrui passar per la l'uccide; e ha natura si malvagia e ria.

Che mai non empie la bramosa voglia, e dopo 'l pasto ha piu fame che pria pusto ha pui fame che. A te convien tenere altro viaggio se vuo campar d'esto loco sel vaggio: che questa bestia, per la qual tu gride, non lascia altrui passar per la sua via, ma tanto lo 'mpedisce che

l'uccide; e ha natura si malvagia e ria ha natura si malvagia e.

Clackmannanshire

Or se tu quel Virgilio e quella fonte che spandi di parlar si largo fiume? O delli altri poeti onore e lume, vagliami 'l lungo studio e 'l grande amore che m' ha fatto cercar lo tuo volume. O delli altri poeti onore e lume, vagliami 'l lungo studio e 'l grande amore.

A te convien tenere altro viaggio se vuo' campar d'esto loco sel vaggio: che questa bestia, per la qual tu gride, non lascia altrui passar per la sua via, ma tanto lo 'mpedisce che l'uccide; e ha natura si malvagia e ria, che mai non empie la bramosa voglia, e dopo 'l pasto ha piu fame che pria pasto ha pui fame che pria.

Dumfriesshire

Or se tu quel Virgilio e quella fonte che spandi di parlar si largo fiume? O delli altri poeti onore e lume, vagliami 'l lungo studio e 'l grande amore che m ha fatto cercar lo tuo volungo studio e 'l grande amore lo tuo volungo studio e 'l grande.

A te convien tenere altro viaggio se vuo' campar d'esto loco sel vaggio: che questa bestia, per la qual tu gride, non lascia altrui passar per la sua via, ma tanto lo 'mpedisce che

1. Open KIT_COL.DOC. Set the margins to .8 inches all around. Redefine Normal to 10-point Times on 14 points of leading, justified, with .5 line (6 points) of space After.

2. Redefine heading 1. The specs are 12-point Bookman bold, flush left and single spaced, with 1 line (12 points) of space Before and 3 points After.

3. Once you've redefined the styles, the entire document takes on the specs for Normal. Go through and apply the style heading 1 to the headings (they're in caps to make them a little easier to find, and there are nine of them). Don't apply heading 1 to the title "Mod Scotland," which is specially formatted in the next step.

4. Set the title in 55-point Bookman bold, flush left and single spaced, with 7 points of space After. Expand the "land" in "Scotland" by 3 points (use the Spacing option in the Character dialog box).

5. Now that the text is formatted, put your cursor in the paragraph *below* the title (nothing's there besides the carriage return—it might be helpful to turn the Show/Hide¶ button on). Select Break from the Insert menu (<ALT> + I, B), and then select the Continuous section break. This allows you to create columns without starting a new page.

6. Put the cursor anywhere in the main text. You might want to check the Status Bar to make sure it's registering that you're in "Sec 2." Select Columns from the Format menu (<ALT> + T, O). Set the Number of Columns to 3, and the Space between columns to .4 inches. If you're in Page Layout view, you'll see the columns snaking across the screen. Otherwise, you'll see one very long, thin column.

7. At this point you should check out your document using the FILE, PRINT PREVIEW command. Look at both pages, and note that they are both in three columns. If the bottom of the columns is uneven, make sure the Widow/Orphan Control option is off (to do this, select Options from the Tools menu, and then the Print category).

8. Position your cursor where you want the first rule to go. Open Microsoft Draw. Select Import Picture from the File menu, and import KIT_RUL1.WMF. Update your Word document, and then return to Word. If you need to, resize the rule so that it fits the column properly, and center it. Continue this until you have all three rules in your document.

9. Once you have the three different rules in your document, you should probably unlink them to reduce the size of your file. To do this, highlight your whole document and then press <CTRL> + <SHIFT> + <F9>. (Remember that Draw's embedded graphics are fields; see Chapter 10.)

10. Notice that the rules tend to be closer to the paragraphs above them than to the headings below. To correct this, add 1 line (12 points) of space Before. You might even create a style called "rule" that includes both the center alignment and the extra space. If you decide to do

---

this, the quickest way is to select a correctly formatted rule, press <CTRL> + s to get into the Style menu, and type "rule" (or whatever name you want to use). Press <ENTER> to save the style definition.

Note: *The first rule in the document is the only one that doesn't need extra space above it. If you put extra space above it, it won't line up with the second column.*

11. Copy and paste the three rules into their other locations in the document.

12. You might want to check your progress by using the FILE, PRINT PREVIEW command. The document should look pretty good.

13. There's one thing left to do. Insert another section break somewhere on the second page of the document. For practice, make it a section break that starts on the Next Page. Then turn to that next page (check the Status Bar to make sure you're really in "Sec 3"). Format this section as a single column. To do this, simply open the Columns dialog box and type "1" in the Number of Columns option.

CHAPTER 14

Templates Save Time

According to the dictionary, a "template" is a pattern, often cut into a thin plate of metal, that artisans use to ensure that certain pieces are made accurately—knobs on a cabinet, for example, or a certain design of handle. Templates are a way to get exactly the same design over and over. Word for Windows uses templates the same way, only for documents. A template for stationery, for example, might contain a stationery heading, a logo, certain styles, and even a glossary entry for the signature line. This ensures that all your letters have a particular style.

Templates save time. Yes, they also take time to set up—anywhere from five to twenty minutes, depending on how fancy you want to get—but as Confucius said, "One great effort, and forever at peace." The effort, however, really isn't that great. Whenever I finally get around to making a template for something that I've been redoing for ages (for example, by renaming an existing document using the Save As command on the File menu, deleting all the text, maybe trying to save *some* of the text, and then typing in all the new text), I'm always glad I finally bothered to do what I should have done in the first place. Templates really do save time.

Templates and styles together can make a powerful design statement. Before you get into this chapter, you should probably review Chapter 7, which covers styles. I strongly recommend that you use styles. Once you think through their formatting and set them up for all the types of publications and presentations you regularly produce, you've finished most of the design for those documents as well. In general, I find that most people actually *like* to use styles, but, for some reason—perhaps out of a mistaken sense that templates are harder to deal with—many of these same people are unwilling to bother with templates. I'd like to think that this chapter can change that.

This chapter covers these topics in the following order:

- How to use existing templates (including the ones that came with this kit).

- How to revise templates, including NORMAL.DOT.

- How to create your own templates.

- How to use the INSERT, DATE AND TIME command.

HOW TO USE TEMPLATES AND CREATE YOUR OWN

In some ways, templates are like styles. For instance, Word for Windows always acts as though you're using styles, even when you think you aren't. The same is true with templates; you might not think you're using them, but you are. You might have noticed that every time you open a new file, Word asks you to select a template from which to work. Even if you just press <ENTER> to get past that screen into the new document, you're still selecting a template—the Normal template, as it's called.

Note: *If you use the New Document button on the Toolbar, Word also uses the Normal template.*

✦ Using Templates

Word comes with several built-in templates besides Normal, for example, FAX.DOT and ARTICLE.DOT (all templates end with a .DOT extension). Some of these are highly sophisticated and come with special macros that prompt you to include certain information in the document. The article template, for example, prompts you to type your phone number and the article's title. At some point, you might want to try a few of these to see how they work. The templates I cover here are much simpler; you don't have to know anything about macros to use or create them.

To use a template:

1. Open a new document by selecting New from the File menu (<ALT> + F, N).

2. Select the template you want from the Use Template scroll box (you can scroll through this menu to find the template you want).

3. Click on OK or press <ENTER> to start a new document using the highlighted template.

Once you have a new document based on an existing template, you can change that document however you like. Using a particular template doesn't constrain you any more than using a particular style—it simply gives you a standardized base from which to start. You can then change it to suit the circumstance.

How to Use the Templates That Come With This Kit

This kit comes with a number of templates for the designs shown in Chapter 2, including:

newsletter	KIT_NEW.DOT
flip sheet or marketing piece	KIT_FLIP.DOT
expense form	KIT_FORM.DOT
letter-fold brochure	KIT_LBRO.DOT
5.5 × 11-inch single-fold brochure	KIT_SBRO.DOT
reports	KIT_RPT1–3.DOT

To use these templates, simply copy them from the disk to your main Word for Windows directory. You can use and revise them just as you can any other template.

✦ Revising Templates

In addition to being able to change the formatting of documents based on a template, you can also change the template itself. Or if you don't want to change the original, you can use one template as the basis for another.

To open and revise a template:

1. Select Open from the File menu to open a template you want to change.

2. Type "*.DOT" in the File Name box and press <ENTER>. (You can also select Document Templates from the List Files menu at the bottom of the dialog box.) Remember that all templates have .DOT extensions. Usually, they are stored in the Winword directory or in another directory that you set up as Word's default.

   Note: *It is possible to store templates in another directory. If you can't find any *.DOT files in the Winword directory, use File Manager to search for them (see the Windows manual if you don't know how to do this).*

3. Scroll through the list until you find the template you want to revise, and then select it.

4. Click on OK or press <ENTER> when you're ready.

5. Revise the template just as you would any document.

6. When you're finished, save and close it.

   Note: *If you don't want to change the original template, use the FILE, SAVE AS command to save your changes as another template.*

TEST RUN: Redefining the Normal Template

A lot of people decide at some point or another to redefine their Normal template to include the style formatting and margins they generally use. Otherwise, they have to change their styles and margins every time they open a new document. (If you have questions about how to redefine styles, refer to Chapter 7.).

To redefine Word's standard styles once and for all:

1. Use the FILE, OPEN command (<ALT> + F, O) to open the Normal template.

2. Select Style from the Format menu (<ALT> + T, Y), and redefine the Normal style.

> **Note:** *If you want, assign Shortcut keys to your styles; you'll be able to use those shortcuts with all your documents.*

3. Redefine headings 1 through 3.

4. Make whatever other changes you want.

5. Save the template, and close it.

The next time you start a new document based on Normal, you've got the basic formatting and styles you want.

✦ Creating a Template from Scratch

You can create a template for just about any sort of document, from stationery to slides to newsletters. A professional writer I know has a template for his draft articles. It has the word "Draft" and the Date field in the header, and page numbers in the footer.

Do You Have the Time?

Word for Windows has several special codes (called fields) that are very useful in templates. One is the Date field, which automatically uses today's date in the document; the other is the Time field, which uses the current time. To see the Date and Time *fields* themselves, turn the VIEW, FIELD CODES option on by selecting Field Codes from the View menu (<ALT> + V, C). To see the actual date and time, turn VIEW, FIELD CODES off.

Note: *If your date and time aren't correct, you need to set them using the Windows Control Panel (see your Windows manual for instructions).*

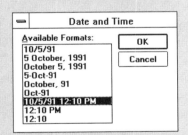

To use the Date and/or Time field:

1. Put your cursor where you want the date or time to go.

2. Select Date and Time from the Insert menu (<ALT> + I, T).

3. The Date and Time dialog box opens. Select the date or time format you like best.

> **Note:** *Word automatically updates these fields to show the current date and time whenever you open the document, and whenever you print it. If you want to update them at whim, use the Update Field command:* <F9>.

4. Click on OK or press <ENTER> when you're done.

To create your own template:

1. Select New from the File menu (<ALT> + F, N).

> **Note:** *To base your template on an existing one, select a template from the Use Template scroll box.*

2. Click on the Template option (<ALT> + T).

> **Note:** *If you click on Summary (<ALT> + S), you can type a description of the template to make it somewhat easier to identify. The description is taken from the Title line in the Summary Info dialog box.*

PUTTING IT ALL TOGETHER: Create Your Own Template

This example shows how to create a template for a 1–2 page informational report that has to be produced on a regular schedule—weekly, for example, or monthly. The layout labeled A is the first page of the report. The layout labeled B is what the template will look like when you're done. If you want, you can use these basic instructions to create a similar template better suited to the work you do.

1. Select New from the File menu (<ALT> + F, N).

2. Click on the Template button (<ALT> + T).

3. Click on OK or press <ENTER>. This template has six main design elements: the header, the footer, the main heading "MUTUAL FUNDS," the table heading "The 10 Best Performers," the column headings ("Assets," and so on), and the outlined rows in the table. I'll briefly explain how to create each element.

4. Select Page Setup from the Format menu (<ALT> + T, U) and set the margins to 1 inch all around.

5. Select Style from the Format menu (<ALT> + T, Y). Define the Normal style as 11-point Times justified, with .5 line (6 points) of space After each paragraph. (See Chapter 7 for information on how to define styles.)

6. Define heading 1 as 16-point Avant Garde caps, with 18 points of space Before and 10 points After. You should probably unlink it from Normal.

7. Define heading 2 as 12-point Avant Garde bold, with 18 points of space Before and 10 points After. Base it on heading 1 instead of Normal.

8. Define three styles for use in the table. (Even if this is the only table in the report, styles will make it somewhat easier to format.) Define the first style, which I call Table, as 10-point Times, with zero points of space After.

3. Click on OK or press <ENTER> when you're done.

4. Set up the template by defining the styles you want to include; adding any appropriate text, table formats, or graphic elements; defining glossary entries; and/or creating macros.

> **Note:** *You can define glossaries and macros for use only with a specific template. To do this, select Template from the File menu, and then select the With Document Template option. Define the glossary entries and create macros just as you would normally.*

5. When you finish creating the template, save and close it.

Banking Group Report

MUTUAL FUNDS

Orem ipsum dolor sit amet, consectetuer adipiscing elit, sed diam nonummy nibh euismod tincidunt ut laoreet dolore magna aliquam erat volutpat. Ut wisi enim ad minim veniam, quis nostrud exerci tation ullamcorper suscipit lobortis nisl ut aliquip ex ea commodo feugiat consequat. Lorem ipsum dolor sit.

Consectetuer adipiscing elit, sed diam nonummy nibh euismod tincidunt ut laoreet dolore magna aliquam erat volutpat. Ut wisi enim ad minim veniam, quis nostrud exerci tation ullamcorper suscipit lobortis nisl ut aliquip ex ea commodo feugiat consequat. Lorem ipsum dolor sit amet, consectetuer adipiscing elit, sed diam nonummy nibh euismod tincidunt ut laoreet dolore magna aliquam erat volut.

Ut wisi enim ad minim veniam, quis nostrud exerci tation ullamcorper suscipit lobortis nisl ut aliquip ex ea commodo feugiat consequat. Lorem ipsum dolor sit amet, consectetuer adipiscing elit, sed diam nonummy nibh euismod tincidunt ut laoreet dolore magna aliquam erat volutpat. Ut wisi enim ad min. Sum dolor sit amet, consectetuer adipiscing elit, sed diam nonummy nibh euismod tincidunt ut laoreet dolore.

Nostrud exerci tation ullamcorper suscipit lobortis nisl ut aliquip ex ea commodo feugiat consequat. Lorem ipsum dolor ex ea commodo feugiat consequat. Lorem ipsum dolor.

Sed diam nonummy nibh euismod tincidunt ut laoreet dolore magna aliquam erat volutpat. Ut wisi enim ad minim veniam, quis nostrud exerci tation ullamcorper suscipit lobortis nisl ut aliquip ex ea commodo feugiat consequat. Lorem ipsum dolor sit amet, consectetuer adipiscing elit, sed diam nonummy nibh euismod. Lorem ipsum dolor sit amet.

The 10 Best Performers

	Assets (millions)	Expense Ratio	Total Return Week	1991	52 Wks	5 Years
Fidelity SI Tech	$223.9	2.07%	-0.26%	34.75%	85.01%	138.54%
Fidelity SI Med	37.8	2.16	3.42	32.92	69.52	N/A
Fidelity SI Hlth	373.2	1.71	-0.19	23.35	68.69	154.92
Fidelity Port: Hlth	161.1	1.11	0.12	28.90	65.82	256.96
Oppenheimer Tch	23.3	1.75	2.05	35.33	55.15	N/A
Putnam Hlth Sci	376.1	1.14	-0.98	18.13	45.21	133.69
Vanguard Hlth	163.6	0.32	-0.87	15.12	39.38	141.81
GT Global Health	175.5	2.30	-0.55	18.44	38.62	N/A
Medical Res Inv	4.4	3.40	-1.49	19.58	31.63	74.72
Fidelity SI Comp	24.2	2.58	-2.34	25.67	29.17	42.25

1

A

Banking Group Report

MUTUAL FUNDS

The 10 Best Performers

	Assets (millions)	Expense Ratio	Total Return Week	1991	52 Wks	5 Years
	$	%	%	%	%	%

1

B

9. Base the second style, which I call Border, on Table, and box it with the thinnest Line style available in the Border dialog box. Even if you don't care to use Shortcut keys with styles, it's very useful to assign one for this particular style, perhaps B.

10. Base the last style—Skinny—on Table also, and format it as 4-point Times with Auto line spacing. Again, it's especially useful to assign a Shortcut key for this style, perhaps s.

    Note: *Although it doesn't usually matter whether you use single or Auto line spacing, it does when you're using very small point sizes, as in this case. If you use single line spacing, the space between outlined rows would be substantially wider.*

11. Type the main heading—in this case, "Mutual Funds"—and apply the heading 1 style. On the next line, type the table heading, and apply the heading 2 style.

12. Create a table with 7 columns and 22 rows. Make the first column 1.4 inches wide, and the others .85 inches wide. (See Chapter 8 for more information on tables.)

13. Highlight the entire table by choosing Select Table from the Table menu (<ALT> + A, A). Format it using the Table style.

14. Type in the column headings and format them as 10-point Avant Garde, centered. The only tricky column heading is "Total Return." You need to highlight the two cells above "Week" and "1991" and merge them by selecting Merge Cells from the Table menu (<ALT> + A, M).

    Note: *Whenever you merge two cells, Word adds an extra carriage return. Delete it so that the rows line up.*

15. Highlight the first column and bold it.

16. Highlight that portion of the table where the numbers go, and set a decimal tab at .38 inches; you need to use the Tabs dialog box to do this. It's probably useful to type dollar and percentage signs where they belong, rather than trying to remember to do it whenever you start a new report.

17. Highlight the first row after the column headings, and apply the Skinny style. Highlight every other row in the table and apply this style. This isn't so hard if you have a Shortcut key. You can also use <F4> (the Repeat command).

18. Highlight each of the other rows, and apply the Border style.

19. The easiest way to position the table and the table heading at the bottom of the page is to highlight and then frame them. Select Frame from the Format menu. To ensure that the frame doesn't cut off the edges of the outlined cells, make the Horizontal Distance from Text .2 inches. Select Bottom from the Vertical Position menu (<ALT> + I). (See Chapter 13 for more information on framing text and graphics.)

20. Create the header by selecting Header/Footer from the View menu (<ALT> + V, H). Open the header by pressing <ENTER>. (See Chapter 12 for information on headers and footers.) Type "Banking Group Report" and format it in 12-point Avant Garde bold, with the second-thinnest rule below.

21. Create the footer by opening the Header/Footer dialog box and selecting the footer (type "F" and press <ENTER>). Format the page number as 10-point Avant Garde bold, centered, with the second-thinnest rule above.

22. Save your template, and give it a name. Word automatically gives every template a .DOT extension (so you don't have to).

CHAPTER 15

Tips for Handling Long Documents

This chapter covers tips and tricks for handling long documents. Whether or not a document is a long one depends as much on what you have inside it as on how many pages it has. A 15-page booklet isn't long unless you have embedded graphics and charts on every page, at which point it can *seem* very long. I try to keep documents with a lot of graphics down to about 15 pages; single-spaced, straight-text documents don't get "long" until they're 40 pages or so. My rule of thumb is that when Word for Windows starts getting sluggish, the document is too big.

When a document is too big, I break it up into two or more files. I try to break documents that are especially long or full of graphics into chapters even if some chapters are quite small. I *always* create a directory and put all the files associated with a large document into that directory, including the original graphics files.

Also, I always keep the *original* graphics and spreadsheet files for images I have pasted into my document until the job is 100% done. The one time I *didn't* do this, several documents got corrupted, and I had to redo a lot of artwork and graphs.

This chapter explains these topics in the following order:

- How to automatically generate a table of contents from your styled headings.

- How to generate an index.

- How to generate a single table of contents and index for a long document broken up into several different files.

CREATING A TABLE OF CONTENTS AND AN INDEX

Word for Windows allows you to generate automatically both a table of contents (TOC) and an index. When Word generates these, it stores them in fields (special sets of codes that tell the program where to find certain information and what to do with it). The great thing about the table of contents and index fields is that you can update them by highlighting them and pressing a single key, the <F9> key. This way, whenever you change your document, all you have to do is update your table of contents or index field, and the whole table of contents or index changes.

To see the fields themselves, you generally select Field Codes from the View menu (<ALT> + V, C). You can see the text of the table of contents by turning Field Codes off (simply select it again from the View menu). There are two Field Codes that work differently than this. To see both the Referenced Document field and the Index Entry field, turn on the Show/Hide ¶ button.

Whenever you change your document, all you have to do to update your index or table of contents is highlight the index or TOC field and press the <F9> key. Word updates it automatically.

✦ How to Create a Table of Contents

Word allows you to generate a table of contents in one of two ways: either from your style headings (you must be using styles to use this feature) or from **table entry fields**, which are codes you use to mark the text you want included in the table of contents. The first method is by far the easier, and I'll cover it here. For information on the second method, refer to your Word for Windows manual.

I have used a very simple example here. (You can find it—unformatted—in the file TOC.DOC on the *Tools of the Trade* disk that came with this book. Just add a few page breaks and apply styles to the headings to create a sample TOC.) However, if you have an actual table of contents you want to do, use these instructions to do it. Because you may not like the formatting for the standard styles that Word uses for its table of contents, I'll go over how to change it. The chapter headings in the following example are from Woody Allen's *Without Feathers*; the bracketed numbers indicate the level of heading you might use to style them (for example, you might apply the style heading 1 to "Examining Psychic Phenomena").

EXAMINING PSYCHIC PHENOMENA [1]
Apparitions [2]
Spirit Departure [2]
Precognition [2]
Trances [2]
Clairvoyance [2]
Prognostication [2]
A GUIDE TO SOME OF THE LESSER BALLETS [1 + page break]
Dmitri [2]
The sacrifice [3]
The spell [3]

To create a table of contents (TOC) *automatically* using your style headings:

1. Create a blank page or two toward the beginning of your document to accommodate the TOC.

2. Put your cursor in the page where you want the TOC to start, and select Table of Contents from the Insert menu (<ALT> + I, C). Word's default values are the ones you'll usually want; they use all your headings to generate the TOC. If you only want to use certain levels of heads (1 and 2, for example), type 1 in the From box and 2 in the To box. Click on OK or press <ENTER> when you're ready.

Table of Contents
Table Of Contents
⦿ Use **H**eading Paragraphs   **OK**
⦿ **A**ll   **Cancel**
○ **F**rom: ▢▴▾ **T**o: ▢▴▾
○ Use Table **E**ntry Fields

3. Word generates a TOC. If Field Codes are on, you see the table of contents field code: {TOC·\o}. When Field Codes are off, you see the actual table of contents, similar to the one that follows.

EXAMINING PSYCHIC PHENOMENA 2
   Apparitions 2
   Spirit Departure 2
   Precognition 2
   Trances 2
   Clairvoyance 2
   Prognostication 2
A GUIDE TO SOME OF THE LESSER BALLETS 3
   Dmitri 3
      The sacrifice 3
      The spell 3

Your automatically-generated table of contents probably looks something like this. Note two things: 1) As soon as your table of contents appears, standard "toc" styles appear on the menu on your Ribbon. You can redefine these styles each time you use them, or you can redefine them permanently by changing the Normal template. 2) As part of your style changes, you might want to redefine how the tabs are set so they line up along the right tab instead of the left.

4. Look at the Style menu on the Ribbon. Word has added three of its standard styles, toc 1–3. You can redefine these styles with the Styles dialog box. If you don't have particular styles in mind, you might try the ones in the following list. I find the half-inch indents of Word's TOC styles to be a bit distracting—they make the whole TOC look lopsided. The following styles use only a quarter-inch indent for third-level heads (toc 3). Remember that changing your styles *here* only affects this one document; you can redefine the default by revising the Normal template (see Chapter 14 for more information). Or, you can use the Add to Template option (<ALT> + E) in the Style dialog box.

Style	Spec
toc 1	12-point Times, with .5 line (6 pts) of space After
toc 2	12-point Times italic, with .5 line of space After
toc 3	12-point Times, with .5 line of space After, indented .25 inches From Left

If you use italics instead of indents to differentiate the levels of headings, the *page numbers* end up italicized as well (remember that styles apply to entire paragraphs). The simple way around this problem is to use your right mouse button to highlight the page numbers and format them however you like.

EXAMINING PSYCHIC PHENOMENA..2
Apparitions 2
Spirit Departure...2
Precognition 2
Trances..2
Clairvoyance..2
Prognostication...2
Dmitri 3
    The sacrifice 3
    The spell..3

If you redefine your TOC styles according to the previous specs, your table of contents now looks something like this. I used my right mouse button to format the page numbers.

✦ Unlinking Fields

Here's how to delete a field, any field. Make sure you can *see* the field. Highlight it, including the braces on either end, and press the <DELETE> key.

In some cases, you may want to change your table of contents substantially—for instance, to add one- or two-sentence summaries describing a chapter's chief points. To do this, you have to **unlink** the TOC from its field.

When you unlink the TOC field, Word substitutes the actual table of contents you generated for the field that generated it. In other words, it gets rid of the field so you can't update it anymore. If you need to change your table of contents after you unlink the TOC field, you have to start over and reinsert your table of contents. (This is not the worst thing in the world, by the way. As you can see, it's pretty fast.)

Note: *You can unlink any field—embedded graphics fields and index fields included.*

To unlink fields:

1. Highlight the entire field, including the braces at either end.

2. Press <CTRL> + <SHIFT> + <F9>, which is known as the Unlink Field command.

✦ How to Create an Index

You create an index in much the way that you create a table of contents using table entry fields—simply insert a code to mark the material you want to be indexed.

To create an index:

1. Highlight the word or phrase you want indexed (if you stick your cursor in a word and double-click, you highlight it). Say that one of the items to be indexed is every reference to the movie *The Big Chill*. Highlight "Big Chill."

2. Select Index Entry from the Insert menu (<ALT> + I, E).

3. Open the Index Entry dialog box. Type ", The" and then click on OK.

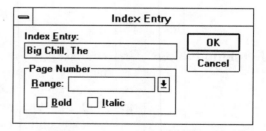

The Index Entry dialog box lets you indicate exactly how you want the indexed word or phrase to appear. If you click on Bold and/or Italic, only the page number itself will use that formatting.

Here's how the indexed phrase will look in your document when the Show/Hide ¶ button is on. Remember that this is a special case; you can't see index entries by turning Field Codes on:

The Big Chill{XE."Big.Chill,.The"}¶

Here's how the entry will look when you generate your index:

Big Chill, The, 3, 4, 5, 6

4. Word's index feature requires that you mark *every single occurrence of a word or phrase* with the Index Entry code. The easiest way to do this is to copy the index entry field (<CTRL> + C), including the braces on either side of the field; use Search on the Edit menu to find every instance of "The Big Chill"; and then paste the index entry field at the end of every "Chill" (<CTRL> + V).

5. When you're done, create a new page at the end of your document for the finished index. Put your cursor on that page and select Index from the Insert menu (<ALT> + I, I). Choose the options you prefer and click on OK or press <ENTER> when you're done. (See the following diagram for an explanation of the options.)

The Normal Index shows index entries and subentries one below the other (see the Word for Windows reference manual for details on using subentries).

The Run-in Index shows index entries and subentries on the same line.

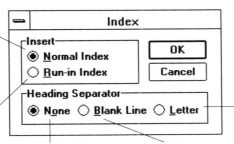

No Heading Separator means that there's nothing to indicate the start of a new alphabetic section.

The Blank Line option uses a single line of space to separate alphabetic sections.

The Letter option uses a letter to indicate the alphabetic section: an A is placed above the A section, a B above the B section, and so forth. The index heading style formats this letter.

6. You can update and unlink the index field exactly as you do the table of contents field, and you can redefine the index and index heading styles in the same manner.

HOW TO CREATE ONE TABLE OF CONTENTS AND INDEX FOR SEVERAL DIFFERENT FILES

Say you're dealing with a 150-page document that you've broken into four files (PART_1.DOC, PART_2.DOC, PART_3.DOC, and PART_4.DOC). You want to create a single table of contents and index for all four. The simplest way to do this is to create a master document that uses Referenced Document fields to create a TOC and index.

Note: *You can also create a master document using Include fields (see your Word for Windows manual for more information).*

To create one TOC and index for several different files:

1. Create a fifth file—call it MASTER.DOC or some such thing (make sure you save it in the same directory as the other parts of your document). You should create both your table of contents and index in this master file. You might also want to put a cover page and other miscellany in it. Since this master document needs to tell Word what other files are in the group, you need to insert some Referenced Document fields. (I usually put these on the page that starts the table of contents.)

2. Select Field from the Insert menu (<ALT> + I, D). Scroll through the Insert Field Type box, and select "Referenced doc." Word automatically puts "rd" in the Field Code box at the bottom of the screen. Type in the name of the first document in the group. Click on OK or press <ENTER> when you're done.

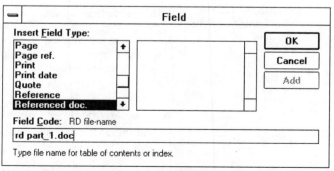

Use the Field dialog box to put a Referenced Document field (also called an RD field) into your master document. The RD field makes Word check the different documents listed to find headings for the table of contents and index entries for the index.

3. Follow the same procedure to create a referenced document field for each of the documents in the group. If you're indeed testing this with four documents called parts 1–4, your master document will look like this when you're done (if the Show/Hide ¶ icon is on).

{rd:part_1}¶

{rd:part_2}¶

{rd:part_3}¶

{rd:part_4}¶

4. You can now create a table of contents and/or an index in your master document exactly as you would any other TOC or index (see the instructions in the previous sections).

5. Two important tips about numbering pages when using referenced documents:

a. To number the pages of your table of contents and/or index, use a section break to separate the two so you can number the pages independently. (If you have a question about this, refer to Chapter 12.)

b. Word for Windows does *not* automatically number the pages between the different documents. You have to go into each document and make sure it starts and ends with the right number so that you can coordinate the numbering with the next document. (Use the PAGE NUMBER command in the Header/Footer dialog box to set starting page numbers.)

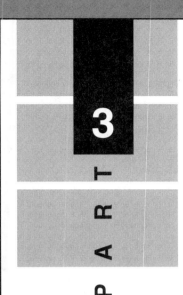

Do It Yourself

This part of the book walks you through the process of creating seven different sample publications and presentations. These projects give you an opportunity to put into practice many of the features covered in this book—from special typesetting characters to positioning to columns.

The projects are short, and each type is covered in a separate chapter (Chapters 16 through 20). You can find materials for five of them on the disk that came with this kit. The other two, *Create Your Own Form* and *Create Your Own Slide Show*, are either extremely simple (as most good slides are) or, in the case of the form, have very little text. If you've done some of the other examples in this book, especially in Chapter 13, each project should take only a half hour or so. Plus, they're broken into stages, so you can take them in even smaller bites. You can find a template for each of these documents on the *Tools of the Trade* disk that came with this kit.

If you happen to be on deadline and want to produce a report or brochure similar to the ones covered here, you can use these instructions to put it together and get it out the door in short order. Chapter 16, *Create*

Your Own Form, covers how to create a computerized expense report, though the instructions there can easily be used as the basis for other computerized forms as well. Word for Windows has two great advantages when it comes to creating recurring forms: its template function enables you to fill out the forms right on the screen, and it can actually add up the columns and rows of numbers once you've entered them.

Chapter 17, *Create Your Own Marketing Materials,* shows how to create two different marketing pieces—a letter-fold brochure and my favorite flip sheet, a design I use quite often. Chapter 18, *Create Your Own Report,* has another favorite design—a single-sided report layout that's nearly perfect. It's simple, yet it has an appealing layout for chapter openers. It has plenty of room for charts and tables, and it can accommodate headers and footers easily. Chapter 18 also shows how to create a landscape report.

Chapter 19, *Create Your Own Newsletter,* contains one of the most difficult designs in this book. You almost have to create a template to use it, because it's not something you'd want to have to set up every month. Although Chapter 20, *Create Your Own Slide Show,* focuses on how to create slides, you can adapt the instruction easily to create overhead presentations and handouts.

Finally, Chapter 21, *P.S. PostScript,* shows how you can edit a PostScript file to create high-quality special effects such as outlining and screening text. ✦

CHAPTER 16

Create Your Own Form

This two-page expense report is proof-positive that forms don't have to be ugly to be useful. It's set up as a template (KIT_FORM.DOT on the *Tools of the Trade disk*), so you can start a fresh one every month, fill it out on your computer screen (Word can even add the rows and columns of numbers for you), and print it when you're done. If you haven't already, you should probably glance at *Forms, Calendars, and Notices* in Chapter 2.

The chief design elements in any good form are simplicity and consistency. Give each element of the form a recognizable style. For instance, the portions of the form in which dollar amounts are entered (from AIR/RAIL to CLIENT #) are formatted with the same column width, a dec tab set at the same measurement, the same line spacing, and so on.

The headings (from DATE to CLIENT #) all have the same amount of space above them, and the account numbers for the various sorts of expenses are at the very bottom of their respective cells. Most text is in 8-point Helvetica caps, which looks suitably utilitarian and form-like. Notice what *isn't* in caps: full-length sentences, subtext such as "From" and "To" under PERIOD, and the company name. The use of upper/lowercase generally makes text easier to read (which is why I've used it in sentences), and in this example it also makes it stand out, since everything else is in caps.

Even the borders and boxes are consistent. There are two types, single and double, each for a different purpose. Single lines generally are used to define information in the form, while double lines are used to accent the headings and the totals.

The top of the report contains the name of the company and of the form itself, along with space for the employee's name, and space to note the period covered by the report. The *in*consistent way these three items are handled gives the form the only conscious design element it has.

The second page provides room to explain the circumstances and purpose of the expenses claimed on the first page, so the design has long lines for information. However, typefaces and borders are much the same. I can't imagine that anyone looking at the two sheets would doubt they go together.

DeZiner Corp.
EXPENSE REPORT

NAME: _____ PERIOD: From _____ To _____

DATE	PLACE VISITED & BUSINESS PURPOSE	AIR/RAIL 21010	BUSINESS MEALS 21011	ENTERTAIN -MENT 21012	HOTELS 21013	TAXIS 21014	AUTO RENTAL 21015	MISC. & TELE 21016	TOTAL: FIRM EXPENSE	CLIENT #

PLEASE NOTE:
- Attach ALL original receipts to this forms.
- Call Joyce Bothers in Accounts Payable (x4444) if you have any questions as to how to complete this form.

TOTAL	
LESS: ADVANCES	

EMPLOYEE SIGNATURE	DATE	APPROVED DEPT HEAD	DATE SIGNATURE	BALANCE DUE

If you want to go through this exercise to create either an expense report of your own or some similar form, take a few minutes to decide the headings you need, the number of columns, and other pertinent details. Then, as you read through my instructions, you can adjust what I'm saying for your own purposes.

Note: *Although I don't explain how to create macros to automate the process of filling in the form, you might want to investigate this. Refer to your Word for Windows manual for information regarding both macros and Fill-in fields.*

SETTING THINGS UP

As always, the first thing you need to do is set up the page. The document is letter-sized in landscape orientation, with top and bottom margins of .4 inches, a left margin of .75 inches, and a right margin of .45 inches. The reason the left and right margins

---

DETAILS OF BUSINESS MEALS, ENTERTAINMENT, AND MISCELLANEOUS

BUSINESS MEALS: This expense classification is reserved for meals which have a clear purpose related to revenue-producing business.

BUSINESS ENTERTAINMENT: The IRS requires the names of the people attending, their position, and the business affiliation (usually company name), and the business purpose of the occasion, in order to justify the expense as *business* entertainment.

BUSINESS MEALS
(Attach All Original Receipts)

DATE	NAMES	COMPANY & POSITION	PURPOSE OF LUNCH/DINNER	AMOUNT
(Attach additional sheets if necessary)			TOTAL	

BUSINESS ENTERTAINEMENT
(Attach All Original Receipts)

DATE	NAMES	COMPANY & POSITION	PURPOSE AND NATURE	AMOUNT
(Attach additional sheets if necessary)			TOTAL	

MISCELLANEOUS EXPLANATION:

---

are so different is that when you border tables, the border over-hangs the left column.

Think for a moment about the typefaces and point sizes you want to use. In this case, the headings are in 8-point Helvetica bold caps, single-spaced and centered, with .5 lines (6 points) of space Before; the notes and explanations are in 8-point Times bold, single-spaced; and the information to be filled in each month or so—the dollar amount and description of the ex-penses claimed (not shown here)—are meant to be in 8-point Times, *not* bold, single-spaced, with .5 lines of space both Be-fore and After so they don't get cramped looking. You also need to place a dec tab in the cells where the dollar amounts will go, in order to get them lined up properly.

After mapping out the formatting I wanted to use for the text, I created four styles: one for the 8-point Helvetica headings (which I called simply 8H); another for the 8-point Times notes (8T); another for the 8-point Times dollar amounts (NO), com-plete with a decimal tab at .5 inches and .5 lines of space Before and After; and the last for 8-point Times text formatted just like NO, but without a decimal tab (which I called TXT). All the styles are upper/lowercase and left-aligned except for 8H.

You'll still need to specially format a few individual cells to get them to look exactly right, but with styles in hand the job's guaranteed to go faster and to turn out to be more consistent.

✦ Laying Things Out

Since you won't be typing data at this point, just creating the form, it's definitely worthwhile to specify the number of rows you want. The form is 11 columns by 21 rows. You should prob-ably turn on the Show/Hide ¶ and Gridlines options so that you can see the invisible formatting characters.

This table uses a number of merged cells, which should be formatted only after the other columns are finished. As a result, I don't start these instructions at the top of the form and pro-ceed through to the bottom. Instead, I save the first two rows until the end.

1. Start at the *third row* of the form. Highlight the entire row, and apply the style I called 8H. Type the headings listed be-low from left to right, placing each heading in its own cell.

The headings are: Date, Place Visited & Business Purpose, Air/Rail 21010, Business Meals 21011, Entertainment 21012, Hotels 21013, Taxis 21014, Auto Rental 21015, Misc & Tele 21016, Total: Firm Expense, Client #. Don't worry if things don't break correctly at this point; they will in a few more steps.

Two things: As you tab from cell to cell to enter the headings, the screen automatically scrolls right, so you don't have to. Although I often work in Draft mode because it's faster, I prefer not to. Working in Draft mode in tables isn't so bad, however, because tables retain their structure. It's only the text that's really "draft."

2. Here's how to change the column widths. In the example, the first column is .6 inches, the second is 1.4 inches, and columns 3 through 11 are all .85 inches. The easiest way to do this is to use the Column Width dialog box on the Table menu (<ALT> + A, W) to set the width for the first two columns. Then highlight the rest of the table (columns 3 through 11), open the Column Width dialog box again, and type .85 in the option that now reads "Width of Columns 3–11." The table should now fill up the page.

3. At this point—when you're not in Draft view—the headings should fit fairly well in their cells. However, you might want to use new line breaks (<SHIFT> + <ENTER>) to break the headings where they look best, and to position the account numbers at the bottom of the cells. The illustration below, complete with invisibles, shows how I handled a few of the headings.

BUSINESS↵ MEALS↵ 21011¤	ENTERTAIN -MENT↵ 21012¤	HOTELS↵ ↵ 21013¤	TAXIS↵ ↵ 21014¤	AUTO↵ RENTAL↵ 21015¤	MISC.-&↵ TELE↵ 21016¤

4. This is as good a time as any to start bordering the cells, which won't complicate the process of merging them together. I'll explain where the single rules go now, and leave the double rules for later.

Highlight the entire table. Open the Border dialog box on the Format menu (<ALT> + T, B). Select the Grid option (<ALT> + G) and the thinnest line style available.

5. Now for merging the cells in the top two rows. Highlight the first three cells in these rows and merge them using the Merge Cells command on the Table menu (<ALT> + A, M). Highlight and merge the last three cells in that row, and then merge the

five cells remaining in the middle. Here's a shortcut for deleting the extra carriage returns that Word adds when you merge cells: Highlight the merged cells and press <DELETE>.

Note: *Remember that these newly created two-row columns are still connected to the rest of the table, even though you want to format them differently. At this point,* don't use your right mouse button to select columns. *If you do, you'll end up selecting the merged cells and the regular columns together, which can get pretty confusing. Instead, select only the particular cells* you want to format.

6. Make the merged cells on either end 3 inches wide, and the middle column 3.65 inches.

✦ Finishing Touches

1. Here are the finishing touches for the top rows. Type "NAME:" in the first two-row column, and "PERIOD From: To:" in the third. I used the 8H style for mine and then made the following adjustments to the text: I got rid of the .5 lines of space Before and aligned it flush left. Here's a shortcut for making text formatted with an all caps style upper/lower case: Highlight the text you want to change, press <CTRL> + A (the all caps hot key), and then use <SHIFT> + <F3> (the Toggle Case key).

   Place a left tab stop at 1.7 inches in the PERIOD cell. Remember that you have to <CTRL> + <TAB> to move text and graphics to a tab stop in tables.

2. Next, highlight the middle two-row column and format it as 12-point Times bold, single-spaced and centered. Type the company's name (in this case, "DeZiner Corp.") in the top row of that column, and the title of the form (in this case EXPENSE REPORT) in the second row.

Use <ALT> + <PAGE DOWN> to get to the bottom of your table with a single keystroke. Use <ALT> + <PAGE UP> to get back up to the top.

3. The last step for these two complicated rows is changing the borders. You could do this in any of several different ways, but this is how I did it. Highlight both rows, and open the Border dialog box. Select None. Go back to the table and highlight the NAME cell. Open the Border dialog box, and select the Box option (<ALT> + B) and the thinnest line available. Here's a nice use for the <F4> "repeat" key. Put your cursor in the PERIOD cell and press <F4>; Word boxes it with a thin rule, too. Highlight the row containing the headings, and box it with a double-lined rule.

4. At the very bottom row, highlight the first three cells and merge them together. Then merge the next three cells, and then the next three. Delete the extra carriage returns, type the text, and format it as 8-point Helvetica bold. Again, I used the style 8H, got rid of the space Before, and realigned the text flush left. I created the two lines of text in these cells using New Line breaks.

To get rid of the border between the newly created columns two and three, highlight them both and select the Box option instead of the Grid in the Border dialog box.

5. Merge the first nine cells in the two rows *above* the bottom row. Type the text and format it with the 8T style. The PLEASE NOTE: is in the first of the two rows. The other text is in the second of the two rows. Again, each line is separated by a New Line break. To border these cells, highlight them both. Select the Preset Box and use the thinnest single line. Then select the top of that box by clicking in the sample area, and select the thinnest double line.

6. You're almost done with this page. In the last three rows of the table's second-to-last column, put in the text for TOTAL, LESS ADVANCES, and BALANCE DUE. I styled it as 8H, and again got rid of the unwanted spacing and center alignment. Highlight the last six cells (these three and the three to their right), and border them with the thinnest double line. Remember that these cells also have gridlines between them.

7. One last thing. Since this is going to be a template, you probably want to format the cells for the text and numbers now, so that when you're ready to type information into them, they'll be ready for you. To do this, format the cells in which the numbers go with the NO style described in *Setting Things Up*. Format the cells where the date and text go with the TXT style.

✦ **Page 2**   **1.** After this table, insert a page break (<CTRL> + <ENTER>). This is one of the reasons it's nice to have a spare carriage return around.

2. This second page is a much easier version of the first page. I'll give only a few pointers:

- The title and notes at the top of the form are *not* in the table. The title is set in 12-point Times bold, centered, as on the previous page.

- I created the first table first—it's 5 columns by 9 rows—and then copied it. You only have to make one change to the second table, and that's to change the heading in the fourth column.

- The text at the top of the form is based on the 8T style; the headings and other text are based on the 8H style. The rows to be filled in are formatted with the style TXT, but only 2 points of space is added Before and After.

- The table is centered. To do this, highlight the entire table; select Row Height from the Table menu (<ALT> + A, H); and then select center alignment.

- The last row of each table also has 2 points of space Before and another 2 points After to make it stand out a little more. The TOTAL cell is 1.5 inches wide; the merged cell to the left of it is 7.1 inches.

- I created the miscellaneous explanation at the bottom by placing a border between and below the last three paragraphs.

Last, but not least: When you're finished with this form, save it as a template.

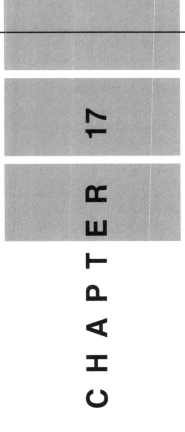

CHAPTER 17

Create Your Own Marketing Materials

This chapter shows you how to create a letter-fold brochure and a flip sheet. In the spirit of Rule of Thumb #1 (Reuse your good ideas), I have used variations on this basic design several times, not only for flip sheets per se, but also for more informal, flyer-type sheets.

Both designs are adapted from Chapter 2. The materials for creating them are on the disk that came with this kit. There is also a template for the letter-fold brochure (KIT_LBRO.DOC), and a template for the flip sheet (KIT_FLIP.DOC).

SETTING UP THE LETTER-FOLD BROCHURE

The text for the cover of this brochure is in KIT_LF1.DOC, and the inside text is in KIT_LF2.DOC. Instead of using a graphic on the very back of the brochure (as was originally done in Chapter 2), this example shows you how to create what's called a "picture window." This window can serve as a placeholder either for a photo that will be stripped in by the print shop, or for computerized artwork that isn't done yet.

The brochure's cover is created using tables, and each of the three panels on the cover is its own cell. The inside of the brochure uses columns. The cover is created in the first page of the document, and the inside text is laid out on the second page.

Set up the document so it's letter-sized and in landscape orientation. Set the margins to .5 inches top and bottom and .3 inches left and right.

✦ Laying Things Out

1. Create a 5-column table for the front cover. Two of these columns will be used for margins (similar to the design for the single-fold brochure covered in Chapter 12). The most difficult part of this example is deciding the width of the columns, and then ensuring that the text and graphics line up exactly

---

The LITTLE
SUPER SAVINGS
ACCOUNT

**Five great ways of
ensuring that *everybody*
can get richer.**

Not just the rich.

1. A minimum balance of $1,000.

2. Free checking.

3. Bounce protection.

4. Free Visa Card (if you qualify).

5. Preferred interest rates.

LITTLE BANK
**We're the little bank
on your corner...**

... wherever you are.

We all need to save for the future. But who can afford to?

At LITTLE BANK, who can afford *not* to?

LITTLE BANK is an insured bank

within each of the three panels. In order to address both of these problems, you have to give yourself a little extra room at the margins, so to speak.

My first inclination was to set the margins at only a quarter inch to leave as much room as possible for the panels themselves. But once I started printing out samples I realized that was cutting it too close. So I set them at .3 inches. To keep an even margin around all three panels of the brochure, I then had to set the two "margin" columns to .6 inches. That leaves about 3.07 inches for each of the three panels. The diagram on the following page shows the basic setup.

2. Now that you see how the layout is set up, highlight the first column—just one cell in this case—and make it 3.07 inches

---

How do I open a Little Super Savings Account?

Ipsum dolor sit amet, consectetuer adipiscing elit, sed diam nonummy nibh euismod tincidunt ut laoreet dolore magna aliquam erat volutpat. Ut wisi enim ad minim veniam.

Quis nostrud exerci tation ullamcorper suscipit lobortis nisl ut aliquip ex ea commodo feugiat consequat.

How is the Little Super Savings Account better than similar accounts at other banks?

Lorem ipsum dolor sit amet, consectetuer adipiscing elit, sed diam nonummy nibh euismod tincidunt ut laoreet dolore magna aliquam erat volutpat.

Ut wisi enim ad minim veniam, quis nostrud exerci tation ullamcorper suscipit lobortis nisl ut aliquip ex ea commodo feugiat consequat.

Dolor sit amet, consectetuer adipiscing elit, sed diam nonummy nibh euismod tincidunt ut laoreet dolore magna aliquam erat volutpat volutpat.

Wisi enim ad minim veniam, quis nostrud exerci tation ullamcorper suscipit lobortis nisl ut aliquip ex ea commodo feugiat consequat. Wisi enim ad minim veniam, quis nostrud.

Quis nostrud exerci tation ullamcorper suscipit lobortis nisl ut aliquip ex ea commodo feugiat consequat aliquip ex ea commodo feugiat consequat.

Dolor sit amet, consectetuer adipiscing elit, sed diam nonummy nibh euismod tincidunt ut laoreet dolore magna aliquam erat volutpat volutpat.

Wisi enim ad minim veniam, quis nostrud exerci tation ullamcorper suscipit lobortis nisl ut

aliquip ex ea commodo feugiat consequat. Wisi enim ad minim veniam, quis nostrud. Quis nostrud exerci tation ullamcorper suscipit lobortis nisl ut aliquip ex ea commodo feugiat consequat aliquip ex ea commodo feugiat consequat.

What kind of benefits do long-time customers get?

Dolor sit amet, consectetuer adipiscing elit, sed diam nonummy nibh euismod tincidunt ut laoreet dolore magna aliquam erat volutpat. Ut wisi enim ad minim veniam.

Quis nostrud exerci tation ullamcorper suscipit lobortis nisl ut aliquip ex ea commodo feugiat consequat. Lorem ipsum dolor sit amet, consectetuer adipiscing elit, sed diam nonummy nibh.

• lobortis nisl ut aliquip ex ea commodo feugiat consequat lobortis nisl ut aliquip ex ea commodo feugiat consequat

• exerci tation ullamcorper suscipit lobortis nisl ut aliquip ex ea commodo feugiat lobortis nisl ut aliquip ex ea commodo feugiat consequat

• enim ad minim veniam, quis nostrud exerci tation ullamcorper suscipit lobortis

• nisl ut aliquip ex ea commodo feugiat

• nostrud exerci tation ullamcorper suscipit lobortis nisl

Lorem ipsum dolor sit amet, consectetuer adipiscing elit, sed diam nonummy nibh euismod tincidunt ut laoreet dolore magna aliquam erat volutpat.

Ut wisi enim ad minim veniam, quis nostrud exerci tation ullamcorper suscipit lobortis nisl ut aliquip ex ea commodo feugiat consequat. Wisi enim ad minim veniam, quis nostrud exerci

tation ullamcorper suscipit lobortis nisl ut aliquip ex ea commodo feugiat consequat.

Ut wisi enim ad minim veniam, quis nostrud exerci tation ullamcorper suscipit lobortis nisl ut aliquip ex ea commodo feugiat consequat. Wisi enim ad minim veniam, quis nostrud exerci tation ullamcorper suscipit lobortis nisl ut aliquip ex ea commodo feugiat consequat.

What other advantages does LITTLE BANK give its customers?

Consectetuer adipiscing elit, sed diam nonummy nibh euismod tincidunt ut laoreet dolore magna aliquam erat volutpat. Ad minim veniam, quis nostrud exerci tation ullamcorper suscipit lobortis nisl ut aliquip ex ea commodo feugiat consequat.

Lorem ipsum dolor sit amet, consectetuer adipiscing elit, sed diam nonummy nibh euismod tincidunt ut laoreet dolore magna aliquam erat volutpat.

Ut wisi enim ad minim veniam, quis nostrud exerci tation ullamcorper suscipit lobortis nisl ut aliquip ex ea commodo feugiat consequat.

How do I get more information?

Ut wisi enim ad minim veniam, quis nostrud exerci tation ullamcorper suscipit lobortis nisl ut aliquip ex ea commodo feugiat consequat.

Enim ad minim veniam, quis nostrud exerci tation ullamcorper Enim ad minim veniam, quis nostrud exerci tation ullamcorper.

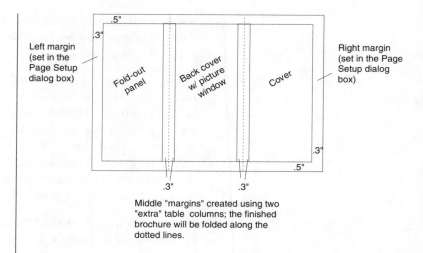

Left margin (set in the Page Setup dialog box)

Right margin (set in the Page Setup dialog box)

.5"

.3"

Fold-out panel

Back cover w/ picture window

Cover

.3"

.5"

.3"

.3"

Middle "margins" created using two "extra" table columns; the finished brochure will be folded along the dotted lines.

wide. Make the second column .6 inches wide; the third column, 3.07 inches; the fourth, .6 inches; and the fifth, 3.07. The easiest way to do this is to use the Column Width dialog box on the Table menu (<ALT> + A, W).

3. The easiest way to get the cover text from KIT_LF1.DOC into your brochure is to open it. There's no need to close the brochure. Highlight the text for one of the three panels, copy it, then use the Window menu to get back to your brochure document. Put your cursor in the cell where you want this text, then paste it in. Repeat this process until you have the text for each of the brochure panels placed in the document you're working on. Then go back and close KIT_LF1.DOC.

Note: *The more documents or windows you have open, the slower Word is likely to run, and the more "low memory" messages you're likely to get.*

Window
New Window
Arrange All
1 BROCHURE.DOC
✓**2** KIT_LF1.DOC

You move back and forth between open documents by selecting the one you want to go to from the Window menu. The document you're presently in is always checked.

4. Here are the specs for each of the three cover panels. I frequently use new line breaks (<SHIFT> + <ENTER>) to break the text in particular places.

Front cover — 36-point Helvetica bold, centered on Exactly 39 points of leading, with 1.5 lines (18 points) of space Before; LITTLE BANK is in small caps.

Back cover — 18-point Palatino bold, centered with single line spacing and .5 lines (6 points) of space After; LITTLE BANK is small-capped and in its own paragraph with 2 lines (24 points) of space Before.

Fold-out panel — The non-numbered text is 18-point Palatino bold, centered, and single-spaced; The LITTLE SUPER SAVINGS ACCOUNT is in its own paragraph with 24 points of space Before; LITTLE and ACCOUNT are small-capped and SUPER SAVINGS is all caps; there's 10 points of space after the paragraph starting with "Five great ways..."; there's 18 points of space between "Not just..." and the numbered text below.

The numbered text is 12-point Palatino, flush left, and single-spaced with 3 points of space After; the numbers themselves are 20-point Times bold, subscripted by 3 points. I set a left tab at .45 inches. You might need to use the Tabs dialog box to do the same.

5. Create a picture window on the back cover. To do this, put your cursor where you want the window, and open Draw. Select Show Guides from the Draw menu (<ALT> + D, W), and then drag the guides until they measure an area 2.75 inches wide and 3 inches high. Choose the Rectangle/Square tool and draw a 2.75 × 3 inch box. You can change the width of the line bordering the box by choosing Line Style from the Draw menu (<ALT> + D, L). When you're done, update the graphic and return to Word. If necessary, you can resize the picture window using the FORMAT, PICTURE command.

6. You should print your document and see what it looks like, making whatever adjustments you feel appropriate. For instance, when I tested it, I decided to move the text in the cover panel slightly to the right by specifying .05 inches in the From Left option in the Paragraph dialog box. I did the same for the fold-out panel. I moved the back panel .06 inches From Left.

◆ Finishing Touches

There's only one finishing touch, and that's placing the text "LITTLE BANK is an insured bank" in the footer. If you prefer, you can frame this text and drag it to the bottom of the page.

1. Open the Header/Footer dialog box. Turn on the Different First Page option (you don't want this footer on the inside of your brochure) and select First Footer from the scroll box. Remember that this option doesn't appear if you're in Page Layout view; you simply have to be in the first page of your document to access the First Footer.

2. Once you're in the footer, type the text "LITTLE BANK is an insured bank" and format it in 12-point Helvetica bold. Put "LITTLE BANK" in small caps.

3. Open the Tabs dialog box and clear all tab stops. Then set a center tab stop at 8.8 inches. Press the <TAB> key once to position the text where you want it.

◆ Page 2

The inside of the brochure is much simpler to do than the cover. It's formatted in three columns with .6 inches of space between each column. The text is in 10-point Palatino, justified, and single-spaced, with .5 lines (6 points) of space After. The headings are in 12-point Helvetica bold, with 1 line (12 points) of space Before and 4 points After. If you want, redefine Normal and heading 1 to follow these specs.

1. In the paragraph after the table, insert a section break that starts on the Next Page. To do this, select Break from the Insert menu (<ALT> + I, B), and then choose the Next Page option.

2. Format the newly created section (section 2) into 3 columns with .6 inches of space between them. (Use the Columns dialog box; remember that the Columns icon on the Toolbar doesn't let you specify the space between columns.)

   Note: *You also specified .6 inches of space between columns when you formatted the cover. The only difference is that you put this space in the column of a table.*

3. Use the Print Preview feature to see how the page looks.

4. Here are some tips for "balancing columns"—in other words, making them even at the bottom:

   • If you've placed space Before headings or other text, you might have to delete it when those headings start a column. Otherwise there will be awkward gaps at the top of the page.

   • Always turn the Widow/Orphan Control option off in the Options dialog box (you can access this through the Print dialog box). If you don't do this, it will be all but impossible to balance your columns.

   • If the columns are still not exactly even at the bottom, add or remove a little space (1 point here and 1 point there) from Before or After paragraphs, around headings, and so forth. If you have extra leading in your document, you might even want to adjust it slightly in a particular paragraph to even things out.

SETTING UP THE FLIP SHEET

One thing I love about this design is how easy it is to do. The text is in the file KIT_FLP.DOC on the *Tools of the Trade* disk. The document is letter-sized in portrait orientation, with 1-inch margins all the way around.

✦ Laying Things Out

1. Open the sample file and take a minute to scroll through it to see where things are. For instance, the title of the piece, "Flip Sheets," and the **overline**, "It's easy to create..." are the first

things you see. (An overline, by the way, is simply an introductory line placed over a main heading. It's sometimes called a kicker.) The two captions are next, and then the two subheads. The footer is at the very bottom.

This is the plan of attack. First, format all the text. Next, create two empty boxes for the picture windows, and then frame them plus their captions.

Note: *Although it's possible to create frames within frames, as of this writing the easiest, most reliable way of creating picture windows within frames is to draw them with Microsoft Draw.*

It's easy to create flip sheets in Word

FLIP SHEETS

What are Flip Sheets?

Ipsum dolor sit amet, consectetuer adipiscing elit, sed diam nonummy nibh euismod tincidunt ut laoreet dolore magna aliquam erat volutpat. Ut wisi enim ad minim veniam. Quis nostrud exerci tation ullamcorper suscipit lobortis nisl ut aliquip ex ea commodo feugiat consequat. Lorem ipsum dolor sit amet, consectetuer adipiscing elit, sed diam nonummy nibh euismod tincidunt ut laoreet dolore magna aliquam erat volutpat dolore magna aliquam erat volutpat dolore magna aliquam erat.

This Design Can Also Be Used to Create Great Informational Flyers

Ipsum dolor sit amet, consectetuer adipiscing elit, sed diam nonummy nibh euismod tincidunt ut laoreet dolore magna aliquam erat volutpat. Ut wisi enim ad minim veniam. Quis nostrud exerci tation ullamcorper suscipit lobortis nisl ut aliquip ex ea commodo feugiat consequat.

Lorem ipsum dolor sit amet, consectetuer adipiscing elit, sed diam nonummy nibh euismod tincidunt ut laoreet dolore magna aliquam erat volutpat dolore magna aliquam erat volutpat dolore magna aliquam erat. Ipsum dolor sit amet, consectetuer adipiscing elit, sed diam nonummy nibh euismod tincidunt ut laoreet dolore magna aliquam erat volutpat. Ut wisi enim ad minim veniam.

Quis nostrud exerci tation ullamcorper suscipit lobortis nisl ut aliquip ex ea commodo feugiat consequat.

Lorem ipsum dolor sit amet, consectetuer adipiscing elit, sed diam nonummy nibh euismod tincidunt ut laoreet dolore magna aliquam erat volutpat dolore magna aliquam erat. Ipsum dolor sit amet, consectetuer adipiscing elit, sed diam nonummy nibh euismod tincidunt ut laoreet dolore magna aliquam erat volutpat. Ut wisi enim ad minim veniam.

Quis nostrud exerci tation ullamcorper suscipit lobortis nisl ut aliquip ex ea commodo feugiat consequat. Lorem ipsum dolor sit amet, consectetuer adipiscing elit, sed.

Ipsum dolor sit amet, consectetuer adipiscing elit, sed diam nonummy nibh euismod tincidunt ut laoreet dolore magna aliquam erat volutpat.

Ipsum dolor sit amet, consectetuer adipiscing elit, sed diam nonummy nibh euismod.

Name of Company ■ Address of Company ■ City, State, Zip
PHONE (212) 444-4444 ■ FAX (212) 444-4555

2. Here are the specs for the text.

Overline	20-point Helvetica italic, single-spaced and flush left, with 7 points of space After.
Title	70-point Helvetica bold on Exactly 72 points of leading, centered, with 1 line (12 points) of space After; condense the whole title by 1.75 points.
Subheads	12-point Helvetica-Narrow italic, single-spaced and flush left, with 2 points of space After; put 1 line of space Before the second sub-head, "This Design Can…."
Main text	10-point Times on 13 points of leading, justified, with .5 lines (6 points) of space After.
Captions	8-point Helvetica bold, single-spaced and centered, with 1.5 lines (18 points) of space After.

3. After you format all the text, use Draw to create a picture window that's 2.5 inches high and 2.85 inches wide. (Remember that you can use the Show Guides option on the Draw menu to measure objects.) Insert the box in the line just above the first caption. Copy the box and paste it above the second caption.

4. Highlight the first picture window and caption, and the second picture window and caption. Create a frame for them and format it as follows: Exactly 2.95 inches wide; Right relative to the horizontal margin; 1.9 inches from the top margin (this setting ensures that the top of the first graphic lines up with the first line of text, *not* with the heading); and a .15-inch distance from the text. Make sure that the Text Wrapping feature is set to Around. When you're done, you might want to check it out with the Print Preview feature.

Note: *There may be border(s) around the frame that you have to delete.*

✦ Finishing Touches

There are three finishing touches: placing the footer, adjusting the captions' width, and preventing the text from wrapping around the bottom of the second picture window and caption. I'll cover the last first.

- To prevent text from wrapping around the bottom of certain frames, simply make the frame longer by dragging the bottom. Or, if you prefer, use the Frame dialog box.

- Now for the footer. Simply *cut* the footer text (the company name, address, phone, and fax). Open the Header/Footer dialog box, and paste it in. If you haven't already, format the text with the specs described above. Notice that there are "n"s dividing portions of the address. These are meant to be square dingbats, so highlight each one and format it as Zapf Dingbats. (If you don't have the dingbats font, you might want to use a bullet instead.) The square dingbats tend to be large to my eye, so I reduced them to 6 points. If you prefer, you can use a frame to position this particular footer. Just remember that if you want a footer to appear on every page, you need to set it as a footer.

- You might find, as I did, that the captions overhang the edge of the picture windows slightly. This is because the window widths are 2.85 inches, and the frame is 2.95 inches. You can either narrow the frame width, or you can simply adjust the Right and Left Indents for each caption. If you choose the latter route, the quickest way might be to adjust the From Right option in the Paragraph dialog box to .1 inches.

CHAPTER 18

Create Your Own Report

These two report layouts should take you only a few minutes to do. They both focus on using styles to create layouts quickly. Once you've defined the styles, you're almost done. In the first report, the outquote on the layout for the chapter opener is defined as a style using Word's Frame commands. If you're not using these instructions as the basis for your own report layout, you can use the file KIT_RTXT.DOC on the *Tools of the Trade* disk.

The second example, ceated using landscape orientation, is a report layout that looks like a presentation. It's meant to be kept brief and to the point, and relies heavily on the use of bulleted lists and captioned charts on the right side of the page. Again, if you're not using these instructions to set up your own report, you can use the sample file KIT_RTX2.DOC.

SETTING UP THE PORTRAIT REPORT

Set up the document as letter-sized in portrait orientation, with 1-inch margins top and bottom, a 1.5-inch left margin (which leaves room for binding), and 1 inch on the right. Although I formatted the example as a single-sided report layout, you can just as easily make it double sided by turning on the Facing Pages option.

✦ Laying It Out

1. Define the styles spec'd below. If you decide to make use of this report in your work, I would define at least four levels of headings, although you only need to define two to finish this example (which covers only the chapter opener). The third heading style I would add is 13-point Helvetica bold, italic, upper/lowercase; the fourth is 12-point Times bold, italic.

B. BACKGROUND

The College's Master Plan, adopted in 1988, defines the mission of the College as follows: "To provide a practical liberal arts education at the baccalaureate level:

- in a small college environment;
- to a varied group of students, male and female, representing a cross-section of society from the United States and the world;
- with a diverse and highly qualified faculty who excel at teaching and who care deeply about students;
- to a varied group of students, male and female, representing a cross-section of society from the United States and the world;
- in a closely-knit campus community which encourages thoughtful self-reflection, ethical development and personal growth."

As will become evident in the body of this report, the College has succeeded, by any measure, not only in achieving its stated mission, but also, in achieving an understanding of it among those constituencies who are aware of the College. To date, however, that understanding has not resulted in desired enrollment growth, and it remains unclear as to whether or not the understanding is broad enough or the mission flexible enough to attain the necessary enrollment growth to ensure future academic and financial viability.

A 1987 financial analysis done for the College indicates that it should have a full-time enrollment of about 600 to remain financially viable.

While the College has experienced a slow but steady enrollment growth over the past five or six years, that growth has come about in only one sector of the enrollment — non-traditional older students — which the College characterizes as "resumers." The number of full-time traditional freshmen has actually declined over that period. These data will be discussed in greater detail in the Internal Environment section of this report, but are worth noting now.

The marketing study comes at a time truly unique in the history of higher education in the United States. The recruiting of students for the Fall 1990 class was, across the nation, the most difficult for private colleges and universities since the years of World War II.

Within the past two years, the College has put almost an entirely new senior administrative team in place. The vice president for finance was hired in 1989 and the vice president for institutional advancement in 1990. Within the past two years, the

"... To date, however, that understanding has not resulted in desired enrollment growth, and it remains unclear as to whether or not the understanding is broad enough, or the mission flexible enough, to attain the necessary enrollment growth to ensure future academic and financial viability."

3

Chapter opener

Remember that you have to redefine Word's standard heading styles if you want to generate a table of contents automatically.

Normal   11-point Times, single-spaced, justified, with 3 points of space After, and a First Line indent of .2 inches.

heading 1   14-point Times bold, centered caps, with single line spacing, a Page Break Before, and 36 points of space After.

College has put almost an entirely new senior administrative team in place. The vice president for finance was hired in 1989 and the vice president for institutional advancement in 1990. Within the past two years, the College has put almost an entirely new senior administrative team in place. The vice president for finance was hired in 1989 and the vice president for institutional advancement in 1990.

I. EXTERNAL FACTORS

Throughout the spring and summer of 1990, major publications throughout the United States headlined the declining enrollment patterns in higher education nationwide among traditional college-age freshmen for the Fall 1990. (See Appendix II).

The March 6, 1991, issue of *The Chronicle of Higher Education* carried a front page story under the headline "Applications Down at Private Campuses, Up at Public Colleges," which contained reported statistics for Fall 1991. Among the facts reported in that story were:

- public institutions are reporting increases of as much as 15% in applications from high school seniors;
- while some private colleges say applications have increased slightly, many report they are down by 5% to 16%;
- small colleges are hurting the most;
- the recession is forcing parents and students who might otherwise consider enrolling at private colleges to look more closely at lower-cost state institutions.

"Colleges in the Northeast have been particularly hard hit by dramatic declines in the number of high school seniors and by the downturn in the region's economy," *The Chronicle* article continues. It further reports that two of the universities cited as among those hardest hit are in Massachusetts.

II. INTERNAL FACTORS

During the course of this study, *RJE Consulting* interviewed a broad spectrum of the College family — students, faculty, staff, administration — to gain a better understanding of the internal environment, including the view of the College's Plan and its impact on the College's goals and strategies. That material will be presented in detail in a later section, but in order to provide perspective in this background section, it is necessary to touch on some of these issues.

In 1983, the College initiated a plan for a Liberal Arts Education. While it received substantial national media coverage in the mid-1980s, the College has not been able to capitalize on that visibility in terms of increased enrollment or, it appears, in terms of the quality of undergraduate students attracted to the College.

a. Academic Challenges and Opportunities

As stated earlier, while the College's enrollment has risen, the increase has not come among traditional residential undergraduates — the group for whom the plan was initially designed. Instead, it has come in the transfer population, especially among non-traditional transfer students (see graph below). While that trend has caused great concern among some at the College relative to its impact on the goals of the plan, it clearly offers some important opportunities. Within the past two years, the College has put almost an entirely new senior administrative team in place. The vice president for finance was hired in 1989 and the vice president for institutional. Within the past two years, the College has put almost an almost new team.

4

Main text

heading 2 — 13-point Helvetica bold caps, flush left, with single line spacing, 22 points of space Before and 7 points After.

outq — 11-point Times bold italic on At Least 17 points of leading, flush right, with 1.25 inches Before (this starts the text at 2.25 inches from the top of the page); the Text Wrapping feature is set to Around; the width of the frame is Exactly 1.7 inches and the height is Exactly 9 inches (this keeps text from wrapping around the bottom); it's positioned horizontally 5.8 inches Relative To Page, and vertically at the Top Relative To Margin, and .2 inches from the text in both cases; the Move with Text option is off.

2. After defining these styles, format the text "Executive Summary" as heading 1, and "This is an Example..." as heading 2. The main text should automatically format in the Normal style, but if it doesn't, apply the style explicitly.

3. Put your cursor anywhere in the first paragraph, and apply the style *outq* to it. If you're in Page Layout view, you should see it automatically reformat itself in the right margin. Drag the outquote frame toward the bottom of the page to keep the main text from wrapping around it.

4. One last thing—a footer. This one is 9-point Helvetica, centered.

And you're done. There are lots of simple variations you can do with this basic structure. For instance, you can make it double sided and add headers and footers, taking advantage of the Different Odd and Even Pages option.

SETTING UP THE LANDSCAPE REPORT

Set up the document as letter-sized in landscape orientation, with a 2-inch margin on top (where the report will be bound), a 1-inch margin on bottom, and 1.25-inch margins left and right. This layout almost has to be single sided; it would be very awkward to read otherwise. Because this report relies so heavily on bulleted lists—it's difficult to read text this wide in paragraph form—and captioned charts, I created styles for each of these design elements.

EXECUTIVE SUMMARY

Lorem ipsum dolor sit amet, consectetuer adipiscing elit, sed diam nonummy nibh euismod tincidunt ut laoreet dolore mag-na aliquam erat volutpat. Ut wisi enim ad minim veniam, quis nostrud exerci tation ullamcorper suscipit lobortis nisl ut aliquip ex ea commodo feugiat consequat. Dolor sit amet, consectetuer adipiscing elit, sed diam nonummy nibh euismod tincidunt ut laoreet dolore magna aliquam. Ad minim veniam, quis nostrud exerci tation ullamcorper suscipit lobortis nisl.

- psum dolor sit amet, consectetuer adipiscing elit, sed diam nonummy nibh euismod tincidunt ut laoreet dolore magna aliquam erat volut
- isi enim ad minim veniam, quis nostrud exerci tation ullamcorper suscipit lobortis nisl ut aliquip ex
- sectetuer adipiscing elit, sed diam nonummy nibh euismod tincidunt ut laoreet dolore ullamcorper suscipit lobortis nisl ut aliquip ex ea commodo feugiat consequa magna aliquam sectetuer adipiscing elit, sed diam nonummy nibh euismod tincidunt ut laoreet dolore magna aliquam
- psum dolor sit amet, consectetuer adipiscing elit, sed diam nonummy nibh euismod tincidunt ut laoreet dolore magna aliquam erat volut psum dolor sit amet, consectetuer adipiscing elit, sed diam nonummy nibh euismod tincidunt ut laoreet dolore magna aliquam erat volut

External Factors

Dolor sit amet, consectetuer adipiscing elit, sed diam nonummy nibh euismod tincidunt ut laoreet dolore mag-na aliquam erat volutpat. Ut wisi enim ad minim veniam, quis nostrud exerci tation ullamcorper suscipit lobortis nisl ut aliquip ex ea com-modo feugiat consequat. Dolor sit amet, consectetuer adipiscing elit, sed diam nonummy nibh euismod tincidunt ut laoreet dolore magna aliquam. Ad minim veniam, quis nostrud exerci tation ullamcorper suscipit lobortis nisl.

Consectetuer adipiscing elit, sed diam nonummy nibh euismod tincidunt ut laoreet dolore mag-na aliquam erat volutpat. Ut

1

---

wisi enim ad minim veniam, quis nostrud exerci tation ullamcorper suscipit lobortis nisl ut aliquip ex ea commodo feugia ea consequat. Dolor sit amet, consectetuer adipiscing elit, sed diam nonummy nibh euismod tincidunt ut laoreet dolore magna aliquam. Ad minim veniam, quis nostrud exerci tation ullamcorper suscipit lobortis nisl.

t wisi enim ad minim veniam, quis nostrud exerci tation ullamcorper suscipit lobortis nisl ut aliquip ex ea commodo feugiat consequat. Dolor sit amet, consectetuer adipiscing elit, sed diam nonummy nibh euismod tincidunt ut laoreet dolore magna aliquam. Ad minim veniam, quis nostrud exerci tation ullamcorper suscipit lobortis nisl.

- onsectetuer adipiscing elit, sed diam nonummy nibh euismod tincidunt ut laoreet dolo
- scing elit, sed diam nonummy nibh euismod tincidunt ut laoreet dolo onsectetuer adipiscing elit, sed diam nonummy nibh euismod tincidunt ut laoreet dolo
- d diam nonummy nibh euismod tincidunt ut laoreet dolore magna aliquam. Ad minim veniam, quis nostrud exerci tation ullamcorper suscipit lobortis n
- incidunt ut laoreet dolore magna aliquam. Ad minim veniam, quis nostrud ex
- ut wisi enim ad minim veniam, quis nostrud exerci tation ullamcorper suscipit lobortis nisl ut aliquip ex ea commodo feugiat consequat.

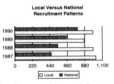

Local Versus National Recruitment Patterns

Lorem ipsum venum minim ad magna aliquam nos-trud nisl ut aliquip exerci ex magna loem ipum.

2

1. Define the styles spec'd below. Remember that you have to redefine Word's standard heading styles if you want to generate a table of contents automatically.

   Normal   12-point Times, on At Least 15 points of leading, flush left, with 5 points of space After, and a First Line indent of .2 inches.

   heading 1   14-point Helvetica bold, centered caps, with single line spacing, a Page Break Before, and 14 points of space After; unlinked from Normal.

   heading 2   14-point Helvetica bold, upper/lowercase, flush left, with single line spacing, 20 points of space Before and 7 points After; based on heading 1.

   bull   Based on Normal + .65 inches From Left, .65 inches From Right, and −.25 inches First Line indent.

   caption   Based on Normal + Helvetica bold, single-spaced, 0-inch First Line indent, and justified.

   graph   Based on Normal + 3 lines (36 points) of space Before and a frame Exactly 3.2 inches wide and 5.65 inches long; horizontally positioned Right Relative To Margin, .2 inches from Text; vertically positioned Top Relative To Margin; and bordered with the thinnest available vertical rule along the left edge; make sure the Move with Text option is off.

2. After defining these styles, format the text "Executive Summary" as heading 1, and "External Factors" as heading 2. The main text should automatically format in the Normal style, but if it doesn't, apply the style explicitly.

3. Select the graph and apply the style *graph* to it. If you're in Page Layout view, you should see it automatically reformat itself in the right margin. You can caption the graph if you want. The only problem I've found with this layout is that, as of this writing, you need to put extra space after the graph

(or extra carriage returns) in order to make the vertical rule reach the bottom margin.

4. One last thing—a header and footer. The footer is 9-point Helvetica bold, centered (like the caption style previously described). The header is simply the thinnest available rule; it is positioned at 1.75 inches from the edge of the paper.

CHAPTER 19

Create Your Own Newsletter

This newsletter stands in stark contrast to the reports in the previous chapter. It's one of the two or three most difficult designs shown in Chapter 2. I strongly recommend that you tackle it only after you feel quite comfortable with all the material presented in this book. In addition, you almost have to use this design as a template—it's definitely not the sort of thing most people want to set up every so often.

Having warned you, I can now go on to say that, in fact, the techniques used to create this newsletter are the same as those used elsewhere. The difficult thing is putting so many techniques into one page and lining them all up correctly.

I focus only on the cover page of the 4-page newsletter shown in the section *Newsletters and Other Periodicals* in Chapter 2, although I do give tips for handling the other pages. Please refer to Chapter 2 to see the entire newsletter. The center spread of that newsletter and the last page, or back cover, are actually quite easy.

SETTING THINGS UP

Before starting, some miscellaneous information: There are two charts that go with this newsletter (KIT_NW1.WMF and KIT_NW2.WMF on the *Tools of the Trade* disk); the text is in KIT_NTXT.DOC. You can get the dingbats used at the end of articles (▲▼) by formatting the letters "st" as 8-point Zapf Dingbats. The complete newsletter is provided as a template in the file KIT_NEWS.DOC (all the templates use only Times and Helvetica fonts so that you can use them even if you don't have a PostScript printer).

Open the file NEWS.DOC. Format it letter-sized, in portrait orientation. The margins are .8 inches top and bottom, and 1 inch left and right. Turn on Facing Pages—this is a double-sided publication—and turn off Widow/Orphan Control in the Options dialog box on the Tools menu, in the Print Category. The center spread is formatted using Word's Column function.

Trumans'
FINANCIAL *news*

Volume 3, Number 7   *June 14, 1991*

Market Analysis

Tu se' lo mio maestro e 'l mio autore; tu se' solo colui da cu' io mi tolsi lo bello stilo che m' ha fatto onore. Vedi la bestia per cu' io mi volsi: aiutami da lei, famoso saggio, ch'ella mi fa tremar le vene e i polsi le vene e i polsi.

A te convien tenere altro viaggio se vuo' campar d'esto loco sel vaggio: che questa bestia, per la qual tu gride, non lascia altrui passar per la sua. Or se tu quel Virgilio e quella fonte che spandi di parlar si largo fiume.

O delli altri poeti onore e lume, vagliami 'l lungo studio e 'l grande amore che m' ha fatto cercar lo tuo volume. O delli altri poeti onore e lume, vagliami 'l lungo studio. O delli altri poeti onore.

Continued on page 4

This Week's Numbers

A te convien tenere altro viaggio se.

Who's Down on the Dollar Now?

O delli altri poeti onore e lume, vagliami 'l lungo studio e 'l grande amore che m' ha fatto cercar lo tuo volume. O delli altri poeti onore e lume.

Or se tu quel Virgilio e quella fonte che spandi di parlar si largo fiume. O delli altri poeti onore e lume, vagliami 'l lungo studio e 'l grande. Or se tu quel Virgilio or se tu quel or se tu quel or se tu qaltri poeti onore e lume, vagliami 'l uel se altri poeti onore e lume, vagliami 'l tu quel se tu quel or se tu quel altri poeti onore e lume, vagliami.

A te convien tenere altro viag-gio se vuo' campar d'esto loco sel vaggio. Non lascia altrui passar per la sua passar per la sua.

Tu se' lo mio maestro e 'l mio autore; tu se' solo colui da cu' io mi tolsi lo bello stilo che m' ha fatto onore. Vedi la bestia per cu' io mi volsi: aiutami da lei, famoso saggio, se tu quel or se tu quel se tu quel se tu quel or se tu quel se tu quel ch'ella mi fa tremar.

A te convien tenere altro viag-gio se vuo' campar d'esto loco sel vaggio: che questa bestia, per la qual tu altr altri poeti onore e lume, vagliami 'l i poeti onore e. ▲▼

INDUSTRY ANALYSIS
Outperforming the Dow 30... Again & Again

Or se tu quel Virgilio e quella fonte che spandi di parlar si largo fiume? O delli altri poeti onore e lume, vagliami 'l lungo studio e 'l grande amore che m' ha fatto cercar lo tuo volume.

Tu se' lo mio maestro e 'l mio autore; tu se' solo colui da cu' io mi tolsi lo bello stilo che m' ha fatto onore. Vedi la bestia per cu' io mi volsi: aiutami da lei, famoso saggio, ch'ella mi fa tremar le vene e i polsi.

A te convien tenere altro viaggio se vuo' campar d'esto loco sel vaggio: che questa bestia, per la qual tu gride, non lascia altrui passar per la sua.

Or se tu quel Virgilio e quella fonte che spandi di parlar si largo fiume? O delli altri poeti onore e lume, vagliami 'l lungo studio e 'l grande amore che m' ha fatto cercar lo tuo volume. O delli altri poeti onore e lume, vagliami 'l lungo studio e 'l grande amore.

A te convien tenere altro viaggio se vuo' campar d'esto loco sel vaggio: che questa bestia, per la qual tu gride, non lascia altrui passar per la sua via, ma tanto lo 'mpedisce che l'uccide; e ha natura si malvagia e ria, che mai non empie la bramosa voglia, e dopo 'l pasto ha piu fame che pria pasto ha pui fame che pria.

E dopo 'l pasto ha piu fame che pria pasto ha pui fame che e dopo 'l pasto ha piu fame che priapria e dopo 'l pasto ha piu fame che pria pasto ha pui fame che pria. ▲▼

Formatting Columns. There are three main layout tools that hold this newsletter together: frames (all are used with the Text Wrapping feature set to Around), tables, and columns. All three of these features enable you to create different kinds of columns. However, only Word's column feature allows you to create snaking, or newspaper, columns, where text flows from column to column.

The following illustration diagrams where each feature—frames, tables, and columns—is used in the newsletter. Remember that even when you think you're not using columns, you are; you're using *one* column. You can add columns created in tables simply by inserting a table; you can add columns created with frames simply by inserting a frame. However, you have to use a

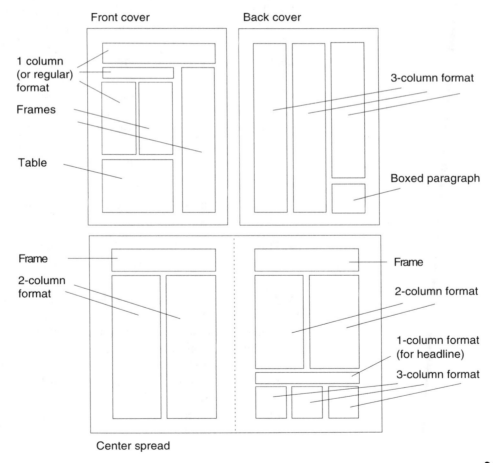

Front cover Back cover

1 column
(or regular)
format

Frames

Table

3-column format

Boxed paragraph

Frame

2-column
format

Frame

2-column format

1-column format
(for headline)

3-column format

Center spread

section break whenever you move from a one-column format to a snaking-column format that uses two or more columns. If you want to change the number of snaking columns you're using on a single page, you have to insert a Continuous section break. As you look at the newsletter diagram, notice that there are no section breaks on the front cover of the newsletter—the columns used there are created with tables and frames. The back cover is in its own section, formatted as three columns.

The second page of the newsletter starts with a Next Page section break. This section—the second section in the newsletter—is formatted as two snaking columns. The headlines at the top of the center spread (on both the left and right pages) are in frames positioned at the Top of the page Relative To Margin. There's a Continuous section break both before and after the headline toward the bottom of the third page of the newsletter.

Although all these section breaks sound complicated, it won't be once you try it a few times. A few reminders about how to deal with sections and columns:

- Use the Break dialog box on the Insert menu to insert a section break (<ALT> + I, B). Word inserts a section break above where your cursor is. If you prefer, you can use the Columns dialog box on the Format menu (<ALT> + T, O) to automatically insert a section break.

- After you insert a section break, use the Columns button on the Toolbar or the Columns dialog box to specify the number of columns you want to use.

- Use either the Columns or the Break dialog box when you want to force text to start a new column.

Styles. The thing about newsletters is that although they should always have styles, you will no doubt adjust them every now and then to suit particular circumstances. For instance, you might lengthen unusually short heads by increasing the point size or expanding certain words to fill the space. You might shorten a head that's too long by reducing the point size, or sometimes by styling it in regular rather than bold text. In some cases, the headline itself might suggest a certain typeface. You might want to set a story about typewriters, for example, in Courier, or a story about Gothic literature in Times caps. Whenever you decide to do something like this, make sure that at least a few elements of the standard style remain, such as alignment, basic point size, type style, and so on. It's important that your dressed-up headline still fit in with the rest of the publication.

The newsletter's front cover includes two frames. One forms the second column, where the two charts go, and the other forms the third column. Both frames use their own heading and text styles; the third-column frame also uses an overline. Remember that in order to apply more than one style to a single frame, you have to define the frames used with the styles in *exactly* the same way. The easiest way to do this is to base one style on another. It's also helpful to define the Next Style as the framed style you actually want to follow the first style.

If you find that your styles are creating frames on top of each other rather than in a single frame, there are three likely culprits: 1) The framed styles might have slightly different definitions. 2) You might need to put a carriage return after the first style in the frame before you select the text for the next style in the frame. 3) You might have selected text to be framed out of order. When I was experimenting with how best to create this document, I had the best results when I styled text in order — in other words, the heading and *then* the text. If nothing works, remember that you can move text into a frame (using either the cut-and-paste or drag-and-drop method) and then format it manually.

These are the styles used for this example:

Normal: 10-point Times, justified and single-spaced, with a First Line indent of .15 inches.

sidebar: Normal + 10-point Helvetica, flush left; boxed with the second-thinnest rule available, and shaded with a 10% screen.

txt: Normal + positioned Right Relative To Margin and .1 inches from Text, 1.9 inches Relative To Page and 0 inches from Text; Exactly 2.1 inches wide and At Least 8 inches high; Text Wrapping set to Around; Next Style = txt.

Note: *This style is used for the* text *in the third-column frame.*

399

continued: Normal + 10-point Times italic, flush right, with .5 lines (6 points) of space After.

heading 1: 36-point Helvetica bold, centered, with .5 lines (6 points) of space After, no First Line indent.

heading 2: Based On txt + 18-point New Century Schoolbook bold, flush left, single-spaced, no First Line indent, Next Style = txt.

> **Note:** *This style is used for the* heading *in the third-column frame.*

heading 3: Normal + 12-point New Century Schoolbook bold, italic, centered, single-spaced; positioned 3.15 inches Horizontal Relative To Page and .1 inch from Text, 2.51 inches Vertical Relative To Page and 0 inches from Text; Exactly 2.1 inches wide; Text Wrapping set to Around.

> **Note:** *This style is used for the* heading *in the second-column frame.*

overline: Normal + 9-point New Century Schoolbook bold, italic, caps, flush left, single-spaced; positioned Right Relative To Margin and .1 inches from Text, 1.9 inches Relative To Page and 0 inches from Text; Exactly 2.1 inches wide and At Least 8 inches high; Text Wrapping set to Around; Next Style = heading 2.

> **Note:** *This style is used for the* overline *in the third-column frame.*

✦ Laying Things Out

1. The first thing to lay out is the masthead. These are the specs:

   "Trumans'" is in 16-point New Century Schoolbook italic; it's positioned at a tab set at .31 inches on the Ruler.

   FINANCIAL is centered in 41-point New Century Schoolbook bold caps on Exactly 39 points of leading.

   "news" is centered in 64-point New Century Schoolbook italic on Exactly 39 points of leading. The reason it's so much bigger than FINANCIAL is that it's set in lowercase letters.

There's an extra carriage return both before "Trumans'" and after "Financial news" that puts some space between the text and the box around it. Both carriage returns are formatted as 10-point New Century Schoolbook on Exactly 3 points of leading.

A box using the thinnest rule available is placed around the two carriage returns and the text sandwiched between.

The date and volume number are in 9-point New Century Schoolbook italic, single-spaced with 1 line (12 points) of space After, and indented .31 inches From Left. (Remember that "Trumans'" is positioned at a tab at .31 inches.) There's a right tab at 6.13 inches to position the date.

2. Once you have the masthead formatted, format the rest of the text. For instance, make the main text Normal, style "Market Analysis" as heading 1, style "Industry Analysis" as the overline, and so on.

When you start styling the text that will be positioned in frames, make sure you style the framed text in the order it's to be placed in the frame. For instance, in the third-column frame you might want to style the overline first, then heading 2, then txt.

Note: *Your position may differ from mine depending on the formatting to use for your text.*

3. After you format "This Week's Numbers" as heading 3, insert the two charts — KIT_NW1.WMF and KIT_NW2.WMF — into that frame using the INSERT, PICTURE command. Scale both of them to about 50% of their original size. Put a single caption covering both charts after the second chart. I set my caption in 8-point Helvetica bold. If you want to, define a style for it.

Note: *If things aren't lining up quite as they should, turn the Show/Hide¶ option on and make sure there are no extra carriage returns anywhere. You might well have to make some adjustments to the numbers provided here, especially if you've spec'd your type somewhat differently, or if you've set different margins.*

4. The last design element for this page is the two-column table at the bottom right. The easiest thing to do is to insert the table, format it so each column is 2.13 inches wide, and cut and paste text into it. Once the text is positioned more or less as

you want it, apply the sidebar style. Unfortunately, the sidebar style borders each column of the table independently, so you have to reborder to make the box go around the outside edge.

As mentioned previously, it can be somewhat awkward to use tables for text that flows from column to column because you have to end the text in one column (put in a carriage return), then start it again in the next. However, for short pieces, this is doable, and the finished design looks nice enough to be worth it. Notice that in the example, the text in the table is formatted flush left, rather than justified. The reason? When you end a justified line with a carriage return, that line loses its justification and aligns itself left—not exactly what you want to happen when you're trying to make text look like it's flowing into another column. If you align the text flush left, this isn't a problem.

✦ Finishing Touches

1. If any of your headings are not looking quite right, size them to fit.

2. Don't forget the dingbats that end each article.

3. You might want to add some space after one of the columns in the table so that the box doesn't crowd the text. (As of this writing, you can't set a border around a table a specified distance from the text, as you can when dealing with regular paragraphs.)

If you want to finish the rest of this newsletter on your own, use the text in the file KIT_NTX2.DOC on the *Tools of the Trade* disk. The rules used in the center spread are in file KIT_NW3.WMF.

CHAPTER 20

Create
Your Own
Slide Show

When done right, charts communicate information more quickly and directly than you could otherwise. But they're no substitute for clear explanations.

"… The idea that you can explain things without explaining them *in words* is pure superstition," writes Rudolf Flesch in his book, *The Art of Readable Writing*. "A favorite proverb of the picture and diagram lovers is 'One picture is worth more than a thousand words.' It simply isn't so. Try to teach people with a picture and you may find that you need a thousand words to tell them exactly what to look at and why…"

Flesch goes on to make the point that even occasional designers of presentations and reports should bear in mind: "If you want to give your reader something to look at," he writes, "well and good; but if you have to tell him something, tell him. In other words, nothing is self-explanatory—it's up to you to explain it. And you have to do it in words." These words can be part of the report, or of an oral presentation made while showing slides or overhead projections. Sometimes people show the chart on a slide or overhead first, followed by a bulleted list of key points made by the chart.

This chapter provides some useful tips for creating slides and other visuals, whether for handouts, overheads, even reports. It also explains how to link your Word documents together so that they always contain the most recent version of the linked information (this is especially valuable for presentations).

LINKING FILES TO CREATE PRESENTATIONS AUTOMATICALLY

In a way, linking files together is just a fancy form of copy and paste. When you link two documents together, all you do is copy a portion of a Word document (called the **source document**) and Paste Link it into the document you're currently working on in Word (called the **destination document**). If you want, you can set the options so that whenever a change is made in the source document, Word automatically makes that change in the destination document as well. If you prefer, you can set the options so that you can manually update the links whenever you want.

Links are actually fields—like the Table of Contents and the embedded graphics created with Draw and Graph—that you can update just as you can any other field. Simply highlight the field (or your entire document if you want to update all its fields at once) and press <F9>. You can also *un*link these fields by pressing <CTRL> + <SHIFT> + <F9>. You can see the actual fields themselves by turning on the Field Codes option (it's on the View menu). If you don't feel particularly comfortable using fields outright, just turn Field Codes off so you don't have to see them, and use the Links dialog box on the Edit menu.

You can also link graphics and charts created in other programs to your Word document. You can do this in one of two ways: 1) You can use the EDIT, PASTE SPECIAL command. 2) You can turn on the Link to File option when using the INSERT, PICTURE command.

Here's an example of how links can be useful. For instance, say your department creates reports documenting the company's monthly sales. The report includes text and tables done in Word and charts done in Graph. You could easily create a monthly presentation based on that full report by linking the appropriate tables and graphs in the presentation (or destination) document to the report (or source) document.

Once you link text or graphics to your Word document, you can format it however you like. When you update your links, your text and graphics will keep their formatting. For instance, if you size and border a linked graphic, the graphic will retain its size and border even after you update it. If you format linked text or a table, it will retain its formatting in the destination document even if it has different formatting in the source document.

1. Copy the portion of your *source* document that you want to link to another document (it can include just about anything—text, tables, charts created in Excel, and so on).

2. Open your *destination* document. Put your cursor where you want the linked information to go, and then select Paste Special from the Edit menu (<ALT> + E, S). Word automatically selects the type of data you're linking (such as Formatted Text). Click on Paste Link (<ALT> + L). The information is now pasted into your destination document and linked with the source document.

3. If you want to specify that the linked information be automatically updated whenever it's changed in the source document, select Links from the Edit menu, select the link you want to automate from the list, and then select Automatic.

Note: *You can treat each link in your document individually: you can update some automatically, some manually, and, if you want, you can lock others so that they can't be updated. When you want to be able to update them again, simply unlock them. You can also use the Links dialog box to cancel links completely—this is the equivalent of highlighting the item and using the Unlink Field key, <CTRL> + <SHIFT> + <F9>. See your Word for Windows manual for information about links.*

PRETTY AS A PICTURE: TIPS FOR CREATING GREAT-LOOKING SLIDES

If you need to do cutting-edge slide presentations, don't use Word. But if you do slide presentations only occasionally, and want high quality without having to learn a new program, go ahead—Word's almost perfect. In fact, Word's linking feature can be a real time-saver if you want to create a presentation based on existing documents.

Naturally, you can use all of Word's design capabilities, Draw, Graph, and WordArt, to create great-looking slides. Here are some ideas to get you started.

- Remember Rule of Thumb #2: Make your headlines "speak" your message, and make sure that every chart, every table, and every list has a meaningful headline.

- One of the most popular slide designs is the bulleted list (see the example in this section). A service bureau employee once told me that most of the slides he processed were of this sort. And why not? They're extremely simple to do, and they are great for reinforcing points. You'll usually want to give your bulleted lists colored backgrounds when creating slides, but *not* when you're creating black-and-white handouts, overheads, or reports.

Bulleted lists are easy to do in Word, and you can dress them up with dingbats, the Symbol font, and oversized numbers. You can also use Word's Border dialog box to put boxes around them, or rules along the top and bottom.

- In fact, you probably should always border your slides and overhead presentations, either with a box or with top and bottom rules. Borders help visually to focus the audience's attention on the message.

- Slides are almost always in color, transparencies for overhead projections are done in black and white as often as not, and most handouts are black and white. If you're creating both color slides and black-and-white handouts that use some of the slide images, don't worry. Color text prints out in black and white unless you're using a color printer.

- You can do simple diagrams using either Word and/or Draw (see the example in this section).

Top 3 Potential Purchasers of Jenret's Plastics Co.

Company Name	Sales/Market Value (000,000)
1. Denton-James, Ltd. (UK)	£4,504.0
	2,110.1
2. Dinfeld Plastics, Inc. (US)	$11,980.3
	5,222.6
3. Kraft & Kelly, Ltd. (UK)	£6,028.7
	3,486.8

This numbered list was created as a table in Word. It's shaded with a 10% screen.

- You can create charts with Graph (see Chapter 10).

- If you have appropriate clip art or a computerized image of your logo, you can add it to your slides, overheads, handouts, and so forth.

- Don't use too many colors in a presentation—it's even worse than using too many typefaces.

- Don't forget to use some of the time-saving devices built into Word—copying and pasting text and tables from existing documents, for instance; linking documents; using glossaries to insert a dingbat or symbol for bulleted lists; or creating presentation templates.

- Remember Dos and Don'ts #11: Be consistent. Use a single style of headline throughout the presentation (you can define a style to include a color). Develop one or two graphic elements—no more—and use them throughout the presentation. Some examples: your company logo, rules created with Draw in one of your standard colors or black, a box created with Word's border command (always use the same line style), a distinctive type of bullet, and so on.

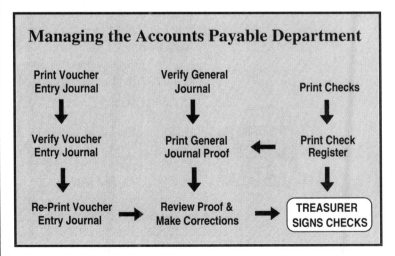

This diagram (arrows and all) was created in Draw; the background was originally yellow. (Remember that you can't shade graphics in Word itself!)

- Remember, Dos and Don'ts #3: Keep it simple. Sometimes the only "visual aid" you need is to outline and shade a single row of numbers in a table. If you try too hard to be visual, you can end up being unsightly.

- When you're using black-and-white graphics, beware of using too many shades of gray. They tend to turn muddy and blur into one another. Thick stripes, thin stripes, diagonal lines, or a grid pattern all add color as surely as red does. And they make for interesting graphics.

HOW TO CREATE SLIDES (OR, NOT POSTSCRIPT AGAIN!)

If your service bureau does not use Word for Windows (and at this writing that's probably the case) you need to create a Post-Script file if you want to produce slides. However, your service bureau might prefer that you create an EPS file for each slide, so they can "print" them using their own presentation graphics program (ask them!). If this is the case, remember to create a separate EPS file for each slide you're producing.

Not all service bureaus do slides, and not all are set up to do them from either PostScript or EPS files. If you have trouble finding a slide shop, there's a national chain of sorts that handles them on a regular basis—AutoGraphix. They produced the test slides you see in this chapter (unfortunately, I can only show a black-and-white print of those slides here). AutoGraphix has an 800 number (1-800-548-8558) and a special kit they'll send with their own PostScript driver. It's all set up for color and includes various amenities that will help you get things right the first time. If they don't have a bureau within driving distance, you can use overnight mail or modem.

To create slides:

1. Whenever you're creating slides, use a letter-sized page in landscape orientation. Use the Page Setup dialog box to set the page width to 11 inches and the height to 8.5 inches. If the printer driver you're using has a paper size option for "note paper" at 8.5 × 11 inches, choose that; otherwise the letter size will do. The note paper option allows you to get very near the 3:2 ratio necessary to produce a quality slide. (Slides

are generally 3 inches long and 2 inches high. Any image you use for a slide should be 1.5 times as long as it is high.)

2. Center the text, graphic, and so on for the slide both horizontally *and* vertically on the page. There are two ways to do this:

- To center text and graphics vertically, you can select Section Layout from the Format menu (<ALT> + T, S) and choose Center for the Vertical Alignment. Just make sure you don't use extra carriage returns because they can throw the image off-balance.

   Note: *The only way you can* see *the vertical alignment on your screen is to use the Print Preview feature.*

   Ordinarily, to center text horizontally you click on the center alignment icon on the Ribbon. But it will look amateurish if the text for all your slides is centered. The easiest way around this is to put your text in a table, and use the Row Height dialog box on the Table menu (<ALT> + A, H) to align the rows on center.

- You can place the text and graphics for your slide in a frame, and then use the Frame dialog box on the Format menu (<ALT> + T, F) to center it both horizontally and vertically on the page.

3. Create a PostScript file by turning on the Print to File option in the Print dialog box. Set up your system to print to a color PostScript printer (if you're creating color slides) such as the QMS ColorScript 100. Make sure you turn on the Use Color option (see Chapter 9 for information on creating PostScript files; see your Windows manual for information on installing printer drivers).

4. Be sure to put in page breaks. Each slide needs to be centered on its own page.

   Note: *If you're creating EPS files for your slides, be sure to print your document page by page (using the From... To... option in the Print dialog box). This puts each slide in its own EPS file.*

5. Create your PostScript file.

If you're creating overheads or handouts, you can simply print them out on your laser printer. (Most stationery stores sell transparencies for laser printers.) If you want color transparencies, any service bureau with a color printer should be able to do them for you.

YOUR SLIDE SHOW

This section walks you through the process of creating the two slides shown in this section. I created all four layouts shown in this chapter in a single document; there's no reason you can't create your whole slide show in a single document, depending on the number of graphics you import from other programs (if your document gets too big, Word slows down to a crawl).

You can use the first set of instructions to create virtually any bulleted list on a slide, overhead, or handout; you can use the second set of instructions to create a combination chart in Graph.

1. Use the Page Setup dialog box on the Format menu (<ALT> + F, U) to set up a letter-sized page in landscape orientation; use 1-inch margins all around.

2. To create the first slide, set a left tab stop at 1.25 inches on the Ruler. (I used a tab rather than a table so I could create a shadow box.)

3. Type and format the text. The main text is set in 18-point Helvetica, double-spaced, with .5 lines (6 points) of space After. The checkmarked boxes (which you can find in the file KIT_CHCK.WMF on the *Tools of the Trade* disk) are subscripted 12 points. The title is set in 26-point Times bold.

4. Place a 4.5-inch frame around the text, and center the frame both vertically and horizontally.

5. Box the text, but not too close to the edges. In my example, the shadow box is 18 points from the text.

Rules of Thumb

☑ Reuse your good ideas.

☑ Don't go overboard.

☑ Keep it simple.

☑ Be consistent.

Although this example is shown in black and white with a shadow box around it, you can easily use color text, a color background, even a color border. If you want to use a color checkmark, you can change the one provided in KIT_CHCK.WMF in Draw.

✦ **Next Slide...**

I created this combination chart in Graph. A combination chart is essentially two different chart types plotted together; in this case, each of the types—a column chart and a line chart—is plotted on its own axis. As it's fairly complex, I recommend that you read *Graph Basics* in Chapter 10 before trying it. Although it's in black and white here, you easily could and should use color for slides.

1. In Word, open Graph.

   Note: *You can create the frame before you create the graph.*

2. Type the numbers and labels in the datasheet. Format the numbers so that they use both decimals and dollar signs. The data used for this chart is shown following. The first row of

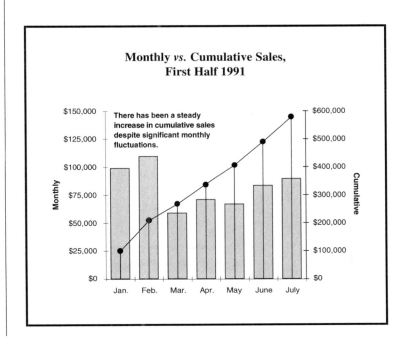

411

numbers is monthly data, which is plotted as a column chart; the second row is cumulative data, which is plotted as a line chart overlay.

3. Because the second row of numbers will be used as the overlay, highlight it and exclude it from the chart for now. To do this, choose Exclude Row/Col from the DataSeries menu (<ALT> + D, E).

4. Select the sample chart, and choose Combination from the Gallery menu. Then choose the second chart type pictured. Delete the legend, resize the chart, format the text in 10-point Helvetica, and select a pattern or color for the columns.

5. Go back to the datasheet and highlight the row containing the data excluded from the column chart, and move it to the overlay. To do this, choose Move to Overlay from the DataSeries menu (<ALT> + D, O). Format the overlay with the pattern you want, including the line width, the color, the marker, and so on.

6. In this example, I changed the scale of the left (Y) axis so that it's somewhat larger; this makes the columns themselves somewhat smaller. To do this, select the axis you want to scale, and then choose Scale from the Format menu (<ALT> + T, S). Enter a maximum value for the axis (in this case, 150,000) and a major unit (in other words, increment; in this case 25,000).

7. To add drop lines—the lines that drop from the markers on the overlay to the bottom of the chart—select the overlay. Choose Overlay from the Format menu (<ALT> + T, O), and select Drop Lines.

8. To place a note on the chart, just start typing. Then format the note (I set the one in the example at 8-point Helvetica bold), and drag it where you want it.

20_CHT.DOC - Datasheet							
	Jan.	Feb.	Mar.	Apr.	May	June	July
	$99,000	$109,500	$59,000	$71,000	$67,000	$83,500	$89,500
	$99,000	$208,500	$267,500	$338,500	$405,500	$489,000	$578,500

9. To label the left axis, choose Titles from the Chart menu (<ALT> + C, T), and then choose the Value (Y) Axis from the list. Type the label; choose Text from the Format menu (<ALT> + T, T); and then choose the orientation for the text. Before leaving the Chart Text dialog box, you might want to click on the Font button to format the text in the font, style, and size you want. Follow this same procedure to create a label for the right axis, which Graph refers to as the Overlay Value (Y) Axis.

   Note: *You can also use this technique to add a title for the chart as a whole.*

10. If you want to give your chart a color background, select the entire chart, including the text. To do this, click toward the edge of the chart window; you know the chart is selected when handles appear around its edge. Choose Patterns from the Format menu, and then select the color you want to use. (Remember that you can't shade a graphic in Word.)

11. Update the chart, return to Word, and finish formatting it.

CHAPTER 21

P.S.
PostScript

As explained in *What Is PostScript?* in Chapter 9, PostScript is a language that tells printers, slide recorders and other output devices what the printed page should look like. After you create a PostScript file (also described in Chapter 9) you can edit that file easily and create sophisticated special effects such as outlining letters and numbers and **screening** them (in other words, coloring them) various shades of gray.

Besides giving you precise control over the size, shape, and position of letters, numbers, and pictures, PostScript has three other advantages that have helped make it a computer graphics standard:

1. PostScript is "device independent." This means it works the same way on any PostScript "device" you might be using: a computer, a standard PostScript laser printer, a color printer, a $30,000 Linotronic imagesetter, or a slide maker (called in the trade a "recorder"). The same PostScript file you create on your computer can be turned easily into many different forms of print and presentation.

2. PostScript is in ordinary text-only files. Other languages— such as Basic, C, Pascal, and LISP (my favorite name for a language)—require an intermediary step before computers

and printers can understand them: You have to **compile** (in essence, translate) them. With PostScript, you don't because every PostScript device has its own built-in "PostScript interpreter." Just send (or **download**) a PostScript file to the printer, slide recorder, or whatever, and the device itself does the rest. You only have to turn your document into a PostScript or Encapsulated PostScript file, as explained in Chapter 9.

3. Because PostScript is a text-only file, you can change words, pictures, and page layouts just by typing a few words and numbers. For instance, you can change black letters into outlined gray letters (or outlined white letters) with a few simple commands. That's what this chapter shows you how to do.

COLOR IT GRAY WITH POSTSCRIPT

PostScript files do more than enable you to get camera-ready copy and slides from service bureaus. They also let you create some professional-quality special effects you couldn't otherwise get in Word for Windows.

Although you can use WordArt to create special effects with text, there's an important difference between WordArt's special effects and the ones discussed in this chapter: the fonts. WordArt's fonts are meant to be fun; they're not professional-quality typefaces in either their design or how well they print. Although Draw does not allow you to create many special effects with text, it has one advantage over WordArt. You can use the same PostScript or other high-quality fonts you usually work with. Although Draw does let you print text in shades of gray, it doesn't let you outline the screened text to finish off its edges; it won't let you color it white; and it won't let you kern text. As of this writing, there are only two ways to do these things. You can use a high-level graphics program (such as CorelDraw!), or you can make a few changes to your PostScript files.

✦ Creating Special Effects with Your PostScript Files

This section explains how to turn the cover design labeled A (taken from an example in Chapter 8) into the one labeled B. The file KIT_PS.PS on the *Tools of the Trade* disk contains the PostScript file for cover A. You can use this file for practice, or you can follow these instructions to add special effects to a publication or presentation you're actually working on.

Don't be intimidated by PostScript's technical look. You don't have to know how to program in PostScript to manipulate the text into doing exactly what you want. You *are* programming when you do this, but you don't need to be a programmer any more than you need to be a designer to come up with a good-looking page. You just need to know a few basics and take the few extra minutes to do it.

Here's the order of business: First, locate the text you want to work with. Second, outline it. Third, color it gray.

To locate the text you want to work with:

1. Turn your Word document into a PostScript or EPS file. If you are using the sample file KIT_PS.PS, this step is already done.

SERVICE
What Membership Means
CREDITS

The Greater New York Consortium

A

SERVICE
What Membership Means
CREDITS

The Greater New York Consortium

B

PostScript Screens

Remember that you don't need a PostScript printer to use PostScript. You only need to install the PostScript printer driver that comes with Windows and create a PostScript or Encapsulated PostScript file. Then you can send that file to your service bureau and get high-quality camera-ready copy or slides. You can also edit that file and create special effects such as screened (or gray-shaded) text.

Screened text is one way to get color into your documents. However, such screens can be tricky to use. For one thing, you have to use high-resolution camera-ready copy (1270 dots per inch with a line screen of 90 lpi) to make the "screens" come out looking professional. You also have to be sure your print shop can handle them; it's not uncommon for screens to get blotched with uneven ink coverage. To be sure you get the quality you need, ask your printer for samples.

Note: *The printing process handles screens rather like photos and scans; see* Photo Opportunities *in Chapter 4 for more information.*

Using PostScript's SETGRAY command, you can specify nine different screens, as shown in the following display. As the numbers get higher, the screen gets *lighter* (0 is black and 1 is white). Although you don't have to outline screened text, I always do because it looks more professional. (By the way, the following numbers started out as 30-point Bookman bold.)

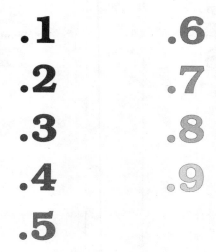

PostScript's Setgray command lets you specify nine different screens. The .1 SETGRAY command creates a screen *almost* indistinguishable from black; .9 SETGRAY gives the lightest screen.

2. After you create the PostScript or EPS file, open it in Word. Since it's a text-only file, Word prompts you to convert it from Text. (Remember to save it as a text-only file when you're finished!)

3. If you're using a PostScript file and working with a Mac-oriented service bureau, delete the problem characters at the very start and end. (You don't have to do this if you're working with an EPS file, or if your service bureau downloads PostScript files directly from a PC.)

4. As you scroll through this file, notice a few things. First, it's huge. Second, all your text is in parentheses. Third, sometimes you see one letter of a word in parentheses, then a slew of numbers (these are PostScript instructions), then another letter of the word and another slew of PostScript instructions, and so on. PostScript can sometimes require a whole page to tell a printer or slide recorder what to do with a single word. This is a nuisance to wade through, but it gives you complete control over each letter.

5. You may recall that in Chapter 8 you kerned several letters in "Service Credits" to close up a few gaps and to prevent other letters from bumping into each other. Well, PostScript handles these kerned letters individually, placing them one by one on the page. Because of this, you're going to find these letters listed in groups of one or two, instead of together as whole words.

   To find these letters, select Find from the Edit menu (<ALT> + E, F) and search for "(SE)"—the first two letters of "Service Credits." (Incidentally, if you turn back to Chapter 8 you'll notice that these letters weren't kerned, so you know they're together.) Word locates this area of the PostScript file. The text is shown following.

   Note: *If you're using these instructions to outline and screen text in a document on which you're currently working, use the Find command to locate the text you want to screen. Remember that in PostScript files, all text is in parentheses.*

```
32 0 0 250 250 0 0 184 /NewCenturySchlbk-Bold /font48 ANSIFont font
1815 183 357 (SE) SB
2172 183 198 (R) SB
2370 183 203 (V) SB
2573 183 496 (ICE) SB
32 0 0 100 100 0 0 74 /NewCenturySchlbk-Bold /font48 ANSIFont font
1786 431 1312 (What Membership Means) SB
32 0 0 250 250 0 0 184 /NewCenturySchlbk-Bold /font48 ANSIFont font
1803 561 195 (C) SB
1998 561 217 (R) SB
2215 561 398 (ED) SB
2613 561 119 (I) SB
2732 561 348 (TS) SB
32 0 0 71 71 0 0 52 /NewCenturySchlbk-Bold /font48 ANSIFont font
1799 2229 1286 (The Greater New York Consortium) SB
```

This is what you see in the part of the KIT_PS.PS PostScript file dealing with the title "Service Credits."

Now that you've located the text you want to work with, you can outline it.

To outline text:

1. Notice that there are three numbers in front of "(SE)" (or whatever other text you're using). These numbers place the letters in a precise spot on the page. You need to change these instructions slightly, and add some new ones, to outline and screen the text. *Whenever you decide to create a special effect in a PostScript file created in Windows, you* must *delete the third number in the series and replace it with a command.* So, delete the third number (in this example, it's "357"), and type "moveto" after the second number in the row (in this example, it's "183"). This tells the printer or slide recorder where the outlining starts.

2. Push "(SE)" onto the next line by putting a carriage return in front of it. Replace the letters "SB" with the two words TRUE CHARPATH, which tell the printer or slide recorder to outline these letters by tracing the path around the characters. Again, you need to make this substitution regardless of the particular text you're working on.

1815 183 357 (SE) SB	1815 183 moveto (SE) true charpath 1 setlinewidth stroke

The code on the left is what you'll find when you locate "(SE)" through the Find command. The code on the right outlines the letters "SE."

3. Press <ENTER> again and type "1 SETLINEWIDTH." This outlines the letters in a very thin line. You could also use 2 SETLINEWIDTH if you wanted a thicker line, or 10 SETLINEWIDTH if you wanted a very thick one.

4. Press <ENTER> again and type "STROKE." This tells the program to go ahead and draw a thin outline around the letters "SE."

   Note: *PostScript ignores extra carriage returns, so you can use them to make the text easier to follow. In the example* Before and After: Outlining "SERVICE," *notice that I used an extra return to separate each group of letters.*

5. Repeat this process for each group of letters in "SERVICE" as shown in *Before and After: Outling Service* on the next page. Notice that the last two lines in each letter group are the same—1 SETLINEWIDTH and STROKE. You can copy and paste them to make the job a little easier. Notice, too, that the second number in each group of letters in this example is "183," which defines the height at which the letters are positioned on the page. Naturally they're all positioned at the same height. The first number describes the position of the letters horizontally, next to one another.

To save time, you might want to define all the PostScript commands necessary to outline and screen text as glossary entries. You need these commands:
MOVETO, TRUE CHARPATH, 1 SETLINEWIDTH, STROKE, .8 SETGRAY, and SHOW.

When you finish outlining "SERVICE," the next step is to screen it. This does not involve changes to existing PostScript commands; rather, you're adding completely new instructions. Add these right after the instructions that outline "SERVICE." Since you are coloring the letters you just outlined, you need to use the exact same MOVETO commands. Complete instructions for making "SERVICE" print light gray appear in the example *How To Color "SERVICE" Gray.*

Note: *If you're using these instructions to outline and screen text in your document, be sure that the numbers you use in the* MOVETO *instructions in the color-me-gray section are exactly the same as those in the outlining section.*

Before and After: Outlining "SERVICE"

```
1815 183 357 (SE) SB        1815 183 moveto
2172 183 198 (R) SB         (SE) true charpath
2370 183 203 (V) SB         1 setlinewidth
2573 183 496 (ICE) SB       stroke

                            2172 183 moveto
                            (R) true charpath
                            1 setlinewidth
                            stroke

                            2370 183 moveto
                            (V) true charpath
                            1 setlinewidth
                            stroke

                            2573 183 moveto
                            (ICE) true charpath
                            1 setlinewidth
                            stroke
```

The column on the left shows the original PostScript code which generates the word "SERVICE." The one on the right shows how the code needs to be edited in order to outline each of the letters in "SERVICE."

How To Color "SERVICE" Gray

```
1815 183 moveto
.8 setgray
(SE) show

2172 183 moveto
(R) show

2370 183 moveto
(V) show

2573 183 moveto
(ICE) show

32 0 0 100 100 0 0 74 /NewCenturySchlbk-
    Bold /font48 ANSIFont font
1786 431 moveto
0 setgray
(What Membership Means) show
```

This box shows the complete instructions for screening "SERVICE."

There are two color-me-gray commands. The first is the SETGRAY command, which controls the darkness of the gray, running from "1" (white) to "0" (black). I generally use ".8," which is a very light gray. You only need to use the SETGRAY command once; then everything from that point on is gray. Since you want "What Membership Means" to be black, you have to SETGRAY back to black.

The second command is called SHOW, which (like STROKE) tells the program to go ahead and do what you told it to—in this case, color the letters gray. Type the instructions shown in the box above to screen the text.

Here's what this "Q" looks like in PostScript.

```
32 0 0 250 250 0 0 185
/AvantGarde-Demi /font36
ANSIFont font
375 317 moveto
(Q) true charpath
10 setlinewidth
stroke

375 317 moveto
1 setgray
(Q) show
```

To screen text:

1. Use the MOVETO command to go back to each of the letters you outlined. Make sure you use the same numbers for the MOVETO commands in both the outlining section (which uses the TRUE CHARPATH command) and in the color-me-gray section (which uses the SETGRAY command).

2. Use the .8 SETGRAY command to screen the outlined text. If you want a darker screen, you might use the .6 SETGRAY command; to make the text white, use the 1 SETGRAY command, and so forth. You only need to give the SETGRAY command once for a given block of text. All the text will be screened until you change it back to black using the 0 SETGRAY command.

3. Use the SHOW command to apply a shade of gray to a particular group of letters.

After you finish coloring "SERVICE" gray, reset the program so that "What Membership Means" prints black. The following two columns show the original code on the left and what you should change it to on the right. Again, you need to add MOVETO, 0 SETGRAY, and SHOW commands.

At this point, you're more than half done. All that remains is to outline and screen the word "CREDITS" using the same commands you used earlier, adjusted to take account of the different letters, and their different positions on the page. The code changes in *Before and After: Outlining "CREDITS"* on the next page show how to do just that.

```
32 0 0 100 100 0 0 74 /NewCenturySchlbk-Bold
   /font48 ANSIFont font
1786 431 1312 (What Membership Means) SB
```

```
32 0 0 100 100 0 0 74 /NewCenturySchlbk-Bold
   /font48 ANSIFont font
1786 431 moveto
0 setgray
(What Membership Means) show
```

After you finish coloring the word "SERVICE" gray, reset the program—so that "What Membership Means" prints black—by changing the code on the left to look like that on the right.

Before and After: Outlining "CREDITS"

```
1803 561 195 (C) SB
1998 561 217 (R) SB
2215 561 398 (ED) SB
2613 561 119 (I) SB
2732 561 348 (TS) SB
```

```
1803 561 moveto
(C) true charpath
1 setlinewidth
stroke

1998 561 moveto
(R) true charpath
1 setlinewidth
stroke

2215 561 moveto
(ED) true charpath
1 setlinewidth
stroke

2613 561 moveto
(I) true charpath
1 setlinewidth
stroke

2732 561 moveto
(TS) true charpath
1 setlinewidth
stroke
```

How To Color "CREDITS" Gray

```
1803 561 moveto
.8 setgray
(C) show

1998 561 moveto
(R) show

2215 561 moveto
(ED) show

2613 561 moveto
(I) show

2732 561 moveto
(TS) show

32 0 0 71 71 0 0 52 /NewCenturySchlbk-
   Bold /font48 ANSIFont font
1799 2229 moveto
0 setgray
(The Greater New York Consortium) show
```

Once you finish outlining "CREDITS," screen it with the instructions listed in *How To Color "CREDITS" Gray.* Remember to reset the color to black when you're finished.

The only thing left is to save the file as a text-only file.

To do this:

1. Select Save As from the File menu (<ALT> + F, A).

2. Select Text Only from the pull-down menu of file types (<ALT> + T). Whenever you use certain features of Word such as copy, paste, Find, and so on, you may find that documents revert to Word's Normal format. If this happens, you have to reselect the text-only format *and* give the file a new name. (Word won't save a file with the same name but a different format.)

3. If you want to, give your file a new name and type a .PS or .EPS extension to make it easier to locate. (You should only give it an .EPS extension if it *is* an .EPS file.)

✦ Downloading Your PostScript Files

I have already mentioned that Adobe Type Manager (ATM) provides real WYSIWYG and helps improve the print quality of non-PostScript printers. However, it has another advantage: It lets you test PostScript and EPS files by downloading them to your PostScript printer *before* you send them to the service bureau. Because a PostScript file is just text, if you printed it using a word processing program, you'd end up printing the actual PostScript commands—which makes for pretty dull reading. So don't print a raw PostScript file. Instead, download (or send) it to a PostScript printer, which interprets and then prints it.

To download files using Adobe Type Manager:

1. In DOS, locate the file PCSEND.EXE. It's probably in the PSFONTS directory. If it isn't, look in the Font Foundary disks that came with ATM.

2. Type "pcsend" followed by the full file name; for instance, "PCSEND FILENAME.PS." You'll get a message saying that the system is sending your PostScript or EPS file to the printer, and shortly, it prints.

> **Note:** *You probably can't use this method to print .EPS files created with a graphics program.*

3. If it doesn't print, you have a bad command somewhere in your PostScript or EPS file. Check for these problems:

- Misspelled commands like SHOW, MOVETO, SETLINEWIDTH, STROKE, and SETGRAY.

- Forgotten commands.

- If you're using a Mac-oriented service bureau and they're having trouble downloading the file, make sure you've deleted the "problem" characters at the very start and end of your PostScript file (see *What If My Service Bureau Has Trouble Printing My PostScript File?* in Chapter 9).

Visual Glossary

Boxes (or Borders)   Word has many boxes (referred to generically as "borders") from which you can choose, included shaded boxes and shadow boxes. You create boxes using the FORMAT, BORDER command; you can box paragraphs of text, pictures, and tables. (See also **Rules**.)

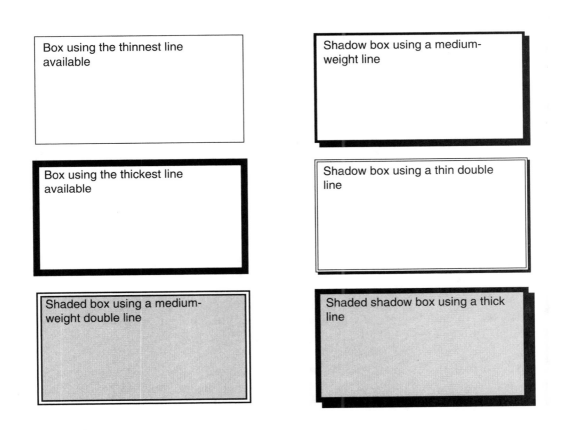

Box using the thinnest line available

Shadow box using a medium-weight line

Box using the thickest line available

Shadow box using a thin double line

Shaded box using a medium-weight double line

Shaded shadow box using a thick line

Cells   Cells are the spaces in a table in which you put text or graphics. Technically they are the intersection of rows and columns.

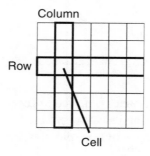

Dingbats   Dingbats are decorative symbols. You can use dingbat *fonts* (such as Zapf Dingbats, which comes standard on most PostScript and compatible printers), and you can also create your own dingbats with Draw.

Drop Caps   Drop caps are often used to start an article in a newsletter, the text of a brochure, and so on. They "drop down" into a paragraph which "wraps around" them. You use *frames* to create drop caps in Word.

Lorem ipsum dolor sit amet, consectetuer adipiscing elit, sed diam nonummy nibh euismod tincidunt ut laoreet dolore magna aliquam erat volutpat. Ut wisi enim ad minim veniam, quis nostrud exerci tation ullamcorper.

Em Dash   An em dash (—) is the typeset equivalent of the double hyphen (--); it's called "em" because it's about the width of an "m." (See also **Typesetters' Punctuation Marks**.)

En Dash   An en dash (–) is the typeset equivalent of a single hyphen (-). You generally use it without space around it in place of the word "through," as in this example: "1990–91." It's called "en" because it's about the width of an "n." (See also **Typesetters' Punctuation Marks**.)

Fields   Fields are special codes that tell Word where to find certain information and what to do with it when it's found. Word uses fields for all sorts of things, including indexes and tables of contents; automatic page numbering; embedded graphics created with Draw, Graph, or WordArt;

and linked documents; and even symbols and dingbats inserted using the Symbol palette. You can usually see the field codes themselves by using the VIEW, FIELD CODES command; however, in the case of a few fields, such as the index field, you have to turn the Show/Hide ¶ option on. When VIEW, FIELD CODES is off, you see what Word calls the field "results"—in other words, the actual text or graphic located or generated by the field.

{INCLUDE C:\\WWCHAPS\\SALES.DOC INTERN_LINK1}

	This Month	Year-to-Date
Briefcases	$104,578	$313,761
Handbags (day wear)	156,897	549,139
Handbags (eve wear)	45,324	131,439
Leather Knapsacks	89,955	275,955
Luggage	67,054	210,270

The top item (in braces) illustrates what a field looks like when you have the VIEW, FIELD CODES option on. When the VIEW, FIELD CODES option is off, you see the results of the field—the actual text or graphic the field locates or generates. In this case, the table (which is linked to another Word document) is the result of the field shown above it.

You update fields—in other words, get the most recent version of the item which they locate or generate—by highlighting them and pressing <F9>. You unlink fields—in other words, get rid of the field and replace it with its result—by highlighting them and pressing <CTRL> + <SHIFT> + <F9>. You delete fields and their results entirely by highlighting them and pressing <DELETE>; you can't just <BACKSPACE> over them.

First Line Indents   First line indents are frequently used to start new paragraphs. You can create this indent by dragging the top half of the Left Indent marker on the Ruler, or by using the FORMAT, PARAGRAPH command to set a measurement in the First Line option. Although you can use a tab to create such an indent, Word has an easier way. It lets you define a style that sets up a first line indent *automatically* for each new paragraph.

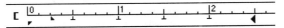

Lorem ipsum dolor sit amet, consectetuer adipiscing elit, sed diam nonummy nibh euismod tincidunt ut laoreet dolore magna aliquam erat volutpat.

Dolor sit amet, consectetuer adipiscing elit, sed diam nonummy nibh euismod tincidunt ut laoreet dolore magna aliquam. Ad minim veniam, quis nostrud exerci tation ullamcorper suscipit lobortis nisl.

This illustration shows what a first line indent looks like on the Ruler.

Hanging Indents   Hanging indents are frequently used for bulleted or numbered lists. Basically, they indent the whole paragraph except for the first line, which begins with the number or bullet. You can create this indent in several ways, from dragging the bottom half of the Left Indent marker on the Ruler, to pressing <CTRL> + T.

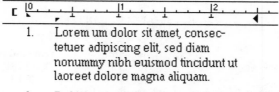

1.   Lorem um dolor sit amet, consectetuer adipiscing elit, sed diam nonummy nibh euismod tincidunt ut laoreet dolore magna aliquam.

2.   Dol it amet, consectetuer adipiscing elit, sed diam nonummy nibh euismod tincidunt ut laoreet dolore magna.

This illustration shows what a hanging indent looks like on the Ruler.

Indents (Right and Left)   While margins affect an entire page of your document, indents affect only the particular paragraphs you choose to indent. For instance, you might choose to indent a long quote or an excerpt from a report. You can do this in one of two ways: by dragging the Right and/or Left Indent markers on the Ruler, or by specifying a measurement in the From Left and/or From Right options using the FORMAT, PARAGRAPH command.

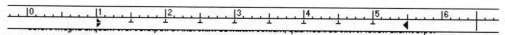

suscipit lobortis nisl ut aliquip ex ea commodo feugiat consequat. Dolor sit amet, consectetuer adipiscing elit, sed diam nonummy nibh euismod tincidunt ut laoreet dolore magna aliquam. Ad minim veniam, quis nostrud exerci tation ullamcorper suscipit lobortis nisl.

Ipsum dolor sit amet, consectetuer adipiscing elit, sed diam nonummy nibh euismod tincidunt ut laoreet dolore magna aliquam erat volutpat ut wisi. Enim ad minim veniam. Ullamcorper suscipit lobortis nisl ut aliquip ex ea commodo feugiat. Sit amet consectetuer adipiscing elit, sed diam nonummy nibh. Minim veniam, quis nostrud exerci tation ullamcorper suscipit lobortis.

The indented text is measured on the Ruler by the Left and Right Indent markers ▶ ◀. The other text is set at the margins for the page.

Kerning (or Character Spacing)   Word allows you to *kern* letters, which means simply to adjust the space between them. Generally you kern text in order to make it longer or shorter to fit the available space. You can also use kerning to improve the appearance of text set at large point sizes, since large letters tend to run into each other. Word has three basic types of kerning or character spacing:

NORMAL,
CONDENSED, and
E X P A N D E D.

Leading (or Line Spacing)   Leading, also known as line spacing, is the amount of space between lines of text. Leading is described as open (for instance, double line spacing), solid (or single line spacing), and negative or tight.

Negative leading   Solid leading   Open leading

Margins   Word enables you to set different margins—top, bottom, right, and left—for each page of your document. You can do this using the FORMAT, PAGE SETUP command. You can also change the margins for each full-page *section* of your document by dragging the appropriate icons on the Ruler and in the FILE, PRINT PREVIEW screen. (See also **Indents**.)

|2 . . . . |3 . . . . |4 . . . . |5 . . . . |6 . . . . |7 . . . .
[   ]

Ipsum dolor sit amet, consectetuer adipiscing elit, sed diam nonummy nibh euismod tincidunt ut laoreet dolore magna aliquam erat volutpat ut wisi. Enim ad minim veniam. Ullamcorper suscipit lobortis nisl ut aliquip ex ea commodo feugiat. Sit amet consectetuer adipiscing elit, sed diam nonummy nibh. Minim veniam, quis nostrud exerci tation ullamcorper suscipit lobortis.

The square-bracket icons on the Ruler indicate the margins. The left margin is set 2.25 inches from the left edge of an 8.5 × 11 inch (letter-sized) sheet of paper. The right margin is 1.25 inches from the right edge—in other words, 7.25 inches from the left edge.

Nonprinting ("Invisible") Characters

When Word's Show/Hide ¶ option is on, you can see the nonprinting or "invisible" characters that represent carriage returns, tabs, spaces between words, and so on. Even when you can see the invisible characters on your screen, they don't print. They simply make it easier to lay out your document by showing you the underlying formatting.

Carriage return	¶
New line break	↵
Spaces	....
Non-breaking spaces	••••••••••••
Tab	→
End-of-cell marker	¤
Page break	....
Section break	════════════════════════

Orientation

Pages can be oriented in one of two ways: in Portrait mode (vertical) or in Landscape mode (horizontal). In Word, you can specify the orientation for each full-page *section* of your document using the FORMAT, PAGE SETUP command.

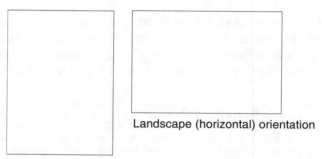

Landscape (horizontal) orientation

Portrait (vertical) orientation

Paragraph Spacing

You can put space both Before and After paragraphs using the FORMAT, PARAGRAPH command.

Paragraph spacing

Rules   Rules are simply horizontal or vertical lines used to emphasize certain elements on a page—headings, for example—or to define sections of a page, such as sidebars. You select and place rules (which Word refers to generically as "borders") using the FORMAT, BORDER command. You can place rules above, below, and between paragraphs. You can also place vertical rules to the right and left of paragraphs. (See also **Boxes**.)

Screens   A screen is a shade of gray made by a dot pattern printed on a black-and-white printer. The quality of shading varies depending on the resolution of your printer. If you want to create truly professional-looking screens, you have to use a high-resolution printer such as a Linotronic. However, depending on the sort of publication or presentation you're working on, the 300-dpi resolution of the everyday laser printer might be fine.

Screens are frequently used as a background to text that is set apart from the main text of a publication—a sidebar in a newsletter, for example. You can create screens in Word by using the Shading function (which you can access through the INSERT, BORDER command). When you use a screen as a background, you should make it fairly light so that it's easier to read the text printed on top of it. You can also create screens by selecting colors—for borders, for instance, or for graphics created with Draw—and then printing them on a black-and-white laser printer. Depending on the type of printer you have, it will translate the color into a shade of gray.

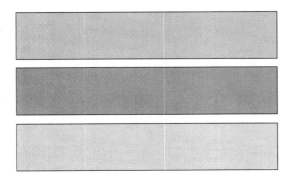

All three screens were printed off a Linotronic imagesetter at a resolution of 1270 dpi with a line screen of 133 lines per inch. The top screen was created by selecting 10% from the Pattern menu in the Shading dialog box while using black (or Auto) as the foreground color and white (or Auto) as the background color. The middle screen was created using cyan as both the foreground and background color, and setting the Pattern to solid. The bottom screen was created in the same way, except using yellow.

Smart Quotes   See **Typesetters' Punctuation Marks**.

Stick-Up Caps   Like drop caps, stick-up caps are often used to start an article in a newsletter, the text of a brochure, and so on. They "stick up" and out of the paragraph in which they occur. You use *frames* to create stick-up caps in Word.

L orem ipsum dolor sit amet, consectetuer adipiscing elit, sed diam nonummy nibh euismod tincidunt ut laoreet dolore magna aliquam erat volutpat. Ut wisi enim ad minim veniam, quis nostrud exerci tation ullamcorper.

Typesetters' Punctuation Marks   Typesetters' punctuation marks have that professional look that immediately distinguishes them from their typewriter-like counterparts. You can use these punctuation marks in Word in two ways: by turning <NUM LOCK> off, holding down the <ALT> key, and typing the codes (from the following list) on the numeric keypad; or by using the Symbol palette. Notice that each typeface draws these punctuation marks somewhat differently. You will sometimes hear the curved open and close single and double quotes called Smart Quotes.

Typesetter versus Typewriter

	Typewriter	Typesetter (Times)	Typesetter (Palatino)	Code <ALT> + code
Open and close single quote	' '	' '	' '	0145 0146
Apostrophe	'	'	'	0146
Open and close double qoute	" "	" "	" "	0147 0148
Bullet	-	•	•	0149
En dash	-	–	–	0150
Em dash	--	—	—	0151
Ellipsis	...	... (Symbol font only)		0188

Note: *As of this writing, Word's Symbol palette doesn't display all typesetters' punctuation marks unless you're using a font manager.*

References

David Ogilvy
Ogilvy on Advertising
Vintage Books, Random House
New York
1985

Alan Swann
Graphic Design School
Van Nostrand Reinhold
New York
1991

Eric Gill
An Essay on Typography
Lund Humphries Publishers
London
1988

Kit Hinrichs
TypeWise
North Light Books
Cincinnati
1990

Allen Hutt and Bob James
*Newspaper Design Today, A Manual for
    Professionals*
Lund Humphries Publishers
London
1989

Rudolf Flesch
The Art of Readable Writing
Harper & Brothers Publishers
New York
1949

Bernard Bailyn
Pamphlets of the American Revolution
Harvard University Press
Cambridge
1965

Index

A

Absolute positioning, 326
Ads, 25-30, 234-235
Alignment
    rows, 238
    text, 89, 127-128
All caps, 20, 123
ANSI character set, 154
ASCII character set, 154

B

Bitmapped formats, 289
Booklets, 46-52
Borders, 7-8, 200, 427
    designing, 198-200, 241
    rules (lines), 433
    shading, 241-242
Break
    column, 345
    dialog box, 314
    page, 117, 201-203
    section, 314-316, 343-344
Brochures, 35-45
    letter-fold, 36-38, 102, 377-383
    single-fold, 103-104
Bullets, 165, 178-179, 213-214, 434
Bullets and Numbering command, 213

C

Calculate, 246
Calendars, 16-21
Camera-ready copy, 4, 5, 106-107
Captions, 62
Catalogs, 46-52
Cells, 428
    delete, 236
    insert, 236
    merge, 238
    shift, 237-238

Character
    dialog box, 131-140
        use as default, 132
    formatting, 120-124
    spacing, 88, 132-136, 150, 431
Checkmarks, 164. *See also* Dingbats
Clip art, 4, 271-272
Color
    blackness of font, 76
    in black-and-white designs, 57-58
    paper, 38
    printer, 252-253
    printing, 36, 139-140
Columns, 340
    breaks, 345
    newspaper-style, 341-342, 397-398
    sections, 314-316, 342-344
Copy and paste, 116
Crop, 96, 292-293
Crop marks, 105-107
Cut and paste, 116

D

Datasheets (Graph), 279-281
Date (field), 353
Design
    Dos and Don'ts, 10-14
    Rules of Thumb, 9-10
Desktop presentation, 5
Desktop publishing, 3-5
Destination document, 404
Dingbats, 84, 155-179, 428
Directories, 46-52
Display type, 69
Dot patterns, 270
Dots per inch, 4, 99
Double-page spread, 8
Download, 255
Draft mode, 114

Draw (Microsoft), 260-272
Drop caps, 90, 336-337, 428

E

Ellipsis, 165, 434
Em dash, 27, 165-168, 428, 434
Embedded graphics, 260-261
En dash, 165, 428, 434
Encapsulated PostScript (EPS), 254-258
Escape key, 116
Extended character set, 161-164

F

Facing pages, 305-307
Field codes, 358-360, 362, 364, 429
Fields, 260, 358, 361-363, 364, 428-429
File command (Insert menu), 313
First line indents, 211-212, 429
Flip sheets, 31-35, 383-386
Flyers, 21-25
Folio, 60, 323
Fonts, 67-68, 73-77
    manager, 121
    menu, 120-122
    printer versus screen, 156
Footers, 5, 63, 307-311, 321-323
Forms, 16-21, 369-376
Frames, 326-327
    deleting, 329
    dialog box, 329
    inserting, 327, 334-335
    moving, 328, 330
    positioning, 332-333
    sizing, 328, 330
    text wrapping, 326, 329
    with styles, 331

G

Glossary entries, 167-170, 206
Go To, 116
Graph (Microsoft), 277-286
Graphics, 7, 287
    borders for, 292
    captioning, 297
    cropping and scaling, 292-296
    formats, 288
    inserting, 290-291
Gridlines, 229, 233

H

Halftone, 96
Hanging indents, 8, 216-217, 430
Headers, 5, 63, 307-311, 321-323
Headings, 7
Height menu, 330
Horizontal printing. *See* Landscape mode
Hot key, 113
House sheet, 93

I

Import filter, 288
Indents
    first line, 211-212, 429
    hanging, 216-217, 430
    right and left, 208-211, 430
Index, 362-365
Insert Table, 228-229
Inside margin, 8
Invisible characters. *See* Nonprinting characters

K

Kerning. *See* Character spacing
Keyboard commands, 113

L

Landscape mode, 21, 31, 390-393, 432
Large initial caps, 90
Laser printer, 4
Leading. *See* Line spacing
Letter-fold brochures, 36-38, 102, 377-383
Line screen, 97
Line spacing, 38, 87, 141-145, 150, 431
Lines per inch, 97
Linking files, 404-405
Lists, 212-217

M

Macros, 170-174, 206
Margins, 231, 302-306, 431
Mechanicals. *See* Camera-ready copy
Monochrome, 97
Monospaced font, 128
Mouse shortcuts, 117

N

Newsletters, 53-59, 395-402
Newspaper-style columns, 341-342

Non-breaking spaces, 19, 163
Non-repro, 106
Nonprinting characters, 124-125, 432
Normal
    style, 186-192
    template, 350
    view, 113-114
Numbered lists, 213-217

O

Object, 260-261
Options dialog box, 115-116
Orientation, 31, 390-393, 432
Orphans, 202
Outline view, 114
Output, 98
Outquotes, 7, 62, 334

P

Page Break Before command, 201-202
Page breaks, 201-203
Page Layout view, 114
Page numbers, 305, 307-308, 317-320
Page Setup, 300
    margins, 302-305
    orientation, 299, 301, 306
    page size, 300-303
    sections, 306-307, 314-316
    use as default, 302
Pagination, 201-203
Paragraph
    dialog box, 140, 201
    formatting, 124-125, 140-141
    indents, 208-212, 216-217, 430
    spacing, 145-148, 432
    styles. See Styles
Paste, 116
Paste special, 404
Paste-up, 4, 105-107
Periodicals, 53-59
Photos, 96-98
Photostats. See Stats
Picture
    crop, 293, 295, 296
    format, 293
    insert, 98, 290-291, 295, 404
    scale, 292-293, 295
Picture window, 47

Plot, 277
Point Size menu, 122
Portrait mode, 31, 388-390, 432
PostScript, 253-256
    creating files, 254-258
    encapsulating, 256-258
    special effects, 416-425
Preprinted color paper, 31
Print
    dialog box, 250-251
    icon, 250
    Preview, 319
Printer
    color, 252-253
    driver, 253
    fonts, 156
    setup, 251-252
Printer spreads, 101
Proportionally spaced, 128
Punctuation marks, 27, 165-168, 434

R

Reader spreads, 101
Referenced Document, 364-365
Relative positioning, 326
Repeat command, 116
Reports, 59-66
    landscape, 392-393, 432
    portrait, 388-390, 432
Resolution, 4
Reverse text, 275
Ribbon, 119-131
Rule. See Borders
Ruler, 119-131

S

Sans serif, 69-72, 82-83
Scaling, 292-293
Scanning, 96
Screen fonts, 156
Screens, 241-243, 248, 433
Section breaks, 314-316, 343-344
Section layout, 306-309, 343-344, 347-348
    on the Format menu, 409
Serif, 69-72, 78-81
Shading, 241-243
Show Guides, 263
Show/Hide ¶, 124-125

Single-fold brochure, 103-104
Slides, 403
    creating slides, 405-408, 410-413
    PostScript files, 408-409
Smart quotes. *See* Typesetters' punctuation marks
Snap to Grid, 263-264
Source document, 404
Spreads, 57, 101
Stats, 25
Stick-up caps, 90, 337, 434
Style, 183-187, 206
Styles
    Based On command, 221-222
    define by example, 194
    defining, 189-193
    dialog box, 187
    menu, 127, 195-197
    Merge command, 220-221
    Next Style feature, 223
    redefining, 187-189
    sheet, 183
    standard, 195-197
Sub- and superscripting, 137-138
Symbol (typeface), 84, 155-181
Symbol Palette, 157-161

T

Table of contents, 358-362, 364-365
Tables, 227-231
    borders, 241-242
    calculating in, 246
    centering, 238, 239
    column width, 231-233
    delete cells, 236
    delete columns, 236
    delete rows, 236
    entering, 238-239
    entry fields, 358
    insert cells, 236
    insert columns, 236
    insert rows, 234-235
    markers (Ts), 231, 233
    menu, 233-240
    merge cells, 238
    row height, 239
    rows, 234-236
    select column, 233, 236
    select row, 236-237
    select table, 233, 238
    split table, 231
Tabs, 128-130
    dialog box, 218-219
    Tables, 240
Template, 20, 206
    creating, 350-351, 353-356
    Normal, 350
    revising, 352-353
Time (field), 353
Toolbar, 118-119
Typeface, 67, 78-84
Typesetters' punctuation marks, 27, 165-168, 434
Type styles, 120-124
Typography, 67-90

U

Undo, 116
Unlinking fields, 361-362

V

View menu, setting up, 113-115

W

Widow/Orphan Control command, 202, 347
Widows, 202
WordArt, 273-276
WYSIWYG, 24

Z

Zapf Dingbats. *See* Dingbats
Zoom, 318-319
Zoom tool (Draw), 266-267

Attention 5 ¼" disk drive users:

The *Tools of the Trade* disk for Word for Windows™ is also available in a 5 ¼" high density format. Please return the coupon below with a check for $10.00 payable to Addison-Wesley to:

Addison-Wesley Publishing Company
Order Department
1 Jacob Way
Reading, MA 01867-9984

Please send me the 5 ¼" disk (ISBN 0-201-60869-3) to accompany *The Word for Windows™ Print and Presentation Kit* by Christine Solomon. I am enclosing a check for $10.00.

Name_____

Address_____

City_____ State_____ Zip_____